ABOUT THE AUTHOR

PETER CLARKE, F.C.A., M.A. (Econ.), Ph.D., currently
lectures in management accounting at the Department of
Accountancy, University College, Dublin at both undergraduate and postgraduate levels. He has published
numerous articles on accounting in professional journals and
has undertaken several overseas lecturing assignments. He
has also presented papers to the annual conferences of the
Irish, European and American Accounting Associations. His
research interests include the changing practice of
management accounting and its historical development.

IRISH STUDIES IN MANAGEMENT

Editors:
W.K. Roche
Graduate School of Business
University College Dublin

Brian O'Kane
Oak Tree Press

Irish Studies in Management is a series of texts and research-based monographs covering management and business studies. Published by Oak Tree Press in association with the Graduate School of Business at University College Dublin, the series aims to publish significant contributions to the study of management and business in Ireland, especially where they address issues of major relevance to Irish management in the context of international developments, particularly within the European Union. Mindful that most texts and studies in current use in Irish business education take little direct account of Irish or European conditions, the series seeks to make available to the specialist and general reader works of high quality which comprehend issues and concerns arising from the practice of management and business in Ireland. The series aims to cover subjects ranging from accounting to marketing, industrial relations/human resource management, international business, business ethics and economics. Studies of public policy and public affairs of relevance to business and economic life will also be published in the series.

ACCOUNTING INFORMATION FOR MANAGERS

2nd edition

Peter Clarke

Graduate School of Business

University College Dublin

Oak Tree Press
in association with
Graduate School of Business
University College Dublin

OAK TREE PRESS
19 Rutland Street, Cork, Ireland
www.oaktreepress.com

A catalogue record is available for this book from the
British Library.

ISBN 1 86076 248 4

Printed in Ireland by Colour Books Ltd.

In memory of Jim Finucane

Contents

SECTION 2: COST ACCUMULATION SYSTEMS

Preface

The essence of management accounting is decision-making. Good decisions require information. This book aims to provide managers with an important type of information — accounting information to be used in decision-making. The discipline it covers is often referred to as management, or managerial, accounting. Throughout this book, two important themes are stressed. The first is concerned with the type of information that is required by managers. This is a technical matter. The second is concerned with the response by managers to that information. This is a behavioural issue. Thus, for accounting information to have any value, it must be technically correct and generate the appropriate response from managers.

Aims

This book aims to meet the needs of students of management accounting, both at undergraduate and postgraduate levels. Business managers may also find this book useful. It attempts to explain the conceptual basis of accounting, setting out the key areas in management accounting in suitable depth. It covers the variety of techniques available to provide relevant information to managers. Each chapter contains illustrations of these techniques. At the end of each chapter, there are discussion questions and problems designed to enhance the learning process. Solutions are to be found in the Lecturers' Resource Pack, available from the publishers (see the end of this book for details).

Contents

Chapter 1 provides an introduction to accounting and its role in decision-making. Chapters 2, 3 and 4 provide an overview of financial statements and their interpretation. Financial statements reflect the financial impact of managerial decision-making. They are a form of accountability. They also provide the basis for evaluating the financial strengths and weaknesses of a business and are therefore a springboard for future decisions. This overview of financial statements facilitates the use of the book as a stand-alone text on management accounting courses, especially since no previous knowledge or experience of accounting is assumed.

Chapter 5 discuss the fundamentals of cost accumulation systems in both manufacturing and service enterprises. However, stock valuation issues for financial reports are not a focus of this book. Instead, the emphasis is on product costing for managerial decision-making. In recent times, product costing systems have been the subject of much criticisms. It is argued that traditional methods of absorbing overheads should be replaced by an Activity-Based Costing (ABC) system. The topic of ABC is discussed in Chapter 6.

Chapters 7, 8, and 9 are concerned with specific aspects of decision-making: Profit planning, relevant costs and capital expenditure decisions respectively. Chapter 10 discusses the issue of control with emphasis on budgetary control. Chapter 11 is devoted to standard costing systems and shows how traditional variances can be computed using either a formula method or a "t-account" method. Chapter 12 is concerned with issues of responsibility, structure and evaluation. Finally, Chapter 13 identifies some of the current developments in management accounting.

Acknowledgements

This book could not have been completed without the help and encouragement of many individuals who need to be acknowledged. Dorothy, Susan and Kevin tolerated my absences without complaining; Brian O'Kane kept up the pressure in a diplomatic and productive way; Bill Roche provided valuable financial assistance. I am grateful to both the Association of Chartered Certified Accountants and the Chartered Institute of Management Accountants for permission to use questions from previous examination papers. Also, UCD colleagues shared their teaching material with me. Finally, generations of students have contributed to its development.

Peter Clarke
Dublin
September 2002

Section 1:

Introduction to Accounting Information

1

Accounting Information and Decision-Making

1.1 THE IMPORTANCE OF DECISION-MAKING

A decision represents a choice among alternatives. If there are no alternatives, there are no decisions to be made. Information is needed in order to make rational decisions. The decisions that business managers make have enormous significance for the business entity itself, for its employees, for customers and for society at large. For example, before deciding which lines should be phased out and/or which should be promoted more vigorously, the manager of a trading company needs to know which products have been successful. Before accepting a job or investing money in a company, potential employees and investors need to satisfy themselves as to the company's financial viability; suppliers will need to satisfy themselves as to the likelihood of receiving payment for goods supplied.

The following diagram outlines the framework in which decisions should be made. Before a decision can be made, the objectives of the decision-maker and the various alternatives must be known.

Exhibit 1.1: A Framework for Decision-Making

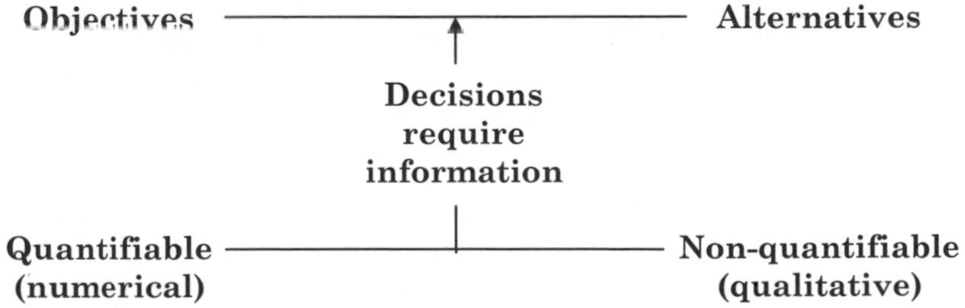

Objectives ——————————↑—————————— Alternatives

Decisions
require
information

Quantifiable ——————————|—————————— Non-quantifiable
(numerical)   (qualitative)

The key element in the decision-making process is *information*. There are different types of information: Accounting information is that subset of information that is expressed mainly in financial (money) terms. For example, the essential ingredient for a successful business is to sell goods or services to customers at a price in excess of the costs of producing or providing them. The excess of sales revenue over cost is "profit" and is a commonly used yardstick of successful business performance. Another type of information is expressed in numerical terms — for example, information on market share statistics. A third type of information is qualitative (that is, non-quantifiable) — for example, information regarding the skills and morale of employees.

Decisions require information, although some decisions are made purely on the basis of intuition or inspiration. Sometimes "hard" information is available but is ignored by the decision-maker. However, the likelihood of making a good decision is enhanced by using, judiciously, the information at hand. The use of such information is the primary focus of this book. Nevertheless, one should appreciate that all information has its limitations — for example, information on future demand will always be subject to an element of uncertainty because the future itself is always uncertain. In addition, information about a particular phenomenon may be presented or calculated in different ways — for example, we will see later that there are many different ways of calculating the cost of a unit of output!

1.2 THE NATURE AND SCOPE OF ACCOUNTING INFORMATION

There are many sources and types of information available to decision-makers, of which accounting information is but one. The discipline and role of accounting have been defined in many ways during the years but it is now recognised that the task of accounting is to record and summarise financial information that is considered most relevant to different interested parties (users) to allow them to assess the performance and financial position of the reporting entity.

This approach to defining accounting was put formally in a document entitled *The Corporate Report*, published in 1975, by a committee representing the accountancy profession in the United Kingdom and Ireland. In relation to reporting by companies it stated:

> The fundamental objective of corporate reports is to communicate economic measurements of and information about the resources and performance of the reporting entity useful to those having reasonable rights to such information.

In other words, the accounting process, and ultimately accounting information, should influence people's decisions regarding a business

entity. As an aside, it is useful to note that there is a difference between "accountancy" and "accounting". Accountancy means the work
of public practitioners — the accountancy profession, comprising
qualified accountants; accounting describes the subject to be studied
and is the focus of this book. Other related terms are that of "auditor"
and "auditing". An auditor, who is a qualified accountant, has a legal
duty to report to the owners of the business on the financial statements prepared by the accountant on behalf of the directors of the
company. The auditor's report contains his opinion on whether the
financial statements show a true and fair view.

For accounting to have any relevance to the modern business
world, it must be decision-oriented. There are at least two important
questions concerning this approach that need to be asked:

1. Who are the users of accounting information?

2. Are the information needs of managers similar to those of other
    parties?

Users of Accounting Information

Users of accounting information are usually grouped under a number
of headings. The relationship of each group to the business entity is
highlighted in Exhibit 1.2. Each user group makes a contribution to
the business entity that is vital to the survival of the business. In return, each group expects to receive something from the enterprise.
Thus, each member of a user group makes an input into the organisation in return for a future reward from the organisation. The decision
whether to participate will be influenced, to some extent, by accounting information. However, it should be acknowledged that the decision will also be influenced by other types of information.

Exhibit 1.2: Users of Accounting Information

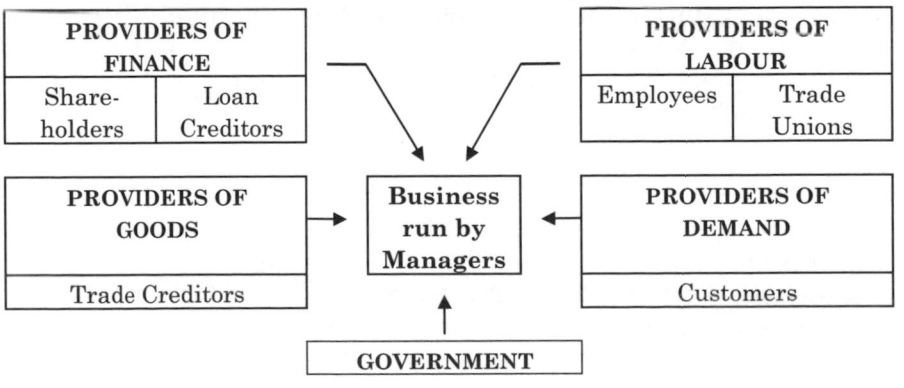

Shareholders

Shareholders provide share capital to the business, usually in the form of cash, in return for a financial benefit in the future. This benefit may be in the form of cash dividends and/or an increase in the market value of the company in which they are shareholders. In evaluating investment opportunities, shareholders are interested in the earnings stream of the company and the portion to be paid out to them by way of dividend. Based on past performance, shareholders make estimates of likely future profits of the company and the dividends that can be paid out of such profits. In addition, they are concerned with the current and future market value of their shares in the company. They are also interested in the performance of other companies, which may be offering higher or lower returns. Information on the entity's future cash inflows and future cash payments may also be relevant to shareholders. Without cash, a company cannot survive in the long-term — no matter how skilled the managers and employees are.

Creditors

Creditors are those individuals or institutions that provide (repayable) finance to the company. Trade creditors supply goods and services to the company. Loan creditors provide finance by way of cash loans.

Trade creditors are interested in the ability of the company to discharge the amount owing to them without delay. Consequently, trade creditors are interested in the liquidity of the company. Liquidity is evidenced by the excess of cash, or near cash assets, over the company's immediate liabilities. Trade creditors are also interested in the time taken by the company to pay its bills and whether the credit period is static, increasing or decreasing compared with previous accounting periods.

The concern of the loan creditor is two-fold. First, whether the agreed interest payments can be made and, second, whether the loan can be repaid on maturity. Loan creditors will be concerned with the company's profitability, cash flow, and whether there are any other loans due to be repaid.

Employees

It is natural that employees, and their trade union representatives, should want information about the cost structures, wage relativities, profitability and job security of their companies, together with comparative information about other companies. This information is, for example, essential to wage negotiation. However, most employees also seek reward in forms other than monetary gain, such as challenge, personal development and recognition of their services.

Customers

Customers may be interested in the financial reports produced by companies from which they intend to purchase goods or services. Usually customers' interest will be to establish the ability of the company to supply the goods or services required and to continue to operate in future years; the latter is important where purchase of long-term assets, requiring future maintenance, is concerned. However, not many customers are interested in looking at a company's financial statements before buying goods — for example, one buys petrol from the local garage without reference to the garage's financial statements. However, the monetary amounts involved in purchasing decisions may vary enormously. Thus, the decision to buy a house would be based to a greater extent on accounting information than the decision to purchase petrol, since the consequences — the inability to have serious building faults put right — are significantly greater than having to buy petrol from a less conveniently located garage.

Government

The use and interpretation of accounting information are essential for Government departments to implement and monitor State policy. Government policy ranges from taxation to the regulation of certain activities. For example, under Irish law, below cost selling in supermarkets is illegal. To prove whether goods are being sold below cost requires the interpretation and analysis of accounting information.

Managers

The managers of a business enterprise will analyse and interpret accounting information to plan and control performance. The use of accounting information by managers to plan and control the activities of a business comprises the area of management, or managerial, accounting. The information required for such purposes is, of necessity, very detailed and specific — for example, cost per unit. Information is reported to managers more frequently and regularly than to any of the other user groups. For example, shareholders may receive information on the sales, costs and profit performance of the company only on an annual basis, while managers receive information more frequently — perhaps monthly, or even weekly.

Detailed and frequent accounting information is provided to managers to influence their decisions. The financial outcomes of all these managerial decisions are reflected in the annual financial statements and reports produced by the business. These financial reports contain highly aggregated data and are typically prepared at the end of the accounting period in compliance with company legislation and other pronouncements by the accountancy profession. They are intended to influence the decisions of users who are external to the company and take no active part in the day-to-day decision-making activities.

1.3   DISTINGUISHING FINANCIAL AND MANAGEMENT ACCOUNTING

For study purposes, accounting is usually divided into two parts: financial accounting and management accounting. The distinction is based mainly on the user groups of accounting information.

The first five of the groups above — shareholders, creditors, employees, customers and Government — are mainly *external* to the organisation in the sense that they take no active part in the day-to-day decision-making within the enterprise. Their information needs should be satisfied by annual financial accounting reports.

Financial accounting information should be of crucial importance to user groups in deciding what action to take in respect of their involvement with the organisation, including, in the extreme, the decision whether to continue or terminate their involvement.

The three principal statements of the financial accounting process are the profit and loss account (or income statement), the cash flow statement and the balance sheet. The profit and loss account reports the results of a business entity's sales revenue and expenses incurred in earning that revenue over a period of time. The cash flow statement reports the inflow and outflow of cash during an accounting period. All outflows, whether of a capital (for example, purchase of fixed assets) or revenue (payment of wages) nature, are reported. The balance sheet reports the financial position of an organisation at the year end — what the organisation owns (assets) and how those assets have been financed (liabilities).

Conversely, the final group of users — that is, managers — are *internal* to the organisation in the sense that they are responsible for the day-to-day functioning of the company. Managers need information to plan and control the organisation.

Planning is the process of formulating a course of action. It involves the setting of goals or targets, identifying alternative ways of achieving those goals, including an estimate of future costs and revenues, and choosing between those alternatives. Planning is a forward-looking activity.

Control can be defined as the process of monitoring the outcome of the chosen alternative and identifying whether the plans are being achieved. This is usually done by translating objectives into financial targets and monitoring performance against those targets. This comparison results in variances being identified, which can be either significant or insignificant. The definition of a significant variance will be discussed in a later chapter but it broadly represents the notion of importance. If the variance is deemed to be not significant, satisfactory progress towards the specific goals can be assumed.

The whole issue of control is much more complex than simply variance analysis. For example, a reported variance may be significant to a manager on one occasion but not another. If the variance is significant, the manager must identify an appropriate response — for example, if a cost overrun has been identified, he must decide whether different production methods can be used to reduce costs, whether the selling price can be increased, or whether additional units can be sold. The difficulty with managerial control is, first, knowing when a variance is significant and, second, identifying the most appropriate corrective action to be taken if the variance is deemed significant. The difference between planning and control decisions can be appreciated from the following questions:

Planning

1. What is the cost of offering a new course at University?

2. How many meals must a restaurant sell each evening to break-even?

3. What selling price should be charged for each unit?

Control

1. Why are the costs out of line with projections?

2. Why were fewer meals sold than anticipated?

3. Why was the actual selling price less than the budgeted price?

The information needed by managers to make such decisions is provided by the management accountant. In essence, management accounting is concerned with providing information to managers in order to help them plan and control the activities of the company. Thus, it is the intended users of accounting information that primarily distinguishes the disciplines of financial and management accounting.

It is also important to stress that the distinction between financial and management accounting is sometimes made for teaching convenience. The reality is sometimes different. Managers are interested in financial accounting reports — for example, to monitor the overall financial position of their company not just the part of it for which they are personally responsible. On the other hand, a potential financier may be interested in a specific piece of information not available in the company's financial statements — for example, the break-even point of a particular project for which he has received a proposal for funding. In other words, all accounting information may be relevant to managers. The relevance of the information will be determined by the decision being made.

However, it is important to realise that both financial and management accounting information are derived from the same, single accounting system. Essentially, it is the way that the accounting information is presented, reflecting the different needs of the respective user groups, that distinguishes financial accounting from management accounting. The main differences are presented in Exhibit 1.3 below.

Exhibit 1.3: Differences between Financial and Managerial Accounting

	FINANCIAL	MANAGEMENT
Primary users of accounting information:	External to company	Internal users (managers)
Type of information:	Summarised: Balance sheet/profit and loss/cash flow	Very detailed and specific reports
Frequency:	Usually once a year	As required by managers
Time focus:	Past orientation (historical)	Past orientation (historical) and future orientation (projections)
Format of accounting reports governed by:	Companies Act and standards issued by accountancy profession	Not governed by legislation or standards

Characteristics of Good Accounting Information

In order to be useful for decision-making, accounting information must possess certain characteristics:

1. **Relevance**: This means that accounting information must relate to the decision being taken. Information may be relevant to one

particular decision but not to another; or relevant to one user group but not to another. Relevance is ultimately determined by the user and the decision being taken. Information is relevant when it influences the economic decisions of users by helping them evaluate past, present or future events.

2. **Understandability**: If accounting information is not understood by users, it is of little practical benefit. It is important to present accounting information in such a way that it is comprehensible to the less informed user of accounts without omitting information which is of value to the informed user.

3. **Timeliness**: To be useful, accounting information should be up-to-date and published as soon as practicable after the end of the period to which it relates, since up-to-date information is of more value to users than stale data.

4. **Accuracy**: If accounting information is not accurate, misinformed decisions by the user will inevitably result. To be accurate, accounting information must represent faithfully the effect of the transactions it reports and must be complete, although some immaterial items may be excluded that would not influence the decisions or conduct of a reasonable person

5. **Consistency of Preparation**: This characteristic has two dimensions — the comparability of a company's performance over time and the comparability of accounting reports between business entities. If accounting reports are not prepared on a consistent basis, then meaningful comparisons between performance in different time periods and between companies are virtually impossible.

Management accounting has, in recent years, been subject to a number of criticisms. There have been suggestions that a decline has occurred in the usefulness and relevance of management accounting. In particular, there are assertions that management accounting:

1. Places too much emphasis on short-term results (a phenomenon referred to as short-termism). This is the tendency to place a major focus on the achievement of the maximum profits in the immediate accounting period, in part because of the expectations of shareholders and other financiers. The reaction of management is to take action to improve short-term profitability, which may seriously undermine long-term viability. Typical examples include a de-emphasis on quality, delayed spending on maintenance and cut-backs in advertising expenditure

2. Fails to present a relevant set of performance measures to managers. Managers are judged on their profitability, especially in the

short term. Many management experts believe that profit is created through attention to quality, customer care, product development, delivery performance and production efficiency; and that profit follows as a natural consequence of these. The profit statement is a useful, if delayed, confirmation of a company's competence. Other performance measures, agreed with the appropriate functional executive, must be monitored if a profit is to be generated at all.

Cost Accounting

The emphasis of this book is on management accounting or providing relevant accounting information to managers. Some writers refer separately to an important branch of management accounting — cost accounting. Cost accounting developed due to the need to provide cost information for the valuation of stocks for profit and loss account and balance sheet purposes. Gradually, this purpose extended to providing cost information to management and has now been integrated within the main discipline of management accounting.

World War I greatly increased the demand for cost information, especially in relation to the pricing and control of Government munitions contracts. It is therefore no great surprise that the Association of Cost and Management Accountants, now known as the Chartered Institute of Management Accountants (CIMA), was formed in the UK in 1919. In the same year, the National Association of Accountants (NAA) was formed in the United States. The distinction between financial and management accounting became institutionalised in the United States in 1972 when the NAA (now the IMA) established a study programme leading to a Certificate in Management Accounting (CMA).

Early cost accountants were concerned with establishing the "absolute truth" — a precise cost for stock valuation purposes. As a result, in its early years, cost accounting was very much subservient to financial reporting requirements.

In addition, the prevailing management philosophy in the early part of this century was that of the classical, or scientific, school of management. Writers such as Taylor and Fayol viewed organisations from a mechanical point of view. Plant and people were to be managed with a view to maximising output for the common good of the owners, employees and society. The management function was centralised and management's proper role was to plan, co-ordinate and supervise the activities of subordinates. This philosophy, which cost accountants adopted readily, was pervasive until the 1930s. Cost accountants' professional concern was with issues of measurement, in sympathy with the concern of classical management theorists. The classical development of performance standards and identification of variances attracted accountants towards developing cost standards and budgets. The attitude of certainty that prevailed within classical management practice was intuitively appealing to accountants.

During the 1930s, the application of economic thinking to accounting began to change cost accounting. In particular, J.M. Clark's work *Studies in the Economics of Overhead Costs* (1923) was an important contribution. In coining the phrase "different costs for different purposes", Clark pointed out that historical cost information must necessarily be revised and amended to make it suitable for decision-making. He pointed out that:

> If cost accounting sets out, determined to discover what the cost of everything is and convinced in advance that there is one figure which can be found and which will furnish exactly the information which is required for every possible purpose, it will necessarily fail, because there is no such figure. If it finds a figure that is right for some purpose, it must necessarily be wrong for others.

Clark alerted accountants to the notion of *conditional* cost rather than *absolute* cost. In other words, cost depends on the particular purpose for which it was required.

Though management accounting systems are costly to develop and maintain, increasingly organisations world-wide are devoting resources to their development. Accounting information is an economic good that is obtainable at a cost. Different levels of information are available at different costs. The cost of information must be related to its value. Information can only have value if it influences human behaviour to make better decisions. Alternatively stated, the absence of accounting information may entail an opportunity cost if poor decisions are made as a result. On the other hand, if accounting information does not influence behaviour, it has no value.

Anyone studying the discipline of management accounting must be aware of its potential, and actual, behavioural consequences. Management accounting exists to influence human behaviour, particularly in the context of planning and controlling the organisation. This influence may be positive in the sense that it encourages individuals to make decisions to achieve the goals of the organisation, a phenomenon often referred to as goal congruence — in some situations, individuals are given incentives by management to perform in a particular manner. However, accounting systems can also have negative consequences — the wrong emphasis on financial results can create tension and anxiety among employees or result in inappropriate behaviour, such as reducing the marketing spend to achieve short-term profit goals. In this instance, short-term advantage — increased profit — might be achieved at the expense of the long-term strategic position of the firm.

While accounting systems can be viewed as a mechanical phenomenon based on the assumption that participants behave in a rational manner, this is not necessarily true. People do not always appear to act in a purely rational fashion, and accounting information is vulnerable to the social and political concerns of those involved in its production and use. Thus, the discipline of management accounting should be viewed not as a purely technical process but in the context of group and individual goals and the complex workings of modern organisations.

While this book is primarily concerned with the financial information available for a commercial (profit-oriented) business, the usefulness of accounting information is not restricted to this particular form of organisation. Other types of enterprise include charities and not-for-profit organisations, for which the generation of profit is not a primary concern. While financial information plays an important part in decision-making, non-financial information, such as the following, is also important:

1. The average length of time it takes for a phone repair.

2. The number of letters delivered per day.

3. The number of broadcasting hours.

4. The number of flights arriving on time.

In brief, both financial and non-financial information is important in making informed decisions.

1.4   END OF CHAPTER QUESTIONS

Question 1.1

Company financial statements, including profit and loss accounts, balance sheets and cash flow statements are used by a variety of individuals and institutions for a wide variety of purposes.

REQUIREMENT

Specify six different types of users of financial statements and explain in each case the aspects of performance or position in which they may be interested.

(*The Association of Chartered Certified Accountants*)

Question 1.2

Comment on the differences that exist between the published financial statements and the internal management accounting information which large companies produce.

(The Association of Chartered Certified Accountants)

Question 1.3

How could traditional accounting reports be made more useful to those outside the business itself?

State **three** classes of people, other than managers and owners, who are likely to need to use financial accounting information.

(The Association of Chartered Certified Accountants)

Question 1.4

In recent years, there have been suggestions that a decline has occurred in the usefulness and relevance of management accounting. In particular, there are the assertions that management accounting:

1. Places too much emphasis on short-term results (a phenomenon referred to as short-termism).

2. Fails to present a relevant set of performance measures to managers.

REQUIREMENT
Discuss these issues.

(The Association of Chartered Certified Accountants)

2

Financial Position and Profitability

2.1 THE REGULATION OF PUBLISHED FINANCIAL STATEMENTS

The next two chapters are concerned with published financial statements — the profit and loss account, balance sheet and cash flow statement — which contain highly aggregated items of information. Because they are of general interest to all users of accounting information, it is useful to review briefly the regulatory environment in which they are produced.

Accounting information can be looked at from a demand/supply perspective as illustrated in Exhibit 2.1 below. User groups, who provide finance and resources, require financial information about the business entity. They represent the *demand* for accounting information. The business entity (the reporting company) uses those resources and represents the source or *supply* of accounting information.

The content and format of these financial statements are regulated by two major sources:

1. Government legislation requires the financial statements of reporting companies to show a "true and fair" view of the financial performance and position at year end. Increasingly, Government legislation is being influenced by European Union membership provisions.

2. The accountancy profession issues pronouncements such as Statements of Standard Accounting Practice (SSAPs) and, more recently, Financial Reporting Standards (FRSs).

Exhibit 2.1: Resource Flows and Regulation

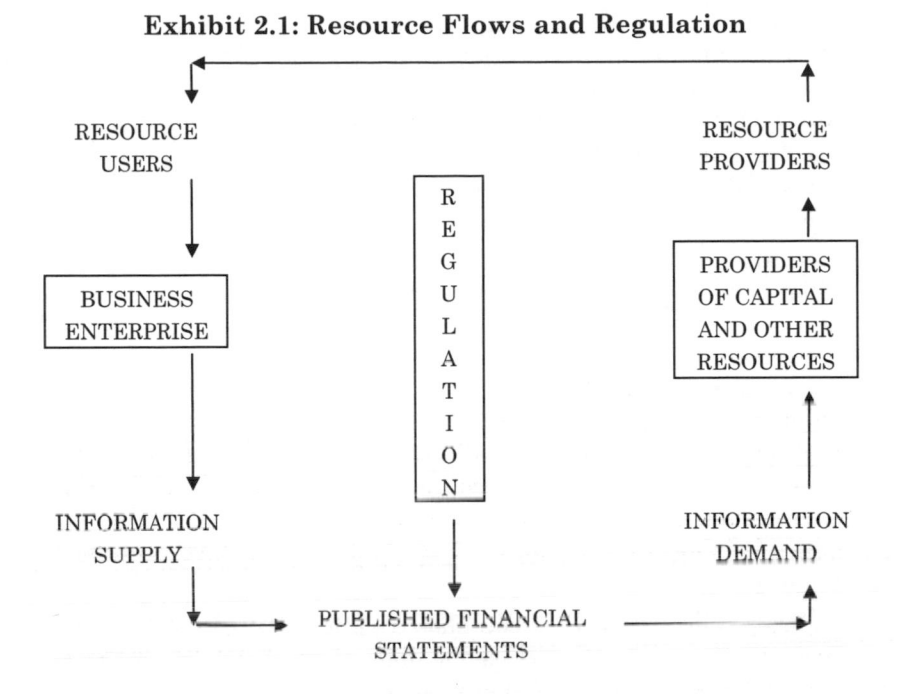

The Impact of Government and the Companies Acts

The Companies Acts contain regulations for all limited companies. Generally speaking, the Companies Acts require a company, once in every calendar year, to present to its members (the shareholders) a profit and loss account and a balance sheet. These accounting statements must be audited by a statutory, or external, auditor who attaches a report to the financial statements.

A typical audit report contains the following points:

REPORT OF THE AUDITORS

We have audited the financial statements on pages * to * and the accounting policies set out on page * .

We conducted our audit in accordance with Auditing Standards issued by the Auditing Practices Board.

In our opinion, the financial statements give a true and fair view of the state of affairs of the company at 31 December, 20x2 and of the results for the year then ended and have been properly prepared in accordance with the Companies Acts.

There are four phrases contained in the audit report that need clarification:

1. "In accordance with Auditing Standards" informs the shareholder that the auditor is not simply bound by his own judgment as to what constitutes satisfactory procedures for the conduct of the audit. The Auditing Practices Board issues auditing standards that lay down basic standards and guidance for auditors. The objective of auditing standards is to ensure a high quality of audit practice and consistency between auditors.

2. "In our opinion" is probably the most important feature of the audit report. The auditor is not certifying that the accounts are correct, since there is a high degree of subjectivity required in the preparation of financial statements and cost prohibits the checking of every detail. Thus the basis of the audit report is the professional judgment of the auditor. One consequence of this is that the auditor cannot be automatically held liable for any errors or fraud that may be found in the accounts at a later stage. If his opinion was formed on the basis of normally adequate work and no negligence is involved, the auditor has fulfilled his obligation to shareholders.

3. "A true and fair view" is the basic requirement of the Companies Acts, though this phrase is not defined in the Acts and is thus open to interpretation. A common understanding of the phrase is that the financial statements of an enterprise give a true and fair view if they, together with related notes, are sufficiently informative of matters that affect their use, understanding and interpretation by those for whom they are intended, and they are prepared in accordance with accounting principles appropriate to the circumstances of the business. It is the view of the professional accountancy bodies and the courts that, except in most unusual circumstances, compliance with accounting standards is necessary to achieve a true and fair view. This is because accounting standards are, in effect, a codification of good accounting practice.

4. "In accordance with the Companies Acts" indicates that the legal requirements covering the preparation of the accounts have been met. The Companies Acts lay down many disclosure and format requirements and contain some valuation rules.

An increasingly important influence on national legislation is the European Union. The EU seeks to promote a number of "freedoms" among member states, of which the freedom of capital movement is one. Free movement of capital requires the harmonisation of the flow of financial information about companies from all parts of the EU. Previously, differences existed between member states as regards the legal requirements governing both the structure and content of financial statements, which could be prejudicial to the investment of capital in member states to the extent that investors might not have sufficient information to make their decisions. This was particularly true as regards purchase of shares in companies in other member states. Harmonisation of financial statements was also necessary in order to harmonise the taxation systems in member states.

The EU influences published financial statements in member states through the use of Directives. These Directives are not law, *per se*, but they require member states to alter, where necessary, their national legislation to make requirements of the Directives legally enforceable. Member states are given a fixed period (for example, two years) to bring their own national legislation into line with a Directive and a further period by the end of which the revised national legislation must be effective.

To date, two important Directives have been issued that directly affect financial statements:

1. The Fourth Directive (1978) applies to both public and private companies, and deals with the format and content of limited company accounts, the valuation rules and the publication of these documents. This was implemented by the Companies (Amendment) Act, 1986.

2. The Seventh Directive (1983) requires the preparation of consolidated accounts for groups of companies, in order to provide a true and fair view of the economic and financial position of the group. It therefore supplements the Fourth Directive, which applies *only* to the accounts of individual limited companies.

The Companies (Amendment) Act, 1990 and the Companies Act, 1990 together represented the biggest overhaul of Irish company law since 1963. Taken together, the two Acts introduced major provisions of which the most important, for the purposes of this book, are the role of the examiner and the responsibilities and restrictions imposed on directors.

The Examiner

The Court can appoint an examiner if it considers that such an order would facilitate the survival of a company, or any part of its undertaking, as a going concern. An examiner is appointed for three months, during which time the company is under the protection of the Courts. During this time, the company cannot be wound up, or have a receiver appointed to it, no steps can be taken to repossess goods taken under a hire purchase agreement or a reservation of title clause nor can legal action be initiated to recover debts.

Once appointed, the examiner is obliged to conduct an examination of the affairs of the company, and report to the Court within 21 days of the appointment or such longer period as may be allowed. The examiner's report must include, *inter alia*:

1. A statement of affairs.

2. Comments on the deficiency or disappearance of any property.

3. A statement of opinion whether the company, or part of it, is capable of survival as a going concern, with any necessary recommendations.

4. A statement whether such a course of action would be more advantageous for members and creditors than a winding up.

Clearly, the examiner needs to rely on accounting information in his deliberations.

Responsibilities of Directors

The impact of the Companies Act, 1990 has been significant, especially in relation to directors' duties and responsibilities. The following are three of the main points:

1. A company shall not enter into any arrangement whereby a director acquires non-cash assets from the company (or vice versa) unless the arrangement is first approved by a resolution of the company in general meeting. This applies to non-cash assets, which exceed 10 per cent of the company's net assets, based on the accounts of the preceding financial year.

2. A company shall not make a loan to a director unless the value of the arrangement is less than 10 per cent of the net assets — all directors being aggregated for this purpose. However, this does not apply if the transaction is conducted as part of the ordinary business of the company. If this provision is breached, on a winding up the Court may make the directors who benefited from such loans personally liable for the debts of the company.

3. A director of a company may be declared personally responsible, without any limitation of liability, for all or part of the debts of the company if he knowingly carried on any business of the company in a reckless manner or with intent to defraud creditors. A director shall be deemed to have been knowingly a party if, having regard to the general knowledge, skill and experience that may reasonably be expected of a person in his position, he ought to have known that his actions or those of the company would cause loss to the creditors of the company.

The Impact of the Accountancy Profession, including SSAPs and FRSs

The accountancy profession has been able to respond to the requirements of changing business practices and structures and to the demands of a sophisticated investing community more speedily and with greater flexibility than company legislation. The Accounting Standards Committee (ASC) was established in 1970 by the professional accountancy bodies in the UK and Ireland. It issued more than 20 Statements of Standard Accounting Practice (SSAPs) with which company accounts are expected to comply. These accounting standards lay down not only what accounting information must be disclosed but also how particular transactions must be recorded and measured — for example, research and development costs.

Moreover, accounting standards require information to be disclosed in a company's financial statements over and above the minimum requirements of company law — for example, a cash flow statement is required of all but the smallest companies. This statement is a requirement of the accountancy profession though not a legal requirement. Likewise, a company's earnings per share (EPS) must be disclosed to comply with accounting standards though it is not required to be disclosed by company law.

The ASC was replaced on 1 August 1991 by the Accounting Standards Board (ASB), which is an independent accounting standards-setting body and has the power to issue Financial Reporting Standards (FRSs) in its own right. The ASB also has legal backing, since it can refer dubious accounts to a Review Panel, which can apply to the Courts to require the company to restate its accounts. An Urgent Issues Task Force (UITF) looks at issues not covered by standards, with a view to producing or revising a standard more quickly than is the normal case. These three bodies operate under the control of the Financial Reporting Council (FRC). Since the ASB and Review Panel are UK bodies, their powers do not extend to Irish companies. However, FRSs issued by the ASB are promulgated in Ireland by the Institute of Chartered Accountants in Ireland.

Against this background, and in order to avoid the confusion that might result from SSAPs having a different source of authority (and one no longer in existence), the ASB passed a resolution formally adopting and re-issuing the 22 SSAPs extant at 1 August 1991 as its own. All these SSAPs have been or are in the course of being reviewed.

2.2 THE BALANCE SHEET — FINANCIAL POSITION

The three major accounting statements prepared by a company are the profit and loss account, balance sheet, and cash flow statement. In this section, we shall concentrate on the balance sheet.

A balance sheet represents an ordered list, in money terms, of the resources owned by a business and the resources supplied to the business by external parties. An alternative term for the balance sheet is a Statement of Financial Position, which is perhaps more descriptive of the statement and is used, for example, in the US.

All balance sheets contain *three* important items of accounting information:

1. Assets.

2. Liabilities.

3. Shareholders' funds.

Assets represent the resources owned and controlled by the enterprise as a result of a past transaction or event. Usually the enterprise generates cash by selling these resources. In other words, assets represent potential cash inflows.

Liabilities are the financial obligations arising out of past transactions or events that must be paid by the enterprise. They represent future cash outflows.

Shareholders' funds represents the portion of the assets of the enterprise financed by the owners. Initially, this represents the capital invested in the business by the owner(s), later to be augmented by profits retained by the business.

The relationship between assets, liabilities and shareholders' funds, whereby total assets are financed by creditors and shareholders, can be depicted as an equation:

$$\begin{matrix} \text{TOTAL} \\ \text{ASSETS} \end{matrix} = \begin{matrix} \text{SHAREHOLDERS'} \\ \text{FUNDS} \end{matrix} + \begin{matrix} \text{TOTAL} \\ \text{LIABILITIES} \end{matrix}$$

Classification of Balance Sheet Items

All balance sheets represent an expansion of the above equation in that they contain six boxes of accounting information. Thus, assets will be subdivided into fixed and current categories; capital will be divided into share capital and retained profits and liabilities will be classified as either long or short-term. Thus:

1. Fixed assets		3. Share capital		5. Long-term liabilities
+	=	+	+	+
2. Current assets		4. Retained profits		6. Current liabilities

Fixed assets are those intended for use on a continuing basis. In accordance with the EU Fourth Directive, fixed assets are categorised as Intangible, Tangible or Financial. Intangible assets include goodwill or brands. Typical tangible fixed assets include land and buildings, plant and machinery, furniture and motor vehicles. A more appropriate description of these assets might be long-term assets. Financial assets include long-term investments made in other companies.

Current assets represent those assets in cash form or expected to be converted into cash during the coming year and are thus short-term in nature. The three principal current assets of a company are:

1. Stock that represents goods and materials held by the business and intended for eventual resale.

2. Accounts receivable, or debtors, which represent amounts due from customers.

3. Bank/cash balances.

Liabilities must be classified as either long-term or short-term (current), based on the time at which payment is expected to be made. Long-term liabilities are those due to be paid beyond the next accounting period, usually one year, whereas current liabilities are expected to be discharged within the next 12 months. Current liabilities consist mainly of two items:

1. Bank overdraft or short-term loans (loan creditors).

2. Accounts payable, or creditors, resulting from the purchase of goods or services on credit.

Shareholders' funds, or equity, represents the portion of total assets financed by the owners. It typically consists of two items:

1. The original share capital invested by the owners.

2. Profits retained within the business (this will be discussed later).

Types of Share Capital

The owners of a limited company are called shareholders. The degree of control that a particular shareholder can exercise will depend on the number of shares that he holds and more importantly, the type of share that he owns. Broadly speaking, there are two classes of share capital: Preference share capital and Ordinary (or equity) share capital.

A preference share is generally entitled to a dividend each year at a specified rate, before anything is paid to the ordinary shareholders. A holder of one 10 per cent preference share of €1 nominal value will receive an annual dividend of 10c each year — the dividend being related to the nominal value of the invested capital rather than to the company's profitability. Preference shares are usually entitled to a cumulative dividend — that is, if a dividend is not paid in any year because of insufficient profits, the dividend is carried forward to be paid in a future year. In the event of the company being wound up, preference shareholders receive back their capital before ordinary shareholders (assuming there are any funds available to repay).

Ordinary shares are the risk-bearing shares. The ordinary shareholders are entitled to receive all profits after tax and preference dividends. As a result, ordinary shareholders stand to gain most when high profits are made by the company and to suffer most when losses are incurred. They also must wait until preference capital has been repaid, in the event of a winding up, before receiving any repayment themselves.

When forming a limited company, Articles of Association must be prepared which, *inter alia*, specify the rights attaching to each class of share. Different classes of share capital with different rights may be needed to attract funds from a variety of sources whose providers may have quite different attitudes toward the mix of risk and reward that they would find acceptable. Some investors are content with stable returns at relatively low risk, others are prepared for opportunities to obtain high returns, albeit at greater risk.

Presentation of Balance Sheets

The balance sheet is a statement of assets, liabilities and shareholders' funds — the financial position of the company at a moment in time. It is, by definition, a historical document. Traditionally, balance sheets were presented in a two-sided format or horizontal format. These six boxes of financial information are shown below:

J. BALL COMPANY
BALANCE SHEET AT 31 DECEMBER 20x1

	€		€
1. Fixed assets	10,000	3. Share capital invested	9,000
		4. Retained profits	3,000
		5. Long-term	4,000
2. Current assets		liabilities	
Stock	3,000	6. Current	1,000
Debtors	2,000	liabilities	
Cash	2,000		
	7,000		
	17,000		17,000

Under the EU Fourth Directive, different formats of balance sheet are permissible — either the traditional two-sided balance sheet or the more modern vertical presentation. A vertical format is presented below:

J. BALL COMPANY
BALANCE SHEET AT 31 DECEMBER 20x1

	€	€
1. Fixed assets		10,000
2. Current assets	7,000	
6. Less: Creditors		
(amounts falling due within twelve months)	1,000	
Net current assets		6,000
Total assets less current liabilities		16,000
5. Creditors		
(amounts falling due after more than one year)		4,000
Capital and reserves		
3. Called up share capital	9,000	
4. Profit and loss account (retained profits)	3,000	
		12,000
		16,000

Two terms that will be subsequently used in evaluating a business's financial position are "shareholders' funds" and "capital employed". The former represents the total funds invested in the company at-tributable to shareholders. In J. Ball's balance sheet, this amounts to

€12,000, comprising share capital subscribed plus retained profits. Capital employed represents the total amount of long-term funds invested within the business. This amounts to €16,000 above, since it combines shareholders' funds and long-term loans.

Definition and Evaluation of Liquidity

Balance sheets reveal important information that is used to evaluate the financial position of the company at the balance sheet date. The two aspects of financial position that can be examined are:

1. Liquidity.

2. The reliance on debt financing, which is described as leverage or gearing.

Liquidity represents the ability of an enterprise to pay its debts as and when they become due. Liquidity must be ranked as one of the principal objectives of any enterprise, because an enterprise without liquidity may be forced by its creditors to stop operations and end its existence. Two ratios are commonly used to assess the liquidity position of a company:

1. The Current ratio

2. The Acid Test ratio.

The Current Ratio can be stated as:

$$\frac{\text{Current assets}}{\text{Current liabilities}}$$

This is a rather crude measure of liquidity, indicating the extent to which current assets are available to meet the current liabilities. It does not take into account the liquidity of the individual components of current assets — for example, the length of time it would take to turn stock and debtors into cash. In addition, the realisable value of accounts receivable may be less than stated, though the realisable value of stock may be considerably higher than the stated amount, which is usually at cost. A Current ratio of around 2:1 is recommended for most businesses.

The Acid Test ratio is considered a somewhat more severe test of liquidity. It is calculated on the same basis as the Current ratio except that stock is specifically excluded. This is to show the immediate liquidity position of the business. Selling stock takes time — the Acid Test ratio shows only the current assets that can be quickly turned into cash. An Acid Test ratio of about 1:1 is recommended but, as with the Current ratio, many businesses survive quite well with ratios considerably less than this. Since service companies generally do not hold large amounts of stock, their Current ratios should approximate to their Acid Test ratios.

As with all ratios, it is important to remember that the trends highlighted are more important than a single year's figures.

Definition and Evaluation of Leverage (Gearing)

Leverage (gearing) refers to the extent to which long-term funds have been financed by borrowing. Some borrowing is usually beneficial to a company since interest payments are tax deductible, making it a cheap form of finance compared with share capital (dividends paid to shareholders are not deductible for tax purposes).

However, excessive leverage increases the risk to ordinary shareholders because large interest payments may depress profits. In addition, all borrowings must be repaid thus creating potential future cash flow problems for the business. Moreover, modern loan agreements often contain restrictive covenants that impose certain restrictions on the business — for example, reduced dividend payments. Should a business be unable to meet the required interest and capital repayments, lenders can appoint a receiver whose express function is to sell off sufficient assets to repay the loan.

The two commonly used gearing ratios are:

Debt/Equity Ratio:

$$\frac{\text{Long-term debt}}{\text{Shareholders' funds}} \quad \text{x} \quad 100 \quad = \quad X\%$$

Debt/Capital Employed Ratio

$$\frac{\text{Long-term debt}}{\text{Capital employed}} \quad \text{x} \quad 100 \quad = \quad Y\%$$

The Debt/Equity Ratio compares the two elements in the long-term capital structure – debt and equity. The Debt/capital Employed ratio expresses one element in the long-term capital structure – debt – as a percentage of the total long-term capital. Thus, both ratios portray the same information but in different ways.

In contrast to the liquidity ratios, there is no commonly accepted desirable ratio for gearing. However, many financial analysts would be unhappy if the debt/capital employed ratio exceeded 50 per cent. A ratio above 50 per cent would indicate that the absolute amount of long-term debt exceeded shareholders' funds and, thus, to some extent, that shareholders were losing financial control over their company.

2.3   THE PROFIT AND LOSS ACCOUNT

Owners and other users of financial statements are concerned with the overall success of an enterprise. Success can be defined in a number of ways — for example, sales growth, market share or even conditions of employment. However, one of the most important measures of success in today's society is "profit". Net profit (net income) represents the growth in shareholders' funds (and net assets) during the period from trading activities.

Since the drive for profit underlies the existence of most business organisations, it follows that an important function of an accounting system is to provide information about profitability. Many users including investors, creditors and employees are interested in last year's profit not so much for its own sake as for the clues it gives to the likely profits of future years. It is important to stress that profit is good for business and good for people. First, profit is a means of indicating how effectively resources are put to use. Functioning in this way, profitability figures help prevent inefficiencies and waste. Second, profit enables companies to pay their business costs and live up to their responsibilities. Without profit, there would be no jobs or customer service.

In determining overall profitability, accountants traditionally have looked to actual business transactions to provide objective evidence on whether a business has been profitable. Using the transactions approach to profit measurement, if a business buys an item for €70 and promptly sells it for €100 cash, we have objective evidence that the business has earned a profit of €30. Decision-making to achieve profit is one of the essential themes of this book. Yet the concept of profit is frequently misunderstood and confused with other concepts such as cash flow. Accordingly, it is worthwhile to outline what accountants mean by "profit".

One way to explain the concept of net profit and show how retained profit appears on the balance sheet of a commercial organisation is to highlight the financial impact of a number of transactions on successive balance sheets. For example, let us assume that the balance sheet of J. Brown, a retailer, on 1 December 20x1 was as follows:

J. BROWN
BALANCE SHEET AT 1 DECEMBER 20x1

	€		€
Fixed assets	10,000	Share capital invested	4,000
		Retained profits	Nil
Cash	1,000	10% Long-term loan	5,000
		Creditors	2,000
	11,000		11,000

The following five transactions subsequently took place:

1. Purchased one stock unit for €2,000 cash.
2. Sold one stock unit for €6,000 cash.
3. Purchased one stock unit for €2,000 cash.
4. Paid wages expense, €500 in cash.
5. Paid interest on loan, €500 in cash.

Transaction 1
The balance sheet after purchasing one stock unit for €2,000 cash is
as follows:

J. BROWN
BALANCE SHEET (1)

	€		€
Fixed assets	10,000	Share capital invested	4,000
Stock	*2,000	Retained profits	Nil
Cash	*Nil	10% Long-term loan	5,000
		Creditors	2,000
		Bank overdraft	*1,000
	12,000		12,000

* Indicates a figure that has changed from the previous balance sheet.

Transaction 2
Since one stock unit has been sold for €6,000 cash, a profit of €4,000
must be recorded. The balance sheet is as follows:

J. BROWN
BALANCE SHEET (2)

	€		€
Fixed assets	10,000	Share capital invested	4,000
Stock	*Nil	Retained profits	*4,000
Cash	*5,000	10% Long-term loan	5,000
		Creditors	2,000
		Bank overdraft	*Nil
	15,000		15,000

Transaction 3

Stock is now replaced at a cash cost of €2,000. The resulting balance sheet is as follows:

J. BROWN
BALANCE SHEET (3)

	€		€
Fixed assets	10,000	Share capital invested	4,000
Stock	*2,000	Retained profits	4,000
Cash	*3,000	10% Long-term loan	5,000
		Creditors	2,000
	15,000		15,000

Transaction 4

Wages expenses of €500 are paid by cash. The resulting balance sheet is as follows:

J. BROWN
BALANCE SHEET (4)

	€		€
Fixed assets	10,000	Share capital invested	4,000
Stock	2,000	Retained profits	*3,500
Cash	*2,500	10% Long-term loan	5,000
		Creditors	2,000
	14,500		14,500

Transaction 5

Interest of €500 is paid on the loan. The resulting balance sheet is as follows:

J. BROWN
BALANCE SHEET (5)

	€		€
Fixed assets	10,000	Share capital invested	4,000
Stock	2,000	Retained profits	*3,000
Cash	*2,000	10% Long-term loan	5,000
		Creditors	2,000
	14,000		14,000

These five transactions all impact on the balance sheet, with some of the transactions impacting on the amount of retained profit. Note that net profit represents the increase in shareholders' funds during the accounting period, resulting from trading.

However, it is neither necessary nor feasible to prepare a balance sheet after each transaction. Instead, a balance sheet is usually prepared at the end of the accounting period, together with a profit and loss account which is a *summary* of all the transactions that impact on the profit performance of the business entity during the accounting period. Using the example above, the net profit for the period, which has been retained within the business, is €3,000.

Alternatively, one could look at the difference between opening and closing net assets. The opening net assets (total assets less total liabilities) of J. Brown were €4,000. At the end of the period (after five transactions), net assets amounted to €7,000. This increase in net assets (€3,000) is matched by an equal increase in shareholders' funds, under the separate heading of retained profit.

Since J. Brown is a retail organisation, the calculation of net profit is done in two separate stages. Initially, sales revenue earned during the accounting period is identified. It is established accounting practice to recognise and record sales revenue at the time when goods are sold to a customer. Various terms are used to describe different types of revenue; companies selling goods usually use the term sales to describe their principal revenue source, while in the professional practice of lawyers, doctors and accountants, revenue is referred to as fees earned. Miscellaneous forms of revenue include deposit interest received, rent received or even bad debts recovered.

J. BROWN
PROFIT AND LOSS ACCOUNT
FOR PERIOD ENDED 31 DECEMBER 20x1

	€	€
Stage 1: Determination of Gross profit		
Sales revenue (1 unit)		6,000
Less: Opening stock	Nil	
Add: Purchases (2 units)	4,000	
Less: Closing stock (1 unit)	(2,000)	
		(2,000)
Gross profit		4,000

The cost of sales comprises three elements:

1. Opening stock at the start of the period.

2. Add: Purchases (or production costs for a manufacturer) of goods for resale.

3. Less: Closing stock at the end of the period.

At the end of any accounting period, some goods may remain unsold. Closing stock should be deducted from opening stock and purchases to provide a "cost of goods sold" figure, which in turn is deducted from "sales" to provide "gross profit". A gross loss would normally indicate that the firm was selling its goods below cost.

The second stage in the profit measurement process is to deduct all the expenses of the business from the gross profit. Expenses represent the various types of expenditure that will not provide any future benefit to the firm. Examples include wages and salaries for employees, rent, rates and advertising. Expenses also include depreciation of fixed assets. Taken together, total expenses are the "cost of doing business" — the cost of the various activities necessary to carry on a business. They include selling and marketing the product or service, distributing the product or supplying the service, administering the business and financing the business.

In many cases, the measurement of expense is straightforward — for example, rent. In other cases, the precise identification and measurement of expenses will not be so clear-cut, and estimates will be called for — for example, amounts to be written off as bad debts.

The difference between gross profit and total expenses will represent either a net profit or net loss for the accounting period. The remaining part of the net profit calculation is as follows, ignoring (for the time being) the impact of taxation and dividends:

J. BROWN
PROFIT AND LOSS ACCOUNT
FOR YEAR ENDED 31 DECEMBER 20x1 (cont'd)

	€	€
Stage 2: Determination of Net profit		
Gross profit (carried down)		4,000
Less:		
Selling and distribution expenses	Nil	
Administration expenses (wages)	500	
		(500)
Profit before interest and tax (PBIT)		3,500
Interest paid (and payable)		(500)
Profit before tax (PBT)		*3,000
and retained for the financial year		

* *To be shown on the balance sheet at the end of the accounting period, under the heading "Retained profits" or "Profit and loss account".*

The profit and loss account indicates the increase in shareholders' funds during the period, resulting from trading. Net profit is a legal concept, representing the amount of funds that are legally available to be paid to shareholders (although, in most cases, a portion of the profit will be retained in the business). Corresponding to this increase in shareholders' funds is an equal increase in *net assets*, which may or may not be in the form of cash sufficient to pay dividends.

ILLUSTRATION

A complete illustration of the preparation of a profit and loss account and closing balance sheet is based on the following balances which were extracted from the books of J. Owens Ltd., on 31 December 20x8. The company has been trading for a number of years.

J. OWENS LTD.
ACCOUNT BALANCES AT 31 DECEMBER 20x8

	€
Share capital invested	4,000
Profit and loss account (1 January)	1,600
Premises	4,800
Plant and machinery	3,100
Debtors	4,100
Creditors	1,400
Distribution expenses	490
Purchases	6,230
Sales	12,900
Income from investments (financial assets)	20
Telephone expenses (admin.)	240
Wages and salaries (admin.)	2,100
Cash on hands	40
Bank overdraft	2,290
Opening stock	1,600
Rent and rates (admin.)	630
Heating expenses (admin.)	510
Stock exchange investments at cost	200
Long-term loan payable	2,000
Interest paid on loan	170

The following information is also provided:

1. Closing stock was valued at €1,800.

2. Dividends of €200 are to be declared (but are unpaid at year end).

3. Business tax on profits is payable at the rate of 40 per cent on profit before tax (PBT).

REQUIREMENT

You are required to prepare a profit and loss account for the year ended 31 December 20x8, together with a balance sheet at that date.

SOLUTION

J. OWENS LTD.
PROFIT AND LOSS ACCOUNT
FOR YEAR 31 DECEMBER 20x8

	€	€
Turnover (sales)		12,900
Cost of sales: Opening stock	1,600	
Add: Purchases	6,230	
Less: Closing stock	(1,800)	(6,030)
Gross profit		6,870
Distribution expenses		(490)
Administration expenses		(3,480)
(240 + 2,100 + 630 + 510)		
Operating profit		2,900
Income from financial assets		20
Interest paid (and payable)		(170)
Profit on ordinary activities before tax		2,750
Taxation (40 per cent)		(1,100)
Profit after taxation		1,650
Dividends		(200)
Profit retained for year		1,450
Profit brought forward 1 January		1,600
Profit carried forward 31 December		3,050

J. OWENS LTD.
BALANCE SHEET AT 31 DECEMBER 20x8

	€	€
Tangible fixed assets		
Premises		4,800
Plant and machinery		3,100
		7,900
Current assets		
Stock	1,800	
Debtors	4,100	
Investments	200	
Cash	40	
	6,140	
Creditors (amounts due within one year)		
Creditors	1,400	
Bank overdraft	2,290	
Taxation payable (Note)	1,100	
Dividends payable (Note)	200	
	4,990	
Net current assets		1,150
Total assets less current liabilities		9,050
FINANCED BY:		
Creditors (amounts due after one year)		
Long-term loan	2,000	
		2,000
Capital and reserves		
Called up share capital	4,000	
Profit and loss account	3,050	
		7,050
		9,050

NOTE: Both taxation and dividends are payable out of profits earned this year. Therefore, they are included in this year's profit and loss account. The immediate impact is to reduce the amount of retained profits on the balance sheet. However, since the relevant amounts have not yet been paid, they are also included on the balance sheet, and classified as short-term liabilities, being amounts due to be paid within 12 months.

2.4 CAPITAL AND REVENUE EXPENDITURE

When preparing financial statements, an important distinction is made between capital and revenue expenditure. Capital expenditure may be defined as any expenditure incurred in creating, acquiring, extending or improving an asset for use in the business. The important point is that the benefit derived from such capital expenditure will accrue to the company over a number of accounting periods. At the end of an accounting period, capital expenditure appears on the face of the balance sheet under the appropriate fixed asset heading. Revenue expenditure may be defined as outlay incurred for earning revenue or maintaining the earning capacity of the business. The benefit derived from such expenditure is used up in the current accounting period. In other words, revenue expenditure comprises the day-to-day running expenses of the business.

The Importance of the Distinction

The distinction between capital and revenue expenditure is important because of the implications involved when preparing financial statements of a business. Capital expenditure is reflected on the balance sheet of a firm under the heading "fixed assets". Revenue expenditure, on the other hand, is written off immediately to the profit and loss account of the business and thereby reduces profit (or increases losses) for that year. If, say, capital expenditure is treated incorrectly in the financial statements of an entity as a trading expense, then the profit (loss) figure for the accounting period will be understated (since expenses are overstated) and the fixed assets on the balance sheet will be understated and thus, the financial statements will not be an accurate reflection of the business's financial position.

Materiality

Underlying the above discussion is the concept of materiality. The term materiality refers to the relative importance or significance of an item or event. For example, should the cost of a pencil sharpener be recorded as an asset and depreciated over its useful life? Even though more than one period will benefit from the use of this asset, the concept of materiality permits its immediate expensing on grounds that it would be too cumbersome to undertake depreciation accounting for such a low-cost asset and that the results of the company would not differ significantly. Generally, an item is material if there is a reasonable expectation that knowledge of it would influence the decisions of prudent users of financial statements.

2.5 DEPRECIATION OF FIXED ASSETS

To prepare a profit and loss account and determine net profit for an accounting period, accountants use the matching or accruals principle. Under the matching principle, revenues are recognised when earned — that is, when realised in the form of cash or when reasonably certain of conversion into cash; revenue is then "matched" with associated costs. In using the matching principle, one must ensure that all expenses are recorded in the period in which they are incurred. One expense that needs careful consideration is depreciation of fixed assets.

Fixed assets have a useful life extending over a number of years. This creates an accounting problem, because to write off the entire cost of the asset in the year of purchase to the profit and loss account would clearly be incorrect. Fixed assets are used over a relatively long period of time and, yet, they do depreciate and at the end of their useful life may have a small or nil residual value.

The accounting problem of fixed assets is solved by providing for annual depreciation. Depreciation may be defined as "a measure of the wearing out, or reduction in the useful economic life of a fixed asset whether arising from use, passage of time or obsolescence". This means that a portion of the historical cost — the purchase price — should be written off by way of depreciation to the profit and loss account each year. The amount depends on the original cost, the estimated realisable value and the estimated useful life of the asset.

Where an asset is deemed to last five years, with no residual value for example, one-fifth of the cost of the asset may be written off as depreciation each year to the profit and loss account. However, depreciation is purely a book-keeping entry and does not involve any cash flow. There are two principal methods of depreciation that are illustrated below.

ILLUSTRATION

A company purchased an asset for €10,000 that has an estimated useful life of four years and is expected to realise €2,000 when disposed of.

Straight Line Method

This method is also referred to as the fixed instalment method. The straight line method spreads the net cost evenly over the estimated useful life of the asset. The formula for calculating annual depreciation under the straight line method is:

<u>Historical cost of asset less realisable value</u>
Estimated useful life

$$= \quad \underline{€10,000 - €2,000} \quad = \quad €2,000 \text{ per annum.}$$
$$4 \text{ years}$$

While it is a simple method, its disadvantage is that an even amount of depreciation is written off each year even though certain assets depreciate more quickly during the initial years of their lives.

Reducing Balance Method

Using the reducing balance method, a pre-determined percentage is applied to the cost of the asset for the first year. In succeeding years, the same percentage is applied to the book value of the asset — that is, cost less total (aggregate) depreciation written off to date. Thus, the annual depreciation charge under this method gets smaller and smaller each year. Its main advantage is that the higher depreciation expense in early years reflects the early obsolescence associated with many fixed assets. This is appropriate where assets depreciate more rapidly in their early years compared with later years.

The appropriate percentage to use for the reducing balance method can be obtained by using the following formula:

$$R = 1 - \sqrt[n]{S/C}$$

where R = annual rate of depreciation; N = Useful life (years) of asset; S = Scrap value at end of life; and C = Historical cost of asset.

For the reducing balance method to apply, there must be a scrap value for the asset. Exhibit 2.2 shows the appropriate reducing balance percentage given the estimated useful life and the scrap value as a percentage of historic cost.

Exhibit 2.2: Annual Depreciation Rates — Reducing Balance Method*

Useful Life	Scrap value (S) as % of Cost (C)				
(years)	20%	15%	10%	5%	1%
2	55	61	68	77	90
3	41	47	53	63	78
4	33	38	43	53	68
5	27	31	37	45	60

* *Based on opening book value of asset.*

Since the fixed asset in the example has an estimated useful life of four years, and the scrap value is 20 per cent of cost, the appropriate percentage to use is 33 per cent. The depreciation charges for the first two years will be as follows:

	€
Cost	10,000
Depreciation (Year 1) (33% x 10,000)	3,300
Book value	6,700
Depreciation (Year 2) (33% x 6,700)	2,211
Book value	4,489

The annual depreciation expense written off to the profit and loss account and the balance sheet presentation for the asset is shown in Exhibit 2.3, which highlights the distinction between "depreciation" and "aggregate depreciation". The former represents the annual expense that is written off to the profit and loss account, while the latter represents the total amount of depreciation written off to date. Aggregate depreciation is shown by way of deduction from the cost of the asset on the balance sheet to give "book value". In the first year and first year only, both depreciation and aggregate depreciation will be the same.

Exhibit 2.3: Comparison of Depreciation Methods

	STRAIGHT LINE €	REDUCING BALANCE €
Depreciation (Profit and loss account)		
Year 1	2,000	3,300
Year 2	2,000	2,211
Balance Sheet — Year 1		
Cost	10,000	10,000
Less: Aggregate depreciation	(2,000)	(3,300)
Book value	8,000	6,700
Balance Sheet — Year 2		
Cost	10,000	10,000
Less: Aggregate depreciation	(4,000)	(5,511)
Book value	(6,000)	(4,489)

The purchase of fixed assets affects the profit for the year via the resulting annual charge for depreciation. However, the profit upon which the liability for corporation tax is calculated (taxable profit) does not include accounting depreciation. Certain categories of fixed assets attract capital allowances that are, in effect, a form of tax depreciation.

In providing for depreciation in the annual financial statements, modern accounting practice requires:

1. The disclosure by way of note in the company's financial statements of the accounting policy — that is, disclose the assets being depreciated, the method being used and the annual rates. In addition, the depreciation charge for the year, the gross cost of the depreciable assets and the related accumulated (aggregate) depreciation must also be disclosed.

2. The method of depreciation to be applied consistently. A change from one method to another is permissible only on the grounds that the new method will give a fairer presentation of the results and of the financial position.

3. It is not appropriate to omit depreciation of a fixed asset on the grounds that its market value is greater than its book value. If account is taken of the increased value of fixed assets (for example, through the revaluation of premises), depreciation should be based on the revised figure.

2.6   THE LAYERED PROFIT AND LOSS ACCOUNT

In October 1992, the ASB issued a new accounting standard (FRS 3 *Reporting Financial Performance*), which introduced radical changes to the format of the profit and loss account and to the calculation of EPS. FRS 3 supersedes SSAP 6 (dealing with extraordinary and exceptional items) and amends SSAP 3, *Earnings per share (EPS)*. It is plausible to argue that FRS 3 was needed to address problem areas in determining a company's overall profitability during an accounting period. The three problem areas that are addressed in FRS 3 are discussed in turn.

First, there was the need to eliminate the confusion and manipulation associated with distinguishing between extraordinary and exceptional items in financial statements. Under SSAP 6 and SSAP 3, extraordinary items did *not* affect the calculation of EPS whereas exceptional items did. Consequently many unusual gains were classified as exceptional items in the financial statements, thereby boosting EPS. On the other hand, many unusual losses were deliberately classified as extraordinary items since they would thus not impact on EPS calculations.

Second was the heavy emphasis placed by users of financial statements on the EPS figure (which, in turn, was used in calculating the company's Price/Earnings Ratio — PER). Intelligent users of financial statements will recognise that the financial performance of a complex organisation simply cannot be distilled into a single accounting number such as EPS.

Third, traditional profit and loss accounts did not separately disclose and differentiate between the results from continuing operations, discontinued operations and acquired companies. Thus, it was difficult to make a realistic prediction of the operating profits of the enterprise for future years, particularly where there was significant change in the activities of the business.

These three problem areas were addressed in FRS 3. The intention behind the standard was to make available to users of financial statements additional and relevant information about financial performance that is presented in a logical manner. FRS 3 should lead to more sophistication in the assessment of a company's performance during an accounting period and produce benefits to users such as a greater ability to more accurately predict future financial performance. It will no longer be credible for those analysing financial statements to concentrate on a single accounting number such as EPS or the net profit for the year and deem that to be the sole indicator of a company's performance. Instead, FRS 3 will enable users of accounts to be more aware of the various aspects of a company's trading performance.

Extraordinary Items

Under FRS 3, extraordinary items will still, in theory, remain. However, their occurrence will be significantly reduced. Traditionally, most extraordinary items related to the sale or restructuring costs of a business segment. Under FRS 3, such events will receive separate disclosure in the profit and loss account relating to discontinued operations. Any extraordinary items that remain are to be included in computing EPS. Thus, all transactions will now impact on the EPS calculation. This will remove one of the major abuses in accounting in these islands.

EPS

It can be argued that, in previous years, too much attention was placed on the single EPS figure published by companies. Under FRS 3, the definition of "earnings" on which the EPS calculation is to be based will include extraordinary items. However reporting companies

will be allowed to present a number of EPS figures. Nevertheless, the
EPS figure required by FRS 3 should be at least as prominent as any
additional version presented and the reasons for calculating the additional version should be explained.

Continuing and Discontinued Operations

The standard also requires separate disclosure of continuing operations and discontinued operations. This represents a significant improvement in the reporting of a company's financial results. In addition, the disclosure relating to continuing operations is to be divided
into normal continuing operations and acquisitions.

In a similar manner, disclosure relating to discontinued operations
will generally be subdivided into the profit (loss) from discontinued
operations together with a separate disclosure for any gain (loss) on
the disposal of discontinued operations.

Thus, under FRS 3, companies must now analyse turnover and
operating profit between acquired, continuing and discontinued operations. The analysis of turnover and operating profit is the minimum disclosure requirement in this respect for the profit and loss
account.

In future, profit and loss accounts prepared under FRS 3 will have
a layered format, designed to highlight four important components of
overall financial performance as follows:

1. Turnover/profits from continuing and acquired operations.

2. Turnover/profits from discontinued operations.

3. Profits/losses on the sale or termination of a business segment,
   with separate disclosure for fundamental reorganisation or restructuring costs. (Profits/losses on sale of assets in continuing operations will also be separately disclosed).

4. Extraordinary items (which are to be included in calculating EPS).

Clearly users of financial statements will now have additional and
more relevant information, presented in a logical manner, to use in
the prediction of future profits of the business entity.

A brief illustration of the new profit and loss account format is
contained in Exhibit 2.4 for reference purposes and readers are encouraged to examine this exhibit and work through the answers to
the following two questions:

1. What would the profit on ordinary activities (before interest) have
   been if the segment was *not* sold during the year? [Answer: €51
   (the loss on disposal would not have incurred)]

2. What profit figure should be used in predicting operating profits for next year? [Answer: €56 (profits on continuing operations)].

Exhibit 2.4: Profit and Loss Account
for Year Ended (date)

	€	€
Turnover		
Continuing operations	550	
Acquisitions	50	
	600	
Discontinued operations	175	
		775
Cost of sales		(620)
Gross profit		155
Net operating expenses		(104)
Operating profit		
Continuing operations	50	
Acquisitions	6	
	56	
Discontinued operations	(5)	51
Loss on disposal of discontinued operations		(4)
Profit on ordinary activities before interest		47
Interest payable		(18)
Profit on ordinary activities before taxation		29
Tax on profit on ordinary activities		(14)
Profit on ordinary activities after taxation		15
Dividends		(5)
Profit retained for financial year		10

2.7   END OF CHAPTER QUESTIONS

Question 2.1

Write a brief essay discussing the issues raised in the following statement:

> There is little to be gained from a balance sheet, as the important feature of a company's performance is the net profit from the profit and loss account.

(*The Association of Chartered Certified Accountants*)

Question 2.2

What do you understand by the phrase "information content of financial statements"?

(The Association of Chartered Certified Accountants)

Question 2.3: Kevin

The accounting equation can be expressed as Assets = Liabilities + Capital. The balances of each item in Kevin's accounting equation are given below for 31 August and for each of the next 12 business days.

	CASH	DEBTORS	STOCK	FIXED ASSETS	CREDITORS	CAPITAL
	€	€	€	€	€	€
Aug. 31 Bal.	5,000	10,000	9,000	6,000	6,000	24,000
Sept. 1	7,000	8,000	9,000	6,000	6,000	24,000
2	7,000	8,000	10,000	6,000	7,000	24,000
3	11,000	8,000	10,000	6,000	7,000	28,000
4	13,500	5,500	10,000	6,000	7,000	28,000
5	10,500	5,500	13,000	6,000	7,000	28,000
8	8,500	5,500	13,000	10,000	9,000	28,000
9	6,500	5,500	13,000	12,000	9,000	28,000
10	5,500	5,500	13,000	12,000	8,000	28,000
11	6,500	5,500	13,000	11,000	8,000	28,000
12	6,500	7,500	11,000	11,000	8,000	28,000
15	6,500	7,500	15,000	11,000	12,000	28,000
16	6,500	8,500	15,000	10,000	12,000	28,000

You should assume that only one transaction occurred each day.

REQUIREMENT

1. State in a single sentence the nature and amount of the transaction that took place on each of the above 12 days.

2. Compute the current ratio at 16 September, assuming all liabilities are classified as current.

(The Institute of Chartered Accountants in Ireland)

Question 2.4: M. Robbins Company

On 31 December 20x8, the following balances were extracted from the books of M. Robbins Company, for the first year of trading.

	€
Share capital	6,000
Premises	4,000
Plant and machinery	3,000
Debtors (Accounts receivable)	5,000
Creditors (Accounts payable)	4,000
Purchases	8,000
Sales	17,000
Investment income	100
Distribution expenses	1,000
Bank overdraft interest	1,000
Cash on hands	1,000
Bank overdraft	1,000
Administration expenses	9,000
Stock Exchange investments at cost	2,000
Long-term loan	5,900

NOTE: Closing stock was valued at €3,000.

REQUIREMENT
You are required to prepare a profit and loss account for the year ended 31 December 20x8, together with a balance sheet at that date.

Question 2.5: O'Dea Ltd.

The following balances have been extracted from the books of O'Dea Ltd., a retail shop which had been trading for a number of years, at 31 December 20x0:

	€
Capital invested	5,500
Profit and loss account (1 January 20x0)	2,500
Debtors	3,800
Creditors	2,936
Purchases	26,419
Wages and salaries expense	6,287
Distribution expenses	3,149
Sales	44,900
Stock (1 January 20x0)	4,100
Rent and rates expense	3,986
Postage and stationery expense	369

	€
Insurance expense	1,219
Premises at cost	10,600
Interest on loan paid during year	400
Plant and equipment	2,500
Bank overdraft	1,493
Long-term loan	7,000
Telephone expense	1,500

The following information is provided:

1. Closing stock was valued at €6,109.

2. Taxation is to be provided on this year's profits before tax at the rate of 40 per cent.

3. Dividends in the amount of €300 are to be declared, based on profits of the year.

REQUIREMENT
Prepare a profit and loss account for the year ended 31 December 20x0 together with a balance sheet as on that date.

Question 2.6: N. Case Ltd.

The following list of balances have been extracted from the books of N. Case Ltd. at 31 December 20x8, the end of the year:

	€
Sales	43,100
Purchases	19,000
Repairs expense	2,100
Distribution expenses	3,100
Creditors	4,200
Debtors	9,300
Stock (1 January 20x8)	8,400
Fixtures and fittings	4,000
Land and buildings	15,000
Light and heat expense	900
Bank overdraft	400
Wages and salaries expense	8,700
10 per cent Loan (long-term)	10,000
Interest expense	1,000
Postage, telephone and stationery expense	700
Deposit account	3,000
Called up share capital	15,000
Profit and loss account 1 January 20x8	2,500

The following information is relevant:

1. Closing stock was valued at €3,500.

2. Included incorrectly in repairs (€2,100) is a sum of €1,200 in respect of new fixtures and fittings.

3. Provide for taxation amounting to €1,225 for the above year.

REQUIREMENT
Prepare a profit and loss account for the year ended 31 December 20x8 together with a balance sheet as at that date.

Question 2.7: P. Wood

The following profit and loss account and balance sheet have been prepared by a junior clerk of a business, which you have now joined. The business has neither generated a profit nor loss until this year. You are required to draft the accounts in a format suitable for presentation to a director (who has little knowledge of accounting).

PROFIT AND LOSS ACCOUNT OF P. WOOD
FOR YEAR ENDED 31 DECEMBER 20x5

	€		€
Opening stock (1.1.20X5)	5,000	Sales	25,000
Purchases	8,000		
Purchases of motor vehicles	3,000	Closing stock	9,000
Advertising	2,000		
Wages	4,500		
Purchase of fixtures	1,000	Trade creditors	4,500
Rent & rates	1,500		
Profit	13,500		
	38,500		38,500

P. WOOD's BALANCE SHEET
AT 31 DECEMBER 20x5

	€		€
Share capital	2,500	Debtors	7,000
Profit	13,500	Closing stock	9,000
	16,000		16,000

Question 2.8: Rapid Ltd.

The balances below were extracted from the books of Rapid Ltd. on 30 June 20x8:

	€000
Share capital	1,000
20 per cent Loan payable	100
Land and buildings (Cost €900)	700
Plant and machinery (Cost €700)	400
Motor vehicles (Cost €200)	180
Stock 30 June 20x8 (Note 1)	400
Debtors	450
Creditors	340
Retained profit (1 July 20x7)	88
Sales	2,600
Cost of sales (Note 1)	1,440
Rent and rates	90
Insurance	120
Wages and salaries	320
Advertising	65
Stationery and telephone	15
Interest on loan	20
Bank overdraft	72

1. The closing stock has already been adjusted for in computing the cost of sales figure above.

REQUIREMENT

You are required to prepare the profit and loss account for the year ended 30 June 20x8, together with the balance sheet as at that date.

Question 2.9: Greyrock Ltd.

Greyrock Ltd. purchased a new item of equipment on 1 January 20x1 for €1,400,000. The asset had an expected life of five years at the end of which its realisable value was expected to be €150,000.

REQUIREMENT

1. Describe and comment on the purpose of depreciation in financial statements.

2. Calculate the charge for depreciation for Greyrock Ltd. for the years ended 31 December 20x1 and 20x2, using the following depreciation methods: (i) reducing balance; (ii) straight line method.

(The Association of Chartered Certified Accountants)

Question 2.10: P. Unter Ltd.

From the following information of P. Unter Ltd. at 31 December 20x7, you are required to prepare a profit and loss account for the year ended 31 December 20x7 together with a balance sheet at that date. The company has been trading for a number of years.

	€
Capital invested	5,500
Profit and loss account (1 January)	2,500
Debtors	3,500
Creditors	2,936
Purchases	26,419
Wages and salaries	6,287
Distribution	3,149
Sales	44,900
Stock (1 January)	4,100
Rent and rates	3,986
Postage and stationery	369
Insurance	1,219
Premises at cost	10,600
Interest on loan paid during year	700
Plant at cost	2,500
Bank overdraft	1,493
10 per cent Loan 200x	7,000
Sundry administration expenses	1,500

The following information is provided:

1. Closing stock was valued at €6,109.

2. Provision should be made for depreciation on all the fixed assets at a rate of 10 per cent on the straight line basis. The fixed assets were all acquired during 20x7.

Question 2.11: Stanton Concrete Ltd.

Stanton Concrete Ltd. had the following balances as of the end of its accounting year dated 31 December 20x8.

	€
Ordinary share capital (50c shares)	77,000
7.5 per cent Loan (repayable 201x)	68,700
Cash	1,000
Stock and work in progress	55,800
Motor vehicles at cost	34,500
Aggregate depreciation	16,000

	€
Plant and machinery at cost	92,900
Aggregate depreciation	47,100
Investments (short-term) at cost	9,300
Current taxation payable	15,700
Trade creditors	59,700
Trade debtors	79,600
Freehold land and buildings	85,800
Aggregate depreciation	11,300
Dividends payable	3,800
Bank overdraft	8,900
Profit and loss account (retained profits)	50,700

REQUIREMENT

1. You are required to prepare a balance sheet at 31 December 20x8, based on the above information.

2. Compute the following ratios based on the balance sheet:

    (a) Current ratio

    (b) Acid Test ratio

    (c) Long-term debt/Capital employed.

Question 2.12: New Dev Ltd.

The following data relates to New Dev Ltd. at 31 March 20x1 based on its first trading year ended on that date:

	€
Trade creditors	60,000
Closing stock	40,000
Debtors	90,000
Plant and machinery at cost	200,000
Aggregate depreciation	15,000
Land at cost	105,000
Buildings at cost	130,000
Aggregate depreciation	20,000
Called up share capital	250,000
Profit retained for year	65,000

NOTE: The figures for cash and long-term liabilities for the balance sheet are the only figures that are missing. However, you may assume that total current assets amount to €175,000.

REQUIREMENT

1. You are required to prepare a balance sheet after the first year of trading.

2. Confirm the following ratios:

   (a) Current ratio: 2.91 times

   (b) Acid Test ratio: 2.25 times

   (c) Long-term debt to Capital employed: 38.9%.

Question 2.13: M. Cod Ltd.

The following balances were extracted from the books of M. Cod Ltd. at the end of his first financial year to 30 June 20x1:

	€
Ordinary share capital	6,000
Premises	2.250
Plant & machinery	2,010
Loan payable — J. Smith (20x5)	1,000
Selling expenses	360
Purchases	6,639
Sales	8,957
Debtors	1,524
Creditors	1,392
Telephone expense	247
Advertising expense	724
Bank interest paid	60
Wages and salaries expense	2,172
Cash at bank	1,363

You are informed that on 30 June 20x1 stock was valued at €1,570.

REQUIREMENT

You are required to prepare a profit and loss account for the year ended 30 June 20x1 and a balance sheet as at that date.

Question 2.14: Shirley Ltd.

The accounting year of Shirley Ltd. ended on 30 June 20x6. The following list of balances was extracted from the company's accounting records:

	€
Purchases	29,140
Sales	38,841
Wages and salaries (admin.)	3,770
Light and heat (admin.)	1,554
Rent and rates (admin.)	482
Bank interest	209
Advertising (selling)	205
Premises — Cost	3,810
Premises — Aggregate depreciation	934
Furniture and fittings — Cost	1,804
Furniture and fittings — Aggregate depreciation	604
Motor vehicles — Cost	2,000
Motor vehicles — Aggregate depreciation	300
Stock 1 July 20x5	8,305
Debtors	8,200
Creditors	5,900
Retained profits brought forward (1 July 20x5)	407
Cash in hand	945
Bank overdraft	1,438
Share capital (Ordinary)	12,000

The following information is also available:

1. Depreciation for the year is to be charged as follows:
    (a) Premises: €176 (administration expense)
    (b) Furniture and fittings 10 per cent on a diminishing balance method basis (administration expense)
    (c) Motor vehicles 10 per cent on cost (Distribution expense)

2. Stocks on hand at 30 June 20x6 amounted to €9,224.

REQUIREMENT
Prepare a profit and loss account for the year ended 30 June 20x6 and a balance sheet as at that date.

Question 2.15: T. O'Mato Ltd.

The following balances were extracted from the books of T. O'Mato Ltd., at 31 March 20x9. The company has been trading for a number of years.

	€
Share capital	233,000
Land and buildings (cost €100,000)	86,000
Furniture and fittings (cost €150,000)	90,000
Motor vehicles (cost €100,000)	60,000
Stock at 31 March, 20x9 (Note 2)	124,000
Trade debtors	155,000
Creditors	119,000
Sales	830,000
Cost of sales (Note 2)	541,000
Wages and salaries (admin.)	104,000
Rent, rates and insurance (admin.)	15,000
Selling and distribution expenses	12,000
Sales commissions	6,500
14 per cent Loan payable	50,000
Stationery and telephone (admin.)	4,000
Interest on loan	7,000
Advertising	45,000
Bank overdraft	7,500
Retained profit (1 April 20x8)	10,000

You are provided with the following additional information:

1. Depreciation is to be provided on fixed assets on hand at 31 March 20x9, at the following rates:

    ◊   Land & buildings: 2 per cent on cost

    ◊   Furniture & fittings: 10 per cent on cost

    ◊   Motor vehicles: 20 per cent on cost

2. Closing stock has already been adjusted for in computing the cost of goods sold above.

REQUIREMENT

You are required to prepare:

1. The profit and loss account for the year ended 31 March 20x9.

2. The balance sheet as at that date.

Question 2.16: Deli Ltd.

Deli Ltd. was incorporated in December 20x6, when it issued 600,000 ordinary shares of €1 each for cash. The company commenced business on 1 January 20x7, and, since that time, has traded in a single product, "tint", which is both purchased and sold for cash.

The company purchased fixed assets at a total cost of €400,000 in January 20x7. These fixed assets were expected to last nine years and have a combined residual value of €40,000.

The following information is provided in respect of the years 20x7, 20x8 and 20x9.

	20x7	20x8	20x9
Number of items bought	13,000	14,000	14,000
Number of items sold	10,000	12,000	14,000
Average purchase price per item	€90	€90	€90
Average sale price per item	€130	€140	€150
Total expenses (excluding depreciation)	€305,000	€346,000	€402,000
Closing bank balance (31 December)	€25,000	€99,000	€537,000

REQUIREMENT

1. Prepare summary profit and loss accounts of Deli Ltd. for each of the three years 20x7 to 20x9, together with the balance sheet at 31 December in each year, depreciating fixed assets on the straight line method.

2. Prepare summary profit and loss accounts of Deli Ltd. for each of the three years 20x7 to 20x9, together with the balance sheets at 31 December in each year, depreciating fixed assets on the reducing (diminishing) balance basis (depreciation rate 22.5 per cent).

NOTES:

(a) Ignore taxation.

(b) No dividends were paid during the years 20x7 to 20x9.

3

Cash Flow Statements

3.1 THE NATURE AND IMPORTANCE OF CASH FLOW STATEMENTS

In accordance with company law, published financial statements of limited liability companies comprise a profit and loss account showing, *inter alia*, the amount of profit generated in the business during the year, and a balance sheet showing the amount and classification of assets and how they were financed. In addition, comparative figures for all items in both the profit and loss account and balance sheet must be provided. These two financial statements are prepared under the accruals (or matching) basis of accounting. However, critics of the profit and loss account argue that the accruals principle frequently leads to a surplus or deficit far removed from the underlying creation or consumption of cash from operations. Accordingly, it is possible that a business may be generating a profit according to the profit and loss account, but experiencing severe cash flow problems. Thus, for a fuller understanding of the company's affairs, it may be necessary to identify the movements in assets, liabilities and share capital that have taken place during the year and the resultant effect on net liquid funds. Net liquid funds are the firm's cash at bank and in hand less other borrowings repayable within one year of the accounting date.

Net profit, prepared under the accruals basis of accounting, will rarely equal cash flow for the accounting period. At least three reasons for this difference can be cited:

1. Some transactions impact on cash flow but not profitability, i.e. the profit and loss account (e.g. purchase/sale of fixed assets, issue of share capital or repayment of loans).

2. Some transactions impact on profitability, i.e. the profit and loss account, but not cash flow (e.g., depreciation of fixed assets, writing off bad debts).

3. There is an inevitable time lag between earning revenue (as in the profit and loss account) and the receipt of the relevant cash (which impacts on cash flow). An excellent example of this is goods sold on credit.

The apparent "inconsistency" between a business generating a profit according to the profit and loss account, but experiencing severe cash flow problems at the same time, is explained by the preparation of a cash flow statement. In simple terms, a cash flow statement explains the movement in cash funds between successive balance sheets. In July 1975, the accountancy profession in these islands issued an accounting standard, SSAP 10 (*Statements of Source and Application of Funds*), requiring companies to produce a statement of source and application of funds as part of their audited financial statements. The objective of SSAP 10 was to show the manner in which the operations of the reporting entity had been financed and in which its financial resources had been used. This was the first accounting standard to require an addition to the basic financial statements of the balance sheet and profit and loss account. However, SSAP 10 did not prescribe a specific format. Indeed, it did not even define the important term "funds". Consequently, the presentation of such statements varied widely, reducing comparability and, therefore, their usefulness. In some cases, companies could present a statement of source and application of funds that could virtually disguise the underlying cash flow position of the entity.

ILLUSTRATION

The following current assets and current liabilities were extracted from the balance sheet of CF Ltd. as at 31 December, 20x2:

	31 Dec. 20x1	31 Dec. 20x2
	€	€
Stock	4,600	4,300
Debtors	1,300	2,600
Cash and Bank	2,500	1,200
	8,400	8,100
Creditors	7,900	6,500
Net current assets	500	1,600

REQUIREMENT

Identify the change in working capital funds and the change in cash funds. Net current assets (or working capital) here comprises of current assets less current liabilities.

ANALYSIS
If we look solely at working capital (defined in this case as total current assets minus total current liabilities) then this provides an *increase* of funds of €1,100 over the year. On the other hand, if we look only at cash funds, we see that the position has *deteriorated by* €1,300 over the same period.

Sources and Application of Funds
The principal sources and applications of cash flow are highlighted in Exhibit 3.1 below.

Exhibit 3.1 Sources and Application of Cash Funds

Sources of cash funds	Application of cash funds
Cash flow from trading i.e. profitable trading.	Negative cash flow from trading i.e. unprofitable trading.
Changes in working capital • Reduction in stocks • Reduction in accounts receivable • Increase in accounts payable.	Changes in working capital • Increase in stocks • Increase in accounts receivable • Decrease in accounts payable.
Miscellaneous income received • Receipt of interest • Receipt of dividends.	Payments of profits • Payment of interest • Payment of taxation • Payment of dividends.
Liquidate fixed assets • Cash on sale of fixed assets.	Purchase of fixed assets • Cash payment to acquire fixed assets.
Generate long-term sources of finance • Issue additional share capital • Issue additional long-term loans.	Repayment of long-term finance • Repayment of share capital • Repayment of long-term loans.

3.2 PREPARATION OF CASH FLOW STATEMENTS

Based on the listing of the various sources and applications of cash (Exhibit 3.1), the following sequence in preparing cash flow statements is recommended. The first is to confirm that comparative balance sheets and a detailed profit and loss account are available. From these financial statements, identify the operating profit for the year. This will be the opening figure in the cash flow statement being prepared. Thereafter, identify the movement (increase or decrease) in cash/bank funds during the period. This will represent the end line in the cash flow statement being prepared. What we are trying to do in preparing cash flow statements is to explain or reconcile the difference between operating profit (or profit before interest and tax) and the cash flow generated over the same period. The cash implications of the following activities – cash flow from trading, changes in working capital and various applications of cash during the period – should then be identified and finally, long-term financing generated during the period. Each of these will be discussed in turn.

Cash Flow from Trading

The most significant source of cash funds generated by an enterprise during the period is that of "profitable trading". If all trading transactions were transacted in cash, ignoring other transactions involving the purchase of fixed assets etc., then net profit earned would correspond to the increase in the cash resources of the firm. (A net loss would represent funds absorbed, i.e. indicate that the firm, ignoring other transactions, was depleting its cash funds). However, the net profit calculation will automatically include non-cash items of expenditure, of which depreciation is the most significant in terms of its magnitude within the financial statements. Depreciation is a charge against profits for a year, effectively an attempt to reflect the partial using up of the life of the company's fixed assets; it is simply a bookkeeping entry and does not itself generate cash.

Therefore, cash flow from trading or operations can be determined by either of two methods to be illustrated using the following simplified example where depreciation is the only item in the profit and loss account not involving cash.

ILLUSTRATION

The following summarised profit and loss account is presented to you (ignoring the impact of taxation and dividends).

Profit and Loss Account for Year ended (date)

	€
Sales	21,000
Less Purchases (all used)	(10,000)
Wages	(5,000)
Administration	(2,000)
Depreciation	(1,000)
Net profit for year	3,000

REQUIREMENT
Identify the figure for cash flow from trading.

ANALYSIS
The simplest or most straightforward method would be to deduct from sales the outlays on purchases and operating expenses such as wages and administration. This surplus (€4,000) is, by definition, the cash funds generated from trading. This method is referred to as the *"direct"* method.

As an alternative, the *addback* or *indirect* method is proposed and is commonly used in preparing cash flow statements. Using this method, cash flow from trading can be determined by taking the net profit figure (given) and adding back the depreciation expense. Unfortunately, this shortcut method of adding back depreciation to net profit may, at first sight, create the false impression that depreciation is a source of cash. Depreciation is purely a book-keeping entry and, as such, can never generate cash flow for the business. Depreciation is never a source of cash. In constructing cash funds flow statements, we add back depreciation to the net profit figure simply because it provides a convenient short cut in arriving at cash flow from trading.

Changes in Working Capital
For the purposes of preparing cash flow statements, working capital consists of stock, debtors and creditors. It is best to prepare a schedule of changes in working capital items. Thus for stocks, debtors and creditors identify whether the items have increased or decreased during the period. Increases in any current assets (or decreases in current liabilities) represent an application of cash flow for the period. Increases in current liability items (or decrease in current assets) represent a source of cash flow for the period.

The cash flow consequences of the management of working capital — stocks, debtors (accounts receivables) and creditors (accounts payable) — are shown in Exhibit 3.2.

Exhibit 3.2: Cash Flow Consequences of Working Capital Management

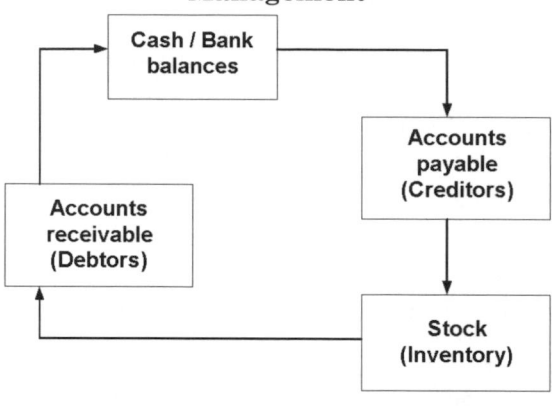

To summarise, operating cash flow is the aggregate of cash flow from trading and changes in working capital. To survive in the long-term, companies must generate positive operating cash flows and such deficiencies can be covered only by external financing from either shareholders or creditors.

Applications (Uses) of Cash during the Accounting Period

There are two main activities that represent applications of cash during the accounting period: (a) payment out of operating profits, and (b) investment in fixed assets. Payments out of operating profits typically consist of interest, taxation and dividends. Investment in fixed assets typically represents purchase of land, building, plant and so forth.

(a) Payment of taxation and dividends (and interest)

Because we start the cash flow statement with the operating profit (PBIT) figure for the year, we must now include the payment of interest as this has negative cash consequences. The figure to be deducted is the expense for the year, as per the profit and loss account. However, it is necessary to prepare a reconciliation of both tax and dividends. The purpose of this reconciliation is to ascertain the cash consequences of paying tax and dividends during the accounting period. Such information will not be directly evident from the financial statements. The following format of reconciliation is suggested:

Reconciliation of tax and dividends

	Taxation €	Dividends €
Opening liability (per balance sheet	XXX	XXX
Add Expense for current year (P/L)	XXX	XXX
Less Closing liability (per balance sheet)	(XXX)	(XXX)
Equals: Cash payments made during the year	XXX	XXX

(b) Investment in fixed assets

The purchase of fixed assets, if relevant, should be obvious from the relevant note to the financial statements relating to fixed assets. In typical examination questions, this information must be created and can be done by preparing a reconciliation of fixed assets in the following format, based on the book amounts (i.e. cost less aggregate depreciation) of the fixed assets:

Reconciliation of fixed assets:	€
Opening book value of fixed assets	XX
Add: Additions during year*	XX
Add: Revaluation of fixed assets	XX
Less: Disposals at book value	(XX)
Depreciation for year	(XX)
Closing book value per balance sheet	XX

* *Must represent the balancing figure. It is only the cash amount paid on the acquisition of fixed assets that will appear in the cash flow statement.*

Disposal of Fixed Assets

It may well be that the company has sold some of its fixed assets during the current accounting period. This represents a source of cash funds and should be reflected as a positive item in the cash flow statement. In many cases, such fixed assets are sold at a profit or a loss and this profit/loss will most likely be included in the operating profit figure for the year. Therefore, in order to arrive at cash flow from operating activities, one further adjustment can be made to the operating profit figure in respect of profit (loss) on the sale of fixed assets. Consider the sale of land with a book value of €10,000 being sold for €12,000, thus generating a profit of €2,000. The cash proceeds of €12,000 represents a cash flow and a distinct source of funds. Since the €2,000 gain may have already been included in operating profit, then the amount of the gain would be double-counted, unless we take steps to eliminate it. Profits from the sale of fixed assets should be eliminated (deducted) from operating profit. Likewise, losses on disposal are eliminated to avoid double-counting by adding them to our operating profit figure in the cash flow statement.

Long-Term Financing Generated During the Period

The main sources of funds generated during the period will be either by way of share issue (including share premium) and/or additional long-term loans obtained. This information may be obtained by comparing opening and closing figures relating to share capital, loans, etc. in order to determine the amount of cash raised (or repaid).

3.3 CASH FLOW STATEMENTS AND FRS 1

FRS 1 is the first Financial Reporting Standard issued by the streamlined Accounting Standards Board (ASB) and replaces SSAP 10. The objective of FRS 1 is to require reporting entities to report on a standard basis their cash generation and cash absorption for a period. Cash flows must be classified under a number of different headings. This structure aims to assist users in their assessment of the reporting entity's liquidity, viability and financial adaptability. A cash flow statement will show the funds generated (absorbed) from operations during the period, in addition to providing information about all the investing and financing activities of the company during the period.

Prescribed Format

FRS 1 was amended in 1996. It contains a standard format and a basic structure that must be adopted. An entity's cash flow statement should list its cash flows under *eight* standard headings as follows, although some of these will not apply to the preparation of every cash flow statement:

1. Cash flow from operating activities
   (profit, adjusted for depreciation and changes in stocks, debtors and creditors)

2. Returns on investments and servicing of finance
   (generally interest paid less interest received)

3. Taxation
   (relating to trading and other income)

4. Capital expenditure and financial investments
   (generally purchase of fixed assets less cash proceeds on disposal)

5. Acquisitions and Disposals
   (the purchase and sale of businesses)

6. Equity dividends paid
   (the amount paid to ordinary shareholders)

7. Management of liquid resources
   (mainly the purchase and sale of government securities)

8. Financing
   (share issues or obtaining or repaying long-term loans)

EQUALS: Increase / decrease of cash during the period.

This net cash flow for the period is added to the balance of cash brought forward at the beginning of the period to give the balance of cash at the end of the year

Reconciliations

Because the information given by a cash flow statement is best appreciated in the context of the information given by the other primary statements, the FRS requires two reconciliations. Neither reconciliation forms part of the cash flow statement but each may be given either adjoining the statement or in a separate note.

The two reconciliations are:

1. A reconciliation between "operating profit" with movement in net cash flow from operating activities during the accounting period. This involves starting with the operating profit figure and adjusting it for depreciation and other non-cash items in the profit and loss account, for example, profit/loss on disposal of assets and changes in bad debt provisions. In addition, adjustments are made for changes in working capital (stocks, trade debtors and trade creditors).

2. A note reconciling the movement in cash during the period with the movements in net debt should be given either adjoining the cash flow statement or in a note. The idea behind this disclosure is to see whether, for example, cash flow is improving as a result of additional debt acquired.

In addition, two notes to the cash flow statement should be published. However, extensive treatment of both these reconciliations and notes are beyond the scope of this introductory book (and probably beyond the comprehension of many students and practitioners!). For learning purposes, the main ingredients of cash flow statements are outlined in Exhibit 3.3 and are based on FRS 1. For teaching purposes, some of this exhibit has been simplified in order to focus on the major ele-

ments of cash flow statements considered appropriate by this author
for teaching introductory accounting courses. Indeed, most of the examples that follow will focus only on identifying the main cash flow
activities of a business together with supporting information.

Exhibit 3.3: Cash Flow Statement for the year ended 31 December 20x2

Reconciliation of operating profit to net cash inflow from operating activities

	€
Operating profit	11,570
Add: Depreciation charges	899
Less: Increase in stocks	(194)
Less: Increase in debtors	(72)
Add: Increase in creditors	234
Equals: Net Cash inflow from operating activities	12,437

Cash Flow Statement	€
Net cash inflow from operating activities	12,437
Returns on investments and servicing of finance (e.g., payment of interest)	(2,999)
Taxation	(2,922)
Capital expenditure (e.g., purchase of tangible fixed assets)	(1,525)
	4,991
Equity dividends paid	(2,417)
	2,574
Management of liquid resources	Nil
Financing	57
Increase in cash	2,631

Under FRS 1, "operating activities" can be prepared using either of
the direct or indirect methods. The indirect method represents operating profit adjusted for non-cash items such as depreciation. The
direct method details operating cash receipts and cash payments.
Both methods result in the reporting of the same amount for net
operating cash flows.

ILLUSTRATION

The following information has been presented to you for Flow Ltd., a retail company, for a recent accounting period:

Balance Sheet as at 31 December

	20x1		20x2	
	€	€	€	€
Fixed Assets (net)		23,500		26,000
Current Assets				
Stock	10,500		12,800	
Debtors	11,000		13,000	
Bank	1,000		100	
	22,500		25,900	
Current Liabilities				
Trade Creditors	(13,900)		(15,500)	
Taxation payable	(2,000)		(1,000)	
	(15,900)		(16,500)	
		6,600		9,400
		30,100		35,400
Financed By				
Share Capital		10,000		12,000
Profit and Loss Account		10,100		13,600
Long-term Loans		10,000		9,800
(repayable 20x9)				
		30,100		35,400

Profit and Loss Account for year ended 31 December 20x2

	€
Sales	100,000
Cost of sales	(73,000)
Gross profit	27,000
Expenses (note)	(16,500)
Profit before interest and tax	10,500
Interest paid	(1,000)
Net Profit before tax	9,500
Taxation	(3,000)
Profit after taxation	6,500
Dividends	(3,000)
Profit retained for year	3,500
Retained profit at start of year	10,100
Retained profit at end of year	13,600

Note: Expenses for 20x2 includes €2,000 depreciation on fixed assets. There were no disposals of fixed assets in 20X2.

REQUIREMENT
Prepare a cash flow statement for the year ended 20x2.

ANALYSIS
Before preparing the cash flow statement, it is first necessary to pre-pare a reconciliation of fixed assets. The purpose of this calculation is to ascertain the cash consequences of buying/selling fixed assets during the accounting period. Such information will not be directly evident from the financial statements.

W1. Reconciliation of fixed assets	**€**
Opening book value of fixed assets	23,500
Add: Additions during year*	4,500
Add: Revaluation of fixed assets	N/A
Less: Disposals at book value	Nil
Depreciation for year	(2,000)
Closing book value per balance sheet	26,000

* *Must represent the balancing figure, i.e. bank transaction. It is the only figure that will not be directly evident from either the profit and loss account or balance sheet.*

Secondly, it is necessary to prepare a reconciliation of both tax and dividends. The purpose of this calculation is to ascertain the cash consequences of paying tax and dividends during the accounting period. Such information will not be directly evident from the financial statements.

W2. Reconciliation of tax and dividends	Taxation €	Dividends €
Opening liability (per opening balance sheet)	2,000	Nil
Add: Expense for current year (P/L)	3,000	3,000
Less: Closing liability (per closing balance sheet)	(1,000)	Nil
Equals: Cash payments made during the year	4,000	3,000

Flow Ltd.
Cash Flow Statement for the year ended 31 December 20X2

Reconciliation of operating profit to net cash inflow from operating activities

	€
Operating profit	10,500
Add: Depreciation expense	2,000
Less: Increase in stocks	(2,300)
Less: Increase in debtors	(2,000)
Add: Increase in creditors	1,600
Net Cash inflow from operating activities	9,800

Cash Flow Statement for year ended 31 December, 20x2

	€
Net cash inflow from operating activities (above)	9,800
Returns on investments and servicing of finance	(1,000)
Taxation paid	(4,000)
Capital expenditure	(4,500)
	300
Equity dividends paid	(3,000)
	(2,700)
Financing	1,800
Decrease in cash	(900)

Information Content of Cash Flow Statements

A cash flow statement highlights differences between the operating profit reported by an entity and the increase/decrease in the cash/bank balance during the same accounting period. As such it should assist shareholders, creditors and others in assessing such factors as:

1. Whether investing activities have been financed from internal sources, e.g., profits generated and/or management of working capital, or from external sources such as borrowing.

2. The company's ability to:
   - ☐ generate positive cash flows in future periods
   - ☐ maintain or expand operating capacity in terms of fixed asset investment
   - ☐ meet its future obligations e.g., repayment of liabilities
   - ☐ pay future dividends.

Historical Cash Flows

A cash flow statement is a record of historical fact in that it reports payments in relation to dividends, interest and purchase of fixed assets. It does not express an opinion whether the expenditure was necessary or whether it will provide long-term benefits for the company. Similarly, it may show an expansion of stock but it does not indicate whether this was due to poor stock or production control, inability to sell the finished product or deliberate company policy to build up stocks.

Likewise, in the case of increased debtors, it does not indicate whether the credit policy of the firm has changed or whether customers are taking additional credit or indeed if the expansion in credit is due solely to the expansion of turnover. Thus, it is advisable to supplement the information contained in a cash flow statement with basic financial ratios and other information available in relation to the company.

3.4 END OF CHAPTER QUESTIONS

Question 3.1: Copeland Antiques

Copeland Antiques reported a net operating profit of €20,000 for the year ended December 31, 20x8. During the same accounting year, the cash balance deteriorated significantly, reducing from €111,300 at the start of the year to €65,300 at the end of the year – a total decrease of €46,000. The Managing Director does not understand how this could have happened since no fixed assets were purchased during the year and the company had not received or repaid any loans.

The following items were included on Copeland's balance sheets at December 31, 20x8 and 20x7:

	20x7	20x8
	€	€
Cash	111,300	65,300
Trade accounts receivable	93,700	123,900
Stock (Inventories)	184,800	222,600
Trade accounts payable	98,000	85,000

Copeland Antiques uses the indirect method to prepare its statement of cash flows. Copeland does not have any other current assets or current liabilities and did not enter into any investing or financing during 20x8. You discover that the depreciation expense for the year amounted to €15,000 during the year. You may ignore tax and dividend payments.

REQUIREMENT

You are required to prepare Copeland's cash flow statements for the year ended 20x8.

Question 3.2: Dublin Company Ltd.

The following are summarised Balance Sheets and Profit and Loss accounts of Dublin Company Ltd., a service company, as at 31 December:

Balance Sheet at 31 December

	20x1		20x2	
	€	€	€	€
Fixed Assets (net)		20,000		30,000
Current Assets				
Debtors	100,000		140,000	
Bank	20,000		5,000	
	120,000		145,000	
Less: Current Liabilities				
Trade creditors	50,000		60,000	
		70,000		85,000
		90,000		115,000
FINANCED BY:				
Share capital (€0.50 each)		60,000		65,000
Profit and loss account		10,000		25,000
Long-term Loans		20,000		25,000
		90,000		115,000

Profit and Loss Account for Year ended 31 December 20X2

	€
Sales (all on credit)	300,000
Selling & distribution expenses	228,000
Depreciation expense	5,000
Administration expenses	38,000
Operating Profit	29,000
Interest	7,000
Net profit before tax	22,000
Taxation	7,000
Profit after taxation and retained for year	15,000
Profit brought forward from previous years	10,000
Profit brought forward at balance sheet date	25,000

REQUIREMENT

Prepare a basic cash flow statement for the year ended 31 December, 20x2 assuming there were no disposals of fixed assets in 20x2. Comprehensive notes to the cash flow statement are not required.

Question 3.3: Wicklow Ltd.

You are provided with the following summarised profit and loss account and balance sheets of Wicklow Ltd., for a recent accounting period.

Balance Sheet at 31 December

	20x1		20x2	
	€	€	€	€
Fixed Assets (net)		37,000		39,000
Current Assets				
Stock (inventory)	231,000		281,000	
Trade Debtors	294,000		408,000	
Bank	1,000		2,000	
	526,000		691,000	
Current Liabilities				
Trade Creditors	387,000		445,000	
Bank overdraft	45,000		104,000	
Taxation payable	5,000		9,000	
	437,000		558,000	
Net Current Assets		89,000		133,000
		126,000		172,000
FINANCED BY:				
Share capital		73,000		83,000
Profit and loss account		38,000		64,000
Long-term Loans		15,000		25,000
		126,000		172,000

Profit and Loss Account for Year ended 31 December 20x2

	€
Operating profit (PBIT)	50,000
Interest	5,000
Net profit before tax	45,000
Taxation on profits	19,000
Profit after taxation	26,000
Retained profits at start of year	38,000
Retained profits at end of year	64,000

Note 1.   Depreciation of fixed assets amounted to €6,000 during 20x2 and is included in arriving at the operating profit figure for the year. There were no disposals of fixed assets.

Note 2.   Dividends are to be ignored.

REQUIREMENT

You are required to prepare a cash flow statement for the year ended 31 December 20x2.

Question 3.4: Longford Company Ltd.

The following summarised profit and loss accounts and balance sheets of Longford Company Ltd., a company that has not borrowed any money, for a recent accounting period are presented to you:

Profit and Loss Accounts for year ended 31 December, 20x8

	€
Profit for year	45,000
Taxation	19,000
Profit after taxation	26,000
Dividend	2,000
Retained	24,000
Brought forward	53,000
	77,000

Balance Sheet as at 31 December

	20x7	20x8
	€	€
Fixed Assets (Net)	37,000	39,000
Current Assets		
Stocks	231,000	281,000
Debtors	294,000	408,000
Cash	1,000	2,000
	526,000	691,000
Current Liabilities		
Creditors	387,000	445,000
Bank overdraft	45,000	106,000
Taxation	3,000	5,000
Dividends	2,000	4,000
	437,000	560,000
Net Current Assets	89,000	131,000
Total Assets less current Liabilities	126,000	170,000

	20x7	20x8
	€	€
FINANCED BY:		
Share capital	73,000	93,000
Profit and loss account	53,000	77,000
	126,000	170,000

Depreciation of fixed assets amounted to €6,000 during 20x8.

REQUIREMENT

Prepare a cash flow statement for the year ended 31 December 20x8. Comprehensive notes to the cash flow statement are not required.

Question 3.5: Cork Ltd.

The following profit and loss account and balance sheets have been prepared for Cork Ltd., a beer manufacturer.

Profit and Loss Account for year ended 31 December 20x8

	€
Operating profit	18,000
Interest on loans	3,000
Net profit before tax	15,000
Taxation	4,000
Profit after taxation	11,000
Dividends	6,000
Profit retained for the year	5,000
Retained profits at start of year	10,000
Retained profits at end of year	15,000

Balance Sheets as at 31 December

	20x7		20x8	
	€	€	€	€
Fixed Assets				
Tangible Fixed Assets (net)		102,000		124,000
Financial Fixed Assets		20,000		23,000
(Investments)				
		122,000		147,000
Current Assets				
Stock	16,000		14,000	
Debtors	32,000		30,000	
Cash & Bank	Nil		43,000	
	48,000		87,000	
Creditors falling due within one year				
Creditors	54,000		69,000	
Bank Overdraft	6,000			
			Nil	
	60,000		69,000	
Net Current Assets		(12,000)		18,000
Total Assets less Current Liabilities		110,000		165,000
Creditors falling due after more than one year				
Long-term Loans		10,000		Nil
Capital and Reserves				
Share capital		90,000		150,000
Profit and loss account		10,000		15,000
		110,000		165,000

Some new fixed assets were purchased during the year but there were no disposals. Depreciation on fixed assets amounted to €12,000.

REQUIREMENT
You are required to prepare a cash flow statement for the year ended 31 December, 20x8. Comprehensive notes to the cash flow statement are not required. Show your workings.

Question 3.6: Wexford Ltd.

The following information has been presented to for Wexford Ltd. for the year ended 31 December 20x5.

Profit and Loss Account for year ended 31 December 20x5

	€
Gross Profit	567,000
Expenses (including depreciation)	(492,000)
Operating profit	75,000
Interest	(7,500)
Net profit before tax	67,500
Taxation	(13,500)
Profit after taxation	54,000
Dividends	(15,000)
Profit retained for the year	39,000
Retained profit at start of year	57,000
Retained profit at end of year	96,000

Balance Sheets as at 31 December

	20x4 €	20x4 €	20x5 €	20x5 €
Fixed Assets (net)		55,500		58,500
Current Assets				
Stock (inventory)	346,500		421,500	
Debtors	441,000		612,000	
Cash	1,500		3,000	
	789,000		1,036,500	
Creditors falling due within one year				
Creditors	575,500		664,500	
Bank overdraft	67,500		156,000	
Taxation	7,500		13,500	
Dividends payable	5,000		3,000	
	655,500		837,000	
Net Current Assets		133,500		199,500
Total Assets less Current Liabilities		189,000		258,000
Creditors falling due after more than one year				
Long-term Loans		22,500		37,500
Capital and Reserves				
Share capital		109,500		124,500
Profit and loss account		57,000		96,000
		189,000		258,000

Depreciation of fixed assets amounted to €9,000 for the year ended 31 December 20x5 and is included in expenses deducted in arriving at profit before interest and tax. There were no disposals of fixed assets during 20x5.

REQUIREMENT

You are required to prepare a cash flow statement for the year ended 31 December, 20x5.

Question 3.7: Belfast Ltd.

The following summary Balance Sheet have been prepared in respect of Belfast Ltd. at 30 June, 20x7, and 30 June, 20x8.

Profit and Loss Account for year ended 30 June 20x8

	€
Operating Profit (PBIT)	47,800
Interest on Loans	1,000
Net Profit before tax	46,800
Taxation	12,000
Profit after Taxation	34,800
Dividends	6,000
Profit retained for the year	28,800
Retained profit at start of year	23,000
Retained profit at end of year	51,800

Balance Sheets as at 30 June

	20x7 €	20x7 €	20x8 €	20x8 €
Fixed Assets (net)		92,000		144,800
Current Assets				
Stock	28,000		30,000	
Debtors	10,000		9,000	
Cash & Bank	5,000		2,000	
	43,000		41,000	
Creditors (amounts falling due within one year)				
Creditors	17,000		16,000	
Dividends payable	5,000		10,000	
	22,000		26,000	
Net Current Assets		21,000		15,000
Total Assets less Current Liabilities		113,000		159,800

	20x7	20x8
	€	€
Capital and Reserves		
Share capital	80,000	97,000
Share premium	10,000	11,000
Profit and loss account	23,000	51,800
	113,000	159,800

Notes:

1. During the year, €70,000 was spent on acquiring new premises.

2. During the year, a machine that has a book value of €1,200 was sold for €1,200, while €40,000 was spent on acquiring new plant.

REQUIREMENT

You are required to prepare a cash flow statement for the year ended 30 June 20x8, (using the indirect method). Comprehensive notes to the cash flow statement are not required. Show your workings.

Question 3.8: Limerick Ltd.

The following information is available in respect to Limerick Ltd., a retail company for a recent accounting period:

Profit and Loss Account for Year ended 31 December, 20x2

	€
Gross profit	109,000
Less: Operating expenses	82,000
Operating profit (PBIT)	27,000
Interest on loans	2,000
Net profit before tax	25,000
Taxation	10,000
Profit after taxation	15,000
Dividends	3,000
Profit retained for the year	12,000

Balance Sheets as at 31 December

| | 20x1 | | 20x2 | |
	€	€	€	€
Fixed Assets				
Land (Freehold)		80,000		90,000
Equipment (net)		35,000		30,000
		115,000		120,000
Current Assets				
Stock	35,000		45,000	
Debtors	40,000		84,000	
Cash & Bank	20,000		1,000	
	95,000		130,000	
Less Current Liabilities				
Trade creditors	(28,000)		(34,000)	
Net current assets		67,000		96,000
		182,000		216,000
Capital and Reserves				
Share Capital		50,000		50,000
(€1 Ord. Shares)				
Revaluation surplus		—		10,000
Profit and loss account		132,000		144,000
		182,000		204,000
Long-term loan		Nil		12,000
		182,000		216,000

Note: Depreciation was provided on equipment only at the rate of 10% on the opening book value. Some equipment was sold at book value during the year. However, the freehold land was revalued by €10,000 during the year.

REQUIREMENT

Prepare a cash flow statement for the year ended 31 December 20x2. Comprehensive notes to the cash flow statement are not required but show your workings for fixed asset movements.

Question 3.9: Sligo Ltd.

Sligo Ltd. is a well-established company engaged in the manufacture and sale of metal products. The following information is obtained from the company's financial records:

Profit and Loss Account for Year ended 30 June 20x2

	€
Sales	900,000
Gross profit	300,000
Operating Profit	176,000
Interest	30,000
Net profit before tax	146,000
Taxation	61,000
Profit after taxation	85,000
Less Dividends Proposed	66,000
Profit retained for year	19,000
Profit brought forward	320,000
Profit carried forward	339,000

Balance Sheets as at 30 June

	20x1		20x2	
	€	€	€	€
Fixed Assets		637,100		767,300
Less Aggregate depreciation		297,500		321,400
		339,600		445,900
Trade investments (Cost)		106,000		106,000
Current Assets				
Stock	230,200		260,100	
Debtors	135,800		196,400	
Bank	Nil		9,300	
	366,000		465,800	
Current Liabilities				
Trade creditors	96,800		101,700	
Taxation	63,800		61,000	
Dividend payable	60,000		66,000	
Bank Overdraft	71,000		Nil	
	291,600		228,700	
Net Current Assets		74,400		237,100
		520,000		789,000
Financed By				
Share capital		200,000		220,000
Share premium		Nil		30,000
Profit and Loss Account		320,000		339,000
		520,000		589,000
15% Debentures		Nil		200,000
		520,000		789,000

Notes:

1. On 31 January 20x2 a share issue was made.

2. During the year ended 30 June 20x2, the company disposed of fixed assets for €17,900 that cost €65,200 some years ago. A loss of €9,600 arising on disposal has been deducted in arriving at operating profit for the year. Also, operating profit for the year includes depreciation in the amount of €61,600.

REQUIREMENT

Prepare a cash flow statement of Sligo Ltd., for the year ended 30 June, 20x2. Comprehensive notes to the cash flow statement are not required but show your workings for fixed assets, taxation and dividends.

Question 3.10: Retail Ltd.

The following information has been presented to you in relation to Retail Ltd., a large retailing company, for a recent accounting period:

Profit and loss account for the year ended 30 September 20x8

	€'000
Turnover	13,984
Cost of sales	7,190
Gross profit	6,794
Operating costs	5,079
Operating profit	1,715
Interest receivable	110
Net profit before tax	1,825
Taxation	668
Profit after taxation	1,157
Less: Dividends proposed	176
Profit retained for year	981
Profit brought forward	661
Profit carried forward	1,642

Balance Sheets as at 30 September

	20x7 €000	20x7 €000	20x8 €000	20x8 €000
Tangible Fixed Assets (Note 1)		1,200		4,559
Current Assets				
Stock	608		2,131	
Trade debtors	258		662	
Cash in hand	3		8	
	869		2,801	
Creditors (Due within one year) (Note 2)	1,358		3,875	
Net Current Liabilities		(489)		(1,074)
		711		3,485
Capital and Reserves				
Called-up share capital (Note 3)		50		1,100
Share Premium		—		743
Retained profits		661		1,642
		711		3,485

Notes to the Accounts
1. Tangible Fixed Assets

	Premises €	Fixtures & Fittings €	Motor Vehicles €	Total €
Cost				
At beginning of year	590	816	56	1,462
Additions	2,520	1,179	32	3,731
At end of year	3,110	1,995	88	5,193
Aggregate Depreciation				
At beginning of year	38	210	14	262
Depreciation for year	117	242	13	372
At end of Year	155	452	27	634
Net Book amount at year end	2,955	1,543	61	4,559

2. Creditors

	20x7 €'000	20x8 €'000
Bank Overdraft	345	1,502
Trade Creditors	693	1,581
Corporation tax payable	320	616
Dividends payable	Nil	176
	1,358	3,875

3. Share Capital
The Share Capital consists of fully paid shares of €0.05 each.

REQUIREMENT

You are required to prepare a cash flow statement for the year ended 30 September, 20x8. Comprehensive notes are not required.

4

Interpretation of Financial Statements

4.1   INTRODUCTION TO ACCOUNTING RATIOS

To help them in interpreting financial statements, users frequently calculate key accounting ratios to show the relationship between two items in the balance sheet or profit and loss account. In order for the ratio to be meaningful, there must be an important relationship between the two elements. Thus the relationship between, say, sales and wages has validity but the relationship between wages and share capital has little significance. There are a number of publications that highlight important accounting ratios across various industries — for example, Dun and Bradstreet produces an annual volume, "Key Business Ratios". In addition, websites such as www.corporate information.com can provide ratios for specific firms. Such data enables the analyst to assess the relative strengths and weaknesses of individual companies.

Ratios can be logically and conveniently divided into *two* main groups:

1. **Financial structure**: Balance sheet structure in relation to liquidity and gearing or leverage.

2. **Profitability**: Profit generated during the year in relation to the resources available.

4.2   BALANCE SHEET RATIOS

The two principal areas of concern in financial (balance sheet) structure are liquidity and leverage (gearing). Liquidity is a measure of the ability of the firm to pay its debts as and when they become due. Gearing (or leverage) is a measure of the relationship between long-term debt and equity, although other definitions are sometimes used.

Liquidity Ratios

The two common liquidity ratios are:

1. The Current ratio.

2. The Acid Test ratio.

The Current ratio is calculated as:

Current assets
Current liabilities

The Current ratio indicates the short-term resources — current assets — that are available to meet current liabilities. While generally it is agreed that a Current ratio of around 2:1 is appropriate for most businesses, some do not experience liquidity problems with ratios considerably less than 2:1 and, conversely, others with ratios of 2 or more may still have liquidity problems.

However, if the current assets comprise, say, €1,000 debtors who when requested to pay are unable to do so, while the current liabilities comprise €500 overdraft repayable on demand, the business is effectively unable to meet its short-term obligations. In such a case, a Current ratio of 2:1 is a misleading measure of liquidity.

While it is similar in form to the Current ratio, the Acid Test ratio is considered a somewhat more stringent test of liquidity as it excludes the least liquid portion of current assets — stock. Stock is specifically excluded for two reasons. First, the net realisable value of stock in a forced sale situation is dubious. Second, and more important, if the business sells its stock and uses the cash to pay off its debts it will be unable to continue trading due to lack of stock.

The Acid Test ratio is calculated as:

Current assets less stock
Current liabilities

In general terms, an Acid Test ratio of about 1:1 is considered to be appropriate for most businesses. However, as with the Current ratio, many businesses survive quite well with ratios considerably less than this and others can have liquidity problems even with ratios in excess of it. As with all ratios, it is important to remember that these liquidity ratios are only indicators of position/trends and do not give a complete picture. Indeed, the trend in the ratios over time is more meaningful than a single year's figures.

Leverage (Gearing) Ratios

The second area of analysis of any balance sheet structure is the composition of long-term funds — capital employed. Capital employed typically comprises invested share capital, retained earnings and long-term debt. Long-term debt consists of financial obligations arising from past transactions or events for which settlement will not take place within the next financial year.

Some borrowing is usually beneficial to a company since interest payments are tax deductible, making it a cheap form of finance compared with ordinary share capital. This is because dividends paid to either ordinary or preference shareholders do not qualify for tax relief and, thus, the after-tax cost of equity is usually higher than the after-tax cost of debt.

Excessive "gearing" or "leverage" increases the risk to ordinary shareholders due to large interest payments, eventual repayment of loans and perhaps the curtailment of borrowing potential in situations of emergency. Usually, the issue of debt is associated with considerable formality and the loan agreement may contain restrictions for the protection of lenders. For example, the loan agreement may contain specific maturity (repayment) dates and dates of interest payments in addition to working capital requirements, dividend restrictions and limitations concerning the issue of additional debt. In many cases, the loan agreement or instrument is held by a trustee who acts as an independent third party to protect the interests of both the lender and the borrower. If a business incurs so much debt that it becomes unable to meet the required interest and capital repayments, lenders can usually appoint a receiver. The receiver may sell the assets of the company and use the cash to pay off the secured loans. Note that a receiver is distinguished from a liquidator, whose job it is to wind up the company. Liquidation of a company is often the eventual outcome of the appointment of a receiver, since in recovering the amounts due to the lenders by selling company assets the receiver may leave little of value to allow the business continue trading.

The commonly used ratios to evaluate gearing can be calculated as follows, although different analysts often modify the ratio in a particular circumstance.

Debt/Equity ratio is calculated as:

$$\frac{\text{Long-term debt*}}{\text{Shareholders' funds}}$$

* *Some analysts include short-term debt, where it is permanent in nature (for example, a "hard core" overdraft).*

This ratio measures the relationship between long-term debt and shareholders' funds. Both are part of the long-term financing of the company. Where this ratio exceeds 100 per cent, long-term debt is providing the majority of the long-term finance of the company. A prudent evaluation of capital structure suggests that this ratio should be less than 100 per cent, so as to indicate that shareholders have provided the biggest part of long-term finance to the company.

An alternative gearing ratio is that of long-term debt as a percentage of capital employed. It is calculated as follows:

- Debt/Capital Employed ratio:

$$\frac{\text{Long-term debt*}}{\text{Capital employed}}$$

* *Some analysts include short-term debt, where it is permanent in nature (for example, "hard core" overdraft).*

Since capital employed is the aggregate of shareholders' funds and long-term debt, both ratios reflect the reliance on long-term debt in slightly different ways. As a result, it is usual to calculate only one gearing ratio relating to the balance sheet of a company.

If the above ratios are defined to include only long-term debt, some analysts argue that the overall borrowing position is *under-* stated. Accordingly, they prefer to focus on the *total debt* of the company and typically calculate:

- Total debt/Total assets ratio:

$$\frac{\text{Total borrowings}}{\text{Total assets}}$$

Like all financial ratios, there is no "absolute" number that is appropriate in relation to gearing levels though many financial analysts would be concerned if a company's debt/capital employed percentage exceeded 50 per cent, and the total borrowings to total assets exceeded 70 per cent. However, it is important to remember that it is often the change in the ratio over time that is more informative than its actual level at a given point in time.

The components to include in the numerator and denominator depend on how one defines both liabilities and shareholders' funds. Unfortunately, there is no general agreement in either the accounting literature or in published financial reports on the precise distinction between liabilities and shareholders' funds. Thus, issues such as preference shares, minority interests, government grants and deferred taxation must be highlighted when computing the above ratios.

It is possible to include preference shares under "debt" since they carry a fixed rate of dividend that must be paid ahead of ordinary dividends. Yet they are not debt since no interest is payable on them. Generally speaking, where preference shares are *redeemable* (the majority of cases), they should be treated as debt.

Minority interests appear only in consolidated financial statements and then only when a subsidiary company is not wholly (100 per cent) owned. In the case of, say, a 90 per cent owned subsidiary, the consolidation process consists of integrating 100 per cent of the assets (and liabilities) of the subsidiary with the assets (and liabilities) of the parent company. However, since the subsidiary is only 90 per cent owned, an adjustment equal to 10 per cent of the net assets not owned by the parent is then shown on the consolidated balance sheet. This 10 per cent adjustment is referred to as "Minority Interests" and is shown on the liabilities side of the consolidated balance sheet. This item is neither equity (shareholders' funds) nor debt, but is part of the total amount of capital employed in the business.

Government grants and deferred taxation should not be treated as debt since they are non-interest bearing sources of funds and do not, strictly speaking, have to be repaid. However, they do represent long-term funds of the organisation and should be included as part of capital employed.

Gearing ratios have been criticised for not focusing on the cash (or funds) necessary to pay for interest payments on long-term debt. This criticism has, in part, motivated proposals for interest coverage ratios as follows:

- Interest cover:

$$\frac{\text{Operating income*}}{\text{Annual interest payments}}$$

* *PBIT (Profit before Interest and Tax)*

The Interest cover ratio indicates the availability of operating profit (PBIT) to cover annual interest payments. Prudent cover would be 3 or 4 times.

One way that companies try to distort this ratio (and improve overall profitability) is to capitalise interest payments. For example, a company may treat the interest on borrowings to finance the construction of fixed assets as part of the cost of those assets. Interest costs incurred during the construction period on major fixed asset additions are capitalised and form part of the total asset cost. Depreciation is charged on total cost, including such interest. Thus, the interest is added to the cost of the asset and is part of the normal depreciation charge on the relevant asset.

4.3   OVERALL PROFITABILITY RATIOS

Perhaps the most important area to evaluate in any company is its overall profit performance in relation to the resources available. This is usually done by calculating a number of financial ratios relating the profit performance of the business to the overall investment and is usually described as *return on investment*. However, "investment" may be defined in any of three ways:

1. Return on capital employed (ROCE).

2. Return on shareholders' funds (ROSF).

3. Return on total assets (ROTA).

It is important that whatever measure is used, it is used consistently. For example, profits can be either pre-tax or post-tax profits. Likewise, the investment can be the opening, closing or average figures for, say, shareholders' funds. These ratios are usually computed as:

- ROCE:

$$\frac{\text{Profit before interest \& tax}}{\text{Capital employed}}$$

- ROSF:

$$\frac{\text{Profit before tax}}{\text{Shareholders' funds}}$$

- ROTA:

$$\frac{\text{Profit before interest \& tax}}{\text{Total assets}}$$

The figure for capital employed, total assets etc. should, strictly speaking, be the average during the year, but for simplicity's sake it is normally satisfactory to use the year-end figure unless there have been major changes in the financial structure of the business.

In computing ROCE, many analysts include short-term bank borrowings in addition to long-term borrowings. The reason is that a company that has perhaps an embarrassingly (even dangerously) large short-term debt would otherwise have a better ROCE than a company that is more prudently funded.

Of the three, ROTA discloses the profit derived from the assets invested in the business (regardless of how they were financed). ROTA (PBIT/TA) has a number of important implications for financial planning and control of any company. Assuming that the long-term goal is to increase the overall return on total assets, Exhibit 4.1 below indicates how the various elements combine (and how they should be influenced) to increase overall profitability.

Exhibit 4.1: How Ratios Combine

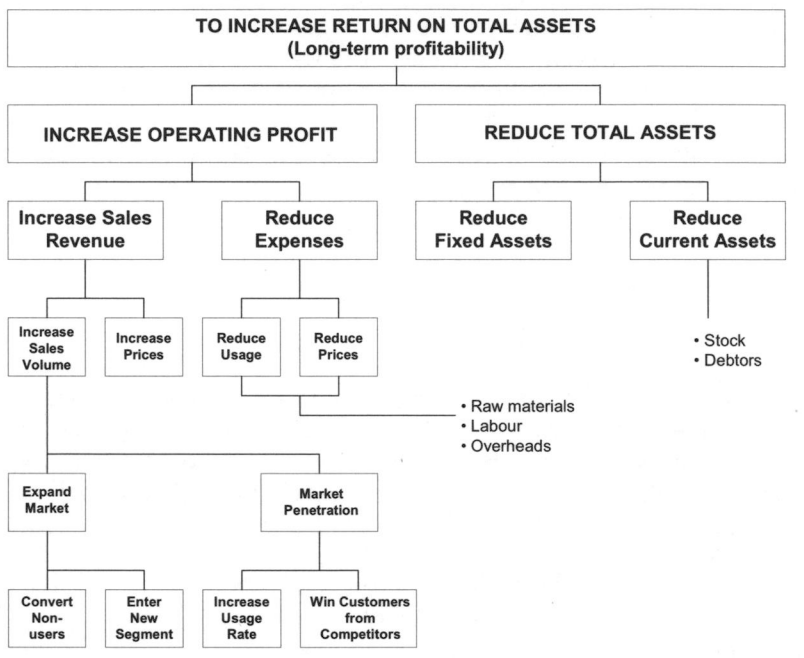

Exhibit 4.2: Pyramid of Accounting Ratios

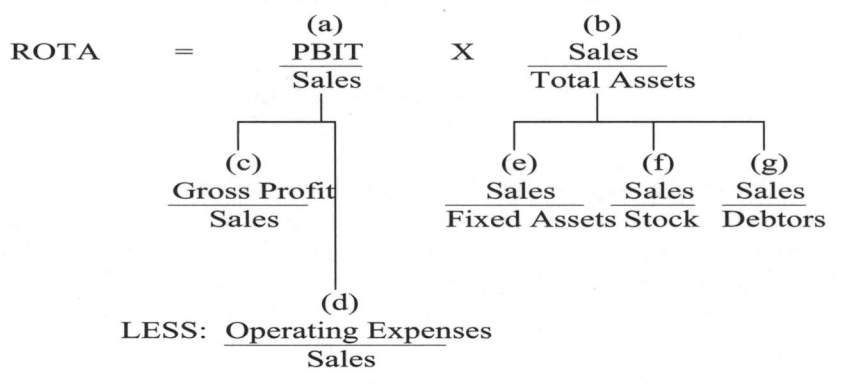

Any of these three profitability ratios can be used to construct a pyramid of ratios. The pyramid of ratios can take many forms, depending on the nature of the company's activities and the preference of the user. One version is shown in Exhibit 4.2 above.

(a) Operating Profit (to Sales) Ratio
This shows the profitability of the business relative to sales after de-

pending on the nature of the company's activities and the preference of the user. One version is shown in Exhibit 4.2 above.

(a) Operating Profit (to Sales) Ratio

This shows the profitability of the business relative to sales after deducting cost of goods sold and all operating expenses but excluding interest and taxation. It is a general indicator of the overall profitability of the business though it does *not* reflect the full impact of the capital structure of the business on profitability. It is calculated as follows:

- Operating profit ratio:

$$\frac{\text{PBIT}}{\text{Sales}}$$

Generally, low operating profit margins are a sign of poor management. Somewhat better than average margins are normally a sign of good management, but unusually high margins may mean that the company may attract future competition unless there are barriers to entry (for example, huge initial capital costs, high technology, patents or other special advantages enjoyed by the company).

Operating profit margins are very important in the context of financial forecasts. This is because management and financial analysts usually base their forecasts of future profitability on projected turnover figures multiplied by estimated future profit margins.

(b) Utilisation of Total Assets

The utilisation of total assets can be calculated by dividing sales by total assets. Its relevance, however, is limited since it is a reflection of three other ratios, which we will examine later:

1. Fixed asset turnover (see (e) below).

2. Stock turnover ratio (see (f) below).

3. Debtor days ratio (see (g) below).

(c) Gross Profit Ratio

This ratio tells us the profitability of the business relative to sales after deducting the cost of the goods sold. In non-manufacturing businesses, the cost of goods sold is usually taken to be purchases adjusted for opening and closing stock. In a manufacturing business, cost of goods sold will include all material, labour and overhead costs incurred in producing the goods that have been sold. The ratio is cal-culated as follows:

- Gross profit ratio:

$$\frac{\text{Gross profit}}{\text{Sales}}$$

The Gross profit ratio can vary widely from one business to the other. For example, there is a broad economic principle that says that ne-cessities should sell at low margins (often strongly supported by gov-ernment price controls), while luxury goods tend to earn much greater margins. Another principle of economics is that businesses that are adapting their products in a fast-changing technology de-serve a high gross margin because of the need to finance new product research and development.

The Gross profit ratio is an indicator of the product pricing policy of the business. If, for example, the ratio has fallen in relation to the previous period, either increased costs have not been passed on to customers in the form of higher selling prices or production ineffi-ciencies have occurred which it is not possible to recover in increased sale prices. Alternatively, low margins may have been deliberately set by management to increase market share. The precise reason for the change can be ascertained only by asking the relevant manager for detailed explanations.

Some typical examples of gross profit margins are as follows:

	%
Retail stores	45–50
Bars/drink	35–50
Food retail	8–16
Pharmacies	20–40
Fashion stores	50–100

(d) Total Operating Expenses Ratio
Total operating expenses must, by definition, be the difference be-tween gross and net profit before interest and tax. The ratio is calcu-lated as follows:

- Total operating expense ratio:

$$\frac{\text{Total operating expenses}}{\text{Sales}}$$

Usually, total expenses would in turn be divided into appropriate classifications such as distribution costs or administration costs. In this way, dominant expense headings can be identified and their trend monitored over time. An alternative and, perhaps, more appropriate way to analyse the company's expense headings is to concentrate on revenue investment items. These are expense items that are important to the company's survival. Important calculations include:

1. Research and development/sales.

2. Marketing costs/sales.

3. Quality costs/sales.

4. Staff training/sales.

Unfortunately, these expense items are usually first to be cut when the company is experiencing financial difficulties.

(e) Turnover of Fixed Assets

This ratio indicates the relative efficiency with which the firm uses its fixed assets to generate sales. However, if the book value of fixed assets is used, this ratio should automatically improve over time, as assets are depreciated. It is calculated as follows:

*   Fixed asset turnover:

$$\frac{\text{Sales}}{\text{Fixed assets}}$$

In addition, the ratio will be affected by the depreciation policy used by the company — for example, one that uses an accelerated depreciation method will have a higher fixed asset turnover than another using straight line, all else being equal, because its denominator is lower. For these reasons, this ratio should be interpreted in the context of the company's underlying accounting policies.

(f) Stock Turnover Ratio

This ratio gives an estimate of the average number of days taken to convert the stock into either cash or debtors. The ratio is sometimes calculated using closing stock rather than average stock and sales rather than cost of sales, though which is used is less important than consistency.

*   Stock turnover:

$$\frac{\text{Average stock x days in period}}{\text{Cost of goods sold}}$$

A deterioration in the stock turnover ratio might indicate:

1. Overproduction of finished goods.

2. Lack of sales demand.

3. Obsolete or old fashioned goods.

(g) Debtor Days Ratio

This ratio gives an estimate of the average number of days credit taken by debtors and is therefore an indicator of the liquidity of the debtors.

•   Debtors days ratio:

Debtors x days in period

Credit sales

However, few companies will provide a figure for credit sales. In such circumstances, the total sales figure is used for the purposes of this calculation.

It is useful to compare the "debtor days" with the company's quoted credit terms, as a measure of the efficiency of credit control in the business (especially when compared to industry norms) and as a guide to the quality of the debtors. For every additional day's credit given, an appropriate amount of finance will be needed to carry the additional debtors. A lack of control in this area very often accounts for excessive borrowing requirements — for example, if a business projects sales of €1,000 for a particular year and quotes credit terms of 90 days but gives *actual* credit of 120 days, how much extra financing is required? Answer: €82, calculated as follows: €1,000 x 90/365 = €246; €1,000 x 120/365 = €328; Difference = €82.

(h) Credit Days Received

Although this ratio has not been previously mentioned, it is always useful to calculate it in the context of the management of working capital. This ratio indicates the average number of credit days taken by the company from its suppliers.

•   Credit days received:

Creditors x days in period

Purchases*

*   *Or Cost of sales.*

If there are no discounts to be received for prompt payments to creditors, the company should seek the longest period possible (without risking the discontinuation of supplies from creditors), as it is a form of free finance.

The aggregate of the stock turnover, debtor days less credit days received ratios reflects the overall length of the operating or working capital cycle. Thus if the relevant periods are 40, 60 and 70 days respectively, it indicates that on average:

1. Stock is on the shelf for 40 days before it is sold.

2. When it is sold, debtors take 60 days before paying.

3. Suppliers give 70 days credit.

Thus the net length of the operating cycle is 30 days!

The following ratios should be taken as a broad rather than a specific guide for the types of business listed.

	SUPERMARKET	JEWELLERS	FAST-FOOD
Sales	100	100	100
Cost of sales %	90	55	50
Gross profit %	10	45	50
Operating & other costs %	8	33	35
Net profit %	2	12	15
Current ratio (times)	0.9	1.0	0.6
Debtor days	2	20	Nil
Stock turnover (days)	20	150	3
Credit days received	35	100	35

ILLUSTRATION

Calculate financial ratios using this information from Magic Carpet Ltd.:

PROFIT AND LOSS ACCOUNT
FOR YEAR ENDED 31 DECEMBER 20x5

	€	€
Sales		150,000
Cost of goods sold		90,000
Gross profit		60,000
Selling & distribution expenses	40,000	
Administration & financial expenses (note)	10,000	
		50,000
Net profit before tax		10,000
Taxation		4,000
Net profit after tax		6,000

NOTE: Includes interest expense of €800.

BALANCE SHEET
AT 31 DECEMBER 20x5

	€	€	€
Fixed assets (book value)			40,000
Current assets			
Stock	21,500		
Debtors	31,000		
Cash	2,500		
		55,000	
Current liabilities			
Trade creditors	25,000		
Current taxation	4,000		
Overdraft	3,500		
		32,500	
Net current assets			22,500
			62,500
FINANCED BY:			
Issued ordinary share capital			30,000
Retained profits			22,500
			52,500
8 per cent Loans (long-term)			10,000
			62,500

You are required to calculate:

1. Current ratio
2. Acid Test ratio
3. Long-term debt to capital employed
4. Total debt to total assets
5. Return on capital employed
6. Return on total assets
7. Return on shareholders' funds (before tax)
8. Gross profit margin
9. Operating profit to sales
10. Total operating expenses to sales
11. Turnover of fixed assets
12. Stock turnover (days)
13. Credit allowed (days)
14. Days credit received.

SOLUTION

1.   Current ratio:

Current assets	=	55,000	=	1.69 times
Current liabilities		32,500		

2.   Acid Test ratio:

Current assets less Stock	=	55,000-21,500	=	1.03 times
Current liabilities		32,500		

3.   Long-term debt to capital employed:

Long-term debt	=	10,000	=	16%
Capital employed		62,500		

4.   Total debt to total assets:

Total debt	=	13,500	=	14.2%
Total assets		95,000		

5.   Return on capital employed:

PBIT	=	10,800	=	17.3%
Capital employed		62,500		

NOTE: Capital employed is defined as shareholders' funds plus long-term loans.

6.   Return on total assets:

PBIT	=	10,800	=	11.3%
Total assets		95,000		

7.   Return on shareholders' funds:

Net profit before tax	=	10,000	=	19%
Shareholders' funds		52,500		

8.   Gross profit ratio:

Gross profit	=	60,000	=	40%
Sales		150,000		

9.   Operating Profit Ratio:

Operating profit	=	10,800	=	7.2%
Sales		150,000		

10.   Total operating expenses to sales:

Total operating expenses	=	49,200	=	32.8%
Sales		150,000		

11.   Turnover of fixed assets:

Sales	=	150,000	=	3.75
Fixed assets		40,000		

12. Stock turnover:

$$\frac{\text{Stock x 365}}{\text{Cost of goods sold}} \quad = \quad \frac{21,500 \text{ x } 365}{90,000} \quad = \quad 87 \text{ days}$$

13. Average period of credit allowed:

$$\frac{\text{Debtors x 365}}{\text{Sales}} \quad = \quad \frac{31,000 \text{ x } 365}{150,000} \quad = \quad 75 \text{ days}$$

14. Average period of credit received:

$$\frac{\text{Creditors x 365}}{\text{Cost of goods sold}} \quad = \quad \frac{25,000 \text{ x } 365}{90,000} \quad = \quad 101 \text{ days}$$

4.4 LIMITATIONS OF RATIO ANALYSIS

A number of financial ratios have been discussed in the above section (and many more could be added). Although ratio analysis may be a useful way of interpreting financial statements, the use of ratios has limitations — in particular:

1. Ratios focus on short-term performance — for example, ROCE reflects the profit performance over the most recent accounting period. However, in generating this profit, certain detrimental activities may have been undertaken, to the long-run disadvantage of the firm. This limitation is often referred to as short-termism.

    Activities that can be restricted by a short-term outlook include: staff training and development, marketing (advertising), quality costs, and research and development. All these costs are usually written off to the profit and loss account as expenses but are vital to the long-term survival of the business. Thus there is a basic conflict in the accounting treatment of these costs (passed through the profit and loss account as short-term items) and their anticipated, but difficult to quantify, long-term benefits. Indeed, faced with an emphasis on short-term profitability, managers may decide to reduce these discretionary costs.

2. Financial ratios are inevitably incomplete — for example, making a phone call to a key client to "wish him well in hospital" is recorded as a cost in the financial statements but may have generated, nevertheless, a great deal of goodwill which will be reflected in future turnover. This intangible benefit is not directly captured in accounting numbers.

3. Financial ratios represent the end result. Thus, increasing attention should be devoted to looking at the activities that are reflected in those results.

4. Ratios must be interpreted in the light of the individual circumstances of the business analysed. For example, a return on capital

employed of, say, 10 per cent cannot be interpreted as being good or bad. If inflation is 20 per cent, the return is inadequate though, in an inflation-free period, a return of 10 per cent may be acceptable for a very low-risk business.

5. Financial analysts constantly search for some standard of comparison against which to judge whether the relationships that they have found are favourable or unfavourable. One such standard is the performance of companies in the same industrial sector. However, intercompany comparisons create their own problems, especially where companies do not employ similar accounting methods. Thus, a business that uses the straight-line method of depreciation is not directly comparable with one that uses the reducing balance method.

   As an alternative to making comparisons with other businesses in the same industry, the analyst may make judgments about a company over a number of accounting periods. However, this approach may not necessarily be informative, especially where the environment in which the firm operates changes or the company enters a different line of business. Past performance is not necessarily the performance that should have been obtained. Thus, a net margin on sales of 3 per cent last year and 5 per cent this year indicates improvement, but if there is evidence that the margin should have been 10 per cent, the return in both years was poor.

6. Ratios reflect past performance, which is not necessarily a reliable guide to what may happen in the future. There are many factors not contained in historic financial statements that are relevant to estimating the future financial performance of an enterprise. What are the future plans of the business? The quality of its workforce? Its distribution and marketing network? All such factors are highly relevant to a comprehensive business analysis.

   The principal benefit of ratio analysis is to suggest questions that need to be answered. Ratios never provide the answers but should lead to an investigation as to what may be right or wrong. In other words, ratios are a tool that should be used in a critical fashion and as an aid to judgment.

4.5   END OF CHAPTER QUESTIONS

Question 4.1

The terms "profitability" and "liquidity" are often used in the context of evaluating the financial statements of a business.

REQUIREMENT

1. Define profitability and liquidity.

2. Explain the difference between them.

(*The Association of Chartered Certified Accountants*)

Question 4.2: Philox Ltd.

The following information relates to Philox Ltd. for 20x1:

	€
Turnover for year (all credit sales)	240,000
Purchases for year (on credit)	140,000
Opening stock	90,000
Closing stock	60,000
Trade debtors at start of year	NIL
Trade debtors at end of year	40,000
Trade creditors at start of year	NIL
Trade creditors at end of year	45,000
Corporation tax due at end of year	20,000
Dividends payable	15,000
Bank and cash balances	55,000
Long-term loans at end of year	80,000
Shareholders' funds (total) at end of year	120,000
Fixed assets (net) at end of year	125,000

REQUIREMENT

1. Calculate both gross profit and cost of goods sold.

2. Calculate the net current assets at the end of the year.

3. Prepare a summarised balance sheet at the end of the year.

4. Calculate stock turnover, credit days given and credit days received from the above data.

5. Calculate both current and acid test ratios.

6. Calculate gearing ratios as follows:

   ◊ Debt to equity

   ◊ Debt as percentage of capital employed.

Question 4.3

A company has annual credit sales of €800,000. Its gross margin is 20 per cent. The company's current assets at the start of the year were €160,000 including debtors of €80,000 and the bank balance of €20,000.

REQUIREMENT

1. Calculate the closing stock the company must carry if management wants the stock turnover period to be 45 days, based on a 360-day year.

2. Calculate how rapidly accounts receivable must be collected if management wants to have €100,000 invested in debtors. Provide your answers in days, based on a 360-day accounting period.

Question 4.4: Hercules Wholesalers Ltd.

Hercules Wholesalers Ltd. has been particularly concerned with its liquidity position in recent months. The most recent profit and loss account and net current assets of the company are as follows:

PROFIT AND LOSS ACCOUNT (extract)
FOR YEAR ENDED 31 MAY 20x2

	€	€
Sales		452,000
Less: Cost of sales		
Opening stock	125,000	
Add: Purchases	341,000	
	466,000	
Less: Closing stock	143,000	
		323,000
Gross profit		129,000

BALANCE SHEET (extract): NET CURRENT ASSETS

	€	€
Current assets		
Stock		143,000
Debtors		163,000
		306,000
Less: Creditors falling due within one year		
Trade creditors	145,000	
Bank overdraft	140,000	
		285,000
Net current assets		21,000

The debtors and creditors were maintained at a constant level throughout the year.

REQUIREMENT

1. Explain why Hercules Wholesalers Ltd. is concerned with its liquidity position.

2. The "operating cash cycle" represents the total of stock turnover days plus debtor days less credit days received. Explain why this concept is important in the financial management of a business. Calculate the operating cash cycle for Hercules Wholesalers Ltd. based on the information above. State what steps may be taken to improve the operating cash cycle of the company.

(*The Association of Chartered Certified Accountants*)

Question 4.5: Modern Developments Ltd.

The following data relates to Modern Developments Ltd., a manufacturing company, at 31 March 200x based on its first trading year ended on that date.

	€
Trade creditors	60,000
Closing stock (completed)	40,000
Debtors	90,000
Plant and machinery (net)	185,000
Land at cost	105,000
Buildings (net)	110,000
Share capital	250,000
Long-term loan (secured)	200,000
Cash and bank balance	45,000
Sales (all on credit)	350,000
Direct materials used	80,000
Production wages	50,000
Production overheads	40,000
Interest paid	25,000
Administration costs	90,000

NOTE: Plant, machinery and buildings have been depreciated and are included in production overhead above.

REQUIREMENT
You are required to:

1. Calculate the amount of profit earned by the company during the year ended 31 March 200x and prepare a balance sheet as at that date. Ignore tax and dividends.

2. Calculate appropriate ratios that will help to explain the performance of the organisation.

Question 4.6

Discuss the main factors that should be taken into account when formulating policy for a business on stocks (inventory), debtors (receivables) and creditors (accounts payable).

(The Association of Chartered Certified Accountants)

Question 4.7

1. Explain the role of the credit manager within a business.

2. Discuss the major factors a credit manager would consider when assessing the credit-worthiness of a particular customer.

3. Identify and discuss the major sources of information that may be used to evaluate the credit worthiness of a commercial business.

4. State the basis upon which any proposed changes in credit policy should be evaluated.

(The Association of Chartered Certified Accountants)

Question 4.8: Memorial Ltd.

The condensed financial statements of Memorial Ltd. are given below.

PROFIT AND LOSS ACCOUNT
FOR YEAR ENDING 31 OCTOBER 20x7

	€
Turnover	112,000
Less: Cost of goods sold	90,000
Gross profit	22,000
Operating expenses	12,000
Operating profit	10,000
Interest	2,000
Net profit before tax	8,000
Taxation	4,000
Net profit for year after tax	4,000
Profits brought forward	26,500
Retained profit at year end	30,500

BALANCE SHEET
AT 31 OCTOBER 20x7

	Cost	Agg. Dep'n.	
	€	€	€
Fixed assets			
Plant and equipment	44,000	4,000	40,000
Motor vehicles	11,000	1,000	10,000
	55,000	5,000	50,000
Current assets			
Stock	22,500		
Debtors	16,000		
Prepayments	1,000		
Bank	4,000	43,500	
Less: Current liabilities: Creditors		18,000	
			25,500
Total assets less current liabilities			75,500

FINANCED BY
Share capital

	€
Ordinary shares of €0.50 each fully paid	20,000
Profit and loss account	30,500
	50,500
8 per cent Debenture stock (202x)	25,000
	75,500

Assuming that the levels of stock and debtors and creditors have all remained constant throughout the year, you are required to calculate the following ratios:

1. Current ratio.

2. Debt/capital employed ratio.

3. Collection period (debtor days).

4. Payment period (days credit received).

5. Stock turnover (days).

6. Interest cover.

7. Earnings per share (PAT divided by number of ordinary shares).

Question 4.9: Threads Ltd.

Threads Ltd. is a company that manufactures nut and bolts, which are sold to industrial users. The abbreviated accounts for 20x8 and 20x7 are given below with the most recent year being presented on the inside column.

THREADS LTD.
PROFIT AND LOSS ACCOUNT
FOR YEARS ENDED 30 JUNE

	20x8		20x7	
	€'000	€'000	€'000	€'000
Sales		1,200		1,180
Cost of sales		(750)		(680)
Gross profit		450		500
Operating expenses	(208)		(200)	
Depreciation	(75)		(66)	
Interest	(8)		(–)	
		(291)		(266)
Profit before tax		159		234
Tax		(48)		(80)
Profit after tax		111		154
Dividend proposed		(72)		(70)
Retained profit for year		39		84
Retained profit brought forward		256		172
Retained profit carried forward		295		256

THREADS LTD.
BALANCE SHEETS AT 30 JUNE

	20x8 €'000	20x8 €'000	20x7 €'000	20x7 €'000
Fixed assets		687		702
Current assets				
Stocks	236		148	
Debtors	156		102	
Cash	4		32	
	396		282	
Creditors (within one year):				
Trade creditors	(76)		(60)	
Accruals	(16)		(18)	
Dividend	(72)		(70)	
Tax	(48)		(80)	
Bank overdraft	(26)		(–)	
	(238)		(228)	
Net current assets		158		54
Long-term liabilities				
Bank loan		(50)		(–)
		795		756
Ordinary share capital of €1		500		500
Profit and loss account		295		256
		795		756

REQUIREMENT
Calculate the following financial statistics for both 20x8 and 20x7, using end of year figures where appropriate.

1. Return on capital employed.

2. Net profit (after interest) margin on sales.

3. Gross profit margin.

4. Current ratio.

5. Acid Test ratio.

6. Average period of credit allowed.

7. Days credit received.

8. Stock turnover ratio.

9. Long-term debt to capital employed.

10. Return on total assets.

11. Operating profit to sales.

12. Fixed asset turnover.

Question 4.10: Shops plc

The following has been extracted from a set of published financial statements of a well-known retail company.

SHOPS PLC
PROFIT AND LOSS ACCOUNT
FOR YEARS ENDED 30 SEPTEMBER

	20x8 €'000	20x7 €'000
Turnover	13,984	6,175
Cost of sales	7,100	3,018
Gross profit	6,794	2,857
Distribution and administrative expenses	5,079	2,089
Operating profit	1,715	768
Interest receivable (net)	110	5
Profit on ordinary activities before taxation	1,825	773
Taxation on ordinary activities	668	295
Profit on ordinary activities after taxation	1,157	478
Dividend	176	–
Retained profit	981	478
Retained profit brought forward	661	183
Retained profit carried forward	1,642	661

SHOPS PLC
BALANCE SHEETS AT 30 SEPTEMBER

	20x8 €000	20x8 €000	20x7 €000	20x7 €000
Fixed assets:				
Tangible assets		4,549		1,200
Investments		80		–
		4,629		1,200
Current assets:				
Stocks	2,131		608	
Debtors	662		258	
Cash in hand	8		3	
	2,801		869	
Creditors: amounts falling due within one year (note 1)	3,865		1,358	
Net current liabilities		(1,064)		(489)
Total assets less current liabilities		3,565		711
FINANCED BY				
Called up share capital (5p each)		1,100		50
Share premium account		823		–
Retained profits		1,642		661
		3,565		711

Note 1. CREDITORS

	20x8 €000	20x7 €000
Bank overdraft	1,492	345
Trade creditors	1,581	693
Corporation tax	616	320
Dividend	176	–
	3,865	1,358

REQUIREMENT

Calculate the appropriate ratios to explain the performance of Shops plc during 20x8 and 20x7, using end of year figures where appropriate.

Question 4.11: Spread Ltd.

The accountant of Spread Ltd. has developed a computer spreadsheet to assist in the prediction of profits and closing balance sheets. The model has been prepared using important accounting ratios and relationships.

By entering the sales forecast and the values of various parameters, the model will print data about profit for the accounting period and a closing balance sheet. The parameters of the model are as follows:

Gross profit as percentage of sales	60
Selling expense as percentage of sales	15
Administration costs, excluding interest	€12,000
Tax rate on profits	40%
ROCE (PBIT/CE)	20%
Debt equity ratio	1:2
Interest rate per cent on debt	10
Ratio of fixed to net current assets	1:1
Current ratio	3
Ordinary dividend pay out per cent	25

The first trial of the model will use sales of €80,000. The only expenses to be deducted from gross profit are selling expenses, administration costs and interest payable on debt.

REQUIREMENT

You are required to:

1. Prepare a profit statement based on the above factors and using sales of €80,000 which shows:

   ◊ Net profit before interest and tax.

   ◊ Profit available for dividend.

   ◊ Dividends.

2. Determine the book value of long-term debt and the current liabilities and prepare a closing balance sheet in as much detail as possible.

(The Association of Chartered Certified Accountants)

Section 2:

Cost Accumulation Systems

5

Fundamentals of Cost Accumulation

5.1 COST ANALYSIS AND CLASSIFICATION SYSTEMS

The previous three chapters were concerned with overall cost levels and their importance in the context of financial statements. However, accounting information needs to be very detailed and specific to enhance managerial decision-making. This chapter explains how costs can be accumulated and used so as to identify, for example, the costs of running a department or the cost of providing a unit of output or service.

Business managers need to know the cost of providing products they make or services they provide for the following reasons:

1. **Stock valuation**: At the end of the accounting period, any unsold stock must be valued at cost in accordance with normal financial reporting requirements. The cost figure represents the actual cost incurred. Consequently, this purpose can be described as accumulating costs on an *ex post* basis.

2. **Planning**: In many situations, selling prices must be determined and agreed with the customer before the work commences. If the selling price cannot be subsequently changed, overall company profitability will depend crucially on the ability to predict costs. This purpose can be described as accumulating costs on an *ex ante* basis.

3. **Control**: Actual costs can be compared with anticipated costs and variances identified. These cost variances can be adverse or favourable, small or significant. The immediate relevance of cost variances for control purposes depends on the stage of production (work in progress or finished goods) and the flexibility of the selling price. Nevertheless, the benefit of cost variances is that they

increase management's knowledge of current operating conditions and can be used to increase the accuracy of future cost projections.

The term "cost" is defined in terms of resources consumed to achieve a particular objective. This objective may be operating a business or a department of the business. It may be the product, a group of products or an activity.

The most familiar concept of cost is that of "historic cost", which represents the cash outlay involved in a transaction. This historic cost is the amount that is recorded in a business's management accounting system. It is used mainly to value closing stocks of finished goods, raw materials and provide for depreciation on fixed assets. The historic amount is *never* relevant for decision-making, since it represents a sunk cost and will not change regardless of the alternative being considered.

In order to summarise cost data in a systematic fashion, a cost classification system is needed. Classification involves systematically grouping costs together according to their common characteristics. Ultimately, the classification system will depend on the purpose for which the cost data is used. One purpose is to provide information for stock valuation needed for external financial accounting reports; another is to provide information for planning decisions, where the information represents future cost estimates; a third is to provide information for control decisions, where the information will initially be backward-looking, with particular reference to what has happened during the past and comparing current results with original plans or targets.

The first stage in the cost accumulation process is to develop a cost classification system. Without this, it is impossible to accumulate costs in a meaningful manner and difficult to plan and control the operations of a business. The six main classification systems are:

1. Cost classification by nature.

2. Fixed and variable costs.

3. Direct and indirect (overhead) costs.

4. Cost classification by function.

5. Cost classification by cost centre.

6. Cost classification in relation to quality.

Classifying Costs by Nature

This classification indicates *what* resources have been consumed in basic categories such as materials, wages, light and heat, advertising and other expenses. This classification system is used extensively in financial reporting and is the classification system with which most people are familiar.

Fixed and Variable Costs

Costs may be classified in relation to their behaviour with respect to output or volume changes. This classification is important in decision-making, especially when an alternative under consideration involves a change in output. For example, in deciding whether to, say, increase output, it is important to understand how costs are affected. This classification system indicates *why* costs have been incurred.

A fixed cost is one that is unaffected by changes in the level of output. Typical examples are rent, insurance and salaries. This definition does not suggest that fixed costs do not change. It is realistic to argue that all costs change due to a number of factors such as inflation and seasonality. However, the important characteristic of a fixed cost is its unresponsive behaviour with respect to output or volume changes, over a range of activity.

A variable cost is a cost that is sensitive to changes in the level of activity. Typical variable costs include materials and power for machines. Variable costs will respond immediately as some change occurs in output.

Fixed and variable costs can be graphed as below. The vertical axis of the graph represents the total amount of the cost whereas the horizontal axis represents output or volume.

Exhibit 5.1: Fixed and Variable Costs

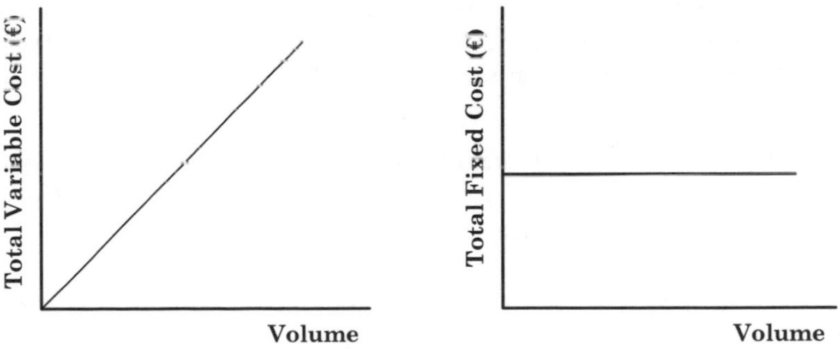

Both graphs above indicate the total fixed (or variable) cost associated with different levels of activity. However, both fixed and variable costs can be defined in terms of average cost per unit rather than in terms of total cost: A variable cost (per unit) will remain constant per unit of output (for example, each unit of output will require a constant input of raw materials); on the other hand, as output increases, the fixed cost per unit will decrease. Exhibit 5.2 below indicates the two ways of describing both fixed and variable costs:

Exhibit 5.2: Fixed and Variable Costs

	FIXED	**VARIABLE**
TOTAL COSTS	Do *not* change with change in volume	Do change with change in volume
UNIT COSTS	Do change with change in volume	Do *not* change with change in volume

The total costs of a business represent the aggregate of both fixed and variable costs and can be graphed as follows:

Exhibit 5.3: Total Cost

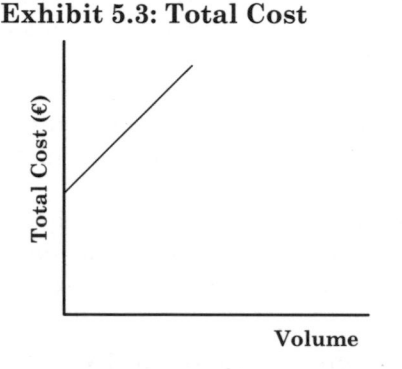

The graph above has been drawn on the assumption of a linear (straight line) relationship between costs and volume. This relationship can be expressed mathematically as follows:

$$Y = A + BX$$

where Y = total cost; A = fixed cost; B = variable unit cost; and X = total output units.

This assumption will not be valid where, for example, quantity discounts on material purchases are available for large orders or where operatives become more efficient as output expands. At this stage, assume that the reduction in unit costs caused by such events is too small to be significant and therefore can be ignored.

Note that fixed costs may behave in a step function. This is because fixed costs are subject to managerial decisions and will rarely remain constant in the long-term — the definition only requires that they remain fixed over a given range of activity. As output increases, additional supervisors or storage space may be required, so that fixed costs will increase in a step-like manner. This does not invalidate the use of graphs as a means of presenting and using cost information; instead, focus on the "relevant range" — the range of activity within which a particular cost/volume relationship remains valid.

A recent criticism of the fixed/variable classification system is that many costs relate to the activities and complexities of the business rather than output alone. In other words, the traditional assumption that output is the most significant factor influencing costs is rather simplistic. In a business, there are quality control costs, set-up costs, purchasing costs, etc., which are not output-led. This criticism has led to the recent emphasis on Activity Based Costing (ABC), whereby costs are linked to activities and then assigned to products.

In many situations, costs are semi-fixed, which means that the cost comprises both fixed and variable elements. For example, a company's electricity bill consists of a fixed charge and a variable charge associated with the amount of electricity used in the accounting period. Semi-fixed costs have the same behaviour pattern as total costs. In some cases, it can be difficult to segregate semi-fixed costs accurately into their fixed and variable components. However, certain techniques are available, such as the "high–low" method and regression analysis, to allow the accurate classification of such costs. These techniques will be explained in a later section.

ILLUSTRATION

The graphs below represent various cost functions. The vertical axis of the graphs represents *total costs* and the horizontal axis represents *volume* or *level of activity*. For each of the following descriptions, write down the letter of the graph that best represents the graph. The same graph may be used more than once.

1. Total material cost.

2. Factory rent.

3. Machine rental for which there is a minimum charge of €1,000, a maximum charge of €10,000, and a usage charge of €10 per hour.

4. Factory power for which there is a fixed charge of €2,000 per month together with a usage charge of €5 per unit produced.

5. Cost of supervisors, where an additional supervisor must be hired if X additional units are produced.

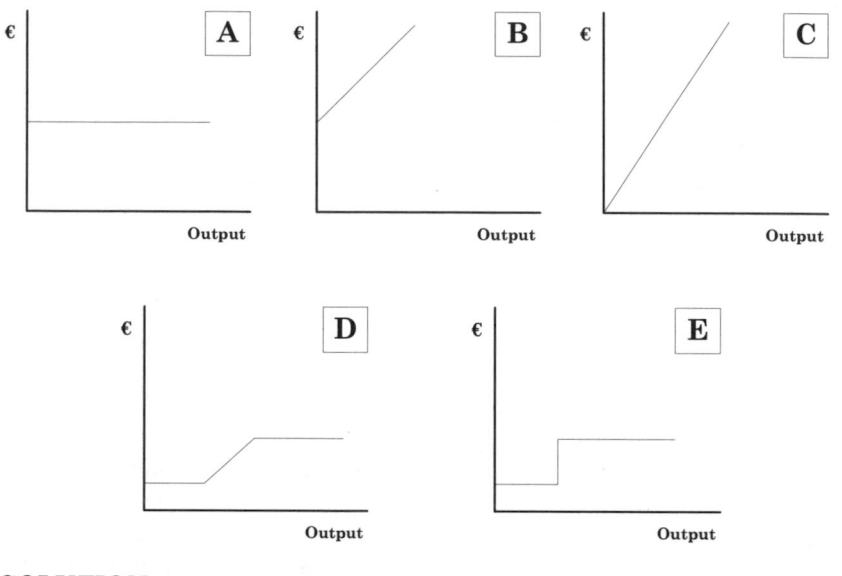

SOLUTION
1C; 2A; 3D; 4B; 5E.

Direct and Indirect (Overhead) Costs

One of the most commonly misunderstood concepts in management accounting is that of direct and indirect costs. A direct cost is a cost that can be identified specifically with, or traced to, a given cost object in an economically feasible way. *Traceability* is the essence of this classification system. A cost object may be a unit of output or an entire department. Thus a cost may be "direct" for one cost object but "indirect" for another cost object. (The more common expression for an indirect cost is "overhead"). For example, a manager's salary may be direct in terms of costing the overall department but would be classified as an overhead if the cost objective were a unit of output. The two main direct costs are:

1. **Direct materials**: Materials that are part of the product being produced — for example, wood for tables, cotton and wool in clothes.

2. **Direct labour**: Work performed on the product itself — one can observe the work being done on the raw materials.

Some direct costs are classified as indirect/overhead, because they are insignificant in relation to overall costs and the cost of detailed record-keeping outweighs any benefit for decision-making purposes — for example, thread in a textile factory. In contrast, some overhead costs — for example, power for machines — can be identified as direct costs by installing special recording meters for each machine. In this case, the power becomes a direct cost of each machine.

The classification of *direct/overhead* can also be used in the context of a service industry in conjunction with the fixed/variable distinction. For example, a hotel would probably want to accumulate its costs by service provided — for example, bedrooms, restaurant and bar. The following exhibit is a useful summary:

Exhibit 5.4: Cost Classification System for Hotels

	DIRECT COSTS			INDIRECT COSTS
COST OBJECTIVE	MATERIALS	LABOUR	OTHER COSTS	
Bedrooms	Soap	Chamber-maid	TV Licence	Advertising
Restaurant	Food	Chef	Plates	Insurance
Bar	Drinks	Bar staff	Glasses	

Associated with the classification of direct and overhead costs are the terms of "cost allocation" and "cost apportionment", though sometimes the distinction is not made. Cost allocation represents the assignment of an entire cost to a single cost objective. Only direct costs, by definition, are allocated. Cost apportionment represents the assignment of an entire cost to two or more cost objectives. Generally speaking, overhead costs will be apportioned among cost objectives.

Cost Classification by Function

In order to build up an overall picture of total costs incurred, costs are usually classified and aggregated by function. This classification system tells us where costs have been incurred. The main functions are:

1. Production.

2. Administration.

3. Advertising/selling.

4. Distribution.

Included under production are all costs starting from the supply of materials and labour and ending with the manufactured finished product together with packaging. Typically, they include:

1. **Direct materials**: A manufacturer buys raw materials and converts them into finished goods. The first basic cost of a manufacturer is that of raw materials.

2. **Direct labour**: In converting raw materials into finished goods, a manufacturer incurs direct labour costs, representing the wages paid to factory employees who work directly on the products being manufactured. Direct labour costs include the cost of machine operators, assembly line workers and others who work on the goods by hand or with tools. When calculating production (manufacturing) costs, it is usual to refer to the aggregate of direct labour and direct material costs as "prime cost".

3. **Production overhead**: All manufacturing costs other than raw material and direct production labour are called factory, or production, overhead.

Examples of manufacturing production overhead costs include:

(a) **Indirect labour**: Supervision and maintenance.

(b) **Occupancy costs**: Depreciation and insurance of buildings.

(c) **Plant and machinery costs**: Power and depreciation of machinery.

Since it is not possible to compile an exhaustive list of all factory overhead costs, manufacturing or production overhead is defined as "all costs incurred in the manufacturing process other than raw materials and direct production labour".

Note that administration, advertising and distribution costs do not relate to the production process and should never be included in manufacturing overhead. Certain costs, such as insurance, may be applicable in part to factory operations and in part to administration. In such cases, these costs should be apportioned between factory overhead and administration costs.

Administration costs represent the costs of running the company and include items such as the salary of the managing director, wages of book-keeping staff and telephone costs.

Advertising and selling costs represent the costs of creating and simulating demand for the company's products. They include advertising costs and also the salaries of sales personnel.

Distribution costs represent the costs of getting the goods to the customers. They include petrol and travel expenses as well as salaries of distribution personnel.

A typical cost statement for a manufacturing company would appear as follows:

COST STATEMENT
FOR YEAR ENDED 31 DECEMBER 20x8

	€	€
1. Production costs		
a. Raw materials consumed:		
Opening stock of raw materials		25,000
Add:		
Purchases of raw materials		140,000
Cost of raw materials available		
for use		165,000
Less:		
Closing stock of raw materials		(20,000)
Cost of raw materials consumed		145,000
b. Direct labour		300,000
c. Factory overhead:		
Supervision	90,000	
Rent and rates	16,000	
Depreciation of plant	11,000	
Depreciation of factory buildings	10,000	127,000
Cost of finished goods manufac-		572,000
tured		
2. Administration		100,000
3. Advertising/selling		150,000
4. Distribution		125,000
Total Cost		947,000

Classification by Cost Centre

A cost centre is a location, person or item of equipment (or a group of these) for which costs may be ascertained and for which an individual is responsible. Charging costs to a cost centre involves charging to that centre all costs that can be traced directly. Suitable cost centres might be maintenance, personnel and general office. It could also be a salesman or group of customers. A cost centre may be an operation cost centre based on all machines, thus ascertaining the cost of a particular operation. In a university, cost centres may be the various departments. This classification system is further discussed in Section 5.2 below.

Cost Classification in relation to Quality

It is argued that companies are becoming increasingly aware that quality can provide a competitive weapon to compete in worldwide markets. Inferior quality products or services can be an important determinant of customer dissatisfaction. The implications of bad quality and dissatisfied customers are evident from the following rules of thumb (Source unknown):

1. About 5% of unhappy customers complain directly to the organisation involved.

2. An average customer with a complaint will tell 10 other people.

3. Customers who have complaints satisfactorily involved will tell 5 other people.

Therefore, quality (and the role of the management in quality measurement) is the first issue to be addressed here.

Quality and Cost of Quality (COQ) reports

An important role for the management accountant in modern organisations is to provide a range of financial and non-financial measurements to management about various aspects of performance. In recent years a great deal has been written in marketing/management and strategy journals about the issue of quality and its importance. Some authors argue, convincingly, that quality is a very important source of competitive advantage. Indeed, one of the leading "quality gurus" argues that "by the end of the century there will be only two types of business: Those that practise Total Quality Management (TQM) and those that are no longer in business" (Deming). At a minimum, quality service can provide protection against litigation.

What is Quality?

Quality is a term that we all use fairly loosely, partly reflecting the fact that there are different dimensions to quality. The ISO (International Organisation for Standardisation – based in Geneva, Switzerland) define quality as: "Quality is the total features and characteristics of a product or service that provide its ability to satisfy stated or implicit needs". However this definition does not make any reference to cost. Thus, related to the definition of quality is the notion of a competitive price which customers are prepared to pay. Thirdly, there is the aspect of customer service before and after sale. These customer perceptions and experiences will influence whether they will become new customers or remain repeat customers. Customer service features may include (among other activities)

1. Provision of pre-sale information.

2. Proper treatment of customers by sales staff.

3. On-time delivery.

4. Follow-up with customer after the sale.

5. Timeliness and accuracy of resolution of questions and complaints.

6. Warranty and repair services.

Attributes/features: It is common to define quality in respect of the features and characteristics of a product or service which taken together determine its ability to satisfy the needs of customers. No matter what individuals within the organisation do, it will always be the customer who is the ultimate judge of quality. While quality considerations apply to products it may even be more important for those in the service industry. A defective product can be replaced subsequently; a defective service leaves the customer with an unpleasant experience, which can be difficult to repair. Obviously quality has many dimensions or attributes and includes the following:

1. Performance - operating characteristics.

2. Reliability – dependability.

3. Durability - operating life.

4. Serviceability - speed and ease of repair.

5. Appeal - appearance, taste, etc.

6. Reputation - perceived quality.

And in relation to service organisations: Cleanliness, Friendliness, Accessibility, Availability and Competence of staff.

The recent emphasis on quality is at variance with the traditional view on quality. In times past it was generally accepted that there was a desirable balance to be achieved between improved quality and higher costs. Thus, statistical sampling was used to ensure that the number of outgoing defective units did not exceed a predetermined, specified limit. Companies, accordingly, established expensive field service operations and provided generous warranty cover. If failures or defects occurred, they could be replaced or repaired by field personnel.

There were other consequences. Typically, companies would keep large amounts of both finished goods and raw materials in stock incurring costs in storage, handling, insurance, breakage and pilferage. Scrap costs were high and, occasionally, production schedules needed to be changed to facilitate rework. These costs were buried in costs of goods manufactured and sold, salaries, travel expenses, insurance, technical services, and so forth. They remain unknown and therefore unmanaged. For many enterprises, one of the greatest opportunities for effective cost management and profit improvement lies in managing costs of quality.

The modern emphasis is on zero defects and consequently no necessity for rework. Also, the modern approach is to design and build quality in, rather than trying to inspect and repair quality into products. For example, products with fewer parts generally place less demand on that product to achieve a required quality level. Some quality experts argue (and provide evidence) that only 20 percent of quality defects can be traced to the production line. The other 80 percent are determined at the design or purchasing stages. Simply put, many manufacturing problems arise because of the difficulty of reliably producing a product that has been designed for performance, but not for manufacture. Companies are now moving away from the traditional "people do what you inspect" approach to quality toward a newer and broader-based "design-it-in" approach. The responsibility for detecting substandard items has been shifted from quality control supervisors to the operators actually performing the work.

The differing views are presented below in Exhibit 5.5.

Exhibit 5.5: Differing Views on Quality

TRADITIONAL VIEW	MODERN VIEW
Improving quality increases costs	Improving quality reduces overall costs
A specified percentage of defects are acceptable	The goal is zero defects
Volume is as important as quality	Without quality, everything is irrelevant

Zero defects means that there are no rejected materials, parts, or finished products, and no rework. It is a state of perfection. While zero defects may seem an unattainable goal, it is important to believe that this level of quality can and will be achieved, no matter how difficult. Quality applies to services as well as to products, although in somewhat different ways. Exhibit 5.6 below lists some of the more critical differences.

Exhibit 5.6: Differences between Products and Services

PRODUCTS	SERVICES
The customer owns an object	The customer owns a memory
The goal of producing objects is to make each product uniform	The goal of each service is unique and each contact is special
A product can be placed in inventory	A service is produced and consumed simultaneously
If badly produced, the product can be recalled and replaced	If a service is improperly provided, apologises and reparations are the only course

Although the quality of service received in hotels, restaurants and hospitals can be a matter of subjective judgement, it can be monitored and improved. Hotel guests, for example, can be asked if the service met their expectations. A service organisation should have a procedure in place to record and deal with customer complaints. It should also hold regular quality review meetings to enable management to discuss and improve the methods of delivering service in order to correct problem areas.

Quality can be achieved by (a) investing in new physical assets and technologies and/or (b) changing practices, policies and systems to encourage experimentation, innovation and learning.

Companies are becoming increasingly aware that quality performance can provide a competitive weapon in worldwide markets. Companies now realise that quality is not just an invigorating slogan or a fad, but is the most profitable way to run the business. Increasing quality can have an enormous impact on company profitability both by reducing operating costs and improving market share and revenues. Excellence in performance should be the norm, not the exception.

Measuring Quality Performance

As companies embrace the quality revolution, they will need to devise and report measures to monitor progress towards specific objectives. Management accountants, as information specialists, are ideally placed to make a positive contribution towards measuring and reporting on quality performance. Reports can be either in financial or non-financial terms. Non-financial performance measures include the following:

1. Suppliers:
    - ☐ Number of defective units delivered
    - ☐ Number of late deliveries.

2. Production process:

   ☐ First-pass rates (percentage of units finished without any rework)

   ☐ Scrap and rework costs including overtime

   ☐ Number and % of production and delivery times not adhered to

   ☐ Number of accidents in plant

   ☐ Number of employee suggestions.

3. Customer satisfaction:

   ☐ Number of customer complaints (say, per 1000 customers)

   ☐ Warranty claims

   ☐ Customer satisfaction questionnaires/surveys

   ☐ Rate of billing/invoice errors (or number of credit notes issued)

   ☐ Customer retention rates (It costs about 5 times more to gain new customers than to retain existing ones).

However, for maximum effect, it is often suggested to highlight the financial impact of quality in a Cost of Quality (CoQ) report. The CoQ report attempts to compute a single aggregate measure of all explicit costs attributable to preventing and correcting defective products. Sometimes managers do not realise the size of the problem or the potential benefits until they see the financial implications. The conventional method for reporting, evaluating, and managing costs of quality is to identify all costs of quality under four major categories as follows:

1. Prevention costs.

2. Appraisal costs.

3. Internal failure costs.

4. External failure costs.

Prevention costs
Prevention costs are those costs incurred by actions to reduce or prevent poor-quality products or services from being produced in the first place. In other words, such costs (and related activities) prevent bad quality work from happening. They include:

1. All costs associated with quality planning.

2. Product design work that ensures specifications for existing and new products meet customer needs.

3. Design, development, maintenance and calibration/set-up of all quality control equipment.

4. Administration of all quality control procedures including the collection, processing and distribution of quality control data.

5. Training of quality control personnel.

Appraisal costs
Appraisal costs are incurred in discovering the condition of products and raw materials and include testing procedures to identify nonconformities before a product or service reaches another activity and is delivered to the ultimate customer. In other words, they are the costs (and related activities) incurred to ensure that quality specifications are met. Appraisal costs include the following:

1. Inspection and testing of incoming materials and goods.

2. Inspection of finished goods.

3. Supervision.

4. Quality data/accounting information gathering, analysis, reporting and audit.

5. Statistical process control.

Internal failure costs
If preventive and appraisal techniques do not work adequately the company begins to spend money on internal failure costs. Internal failure costs are those costs incurred when products or services fail to meet quality standards, and the defects are identified after the products or services are produced but corrected before they are delivered to the external customer. They are the cost of rectifying defective work before the product is delivered to customers. These internal failure costs entail:

1. The costs of any materials scrapped for failure to meet specifications.

2. Reprocessing, rectifying and re-inspection and re-testing of substandard products including any overtime costs.

3. Losses arising from temporary shut-downs of production equipment

4. Revenue losses from price reductions of sub-standard products.

5. The costs of reviewing product specifications as a result of product failures.

External failure costs

These costs are potentially the most expensive because they can involve the only reason why the company is in business – the customer. External failure costs are those costs incurred because poor quality products or services are delivered to external customers. The nonconformities are identified only after the product or service reaches the ultimate customer. These are the costs associated with rectifying defective work delivered to customers. External failure costs are associated with the following:

1. Customer complaints department.

2. Sales returns and allowances.

3. Recall of defective products.

4. Replacements, warranties and repairs.

5. Product liability insurance.

6. Lost sales and lost customers (but this may be difficult to identify).

A typical Cost of Quality report could be presented as in Exhibit 5.7.

Prevention and appraisal costs are sometimes called costs of conformance (adherence to quality standards). Internal failure and external failure costs are sometimes referred to as costs of non-conformance. Prevention and appraisal costs are voluntary; that is, these costs do not have to be incurred. Internal failure and external failure costs are involuntary, because they are costs that the company must pay. Thus,

PC + AC = Cost of conformance

IF + EF = Cost of non-conformance

CoQ   = Cost of conformance and non-conformance.

Exhibit 5.7: Costs of Quality Report for the Period ended ...

Cost Category	Actual €	Budget €	Variance €	
Prevention costs:				
Employee Training	6,000	8,000	2,000	F
Design department	15,000	10,000	(5,000)	A
Total prevention costs	21,000	18,000	(3,000)	A
Appraisal costs:				
Inspection of raw materials	5,000	10,000	5,000	F
Supervisors	7,000	5,000	(2,000)	A
Total appraisal costs	12,000	15,000	3,000	F
Internal failure costs.				
Scrap	50,000	45,000	(5,000)	A
Price reductions	10,000	12,000	2,000	F
Total internal failure	60,000	57,000	(3,000)	A
External failure costs:				
Customer complaints dept.	10,000	25,000	15,000	F
Warranties and repairs	20,000	45,000	25,000	F
Total external failure	30,000	70,000	40,000	F
Total costs of quality	123,000	160,000	37,000	F
CoQ as % sales	19%	25%		

Intangible costs and benefits of quality/bad quality
Some of the above costs are easy to identify, e.g., warranties and repairs. However, the opportunity cost of bad quality is difficult to quantify since it represents lost future sales and deteriorating reputation. In many cases, dissatisfied customers do not complain directly to the company. Rather, they take their business elsewhere and tell others about their unsatisfactory experience. It is also difficult to estimate the benefits arising from improved customer goodwill and changes in market position as a direct result of improved quality. Any attempts to quantify these potential gains are likely to be highly subjective.

Advantages of CoQ reports
A number of advantages of Cost of Quality reports may be cited:

1. Since they are a financial summary of the entire quality programme within organisations, they are an ideal vehicle for getting managerial attention. While non-financial indicators relating to quality are

more important, managers often pay more attention to the financial implications of their activities. In turn, the total quality spend can be expressed as, say, a percentage of sales revenue. In turn such financial performance measures can be compared with predetermined targets or even the previous year. Also, this generally accepted classification of quality costs facilitates external benchmarking with other similar organisations. Most companies are surprised to learn that spending on quality-related costs can amount to 15-30 per cent of sales revenue. Such information can be used as a lever to get management's attention that perhaps, greater awareness and commitment to quality issues can reduce this large amount of money. Literature on the topic of quality performance suggests that well-run manufacturing companies can limit their overall quality costs to less than 5 percent of sales revenue.

2. The CoQ report is logical and sequential in that it portrays the four main elements of quality programmes: Prevention, appraisal, internal and external failure. On the other hand, a listing of several non-financial indicators is more random. Also, managers can appreciate the priorities and trade-offs associated with quality programmes. For example, it is desirable to spend additional resources on conformance activities rather than non-conformance activities.

3. The additional attention of quality performance encourages managerial action and decision making, with the financial implications of their proposed decisions becoming apparent.

Conclusion

The focus of quality rather than cost as a key success factor for all organisations is stressed in all management literature in recent years. Companies are emphasising quality in a number of ways. First, they are planning quality into products at the design stage rather than focusing on quality at the inspection stage. After all, quality has to be built into one's products and services, not inspected into them. Secondly, companies are working closely with suppliers in order to ensure that high-quality components are received into the factory. Suppliers become certified when they demonstrate that they can produce zero defects output. Their deliveries can then enter the production process with no incoming inspection performed. Thirdly, companies are increasing the time and resources spent on staff training and development and actively seek suggestions from employees.

Management accountants can pay an important role in helping organisations achieve their objectives by providing an appropriate range of financial and non-financial measures of quality performance. After all, the end result of accounting information should be actions. Indeed, accounting information that does not stimulate action is of rather poor quality. Accountants should realise that they are in the quality business too!

5.2 ASSIGNING COSTS TO COST CENTRES — ALLOCATION AND APPORTIONMENT

There can be a variety of cost objectives within an organisation. For example, in the context of a university, the cost objective may be relatively broad — to ascertain the costs of running the university; on the other hand, it may be very narrow — to ascertain the cost per graduate. This section looks at how costs may be ascertained for a cost centre. A cost centre is a location, person or item of equipment (or group of these) for which costs may be ascertained and for which an individual is responsible. In other words, the use of cost centres allows identification of specific areas where costs have been incurred. Suitable cost centres in a factory might be maintenance, personnel or administration; suitable cost centres in a university might be the various teaching and service departments.

For the purpose of this section, assume that a cost centre is equivalent to a department. Assigning costs to a cost centre involves charging to that centre all costs that can be traced directly. Usually, a business consists of several cost centres (departments). The advantages of cost centres are:

1. Accumulating costs by cost centre allows managers to identify whether the cost centre is becoming more or less efficient, by comparing cost data from different time periods. Normally an individual is held responsible for costs incurred in the cost centre under his control, in which case, accumulating costs by cost centre may increase the motivation of managers to be efficient. Where related revenue can be directly traced, it allows the overall profitability of that centre to be established. This could be an important consideration in the context of deciding to expand or reduce capacity in that centre.

2. In order to establish unit cost to be used in pricing and stock valuation decisions, one usually begins by accumulating costs by cost centre. This allows a unit cost figure for each department (cost centre) to be ascertained through the use of overhead recovery rates. And, since it is unlikely that each unit of output will pass through each department or cost centre, accumulating costs

by cost centre ensures that only if work is performed in a specific department will costs be charged for that department. In addition, a number of cost centres allows different methods (bases) of recovering (absorbing) costs in the different departments. Thus, for example, costs in one cost centre may be assigned to products on the basis of direct labour hours; and on the basis of machine hours in another. (The issue of overhead recovery will be addressed in the next section).

Before discussing the issue of assigning costs to cost centres, it may be useful to review the distinction between cost allocation and cost apportionment.

Cost *allocation* represents the assignment a cost to a single cost object. The cost object can be broad — for example, the cost of running a school — or it can be very narrow — for example, the cost of a unit. Allocation means that there is no requirement to share this cost between cost objects. Direct costs are allocated.

On the other hand, cost *apportionment* represents the assignment of a cost between two or more cost objects. Again, the cost objective can be broad or narrow. Indirect (overhead) costs are apportioned. However, apportionment is very much an arbitrary task — there is no such thing as a single, best method of apportioning costs. Cost apportionment is ultimately a matter of judgment and opinion. Different bases of apportionment will give different results. Consequently, cost apportionment can easily mislead users of accounting information because users do not often appreciate how arbitrarily businesses apportion costs.

Remember that a cost may be direct for one purpose and indirect for another — for example, the production manager's salary is a direct cost of the production process (and thus allocated), while it would be classified as an overhead in ascertaining the production cost per unit of output from the department.

Usually costs are assigned to cost centres using the benefit principle. This means that costs should be assigned to the cost centres that benefit from the expenditure. In other words, try to identify a cause and effect relationship. However, clerical convenience and cost may lead to the arbitrary use of one method of apportionment and not another.

Bases of Apportionment

The following bases of apportionment are commonly used within organisations:

BASIS OF APPORTIONMENT	COSTS
Relative area	Rent and rates
	Insurance
	Light and heat
Machine running hours	Power for machines
	Machine maintenance
Number of employees	Administration costs
	Canteen costs
Sales revenue	Advertising costs
Book value of machinery	Insurance costs
	Depreciation of machinery

In some cases, costs will be apportioned between cost centres on the basis of some agreed fraction of total costs. This is usually because no logical cause and effect relationship can be established.

ILLUSTRATION

Rialto is a small family-owned fish and chip shop. During its most recent financial year Rialto made a profit of €26,300 as detailed in the profit and loss account below:

SUMMARISED PROFIT AND LOSS ACCOUNT
FOR YEAR ENDED 31 DECEMBER 20x1

	€	€
Sales:		
Fried fish	40,000	
Chips	50,000	
Confectionery	10,000	100,000
Less: Expenses:		
Fish	28,000	
Potatoes	9,000	
Confectionery	8,000	
Frying oil	8,100	
Depreciation	5,000	
Rent and rates	6,600	
Wages	9,000	73,700
Net Profit		26,300

Depreciation, rent and rates and wages are classified as fixed costs.

REQUIREMENT

Prepare a departmental profitability report, allocating and apportioning costs and revenues as appropriate. Distinguish between fixed and variable costs. For sake of convenience, costs can be apportioned on the basis of sales turnover. Should sales of confectionery be discontinued? Give your reasons.

RIALTO SHOP
CONTRIBUTION FORMAT STATEMENT

	FISH €	CHIPS €	CONFECTIONERY €	TOTAL €
Total Sales	40,000	50,000	10,000	100,000
Less: Variable costs:				
Fish	28,000	–	–	28,000
Potatoes	–	9,000	–	9,000
Confectionery	–	–	8,000	8,000
Frying oil	3,600	4,500	–	8,100
Total variable cost	31,600	13,500	8,000	53,100
Contribution	8,400	36,500	2,000	46,900
Less: Fixed costs (W1)	8,240	10,300	2,060	20,600
Product profit (loss)	160	26,200	(60)	26,300

(W1) FIXED COSTS	€
(to be apportioned on the basis of sales revenue)	
Depreciation	5,000
Rent and rates	6,600
Wages	9,000
	20,600

NOTE: In this example, since the information will be used in decision-making, it is useful to report fixed and variable costs separately. The term "contribution" refers to the surplus of sales revenue over total variable costs and this surplus, if any, is available to cover fixed costs. The sales of confectionery should be continued, since they provide a contribution of €2,000. The apportioned fixed costs (€2,060) will be incurred whether confectionery is sold or not.

5.3 ASSIGNING COSTS TO COST UNITS — OVERHEAD ABSORPTION

The purpose of this section is to establish the *cost* of an end product, which in many cases will be a unit of output. Total cost can be divided into *production* and *non-production* costs. Production costs comprise three elements:

1. **Direct labour**: The work performed on the product.

2. **Direct materials**: The materials in the product.

3. **Production overheads**: A share of general production costs such as factory depreciation.

There should be little difficulty in tracing direct material and labour cost to units of output — for example, by way of goods requisition notes. Direct labour is usually traced to the product by way of job cards, or time sheets in the case of a service business. The third category of cost — overhead — is more problematic, because there is no single, correct method of absorbing overhead into cost units. This means that different methods of absorbing overheads into cost units will give different cost figures.

In recent times, production overhead is becoming increasingly important due to the diminishing importance of direct labour — attributable to increased automation. Increased automation generally increases factory overhead due to increased machine maintenance, insurance and depreciation. The switch to automation is likely to continue in the future so that direct labour will become relatively unimportant and production overheads will become increasingly important. In some manufacturing businesses, direct labour can be as low as 10 per cent of total costs, whereas production overhead can be as high as 30 or 40 per cent of total cost.

A knowledge of *total* unit cost is necessary for three purposes:

1. To price a product or service, one must know how much it costs. No profit can be earned unless the selling price covers cost. However, sometimes selling prices are deliberately set below cost so as to entice new customers (although, for certain consumer products such as milk and bread, this is illegal). Also, selling prices take into account a number of factors, of which, cost is only one.

2. Product (or service) costs must also be ascertained in controlling operations. For example, managers want to know whether planned costs are being adhered to (the control function); also managers may learn from cost overruns and use this information in planning for the future.

3. Any unsold goods at the end of the accounting period must be valued for financial accounting purposes. In accordance with accounting standards (SSAP 9), closing stock must be valued at cost (subject to the lower of net realisable value).

The focus of this section is how to assign production overheads to units of output. A simple answer might be to divide total production overhead by the number of units produced. For example, this might be done in a university to calculate the cost per student. However, this simple approach of dividing overheads by units of output is unfair if a variety of products are produced that consume different amounts of overhead resources (students are considered a rather homogeneous lot!).

Overhead absorption represents the third "A" of cost accounting, the other two As being cost allocation and cost apportionment. Overhead absorption (or recovery) is the assignment of overhead costs to units of output. The problem of how to assign overhead costs to units of output in an equitable manner is depicted in Exhibit 5.8 below.

Exhibit 5.8 suggests that costs are accumulated by department. Charging costs to a cost centre involves assigning costs that can be traced to that particular centre (a cost centre is any area of activity for which costs may be ascertained and for which an individual may be held responsible). In many cases, cost centres will be departments and consequently we may use these terms interchangeably.

It is necessary to establish a number of cost centres because:

1. It is most unlikely that all jobs will pass through all production departments. Some jobs will pass through some cost centres but not others.

2. The amount of production activity in the different cost centres (departments) will differ. Thus some products will receive a lot of work in one department but not in another.

3. A number of different cost centres allows different methods (bases) of recovering costs in the different departments. In one cost centre, overhead costs may be assigned to products on the basis of direct labour hours and on the basis of machine hours in another.

Exhibit 5.8: Assigning Overhead Costs to Cost Units

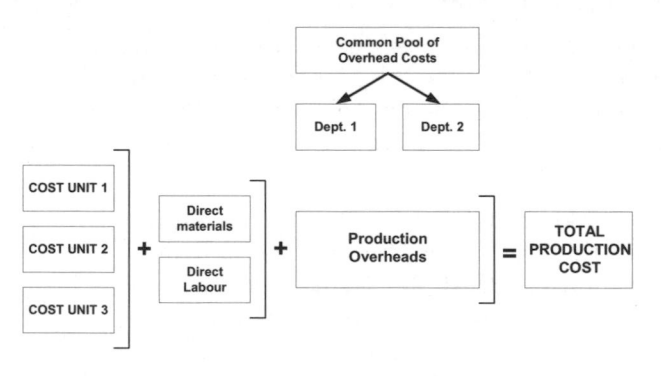

As a result of the cost allocation and apportionment process, total costs assigned to a department will be identified. Usually, the total of such costs will represent three separate elements:

1. Costs that are allocated to a department — that is, direct costs. This means that certain costs are assigned in total to the department. Since no other department benefits from this expenditure, it is not necessary to share such costs between other departments. Examples of such expenditure are the salary costs of the department manager or insurance costs of departmental equipment.

2. Those that are shared among several cost centres. Thus, rent payable on the factory must be shared among the various cost centres in the factory. This sharing is referred to as "apportionment" and should be done as fairly as possible using one of the many different methods of cost apportionment.

3. Service department costs — for example, maintenance. These costs are usually accumulated by service department before being apportioned among the various production departments. (Service department apportionments are covered in the next section).

There are basically two ways that overheads can be assigned to cost units. The first method is simply to divide total overhead cost by the number of units produced. This results in an overhead per unit being identified. Unfortunately, this simple method is not generally acceptable for a business that is producing a number of different products. Different products consume different amounts of overhead resources and therefore another method of assigning (recovering) overheads to cost units must be developed. A commonly-used technique is to calculate overhead absorption rates (OHARs).

The steps needed to calculate a predetermined OHAR are:

1. Estimate activity (output) the forthcoming period to be absorbed.

2. Estimate overheads to be incurred for that level of activity.

3. Divide 2. by 1. to arrive at an OHAR.

Suppose for illustration purposes that a company has departmental overheads of €100,000 per annum and the direct labour hours to be worked are estimated to be 20,000. The overhead absorption rate is calculated as:

$$\text{OHAR} = \frac{\text{Total overhead}}{\text{Direct labour hours}} = \frac{€100,000}{€20,000} = €5 \text{ per direct labour hour}$$

The OHAR states, in effect, that €5 overheads will be added to each unit for every direct labour hour worked on that particular unit. If a certain unit (or job) required 10 hours of direct labour, the overheads assigned (in addition to direct labour and material costs) to this product would be €50 (10 hours @ €5). It is not surprising, therefore, that overheads are sometimes described as what accountants drop on unsuspecting managers!

In setting OHARs, there are four important points that need to be addressed:

1. Departmental or plant-wide rates.

2. Choice of activity base for overhead absorption.

3. Annual or seasonal rates.

4. Predetermined or actual OHARs.

Departmental Rates

Departmental OHARs are usually preferred to plant-wide rates because, with departmental rates, a separate absorption rate is established for each department. Thus, only if work is carried out in a department will overheads be assigned to units as they are processed in that department. On the other hand, using a single plant-wide OHAR, the total overheads of the organisation are divided by some measure of activity — for example, direct labour hours. This means that a share of all overheads will be assigned to units even though they are not processed in all departments.

ILLUSTRATION: Comparison of departmental and plant-wide production overhead rates

The Sayther Company manufactured two products A and B during the first year of its operations. It budgeted factory overhead at €340,000 and 200,000 budgeted direct-labour hours, as shown below:

	BUDGETED OVERHEAD €	BUDGETED HOURS
Department 1	240,000	100,000
Department 2	100,000	100,000
Total	340,000	200,000

The number of labour hours required to manufacture each of these products was:

	PRODUCT A	PRODUCT B
In Department 1	4	1
In Department 2	1	4
Total	5	5

REQUIREMENT

1. Calculate overhead absorption rates for Departments 1 and 2 using direct labour hours (DLH) and indicate the overheads assigned to products A and B based on your calculations.

2. Calculate a plant-wide overhead absorption rate using direct labour hours (DLH) and indicate the overheads assigned to products A and B based on your calculations.

SOLUTION
1. DEPARTMENTAL OVERHEAD RECOVERY RATES:

Dept. 1   €240,000 / 100,000 = €2.40 per DLH
Dept. 2   €100,000 / 100,000 = €1.00 per DLH

Overhead assigned to products using departmental OHARs:

	A	B
Dept. 1	9.60	2.40
Dept. 2	1.00	4.00
	10.60	6.40

2. PLANT-WIDE OVERHEAD RECOVERY RATE:

$$\frac{€340,000}{200,000} = €1.70 \text{ per direct labour hour}$$

Overhead assigned to products using plant-wide rates:

	A	B
Factory overhead	8.50	8.50

Using plant-wide absorption rates, the overhead assigned to each product is the same because they both require the same amount of labour hours. However, this ignores the fact that Department A is relatively more expensive to operate and that there is an unequal amount of labour performed in each department.

Choice of Activity Base for Overhead Absorption

The choice of the overhead absorption, or recovery, base is sometimes a matter of controversy. Many overheads are related to time and so it is logical to charge those products that use factory facilities for the longest time with the largest share of overheads. Therefore, overheads are best absorbed on a time basis — for example, direct labour hours, direct labour cost or machine hours.

In principle, there are four main bases:

1. **Direct labour hours**: Many overhead costs are time-related or associated with the amount of labour input — for example, supervision. Thus overheads are absorbed on the basis of direct labour hours. In a service business, overheads are absorbed (and later charged out) on the basis of direct labour hours. However, this assumes that all labour hours generate the same proportion of overheads. The amount of direct labour hours is usually determined by job cards/time sheets etc.

2. **Direct labour cost**: This should only be used when the labour hourly rates for each operation are similar. If employees are paid at different rates, overheads charged to units of production worked on by higher-paid employees will be greater than those charged to units involving lower-paid employees. Having said that, in some service businesses, overheads are charged out on the basis of direct labour cost because the more expensive labour (senior staff) consume more overheads (larger offices, secretarial assistance) than junior staff. Thus, direct labour cost is a simpler system to operate than having several different recovery rates for different grades of labour. The advantage lies in its simplicity.

3. **Machine running hours**: Many costs are clearly related to machine capacity and utilisation — for example, depreciation of machines and indirect (preventive) maintenance. This argument is particularly relevant where production is highly mechanised. However, for some manufacturing businesses with crude accounting systems, machine running hours may be difficult to obtain. It is not widely used in very small businesses because of the added clerical time involved in its application.

4. **Direct material cost**: This method can only be justified where a major part of overheads is associated with materials handling.

Annual or Seasonal Rates

In setting OHARs, annual rather than seasonal rates are used. This is to eliminate possible distortions due to, say, quarterly fluctuations in either the overhead costs or level of activity. If quarterly rates are used, the following distortion could arise where there is a monthly fluctuation in activity (output):

ILLUSTRATION

	Q 1	Q 2	Q 3	Q 4	TOTAL
	€	€	€	€	€
Fixed overheads	12,000	12,000	12,000	12,000	48,000
Activity (hours)	6,000	2,000	10,000	8,000	26,000
Overhead rate per hour	2.00	6.00	1.20	1.50	1.85

What is required is a *normal* product cost based on average production and average costs rather than actual production cost, which is affected by seasonal fluctuations in production volume. In the illustration above, an average absorption rate of €1.85 per hour would be selected rather than computing separate absorption rates for each month.

Predetermined or Actual OHARs

The OHAR is predetermined for a given time period as this allows an estimated amount to be charged to a unit rather than waiting for the end of the financial year to determine "actual" overhead rates. Basing recovery rates on the basis of actual, rather than predetermined, data involves undue delay and would not be generally acceptable in setting selling prices. Because overhead recovery rates are predetermined, they can only be best estimates. Consequently, if actual activity or spending is different from expected activity or expected spending, there will be an over/under recovery of overheads.

Suppose anticipated fixed overheads and estimated activity for a forthcoming year are as follows:

Estimated fixed overheads	€200,000
Estimated activity	100,000 hours
OHAR	€2 per hour

Two situations can develop during the year:

1. The actual activity will be less (or more) than anticipated.

2. The actual spending will be more(or less) than anticipated.

Situation 1

Actual activity (hours)	90,000
Actual overhead spending	€200,000
Overheads recovered	€180,000
Under-recovery of overheads	(€20,000)

In this situation, the overheads recovered (absorbed) into cost units amount to €180,000. This is less than the actual spending (€200,000). Thus, €20,000 overheads have been incurred but, due to activity being less than anticipated, have not been charged to units of output. This is an under-recovery of overheads and arises from an adverse volume variance.

Situation 2

Actual activity (hours)	100,000
Actual overhead spending	€210,000
Overheads recovered	€200,000
Under-recovery of overheads	(€10,000)

In this situation, the overheads recovered (absorbed) into cost units amount to €200,000. This is less than the actual spending (€210,000). Thus, €10,000 overheads have been incurred but, due to spending being more than anticipated, have not been charged to units of output. This is an under-recovery of overheads and results from an adverse spending variance.

In most situations, under- or over-recovered overheads are written off immediately to the profit and loss account as a separate line item, in internal reports.

5.4   SERVICE DEPARTMENT APPORTIONMENTS

There are typically three levels of costs in a department:

1. Costs that are allocated to a department (direct costs).

2. Those that are apportioned (shared) between several cost centres.

3. Service department costs, accumulated by service department before being apportioned among the various production departments.

The previous section was concerned with the first two levels of cost. This section is concerned with service department costs. In keeping with the concept of responsibility accounting, service costs are accumulated separately. This allows one to assess whether an individual manager is keeping his spending under control. However, for the purposes of calculating overhead absorption rates and cost per unit, the costs of the service departments must be assigned to production (output) departments. Since the production departments produce goods (or services) for sale to customers, they alone can bear overhead costs. Failure to apportion service department costs to production departments will result in setting overhead absorption rates too low to cover all overhead costs.

There are various methods by which service department costs are apportioned to production departments. For the purposes of this book, we shall focus only on the direct method. Under the direct method, service department costs are assigned only to production departments and not to other service departments.

ILLUSTRATION

Parker has two production departments (cutting and assembly) and two service departments (maintenance and administration). Each year, Parker develops predetermined departmental overhead rates on a full costing basis for the cutting and assembly departments. Costs and other data at normal volume are budgeted at the following levels:

| | SERVICE | | PRODUCTION | |
	MAINT.	ADMIN.	CUTTING	ASSEMBLY
Factory overhead costs	€94,000	€48,000	€188,000	€49,200
Direct labour hours	—	—	15,000	10,000
Number of employees	5	20	9	36
Square feet occupied	10,000	20,000	30,000	30,000
Machine hours	—	—	20,000	40,000

Parker is now deciding on the most appropriate method of assigning service department costs to individual job orders. It has been agreed that maintenance department costs should be apportioned on the number of square feet occupied in each department, while the costs of the administration department should be apportioned on the basis of the number of employees.

REQUIREMENT

1. You are required to apportion service department costs to production departments using the direct method.

2. Develop overhead absorption rates for each production department on the following basis:
   ◊ Cutting — machine hours
   ◊ Assembly — labour hours.

SOLUTION
1. SERVICE DEPT. APPORTIONMENTS — DIRECT METHOD

| | SERVICE | | PRODUCTION | |
	MAINT.	ADMIN.	CUTTING	ASSEMBLY
Overheads pre-apportionment	€94,000	€48,000	€188,000	€49,200
Apportionment of Maintenance (sq. ft.)	(94,000)	–	47,000	47,000
Apportionment of Administration (Employees)	–	(48,000)	9,600	38,400
Overheads post-apportionment	–	–	244,600	134,600
Estimated machine hours			20,000	
Estimated direct labour hours				10,000
OHAR (predetermined)			€12.23	€13.46

5.5 COSTS FOR STOCK VALUATION AND PROFIT MEASUREMENT

This section focuses on ascertaining costs to value stock at the end of the accounting period. There are three main categories of goods to be valued at the end of the accounting period: Raw materials, finished goods purchased for resale and finished goods manufactured by the company during the period. In the first two cases, stock will be valued at cost (subject to the lower of cost and net realisable value). The third category — manufactured goods — must be valued at cost of production.

In a manufacturing company, the definition of cost of production can be complex and normally includes the three elements of raw materials, direct labour and production overheads. Clearly the raw materials used to make the product must be included. Direct materials can be physically traced to the product — for example, flour for bread. The second cost ingredient in manufactured goods is the direct labour that is performed on the product. One could go into the factory and see this work being performed — for example, the baking of the bread. The third cost ingredient is manufacturing overhead, which is the aggregate of indirect expenses (for example, factory light and heat) and indirect labour (for example, factory supervisors). By their nature, such costs are necessary for production though they cannot be directly traced to an individual product. For example, light and heat is incurred in respect of total production and not a single unit.

The total cost structure of a manufacturing company can be displayed as follows, with only the costs associated with production being assigned to closing stock valuation:

Exhibit 5.9: Total Cost Structure

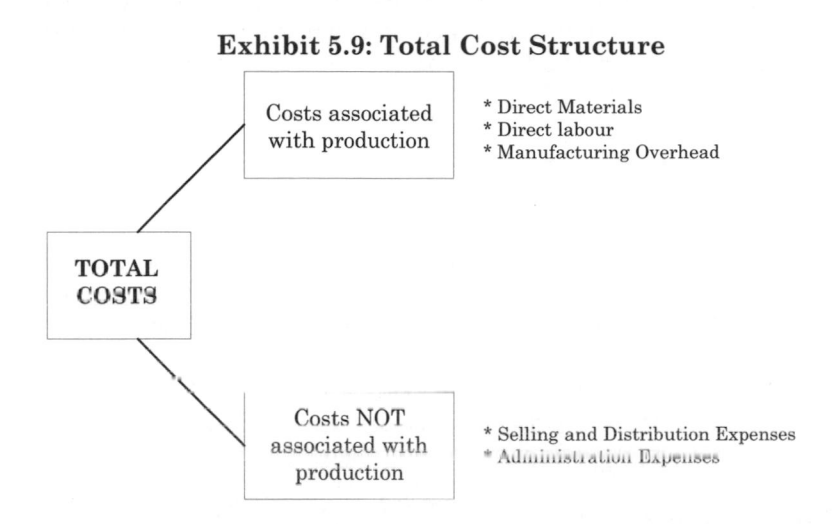

For stock valuation purposes, only costs associated with production are used, because the appropriate costs are those incurred in bringing the product to its present state and condition. Costs not associated with production (for example, administration costs) should *never* be assigned to closing stock.

The major problem in valuation of closing stock is the accounting treatment of "manufacturing overhead". This is an area in which financial and management accounting overlap. It is also an area of controversy and leads to two separate schools of thought, the "Absorption" and the "Variable" school. The controversy concerns *only* the accounting treatment of *fixed* production overhead.

The absorption school argues that both fixed and variable production overheads should be included in stock valuation since both have been incurred in bringing the product to its present location and condition. They argue that one cannot produce goods without incurring fixed production costs. They add that the classification between fixed and variable production overhead can be vague and imprecise.

The variable (or direct) costing school argues that these fixed production costs are associated with providing productive capacity as distinct from using it. They argue that fixed overheads would be incurred regardless of the level of output and represent period, not product, costs and so should not be included in stock valuation but written off in total to the profit and loss account immediately.

The relevant accounting standard (SSAP 9) resolves the argument by requiring companies to use the "full" or "absorption" method of stock valuation for financial accounting purposes. However, for management accounting (internal) purposes, the company may use whatever method it likes. The difference between the reported net profit figures under both methods depends on the change in stock levels over the accounting period.

ILLUSTRATION

A manufacturing company produces only 10,000 units of similar output annually. Direct costs amount to €3 per unit. Each unit is machine processed for 30 minutes and production overhead is re-covered on the basis of machine hours. The estimated running hours per annum are 5,000. Total annual overhead is estimated as follows:

	€
Depreciation of machinery (Variable)	5,000
Other factory overheads (Fixed)	10,000
Administration expenses	10,000

REQUIREMENT

1. Calculate appropriate overhead absorption rates.
2. Compute the valuation of 1,000 units of closing stock under both absorption and variable costing.

SOLUTION

First, calculate an overhead absorption rate, which excludes non-production costs. The absorption method includes both fixed and variable production overheads, whereas the variable method absorbs only the variable cost of production as follows:

OVERHEAD ABSORPTION RATES	ABSORPTION COSTING	VARIABLE COSTING
Overhead to be absorbed	€15,000	€5,000
Machine hours	5,000 hours	5,000 hours
Overhead absorption rate	€3 per machine hour	€1 per machine hour

The closing stock valuation (per unit) is as follows:

	ABSORPTION	VARIABLE
Direct costs	3.00	3.00
Production overhead	1.50	0.50
Total production cost	4.50	3.50

The difference between overhead (and cost) per unit is explained by the treatment of fixed production overhead. As a result, the differences in reported profit between variable and absorption costing methods for financial accounting purposes can be significant. Generally, absorption costing will provide less volatile net profit figures than variable costing. However, over the life of the enterprise, the *total* profit figures will be identical.

The profit difference depends on the changes in opening and closing stock levels. Basically there are only three possible situations in relation to changes in stock levels:

1. When production equals sales, both methods will provide identical net profit figures.

2. When production exceeds sales (a stock build-up), absorption costing provides higher profit figures, because a portion of the fixed production overhead attributable to production will be included in the closing stock valuation figure. Thus, a portion of the period's fixed production overhead is carried to the balance sheet rather than being written off immediately to the profit and loss account. The drawback of absorption costing is that an enterprise could, in theory, boost its reported profit performance by over-producing and thus engage in a stock build up at the end of an accounting period.

3. When sales exceed production (a stock run-down), variable costing will provide higher profit figures, because under variable costing only the fixed overheads applicable to the period in question are being written off. Under an absorption costing system, the overheads for the period in question are being written off *in addition* to a portion of the previous period's fixed overheads which were included in the valuation of opening stock.

ILLUSTRATION

A project to manufacture a new product is under consideration by the management of New Xmas Products Ltd. The following information applies:

Selling price per unit	€6
Advertising and promotion costs	24% of sales price
Variable manufacturing costs	€1.20 per unit

Fixed production costs are estimated at €8,000 per month and the normal production capacity is 5,000 units. Fixed administration costs will amount to €3,000 per month. Production and sales will be:

	JULY	AUGUST	SEPT.	TOTAL
Production (units)	5,000	5,000	5,000	15,000
Sales (units)	3,000	5,000	7,000	15,000

REQUIREMENT

You are required to:

1. Indicate closing stock valuations for July, August and September under both variable and absorption methods.

2. Prepare a forecast profit statement for the above three months under both variable and absorption costing.

SOLUTION

First, ascertain the cost per unit under both variable and absorption costing as follows:

Variable costing	€
Variable manufacturing costs (given)	1.20
Fixed production costs	Nil
	1.20
Valuation	
End of July (2,000 units @ €1.20)	€2,400
End of August (2,000 units @ €1.20)	€2,400
End of September (None)	Nil

Under absorption costing, the unit cost figures are different because of the treatment of fixed production overheads amounting to €8,000 per month. The unit cost figure is as follows:

Absorption costing	€
Variable manufacturing costs (given)	1.20
Fixed production overhead (€8,000/5,000)	1.60
	2.80
Valuation	
End of July (2,000 units @ €2.80)	€5,600
End of August (2,000 units @ €2.80)	€5,600
End of September (None)	Nil

The projected profit and loss accounts for the three months are computed as follows:

PROFIT AND LOSS ACCOUNTS — VARIABLE COSTING

	JULY	AUGUST	SEPT.
Units	3,000	5,000	7,000
Sales price	€6	€6	€6
Total sales	€18,000	€30,000	€42,000
		€	€
Opening stock	–	2,400	2,400
Variable production costs	6,000	6,000	6,000
Fixed production costs	8,000	8,000	8,000
Less: Closing stock	(2,400)	(2,400)	–
Cost of sales	11,600	14,000	16,400
Gross profit	6,400	16,000	25,600
Advertising	(4,320)	(7,200)	(10,080)
Administration	(3,000)	(3,000)	(3,000)
Net profit	(920)	5,800	12,520

PROFIT AND LOSS ACCOUNTS — ABSORPTION COSTING

	JULY	AUGUST	SEPT.
	€	€	€
Total sales (above)	18,000	30,000	42,000
Opening stock	–	5,600	5,600
Variable production costs	6,000	6,000	6,000
Fixed production costs	8,000	8,000	8,000
Less: Closing stock	(5,600)	(5,600)	–
Cost of sales	8,400	14,000	19,600
Gross profit	9,600	16,000	22,400
Advertising	(4,320)	(7,200)	(10,080)
Administration	(3,000)	(3,000)	(3,000)
Net profit	2,280	5,800	9,320

It should be noted that the reported profit difference between the two costing methods can be calculated using the following formulae based on the following notation:

F = Fixed production costs
O = Other fixed costs
C = Contribution margin per unit
Y = Actual sales volume

X　　= Actual (current) production volume
N　　= Normal production volume
PA　= Net profit under absorption costing
PD　= Net profit under direct (variable) costing

The unit contribution (sales price less variable costs) is calculated as:

$$6.00 - 2.64 = €3.36.$$

Profit under direct (variable) costing for July is:

$$PD = C \times Y - [F + O] = €3.36 \times 3,000 \text{ units} - [€8,000 + €3,000] = (€920)$$
loss

Profit under absorption costing for July is:

$$PD - PA = \frac{F(Y - X)}{N} = \frac{€8,000(3,000 - 5,000)}{5,000 \text{ units}} = (€3,200)$$

$$PA = €2,280.$$

The difference in profit for the month of July between the two costing methods is €3,200 (a profit of €2,280 compared with a loss of €920). This is explained by the different accounting treatment of fixed production overheads. The fixed overhead per unit is €1.60 (€8,000/ 5,000 units). During the month of July, an additional 2,000 units were placed in stock. In addition to the variable production costs, absorption costing values this increase in closing stock at €3,200 (2,000 units @ €1.60 per unit), more than under direct costing.

Arguments in Favour of Absorption and Direct Costing

When valuing stock for financial reporting (accounting) purposes, absorption (full) costing must be used in order to comply with the relevant accounting standards. However, internal (management accounting) reports are not constrained by reporting regulations. Thus, management has the option to value stock at either absorption or variable costing for management accounting purposes.

The advocates of variable costing argue as follows:

1. Fixed costs essentially relate to time. They are incurred whether production takes place or not and thus they cannot be regarded as part of production.

2. The use of variable costing avoids the variation of unit cost with every change in the level of output as illustrated below:

	100 UNITS	150 UNITS	200 UNITS
	€	€	€
Fixed cost	1,000	1,000	1,000
Variable cost €5 per unit	500	750	1,000
Total cost	1,500	1,750	2,000
Cost per unit	€15	€11.67	€10

The variable cost is €5 per unit irrespective of the volume of output.

3. Variable costing enables the calculation of unit contribution, which is fundamental in managerial decision-making. Contribution is defined as the amount by which sales revenue exceeds variable cost to provide a surplus from which fixed costs are met and profit made.

4. The use of marginal/variable costing assists pricing policy when considering the use of spare capacity.

On the other hand, those who favour absorption costing put forward the following arguments:

1. Production receives the benefit of services for which fixed costs are incurred and should therefore bear a due share of these costs so that the cost of finished goods includes a charge for fixed overheads.

2. Over the long term, prices cannot be set without regard to total cost including a proportion of fixed overhead costs. If a large proportion of output is priced by reference to variable cost, contribution may not be sufficient to meet fixed costs.

3. It is not always easy to segregate fixed and variable overheads — with absorption costing any such difficulty is avoided.

4. In industries that deal in contracts which take a long period to complete (for example, bridge building), unless fixed overheads are apportioned and added to closing work in progress, substantial losses would be shown over the period of the contract, followed by a year of exceptional profit in the year of completion.

5.6   COSTS FOR PRICING PURPOSES

The previous section concentrated on building up a picture of unit costs. The main purpose was to calculate cost figures for stock valuation purposes. However, cost information is also required for planning and control purposes. A particular situation will be discussed below — that of a job costing system.

A job costing system is usually operated in a business that undertakes different types of jobs for clients rather than mass-producing a single product. Typically, in a job costing system, work is carried out on a "once-off" basis as in the case of a special order — for example, printing diaries or car repair work.

Most of the following section represents a revision and integration of the material already covered. The principles and techniques can be applied to many different situations. However, by concentrating on a particular situation (a job costing situation) that is easy to envisage, the principles may be better understood and subsequently applied.

The main features of a job costing system are:

1. Each job is *different* and needs to be costed separately. The total cost of each job comprises direct materials, direct labour and an appropriate share of overhead. The direct materials costed to the job are based on materials requisition notes. Direct labour hours are based on clock cards or time sheets and the relevant number of hours are multiplied by the appropriate wage rate per hour. Other direct costs are included — for example, hire of special machines for the particular job. In addition to the direct costs of each job, each job should receive a share of departmental overheads through which it passes (this automatically assumes that the company is operating a departmental, rather than plant-wide, overhead recovery rate). The OHAR will be predetermined at the start of the year, based on the following formula:

$$\text{OHAR} = \frac{\text{€ Estimated overheads to be recovered in year}}{\text{Estimated level of activity}}$$

2. Each job can be accurately identified against a specific order (and should be given a specific job number to distinguish it from all other jobs). Each job has a separate job card, on which the required activities to be performed are written and on which all the data is collected. Thus, at any time, it should be possible to see the stage of completion of the job, simply by looking at the job card. And when the job has been completed, cost details will be added.

Job costing systems are usually found in:

1. The construction industry.

2. Professional service firms — for example, accountants.

3. Printing companies.

4. Car service/car repair firms.

ILLUSTRATION

Speciality Products Ltd. computed predetermined overhead rates for the coming year ended 31 December 20x1 for its two departments. Department A is labour-intensive and Department B is machine-intensive.

The total overheads are estimated to be as follows:

	DEPT. A	DEPT. B
	€	€
Total production overhead (fixed)	450,000	415,000

Estimates of direct labour hours and machine hours for 20x1 are as follows.

	DEPT. A	DEPT. B
Direct labour hours	150,000	25,000
Machine hours	100,000	415,000

During January 20x1, the firm completed only *two* orders. Details of costs and other data pertinent to these orders are given below:

	JOB 101	JOB 102
Direct materials cost	€1,000	€ 800
Direct labour costs		
Dept. A	€2,000	€2,500
Dept. B	€ 500	€ 300
Direct labour hours		
Dept. A	1,600	2,000
Dept. B	1,000	1,300
Machine hours		
Dept. A	800	600
Dept. B	2,000	2,500

REQUIREMENT

1. Compute predetermined overhead rates for the two departments, using direct labour hours for Department A and machine hours for Department B.

2. What is the total production cost of each job?

3. What is the normal selling price for both products, assuming a profit margin on sales of 25 per cent?

SOLUTION

1. The predetermined departmental overhead recovery rates are computed as follows:

	DEPT. A €	DEPT. B €
Overheads	450,000	415,000
Activity base	150,000	415,000
	= €3 per labour hour	= €1 per machine hour

2/3. The estimated cost for each job comprises direct costs (materials and labour) together with an estimated amount of overhead as follows:

	JOB 101 €	JOB 102 €
Materials	1,000	800
Labour		
Dept. A	2,000	2,500
Dept. B	500	300
Overhead		
Dept. A	4,800	6,000
Dept. B	2,000	2,500
Total cost	10,300	12,100
Profit *	3,429	4,029
Price	13,729	16,129

*   *The margin given is that of 25 per cent on selling price. Thus, costs must represent 75 per cent of final selling price. The selling price represents a mark-up on cost of 33.3 per cent.*

Under-/Over-Recovery of Overhead

One of the problematic aspects of ascertaining costs for pricing purposes is deciding on the appropriate amount of overheads to be assigned to production units or jobs. Usually, overheads are charged to production on the basis of predetermined absorption rates. This is appropriate when costs must be estimated in advance of performance — for example, when tendering for a contract. In such cases, the selling price is virtually agreed before the work commences.

But using predetermined overhead recovery rates creates the possibility of prediction errors, because of the difficulty of estimating in advance both the level of overheads and the level of activity. In many cases, the actual overheads incurred will differ from the amount predicted. Likewise, the actual level of activity (hours worked) may be different to the hours predicted.

Prediction errors can be favourable or adverse. For example, overheads incurred may be greater than predicted with the result that the company has under-absorbed its overheads during the accounting period. Alternatively stated, the products produced during the period have been under-costed. This under-recovery of overhead represents an additional (and unanticipated) cost to the company and is usually written off immediately to the profit and loss account. If, on the other hand, the actual level of activity is greater than planned, overheads will be over-recovered. This represents miscellaneous revenue and is usually taken as a credit to the profit and loss account. However, it means that customers are being, technically, overcharged which could have long term consequences for the business.

ILLUSTRATION

The Maynooth Manufacturing Co. Ltd. predicted the following figures for the year beginning 1 July 20x0:

	MACHINE DEPT. A	MACHINE DEPT. B	ASSEMBLY DEPT
Direct materials	€100,000	€120,000	€40,000
Direct labour (hours)	20,000	16,000	6,000
Direct labour cost per hour	€2.00	€2.00	€1.50
Hours of machine time	10,000	10,000	9,000
Production overhead	€36,000	€28,000	€13,500

All production expenses other than direct materials and direct labour are included in production overheads. Production overheads are all fixed in nature. The company calculates an overhead rate at the beginning of each year in order to estimate the total cost for each job undertaken. The overhead rates are calculated on the basis of machine-hours in the case of the two machining departments and on the basis of direct labour hours in the assembly department.

The company normally earns a profit margin of 25 per cent on sales (33.3 per cent mark up on cost).

The following estimates related to job number 153, which could be completed during the three months to 30 June 20x1, traditionally a slack time for the industry:

	MACHINE DEPT. A	MACHINE DEPT. B	ASSEMBLY DEPT
Direct materials	€800	€900	€350
Direct labour hours	150	160	40
Hours of machine time	75	80	50

Wage rates were as predicted at the beginning of the year.

REQUIREMENT

1. Calculate the cost of job number 153 and its *normal* selling price.

2. Calculate the under/over recovery of production overheads for the year, assuming that production overheads incurred amounted to €77,500 but that labour and machine hours worked were 80 per cent of budget in all three departments.

3. Comment on the possible effects of the pricing system adopted.

SOLUTION

1. Departmental overhead absorption rates are calculated as follows:

	DEPT. A	DEPT. B	ASSEMBLY
Estimated overheads to be absorbed	€36,000	€28,000	€13,500
Activity (hours)	10,000	10,000	6,000
OHAR:			
per machine hour	€3.60	€2.80	
per labour hour			€2.25

The normal price for Job 153 is calculated as follows:

	DEPT. A	DEPT. B	ASSEMBLY
Materials	€800	€900	€350
Direct labour	300	320	60
Overheads:			
75 x €3.60	270		
80 x €2.80		224	
40 x €2.25			90
	1,370	1,444	500

Total cost	€3,314
Add: Profit margin (25% of sales)	1,104
Normal quotation/sales price	4,418

2. The over-/under-recovery of overheads can be ascertained by comparing the amount of overheads absorbed during the year (actual hours worked multiplied by the predetermined overhead recovery rate) and comparing this with the actual overhead spend.

ABSORPTION OF OVERHEADS	€
Department A: 80% x 10,000 x €3.60	28,800
Department B: 80% x 10,000 x €2.80	22,400
Assembly: 80% x 6,000 x €2.25	10,800
	62,000
Actual overheads incurred (given)	77,500
Under recovery of overheads	15,500

3. The company operates a full cost pricing system that ignores what the customer is prepared to pay. It may be appropriate to set prices to cover variable costs (€2,730), as this would allow a contribution towards fixed costs to be generated. This could be appropriate in the context of spare capacity.

Factors influencing the pricing decision

Pricing decisions represent one of the truly interdisciplinary tasks in any business. Marketing staff have a major input to the product pricing decision based on their judgement and intuition, since price is one element of the marketing mix. However, the marketing person will also rely on his foundations in behavioural science before making a final decision. The accountant also plays a part in providing information and evaluating different pricing policies and is always conscious of the financial dimensions. The production manager is also consulted to ensure that anticipated demand can be satisfied.

The pricing decisions taken by management have inevitably wide-ranging implications both for the business itself and the environment in which it operates. These decisions must be taken as it is only in rare situations (purely competitive markets) that the business is a "price taker" rather than a "price maker". In other words, selling prices are rarely "given". Unfortunately, owners and managers of businesses too frequently fail to recognise the fundamental importance of pricing decisions and their implications in the following areas:

1. Pricing is a major determinant of both the profitability and cash flow of a business. If prices are too low, costs will not be covered and the firm will incur a loss. Alternatively, if prices are high in order to cover "costs", demand may be restricted and again total sales revenue may be insufficient to cover costs.

2. Prices are an essential element in generating market share. However, pricing is only one of the ways in which the business can influence the demand for its products. It can advertise, expand its sales force, improve its selling style, and improve product presentation, in addition to lowering the selling price.

3. Prices help to generate a particular "image" for the product, which will influence future growth. Thus, a product may be considered "exclusive" or a luxury item because of its high sales price.

4. Prices may have an impact on the whole national and international economy. This is particularly true for key raw materials such as oil, gas and steel or post office charges and transport prices.

A number of factors impact on the pricing decision. Five important factors are outlined below:

1. **Company objectives**: Pricing decisions are not an end in themselves; instead, they are a means of attaining the objectives of the company. Company objectives (the specific goals to be achieved within a specific time period) are fundamental to the determination of pricing policy. A frequently assumed objective is that of profit maximisation, though it is doubtful if this is adopted in practice because managers, like most individuals, tend to opt for a satisfactory rather than an optimal solution. Also, in order to maximise profits, one needs to know the parameters of the company's demand curve, which can be difficult to obtain.

   Instead, target profits are a more intuitive objective, which require a company to earn a specific rate of return, with prices set accordingly. The target profit may be determined by last year's profit (an indirect stability objective). Alternatively, the firm may adopt survival objectives, seeking to earn a profit that is just sufficient to guarantee the continued existence of a business for a specific period of time. Pricing policy in such a situation may be very close to variable cost or would at best just cover all costs.

   Finally, a company may set its objectives in terms of sales volume and market share. A company may have a high sales volume objective in which case a low price may be needed to establish a dominant market share. This share can be determined in terms of unit sales or sales revenue. However, this volume objective is not necessarily at variance with the previously mentioned objectives.

2. **Demand**: Demand determines the relationship between price and consumer behaviour and, consequently, is an important factor in any pricing decision. It is common to argue that extra units can

only be sold at reduced prices (the concept of elasticity). If a small change in price brings about a large change in volume, the product is said to be very elastic. For price-inelastic products (for example, birthday cards), changes in price are not associated with changes in demand. Obviously, the availability of substitutes has an important bearing on price elasticity.

3. **Competition**: The very existence of competition in a market tends to set an upper limit on the price that can be charged. In a monopoly situation, one can charge as high a price as one likes though this runs the risk of attracting potential competition. Much depends on whether potential competitors can enter the market quickly and cheaply.

   Competitors' products may be perceived by customers as homogeneous, in which case a price cut on one product would greatly increase sales at the expense of the other (homogeneous) products. Consequently, retaliatory price cuts can be expected from the competition with the only gains accruing to customers in the form of lower prices. If the products are viewed as heterogeneous that is, different in quality or value, some degree of brand loyalty can be expected and so price changes would not necessarily be associated with retaliation.

4. **Costs**: Pricing must ultimately cover costs to ensure the profitability and financial viability of the business. Consistently selling below full costs cannot be a long-term option. If the business is to survive, it must sell at prices that will not only cover costs but also yield a sufficient profit. This consideration has led to the development and popularity of cost-plus pricing policies. Since there is generally less uncertainty about costs than about demand, by relating price to unit costs the business simplifies its pricing task considerably and does not have to make frequent adjustments as demand or market conditions change. Plausible prices can be found with ease and speed.

   Costs can either be "marginal" or "full" costs. Both approaches will give a different cost figure. The marginal cost represents the total variable cost required to get an additional unit to the point of sale. This approach is particularly suited to short-run pricing decisions, especially pricing in the context of spare capacity situations. Alternatively, unit cost can be based on full cost which, in addition to all the relevant variable costs, takes into consideration the fixed costs. The paradox of this approach is that in order to cover fixed costs you need to first know the units sold. Thus sales volume determines unit costs and sales price, whereas theory suggests that unit costs and sales price should determine sales volume and demand. Cost-plus pricing does not guarantee profits since profits are a function of sales volume. Thus a high price that attempts to cover all costs may reduce sales volume.

5. **Marketing strategy**: A company's strategy is one component of its marketing mix and, as such, it must be integrated with the other components to meet the requirements of the corporate marketing strategy. In the long term, the revenue from a product should cover all the associated costs and provide an acceptable profit, but other objectives might prevail in the short term. Basically, two different strategies can be identified:

(a) Price Skimming (Market Skimming): This involves setting a high selling price to cream off the top of the market. The selling price includes a premium that will be paid by a group of buyers who are willing to pay more for that product than other groups of buyers. The reason could be that of status or prestige. This strategy is usually associated with luxury or status goods. It only applies, however, when unit costs remain fairly constant since otherwise the unit costs of a low volume of production may be high enough to offset the premium selling price.

It is basically a short-term policy since, once the "premium" segment is saturated, price is gradually reduced to appeal to the more price-sensitive segments of the market. The principal disadvantage is that the premium itself may entice competition earlier than might otherwise occur.

(b) Penetration Pricing: This involves initially setting a low price to generate a high demand. The principal problem associated with this approach is that prices may be set too low, generating excess demand and resulting in profits foregone that could have been earned at a higher selling price.

There are three conditions which favour such a strategy: (i) A low initial price has the benefit of discouraging actual and potential competition; (ii) If the market is highly price-sensitive, it may prove very effective in generating additional demand; (iii) Where unit costs are falling due to economies of scale, a low initial price coupled with a large volume of production enables a company to lower its unit costs even further.

5.7   END OF CHAPTER QUESTIONS

Question 5.1

Cost allocation and apportionment, used in determining the cost of a department, product or service, occurs in many facets of management accounting.

REQUIREMENT

1. Describe the processes of cost allocation and cost apportionment and their relevance to management accounting.

2. Comment briefly on typical criteria for allocation and apportionment.

(The Association of Chartered Certified Accountants)

Question 5.2

A company produces a wide range of tableware products — for example, plates, cups, etc. Classify the following costs as direct or indirect (D or I) with respect to each *product unit*, and as variable or fixed (V or F). Thus, the essential tests are (a) whether the cost item in question can be traced specifically to a given unit of output (or traced to a cost unit in an economically feasible way) and (b) whether the cost item varies with changes in output, over a relevant range of activity. Thus, you will have two answers, D or I and V or F, for each of the items. State your assumptions.

1. Factory rent.

2. Salary of a factory storeroom clerk.

3. Clay materials for plates, cups, etc.

4. Supervisory salaries, production control.

5. Supervisory salaries, assembly department.

6. Postage of products (each unit is posted separately).

7. Factory power for machines.

8. Sales commission paid on a unit basis.

9. Salaries of salespersons who sell a wide range of product

10.Gold paint (each item is hand painted).

11.Heat and light of factory.

12.Straight-line depreciation, salespersons' cars.

Question 5.3: Desk Ltd.

The following information has been obtained from the books of Desk Ltd., a manufacturer.

	€
Raw materials, 1 January 20x1	75,000
Finished goods, 1 January 20x1	50,000
Purchases	195,000
Direct labour	125,000
Indirect labour	40,000
Heat, light and power (factory)	35,000
Insurance on factory	6,000
Factory and machine maintenance	8,000
Factory supplies	6,000
Depreciation: factory building	9,000
Depreciation: equipment	39,000
Rent and rates	4,000
Sales	630,000
Closing stock of raw materials, 31 December 20x1	83,000
Closing stock of finished goods, 31 December 20x1	60,000

REQUIREMENT

1. Prepare a statement of cost of goods manufactured and compute the gross profit for the year 20x1.

2. Suppose that both the direct materials and the depreciation of equipment were related to the production of the equivalent of 200,000 units. What is the unit cost for the direct materials and depreciation on the equipment? Assume that depreciation is a straight-line, fixed cost.

3. Which of the unit costs in (2) above are likely to change with additional output? Explain why.

Question 5.4: TPL Ltd.

The following information relates to TPL Ltd., a manufacturing company for the year ended 31 December 20x6.

	€
Raw materials:	
Stock at 1 January 20x6	39,000
Purchases	152,000
Stock at 31 December 20x6	41,000

	€
Finished goods:	
Stock at 1 January 20x6	51,000
Purchases	9,000
Stock at 31 December 20x6	57,000
Sales	400,000
Manufacturing wages	60,000
Indirect materials	25,300
Repairs and maintenance of plant and machinery	13,500
Depreciation:	
Factory	38,000
General offices	5,000
Warehouse	7,000
Power	10,000
Light and heat:	
Factory	2,400
General offices	2,100
Administration expenses	16,200
Selling and distribution expenses	32,700

REQUIREMENT

You are required to compute:

1. Cost of raw materials used or consumed.

2. Prime cost.

3. Cost of finished goods produced.

4. Cost of the finished goods sold (manufactured internally and purchased externally).

5. Gross profit.

6. Net profit before taxation.

Question 5.5: Crawfield Company

The Crawfield Company Ltd. makes a single product and you are provided with the following information for the week ended 31 December 20x1.

1. Opening stock of raw materials:
    Material X, 1,500 kilos at 110c per kilo
    Material Y, 1,200 kilos at 112c per kilo
    Material Z, 300 gallons at 55c per gallon.

2. Purchases during the week were 560 kilos of material X at 110c and 400 gallons of Z at 55c.

3. Closing stocks are 1,100 kilos of X, 200 kilos of Y, and 460 gallons of Z.

4. Direct labour used during the week was as follows:
    Skilled   475 hours @ 135c per hour
    Unskilled   540 hours @ 90c per hour.

5. Production overhead: This amounted to €1,320 for the week.

6. 11,000 units have been produced during the week and passed to the finished goods store.

7. There were no work in progress stocks or finished goods at the beginning of the week.

8. Administration costs amounted to €1,250, selling and distribution costs amounted to €2,100 during the week.

9. All units were sold at €1 each.

REQUIREMENT

You are required to produce a total cost statement based on the above information showing the profit/loss for the week. You should clearly distinguish between the various functional cost areas.

Question 5.6: PQR Compounds Ltd.

PQR Compounds Ltd., manufactures three products, P, Q, and R. The profit statement of the company for week 3 is as follows:

	€	€
Sales		800,000
Less Production cost of goods sold		550,000
Gross Profit		250,000
Less: Selling and distribution costs		
Advertising and publicity	40,000	
Salespersons' salaries	2,550	
Salespersons' commission	8,000	
Sales office expenses	8,400	
Distribution and packing	40,950	
	99,900	
General administration costs	20,000	
		119,900
Net profit		130,100

Discussions with the management result in the adoption of the following bases for the apportionment of revenue and costs

	PRODUCT P	PRODUCT Q	PRODUCT R
Sales	€100,000	€300,000	€400,000
Production cost of goods sold as percentage of sales value	70%	60%	75%
Advertising and publicity: proportion per product	25%	25%	50%
Salespersons employed, each paid €150 per week	4	5	8
Salespersons' commission, 1% of sales value			
Sales office expenses, on basis of orders received	100	120	200
General Administration costs, basis of sales revenue			

REQUIREMENT

Assuming all the above costs are fixed except cost of goods sold, distribution and packing and commission, indicate the contribution and profit generated by each product.

Question 5.7: Food Products Company

Food Products Company manufactures three major product lines: Cereals, bars and dog food. The profit and loss account was prepared by product line but did not distinguish between fixed and variable costs.

FOOD PRODUCTS COMPANY
PROFIT AND LOSS ACCOUNT
FOR YEAR ENDED 30 APRIL 20x8

	CEREALS	BARS	DOG FOOD	TOTAL
	000 Kg	000 Kg	000 Kg	000 Kg
Sales	2,000	500	500	3,000
	€000	€000	€000	€000
Sales revenue	1,000	400	200	1,600
Cost of goods sold				
Direct materials	330	160	100	590
Direct labour (variable)	90	40	20	150
Factory overhead (note 1)	108	48	24	180
Total cost of goods sold	528	248	144	920

	€000	€000	€000	€000
Gross margin	472	152	56	680
Operating expenses				
Selling expenses				
Advertising (note 2)	50	30	20	100
Commissions (note 3)	50	40	20	110
Salaries (note 5)	30	20	10	60
Total selling expenses	130	90	50	270
Administration expenses				
Licences (note 4)	50	20	15	85
Salaries (note 5)	60	25	15	100
Total administration expenses	110	45	30	185
Total operating expenses	240	135	80	455
Operating profit	232	17	(24)	225

1. Variable factory overhead is estimated at 30 per cent of direct labour cost.

2. An annual advertising program is implemented for each product line. Each product line is advertised independently of the others.

3. Sales commissions are paid to the salesforce at the rate of 5 per cent on the cereals and 10 per cent on the bars and dog food.

4. Various licenses are required for each product line. These are renewed annually for each product line.

5. Sales and administrative personnel devote time and effort to all product lines. Their salaries and wages are assigned on the basis of management's estimates of time spent on each product line.

REQUIREMENT

The managing director has requested that you prepare a revised profit and loss account for Food Products Company that shows the contribution for each product line and the operating profit for the company as a whole.

Question 5.8: Taurus Company

The Taurus Company is divided into four production departments: A, B, C, and D. Each production department is the responsibility of a single manager. The managing director wants to find out the cost of running each department and has provided you with the following information:

	A	B	C	D	TOTAL
Space occupied in sq. ft.	2,000	800	800	400	4,000
Capital cost of machines	€20,000	€20,000	€10,000	€10,000	€60,000
Total staff	25	20	15	20	80
Machine maintenance hourrs	1,000	1,000	600	400	3,000
Machine running hours per Dept	20,000	20,000	10,000	10,000	60,000
Tooling cost	To be APPORTIONED equally between departments				
Kilowatt hours	20,000	15,000	10,000	5,000	50,000

The cost of each department comprises, for the purpose of this exercise, two separate elements. The cost of supervisory personnel in each department and a share of common factory overheads. The cost of supervisors traced to each department is €4,200 for Department A and €2,100 each for the other three departments. The general (common) overheads are listed as follows and are to apportioned using appropriate bases:

	€
Tooling cost	10,400
Machine maintenance	6,600
Electricity	3,000
Insurance of machinery	12,240
Rent, rates and insurance	4,400
Depreciation of machinery	21,000
	57,640

REQUIREMENT

1. Apportion the above costs among the four departments. Specify the assumptions you have made, if any.

2. You are required to calculate an overhead absorption rate for each department. The company absorbs overheads on the basis of machine hours.

Question 5.9: NEW University

The NEW University has three teaching faculties, an administrative function and a sports area. For cost accumulation purposes, costs are assigned to these five responsibility centres. The following data is available for the year ended 30 June 20x7:

1. The direct costs, mainly salaries, are traceable as follows:

FACULTIES	€000
Business studies	1,556
Engineering	2,593
Medicine	2,075
Administration	1,775
Sports	1,000

2. Occupancy costs including light, heat, maintenance, etc. amount to €1,500,000 for the entire University. Such costs are apportioned on the basis of floor area used which is:

FACULTIES	SQUARE FEET
Business studies	7,000
Engineering	7,000
Medicine	13,500
Administration	7,000
Sports centre	3,000

3. **Sports centre**: The direct costs, including salaries, amount to €1,000,000. In addition, it receives a portion of general occupancy costs but not administration. Sports centre costs are apportioned to teaching faculties based only on the number of students.

4. **Administration costs**: The direct costs, including salaries of personnel, amount to €1,775,000. It receives a portion of general occupancy costs. Costs of administration are charged only to teaching faculties on the basis of number of employees.

5. The number of faculty members and other staff is:

FACULTIES	FACULTY & STAFF
Business studies	30
Engineering	50
Medicine	40
Administration	20
Sports centre	10

6. The number of students is:

FACULTIES	STUDENTS
Business studies	800
Engineering	500
Medicine	120

REQUIREMENT

1. Calculate the average cost per student for each faculty.

2. Why are there differences in the average cost per student, and discuss briefly the relevance of such information.

(The Association of Chartered Certified Accountants)

Question 5.10: FULL Company

The FULL Company has budgeted the following situations for the coming year:

	UNITS	€
Actual sales volume	2,000	
Actual production volume	1,640	
Normal production volume	1,800	
Selling price per unit		50
Variable costs per unit		25
Fixed production costs		15,000
Other fixed cost		25,000

REQUIREMENT

1. Calculate profit under direct (variable) costing using the formula:

   $PD = C \times Y - [F + O]$

2. Calculate profit under absorption costing using the formula:

   $PD - PA = F(Y - X)/N$

Question 5.11: MI Manufacturing

MI Manufacturing is a company that commenced operations on 1 January 20x8 at its new Dublin plant. The accounting results for the year to 31 December 20x8 prepared by clerical staff are as follows:

DUBLIN

Units produced	30,000
Units sold	10,000
Selling price per unit	€12

MANUFACTURING COST SCHEDULE

	€
Materials (€4 per unit)	120,000
Labour (€3 per unit)	90,000
Variable overhead (€2 per unit)	60,000
Fixed manufacturing overhead	60,000
	330,000

The accounting clerk is unsure how to value closing stock.

REQUIREMENT

1. Calculate the value of closing stock under both absorption and variable costing. You may assume that 30,000 units represents the normal production quota.

2. Prepare a summarised profit and loss account under both absorption and variable costing.

3. Use the appropriate formulae to calculate both PD and PA.

(*The Association of Chartered Certified Accountants*)

Question 5.12

A company operates with a budgeted capacity of 400,000 machine hours per quarter. Activity levels are set by reference to this capacity, with the result that typical budgeted quarterly production and sales, at a standard product mix, are 100,000 units.

The average selling price of the company's product range is €80 per unit. The average unit contribution is €32. One-quarter of the variable costs are related to selling and distribution, the remainder are manufacturing. The budgeted fixed manufacturing costs are €1,400,000 per quarter while fixed selling and distribution costs are €500,000 per quarter.

It is the management's policy to hold only a minimum level of stocks but, at times, they have found it difficult to co-ordinate production and sales. In Quarter 3, sales of 75,000 units were achieved, while 120,000 units were produced. Opening stocks of Quarter 3 were minimal.

REQUIREMENT

1. Calculate the reported profit for the quarter under both absorption and variable costing methods.

2. Explain and account for any difference between the reported profits.

(*The Association of Chartered Certified Accountants*)

Question 5.13: Aaron Company

The Aaron Company uses a predetermined overhead rate in applying overhead to production orders on a labour cost basis for Department A and on a machine-hour basis for Department B. At the beginning of 20x1, the company made the following predictions:

	DEPT. A	DEPT. B
Direct labour cost	€128,000	€35,000
Factory overhead	€144,000	€150,000
Direct labour hours	16,000	5,000
Machine hours	1,000	20,000

REQUIREMENT

1. What predetermined overhead rate should be used in Department A and Department B?

2. During the month of January, the cost sheet for production order No. 200 shows the following. What is the total cost (direct and overhead) of order No. 200?

	DEPT. A	DEPT. B
Materials requisitioned	€20	€40
Direct labour cost	€32	€21
Direct labour hours	4	3
Machine hours	1	13

3. At the end of 20x1, it was found that actual factory overhead costs amounted to €160,000 in Department A and €138,000 in Department B. Give the over-applied or under-applied overhead amount for each department and for the factory as a whole. *Assume* that total actual direct labour costs amounted to €120,000 in Dept. A and machine hours of 19,000 were worked during the year in Dept. B.

Question 5.14

A factory uses a job order costing system. A careless bookkeeper has lost the file of job order cost sheets covering the work done last week, but the underlying documents are still available. You have the following data:

1. The factory had no work in process at the beginning of the week.

2. A predetermined overhead rate was used, based on direct labour hours at a volume of 18,000 direct labour hours a year. At this volume, overhead costs were expected to total €90,000 a year.

3. Requisitions and time tickets showed the following usage of direct labour and direct materials last week:

JOB ORDER	DIRECT MATERIALS €	DIRECT LABOUR HOURS
498	1,500	116
506	960	16
507	415	18
508	345	42
509	652	24
511	308	10
512	835	30

4. The rate for direct labour was €8 an hour.

5. Actual indirect labour (overhead) last week cost €740; other overhead costs amounted to €868.

6. Work on jobs 498, 506, and 509 was completed during the week; the completed units were transferred to the finished goods inventory.

REQUIREMENT

1. Calculate the predetermined annual overhead rate the factory used in product costing.

2. Prepare a summary table that will show the amount of each cost element and of all costs in total assigned to each job last week.

3. Calculate the cost of the work in process at the end of last week.

4. Calculate the amount of under/over-applied production for the week.

Question 5.15: Franklin Associates

Franklin Associates is a management consulting firm. Each engagement is covered by a contract. The contract price is negotiated in advance, sometimes as a fixed fee, sometimes as professional staff time plus traceable expenses. The billing rates for the various members of the professional staff are always fixed in advance and are expected, in the aggregate, to cover non-traceable (indirect) costs and provide a margin of profit.

The company uses a job costing system to measure the costs of each contract.

All costs not directly traceable to specific contracts are recorded as indirect costs; a single predetermined indirect cost rate is used to assign indirect costs to contracts, based on the number of professional staff hours.

Budgeted time and costs for the year are as follows:

ANNUAL BUDGET

	HOURS	COST €
Analysis of costs		
Professional staff	25,000	300,000
Secretarial staff		80,000
Office costs including telephone, postage, office supplies, etc.		200,000
Total		580,000
Budgeted net profit		120,000

REQUIREMENT

What is the amount of the fee note for February for a client, assuming 70 professional hours were recorded?

(The Association of Chartered Certified Accountants)

Question 5.16: Promptprint Ltd.

Promptprint Ltd., a printing business has received an enquiry from a potential customer for a quotation for a job. The business pricing policy is based on the master budget for the next financial year shown below. The company operates a plant-wide rather than departmental recovery rate due to the small size of the business and most overheads are associated with the printing process.

MASTER BUDGET 20x5

	€
Sales (billings to customers)	189,800
Materials (direct, variable)	38,000
Labour (fixed)	32,000
Total overheads (fixed)	76,000

NOTE: All overheads are recovered on the basis of direct *material* costs. In addition, the required profit margin is based on total cost.

A first estimate of the direct costs for Job 101 is shown below:

	€
Direct materials	4,000
Direct labour	3,600

REQUIREMENT

1. What is the normal profit margin (mark-up) on cost?

2. Prepare a recommended *selling price* for Job 101 based on the master budget, commenting on your method.

3. Comment of the validity of using a master budget in pricing.

4. During the year in question, the printing business went through a severe recession and the business operated only at 70 per cent of its projected output. For example, raw material consumed on all jobs amounted to €26,600. Although labour was paid in full, only 70 per cent of this amount was charged to jobs. Actual overheads incurred amounted to €80,000. Compute the actual sales for the year together with the overall profit or loss.

(The Association of Chartered Certified Accountants)

Question 5.17: Phil and Ken

Phil and Ken were trained in carpentry and draughtsmanship. They had observed a growing market for fitted kitchens and agreed to combine their skills in a partnership. They fitted out a workshop with a range of new powered woodworking tools and equipment. They developed an expertise in fitting kitchens to customer specifications. With the exact measurements and specifications, they were able to prepare a number of units in their workshop and then deliver to the site and fit them. It took some extra time when "one-off" cupboards or other units were required and these needed to be prepared on the customer's premises.

Business increased *rapidly*. A room over their workshop became available and this was used as a showroom for the various styles of doors and drawers that were available. Ken drew up the plans of each kitchen and negotiated a price with each customer. Ken's rule of thumb for quoting was based on the material cost of cupboards plus 40 per cent, which he believed was a long-standing trade practice. However, he was aware of the prices charged by DIY companies for their units and always endeavoured to stay roughly in line with these competitors.

They were fortunate to employ some good people at above average rates of pay. This expansion placed Phil and Ken in almost a permanent management role, only occasionally doing practical work on kitchen units.

Their product quality claim was reinforced by issuing an invoice only when the customer was completely satisfied. No deposit was taken. The job of invoicing and follow up of accounts fell to Ken because he first prepared the quotes.

Ken was an eternal optimist. No job was ever too difficult. But the staff were finding the schedules a little too tight. Deadlines were being missed as each job took a little longer than expected. There seemed to be more and more jobs that were not quite finished as they tried but often failed to start new jobs on time. The order book was healthy but they were reluctant to recruit any more staff as their balance at the bank was low and the quarterly profit statements were not showing an increasing trend. This latter point was of concern to Ken.

REQUIREMENT

Suggest brief reasons why the quarterly profit statements were not showing an increasing trend and the bank balance was low, despite the costing calculations undertaken and the existence of a healthy order book. What action might be taken to improve profit and cash flow?

(The Association of Chartered Certified Accountants)

Question 5.18: Widgets Ltd.

Widgets Ltd. manufactures a single product that is marketed in three grades of finish — Presentation, De Luxe, and Standard. The variable cost of the basic unit is €6 and the cost of finishing and packing is as follows:

	€
Presentation model	4
De Luxe model	2
Standard model	1

The selling prices are:

	€
Presentation model	15
De Luxe model	12
Standard model	10

The marketing manager has estimated demand in units for the year 20x4 as follows:

Presentation model	20,000
De Luxe model	30,000
Standard model	40,000

The production manager has estimated the production capacity of the factory at 150,000 units per annum.

Fixed costs have been estimated at €100,000 for the forthcoming year.

An enquiry has been received from a manufacturer, Green, who is considering using the basic unit as a sub-assembly in his own product and, at an acceptable price, would be willing to buy 30,000 units a year.

The company's pre-taxation profit objective is €300,000 for 20x4.

REQUIREMENT

1. Calculate the lowest price that could be quoted for the supply of the 30,000 units to Green.

2. Comment upon any business policy matters you consider relevant in these circumstances.

Question 5.19: Rappup Ltd.

Rappup Ltd. is engaged solely in coating other manufacturers' metal fabrications with a preservative. The fabrications are at no time the property of Rappup Ltd. and their value does not appear in the company's accounts. Rappup Ltd. has prepared the following budget for the six months ending 31 December 20x1.

BUDGET	QUANTITY	VALUE
		€
Preservative	50,000 cans	200,000
Direct labour	150,000 hours	50,000
Variable overhead		150,000
Variable costs		400,000
Fixed overhead		250,000
Total cost		650,000
Profit		130,000
Sales		780,000

Variable overhead can be assumed to vary in direct proportion to direct labour hours.

Early in May 20x1, the company was asked to quote for coating for a new customer, the contract to be completed by 31 August 20x1. The technical director estimates that each fabrication unit will require 1,000 cans of preservative and 7,000 direct labour hours to complete, and asks the accountant to calculate a selling price.

REQUIREMENT

Calculate a price for the new contract, assuming normal absorption costing principles with fixed overhead cost absorbed on variable factory cost and a profit loading based on total cost.

Question 5.20: Mr Colley

Mr Colley runs a small printing business. Each job is undertaken according to special instructions from the customer. Mr Colley uses a system recommended by his trade association to fix the price that he charges to his customers.

The cost structure of the business consists of paper and consumables, wages of printing and administrative staff and fixed overheads. In determining quotation prices for his clients, Mr Colley charges out paper and consumables on the basis of actual material consumed. Due to his extensive experience in the printing business, he considers himself very accurate in his estimating of direct materials to be used. Also, direct labour is charged out on the basis of actual hours worked.

Finally, overheads are absorbed on the basis of direct labour cost. The sum of all these items gives a "total cost" for the job and he adds 10 per cent to total cost for his profit margin.

The budget for the forthcoming year (equivalent to 100 per cent capacity) is as follows:

SUMMARISED BUDGET FOR THE COMING YEAR

	€	€
Sales		265,100
Cost of materials	25,000	
Wages	120,000	
Fixed costs	96,000	241,000
Projected net profit for year		24,100

At the end of the year Mr Colley was surprised to discover that the business incurred a loss in spite of stringent cost control. Admittedly, business had fallen by 15 per cent. Since Mr Colley considered that an economic upturn would occur eventually, no one was laid off. No special prices had been given on any jobs during the year.

The summarised actual performance for the year is provided as follows:

	€	€
Sales		225,335
Cost of materials	21,250	
Wages	120,000	
Fixed costs	96,000	237,250
Actual loss for year		11,915

REQUIREMENT

1. How were the actual sales figures computed by Mr Colley?

2. Explain the decline in the profitability of the printing business this year. Annual labour is a fixed cost.

Question 5.21

Classify the following costs of quality by inserting an X under the appropriate category, where:

A = Prevention
B = Appraisal
C = Internal failure
D = External failure

	A	B	C	D
1. Final inspection				
2. Warranty repairs				
3. Goods returned				
4. Quality training				
5. Settlement of product liability action				
6. Field service personnel				
7. Packaging inspection				
8. Complaint department				
9. Rework units from work-in-progress				
10. Replacement of defective product				
11. Lost sales				
12. Scrap				
13. Recalls				
14. Downtime caused by defects				
15. Inspection of raw materials				
16. Maintenance of test equipment				
17. Calibration of test gauges				
18. Design improvements				
19. Quality improvement projects				
20. Re-inspection of rework				

Question 5.22

From the following information calculate the prevention, appraisal, internal and external failure costs:

	€
1. WIP written off due to faulty work	60,000
2. Servicing of customer complaints	20,000
3. Employee training	10,000
4. Inspection of raw materials	5,000
5. Cost of replacement goods to customers	45,000
6. Preventive maintenance	5,000
7. Design department	15,000
8. Supplier (Vendor) liaison	2,500
9. Product liability insurance	25,000
10. Machine breakdowns due to faulty parts	25,000

REQUIREMENT
Prepare a detailed cost-of-quality report.

Question 5.23: Ronnoco

Having employed the services of the quality consultants Eyre and Associates, to introduce a quality improvement programme into the company, the management of Ronnoco requires a detailed quality report comparing the costs of quality for 20x6 with those for 20x5 before any quality initiatives were undertaken.

	20x6 €	20x5 €
WIP written off due to faulty work	50,000	45,000
Servicing of customer complaints	10,000	25,000
Employee training	6,000	8,000
Inspection of raw materials	5,000	10,000
Cost of replacement goods to customers	20,000	45,000
Preventive maintenance	7,000	5,000
Design department	15,000	10,000
Machine breakdowns due to faulty parts	10,000	12,000

Question 5.24: Q Company

At the beginning of the year, Q Company installed a TQM system. By the end of the year, managers were reporting good results — for example, the production manager stated that scrap and rework had both decreased. The directors now want a report of the financial impact of the quality improvements. To prepare this report, the following financial data was collected for actual and projected costs for 20x5. Actual and projected sales for 19x5 were €10 million.

TYPES OF COST	ACTUAL €	PROJECTED €
Scrap	300,000	400,000
Rework	300,000	500,000
Training	200,000	100,000
Incoming inspection	200,000	100,000
Process inspection	100,000	150,000
Final inspection	200,000	100,000
Warranty repairs	100,000	300,000
Recall of products	200,000	800,000

REQUIREMENT

Prepare a detailed cost-of-quality report.

6

Activity-Based Costing

6.1 LIMITATIONS OF TRADITIONAL COSTING SYSTEMS

There are a number of criticisms directed at traditional management accounting practices. One of these concerns the method by which manufacturing overheads are assigned to products. The traditional method of product costing is to assign production overheads to products using volume-based recovery bases. Initially, production overheads are generally accumulated by department (cost centres) and are, in turn, assigned to products using, typically, direct labour hours. The essential feature of such a system is that overhead costs are assigned in proportion to volume. This system has three major limitations:

1. In the new manufacturing environment, products have a very low direct labour content, perhaps as low as 10 per cent of total cost. Coupled with the decline in direct labour costs is a dramatic increase in overhead costs, resulting from expensive machines and skilled indirect labour. The impact of this explosion of overhead costs is twofold: First, as factories increase the pace of automation, overhead grows in percentage terms as direct labour costs fall and second, overheads grow in real terms because of the increased support costs associated with maintaining and running automated equipment.

2. Increasingly, overheads are transaction-driven rather than volume-driven. These transactions involve exchanges of materials and/or information necessary to move production along but do not directly result in physical products.

3. Also, overheads relate to the complexity of business operations because, in the modern competitive environment, companies must become more responsive to customer needs. This involves rapid

development of new products, enhanced product characteristics, wider range of choice and shorter lead times. Meeting these needs has created a growing demand for support functions such as engineering and product development, quality control and staff training. These costs are influenced by factors such as how many parts and products the company handles and how many customer orders it processes — factors that reflect the complexity of the modern manufacturing environment.

An alternative product costing system has been suggested — Activity-Based Costing (ABC). ABC is based on a fundamental concept: Products consume activities and activities consume resources. For example, when a machine is changed from producing one product to another, resources are consumed by the set-up requirements involved and the consumption of resources is independent of the number of units produced in that particular batch. The use of complexity-related variables to absorb overhead costs can affect the estimates of individual product costs. For example, low-volume products create more transactions per unit manufactured than their high-volume counterparts. The per unit share of these costs should therefore be higher for the low-volume products.

Hence, the traditional product costing system, which absorbs production overhead based on volume only considerations, may distort actual product costs. Traditional costing systems, which use volume-based recovery rates, tend to over-cost high-volume products and to under-cost low-volume products. The implication is that companies which use the traditional system of overhead recovery may drop profitable products from the product line while still retaining products that are, in fact, unprofitable! After installing ABC systems, managers have frequently found that the low-volume products should be assigned more overheads since they may be more specialised, requiring more machine set-ups and inspection.

6.2   THE NATURE OF ACTIVITY-BASED COSTING

ABC focuses on activities that cause costs to be incurred. Basically, it divides activities into a three-category hierarchy as follows:

1. **Unit level** activities, which are performed each time a unit is produced (for example, machine power or machine depreciation).

2. **Transaction-based** activities, which are performed each time a transaction (internal or external) takes place (for example, inspection and quality control, machine set-up and materials movement).

3. **Plant level** activities, which contain costs that are common to a variety of products and can only be assigned to products in an arbitrary manner (for example, administration, overall factory services).

The major difference between the traditional product costing systems and ABC lies in the way in that "transaction"-related costs are treated. Traditionally, companies cost their products by assigning overheads to production departments (cost centres); the overheads are then assigned to products using a volume-related measure such as direct labour hours. Activity-based costing also uses a two-stage process to assign overheads costs to products using initially activity centres and then "cost drivers". This process is depicted in Exhibit 6.1.

Exhibit 6.1: Activity-based Costing

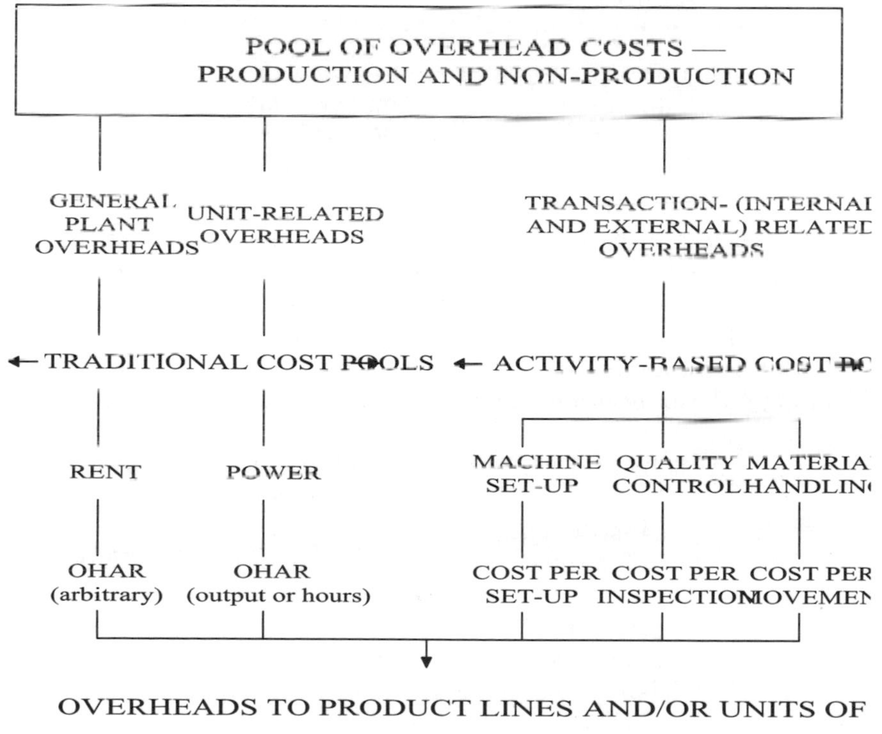

```
┌─────────────────────────────────────────────────────────┐
│           POOL OF OVERHEAD COSTS —                       │
│        PRODUCTION AND NON-PRODUCTION                     │
└─────────────────────────────────────────────────────────┘
       │          │                        │
  GENERAL    UNIT-RELATED        TRANSACTION- (INTERNAL
   PLANT      OVERHEADS          AND EXTERNAL) RELATED
 OVERHEADS                            OVERHEADS
       │          │                        │
← TRADITIONAL COST POOLS  ← ACTIVITY-BASED COST P

       │          │              ┌─────────┬─────────┬─────────┐
     RENT       POWER          MACHINE  QUALITY  MATERIA
                               SET-UP   CONTROL  HANDLIN
       │          │                 │        │        │
     OHAR       OHAR           COST PER COST PER COST PER
   (arbitrary) (output or      SET-UP  INSPECTIO MOVEMEN
                hours)
```

OVERHEADS TO PRODUCT LINES AND/OR UNITS OF

Activity-based costing involves the following three steps:

1. Identify the activities that consume resources and assign costs to those activities. Cost pools represent a section of the organisation that performs some activity. With ABC, costs are grouped into

"pools" according to specific activities. Cost pools may cover more than one conventional cost centre — for example, the decision to raise a purchase requisition may result in costs being incurred in purchasing, materials handling and accounts payable. All these costs would be included in the same cost pool under ABC.

2. Identify the appropriate cost driver. Cost drivers represent those activities or events that are significant determinants of cost. For the activity of purchasing raw materials, the cost driver might be the number of purchase orders. The cost driver rate, therefore, might be the cost per purchase order. There are two types of cost drivers:

(a) *Volume-based cost drivers*: These include volume-based measures such as direct labour hours, machine hours and direct material usage. These cost drivers are the primary determinants of conventionally defined variable costs. They should be traced to products using volume-related cost drivers.

Some examples of cost pools and volume-based cost drivers are:

ACTIVITY (COST POOL)	SPECIMEN COST DRIVERS
Maintenance	Number of machine hours
Production	Volume of production
Packaging	Volume of production

(b) *Transaction-based cost drivers*: These include the output of support departments such as purchasing, personnel and quality control. Generally speaking, these costs will not vary in the short run with the level of output but they will tend to vary in the longer term, as the increasingly complex nature of the production process places additional burden on the support departments.

ACTIVITY (COST POOL)	SPECIMEN COST DRIVER
Stores	Number of issues
Inspection	Number of inspections
Training	Number of people trained
General accounting	Number of suppliers
Personnel	Number of employees
Customer services	Number of customer orders
Purchasing/procurement	Number of purchase orders

3. The third stage in ABC is to assign costs to products by multiplying the cost driver rate by the number of cost driver units consumed by the product. For example, the cost per purchase order multiplied by the number of purchase orders required for product

A for the month of May measures the cost of the purchasing activity for product A for May. In practice, the selection of cost drivers is probably the most important decision to be made in implementing an ABC system. It requires an understanding of all the activities required to make the product (or provide services to customers).

In identifying cost drivers, a sensible starting point is to consult departmental managers and supervisors and ask them what activities cause costs to be incurred in their departments. In other words, ask them what actually happens in their departments!

Two points are worth stressing at this stage. First, if employees perceive that possible redundancies will take place in the future as a result of the implementation of ABC, uncooperative behaviour and general resistance can be expected. Second, react with patience to employees' likely initial response that the system is too complicated to be reduced to a simple classification. Ask the manager how much of his time has been devoted to a particular task over the past six months on average? Is it 10 per cent or is it 90 per cent? In this way, some progress will be made.

One of the lessons of ABC is that costs are a function not only of volume but also complexity. While it may be obvious that a greater volume of output consumes greater resources, it is not so clear why complexity is important in driving costs. To understand the role of complexity, consider two separate manufacturing plants, each of which produces 1 million pens.

In the first plant, only blue pens are produced. In the second plant, 900,000 blue pens are produced in a single batch, 80,000 black pens are produced in a few batches and 20,000 green pens are produced in many small batches. Although both plants have the same volume of output, it is clear that overall costs in plant 2 will be relatively higher because it has a more complicated ordering, set up and delivery system.

If each pen uses the same number of hours (labour or machine), traditional costing system assigns the same amount of overhead to each unit in plant 2. This does not seem to be intuitively correct since the three different types of pens are likely to place different demands on the company's resources.

The dramatic difference in *unit* product costs obtained using the traditional and ABC systems is illustrated in the Alpha Company example below. (Note that the *total* costs of the organisation do not change under ABC. Instead, it is the way that overheads are assigned to products and therefore the individual product costs that change).

ILLUSTRATION

The Alpha Company produces two products, X and Y and provides you with the following information:

		PRODUCT X	PRODUCT Y	TOTAL
Production and sales	(units)	25,000	5,000	30,000
Unit cost data				
Direct materials cost	(€)	25	20	
Direct labour cost	(€)	15	5	400,000
Machine hours		1	2	35,000
Other operating data				
Labour rate per hour	(€)	1	1	
Number of set-ups		4	20	24
Number of inspections		40	80	120

Overhead costs	€
Production processing	700,000
Set-up	120,000
Inspections	180,000
	1,000,000

For illustration purposes, we shall assume that the traditional product costing method is to absorb overheads on the basis of direct labour hours as follows:

$$\text{OHAR} = \frac{\text{Overheads}}{\text{Labour hours}} = \frac{\text{€1,000,000}}{400,000} = \text{€2.50 per labour hour}$$

All production overheads (processing, set-ups and inspection) are included in a single cost pool. Using this labour-based overhead recovery rate, the unit costs of products X and Y are:

	€ X	€ Y
Direct labour (given)	15.00	5.00
Direct materials (given)	25.00	20.00
Overhead (€2.50 per DLH)	37.50	12.50
Total cost	77.50	37.50

Based on the information above, three ABC cost pools can be identified: Production processing, set-up and inspection. Once the cost pools have been identified, costs can be assigned using cost drivers and cost driver rates. In some cases, this can be an easy task; in other situations, inevitably, some arbitrary cost apportionment must take place. Next, cost drivers must be identified. Assume that these are:

COST DRIVER	BASIS
Production processing	Number of machine hours
Machine set-ups	Number of machine set-ups
Inspections	Number of inspections

The overheads per cost pool and the rate per cost driver can be computed as follows:

PRODUCTION PROCESSING COSTS

Production overhead = $\dfrac{\text{Production overhead}}{\text{Machine hours}}$ = $\dfrac{€700,000}{35,000}$ = €20 per machine hour

SET-UP COSTS

Cost per set-up = $\dfrac{\text{Set-up cost}}{\text{Number of set-ups}}$ = $\dfrac{€120,000}{24}$ = €5,000 per set-up

INSPECTION COSTS

Cost per inspection = $\dfrac{\text{Inspection cost}}{\text{Number of inspections}}$ = $\dfrac{€180,000}{120}$ = €1,500 per inspection

The final part of the ABC process is to use the cost driver rates to assign overhead cost to products as shown below. The treatment of direct costs (materials and labour) is identical to the traditional method. The significant difference is the amount of overheads assigned to each product.

ABC PRODUCT COSTS

	X	Y
	€	€
Direct labour (given)	15.00	5.00
Direct materials (given)	25.00	20.00
Production overhead (i)	20.00	40.00
Set-up costs (ii)	.80	20.00
Inspection (iii)	2.40	24.00
	63.20	109.00

(i)   X = €20 x 1 machine hour = €20; Y = €20 x 2 machine hours = €40

(ii)   X = (€5,000 x 4 set-ups) / 25,000 units = 80c;

        Y = (€5,000 x 20 set-ups) / 5,000 units = €20

(iii)   X = (€1,500 x 40 inspections) / 25,000 units = €2.40;

        Y = (€1,500 x 80 inspections) / 5,000 units = €24.

The comparison of unit costs under the two systems is highlighted below:

| | PRODUCT X | PRODUCT Y |
	€	€
Traditional approach	77.50	37.50
Activity-Based Costing	63.20	109.00

The difference is explained by the different demands each product places on the resources of the company. Traditional costing systems, which use volume-based recovery rates, tend to over-cost high-volume products and to under-cost low-volume products. ABC, on the other hand, is based on the fundamental concept that products consume activities and activities consume resources. For example, low-volume products create more transactions per unit manufactured than their high-volume counterparts. The per unit share of these costs should therefore be higher for the low-volume products.

6.3   ACTIVITY-BASED COST MANAGEMENT (ABCM)

If managers want their products to be competitive, they must know (a) what activities go into making the goods or providing the service and (b) the cost of those activities. To reduce a product's costs, managers have to change the activities consumed by the product. After all, people manage activities, not costs. ABC focuses attention on the things that matter – activities and their related costs.

Because ABC focuses attention on the cost of activities, it allows managers to ask whether they can perform an activity more efficiently by changing the production process or by acquiring new technologies or whether they can perform an activity less frequently by changing product design or product mix. When action is taken to reduce what causes the activities that consume resources, a lasting reduction in costs takes place. For example, material handling costs may be driven by the number of separate parts that need to be stored and issued. Material handling costs, under an ABC system, would be charged to products on the basis of number of parts required. Accordingly, if the number of parts per product is reduced, product costs are reduced. Designers are thus motivated to simplify product design.

ABC can also be used to identify and eliminate activities that add costs but not value to the product. Non-value added costs are costs of activities that could be eliminated without reducing product quality, performance or value. The following types of activities are possibilities for elimination because they do not add value to the product:

1. **Storage**: Storage of raw materials and finished goods is an obvious non-value added activity. Many companies are turning to the Just in Time (JIT) philosophy for both purchasing and production. JIT systems are designed, *inter alia*, to reduce or eliminate storage of both raw materials and finished goods.

2. **Moving items**: Moving materials around the factory floor is another activity that does not add value to the end product. Materials movement can be reduced by redesigning the production process.

3. **Waiting for work**. Idle time does not add value. Reducing the amount of time that workers wait on work reduces the overall cost of idle time. This can be achieved by better planning and co-ordination of production.

Many companies are using ABC information to help them "re engineer" or "reprocess" the organisation. By this is meant that all the activities and processes in the organisation are analysed — for example, purchasing, production, inspection, distribution, etc. — to identify the extent to which they are necessary and how they can be made more efficient. Processes should be simplified and restructured with non-value added activities targeted for future elimination. Failure to do so is clearly a missed opportunity for cost management.

ABC also has a role to play in determining customer profitability. The needs of different customers can vary significantly and, in their efforts to retain existing customers and attract new ones, companies can be drawn into providing widely different levels of service — for example, special delivery requirements. Each of these service levels has associated costs that traditional cost systems rarely recognise. As a consequence, companies often do not know the true profitability of selling to individual customers. Using ABC information, overhead costs are assigned to those customers to whom services are provided. In addition, the revenue generated by each customer and all direct costs are considered. The net result is the establishment of a customer profitability portfolio showing the financial contribution of each customer to the company's overall profitability. The much publicised Cooper and Kaplan case study of Kanthal, a wire manufacturer, showed that 20 per cent of its customers were generating 225 per cent of profits, 70 per cent were breaking even and 10 per cent were losing 125 per cent of profits! The customers generating losses actually commanded the biggest sales volume. These same customers demanded lower prices, frequent delivery of small quantities and different product characteristics.

Exhibit 6.2: Activity-Based Costing and ABC Management

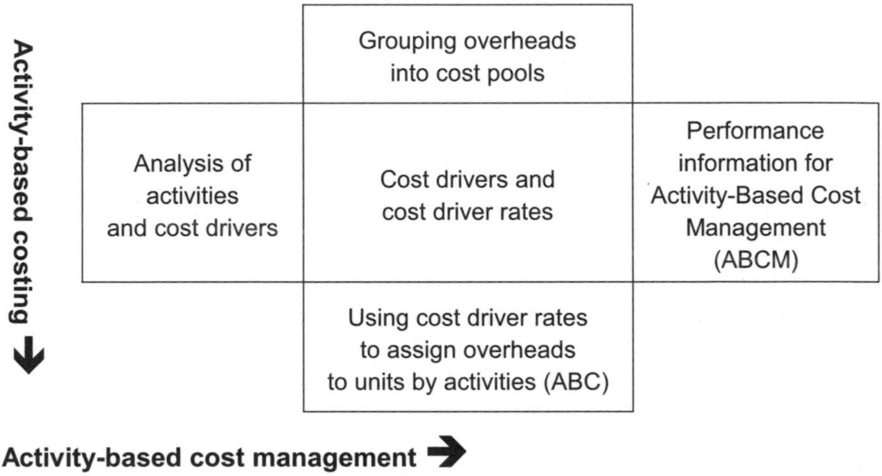

Activity-based cost management ➡

The fundamental aspects in the relationship between ABC and ABC Management (ABCM) are depicted below in Exhibit 6.2 above. In brief, ABC information (shown running from top to bottom) seeks to provide more accurate information for product costing. On the other hand, ABCM (shown running from left to right) is concerned with managing costs rather than simply counting them.

6.4   LIMITATIONS OF ACTIVITY-BASED COSTING

ABC is not without its limitations and critics. First, ABC does not eliminate the arbitrary apportionment problem in cost accounting — for example, a single purchase order may contain items used on several different products. The number of actions performed in a business is typically vast. Ordinarily many actions must be aggregated into each activity. Unfortunately, as more and more actions are aggregated into an activity, the ability of a cost driver to trace accurately the resources consumed by products decreases.

Little is known about the potential behavioural and organisational consequences of ABC. For example, where a manager reduces the number of set-ups because of their costly nature, the effect is to produce more units per batch and thereby increase stock levels with all its related costs. In addition, the new product information associated with ABC may sometimes meet resistance within the organisation — for example, the sales department of the company may not be happy with the new ABC costings which suggest eliminating some of the products in the product line. Furthermore, employees may perceive the introduction of ABC as part of a process to justify subsequent redundancies. In such circumstances, employees may be reluctant to co-operate and provide the initial information on which the operation of the ABC system will be based. The behavioural dimension is important since it will require a fundamental redirection in thinking for all participants together with employees' willingness to accept new ideas.

Also, some accountants are reluctant to change the accounting system with which they are familiar. This is particularly the case in the context of financial reporting. For financial reporting purposes, stocks must be valued at cost, which comprises purchase costs, direct conversion costs, production overhead and any other overheads in bringing the product to its present location and condition. On the other hand, under ABC, some costs which do not come within the conventional ambit of "present location and condition", such as market research, payroll administration and accounts payable, should be considered as product costs. However, the relevant accounting standard (SSAP 9) states: "The costs of general management, as opposed to functional management, are not directly related to current production and are, therefore, excluded from cost of conversion". It is unlikely that ABC product costs would be acceptable for stock valuation purposes for external reporting purposes. It is also debatable whether such a system would be acceptable to the taxation authorities in computing corporation tax liabilities. Indeed, even if it were acceptable, given the many steps that require subjectivity and a degree of arbitrariness (for example, activity identification, and selecting cost drivers), it can be argued that ABC would reduce the degree of comparability of reported results between companies.

The introduction of a new system must be evaluated in the context of cost/benefit analysis. There are many reasons why ABC systems might not provide net benefits for some companies: The cost of implementation, small company size, low overheads and unstable activity patterns. Given the work and time required to establish an ABC system, it would be inappropriate to expect all companies to adopt it. However, it should be noted that an ABC system can be used in parallel with the regular accounting system by loading the relevant data into appropriate computer software every quarter. In this situation, the ABC data can be manipulated in a spreadsheet format, viewed and arranged to provide relevant information to managers.

Finally, and perhaps most important, there is as yet insufficient evidence, that the introduction of an ABC system significantly improves company profitability in all situations. However, some recent research does highlight the fact that ABC-adopting firms outperform their non-adopting competitors.

6.5　END OF CHAPTER QUESTIONS

Question 6.1

What is activity-based costing and what is its relevance to management accounting?

(*The Association of Chartered Certified Accountants*)

Question 6.2

Suggest why companies may decide to introduce an ABC system and indicate what difficulties might companies experience with trying to implement it.

Question 6.3

The traditional methods of cost allocation, cost apportionment and absorption into products are being challenged by some writers who claim that much information given to management is misleading when these methods of dealing with fixed overheads are used to determine product costs.

REQUIREMENT

You are required to explain what is meant by cost allocation and absorption and to describe briefly the alternative approach of activity-based costing in order to ascertain total product costs.

(*The Chartered Institute of Management Accountants*)

Question 6.4: BETA Company

The BETA Company produces two products, X and Y and provides you with the following information:

		PRODUCT X	PRODUCT Y	TOTAL
Production and sales	(units)	20,000	10,000	30,000
Unit cost data				
Direct materials cost	(€)	20	10	
Direct labour hours	(hours)	1	0.5	25,000
Direct labour cost	(€)	10	5	
Other operating data				
Number of set-ups		5	20	25
Number of deliveries		10	40	50

Overhead costs	€
Production processing	500,000
Set-up	100,000
Delivery	200,000
	800,000

REQUIREMENT

1. Calculate product costs, assuming all overheads are absorbed on the basis of direct labour hours.

2. Calculate product costs using processing, set-ups and delivery as cost pools and using direct labour hours, number of machine set-ups and number of deliveries as cost drivers.

Question 6.5: XYZ Ltd.

The following information provides details of the costs, volume and transaction cost drivers for a cost centre and the appropriate service departments, for a particular period in respect of XYZ Ltd., a hypothetical company with a single production cost centre:

	PRODUCT X	PRODUCT Y	PRODUCT Z
Production and sales (units)	30,000	10,000	5,000
Unit material cost (€)	28	22	20
Labour hours (unit)	2	3	2
Machine hours per unit	1	3	2
Unit labour cost (€)	14	21	14
Number of set-ups	4	8	20
Number of receipts/inspections	12	24	100
Number of dispatches	36	12	80

Overhead costs	€
Machine	900,000
Set-up	100,000
Inspection of incoming goods	300,000
Packaging	200,000
	1,500,000

REQUIREMENT

1. Calculate the cost of each product under the traditional approach to product costing, assuming all production overheads are absorbed on the basis of direct labour hours.

2. Calculate the cost of each product under Activity-Based Costing (ABC), assuming that machine overheads (€900,000) are to be absorbed on the basis of machine hours but that other production overheads are to be absorbed by using the appropriate cost driver.

Question 6.6: Group E Company

Group E Company produces three products. The data below is available with respect to year ended 31 December 200x.

	A	B	C	TOTALS
Production and sales (units)	50,000	30,000	5,000	
Selling price per unit (€)	25	30	35	
Direct materials (€)	3	2	1	
Direct labour (€)	6	8	4	
DLH per unit	1.5	2	1	140,000
Machine hours per unit	4	2	6	290,000
No. of Production runs	5	10	15	30
No. of Orders	10	20	20	50
No. of Employees	2	13	15	30

Overhead costs	€
Set-up costs	100,000
Machining costs	600,000
Packaging	100,000
Selling costs	200,000
Administration costs	300,000

REQUIREMENT

1. Calculate the profitability of each product under the traditional approach to product costing — that is, that all production overheads are absorbed on the basis of direct labour hours.

2. Calculate the profitability of each product under Activity-Based Costing (ABC), assuming that machine overheads (€600,000) are to be absorbed on the basis of machine hours but that other overheads are to be absorbed by using the appropriate cost driver.

Question 6.7: Italy Company plc

The Italy Company plc produces three products P, Q, and R. The data which follow are for the year ended 31 December, 20x2:

	P	Q	R	TOTALS
Production and sales (units)	25,000	15,000	10,000	
Selling price per unit (€)	70	55	45	
Short-run variable costs per unit:				
Direct materials (€)	15	13.5	12	
Direct labour (€)	9	7.5	6	
Direct labour hours per unit	3	2.5	2	132,500
Machine hours per unit	4	2	6	190,000
No. of production runs	5	10	10	25
No. of orders	5	20	25	50
No. of customers	8	20	32	60

Factory overhead costs	€
Set-up	150,000
Machining	760,000
Packing	150,000
Shipments	100,000
Administration costs	250,000

Assume that the company has analysed its activities and concludes that the main cost drivers are:

COST DRIVER	BASIS
Direct materials	Units
Direct labour	Units
Machining	Machine hours
Set-up	No. of production runs
Packing	No. of orders
Shipments	No. of orders
Administration	No. of customers

REQUIREMENT

1. Calculate the full production cost per unit of P, Q and R, assuming that overheads are absorbed on the basis of direct labour hours.

2. Prepare a profit and loss account by product using traditional absorption costing.

3. Prepare a profit and loss account by product using activity-based costing.

4. What are the benefits of activity-based costing when compared with traditional costing methods?

Question 6.8: Dalkey Products Ltd.

The current manufacturing costing system of Dalkey Products plc has two direct product cost categories (direct materials and direct labour). Indirect manufacturing costs are applied to products using a single indirect cost pool. The indirect manufacturing cost application base is direct labour hours. The indirect cost rate is €115 per direct labour hour.

Dalkey Products plc is switching from labour-based to a machine-based manufacturing approach at its aircraft components plant. Recently, the plant manager set up five activity areas, each with its own supervisor and budget responsibility.

Relevant data relating to cost pools, cost drivers and cost driver rates are as follows:

COST POOL	COST DRIVER	COST DRIVER RATE €
Material handling	Number of parts	0.40
Lathe work	Number of turns	0.20
Milling	Number of machine hours	20.00
Grinding	Number of parts	0.80
Shipping	Number of orders shipped	1,500.00

Information technology has advanced to the point where all the necessary data for budgeting in these five activity areas are automatically collected.

The two job orders processed under the new system at the aircraft components plant in the most recent period had the following characteristics:

	JOB ORDER 410	JOB ORDER 411
Direct materials cost per job (€)	9,700	59,900
Direct labour cost per job (€)	750	11,250
Number of direct labour hours per job	25	375
Number of parts per job	500	2,000
Number of turns per job	20,000	60,000
Number of machine hours per job	150	1,050
Number of job orders shipped	1	1
Number of units in each job order	10	200

REQUIREMENT

1. Compute the per unit manufacturing cost of each job under the existing manufacturing-costing system (that is, indirect costs are collected in a single cost pool with direct labour hours as the application base.)

2. Assume that Dalkey Products plc adopts an activity-based accounting system. Indirect costs are applied to products using separate indirect costs pools for each of the five activity areas (materials handling, lathe work, milling, grinding and shipping). The application base and rate for each activity area are described in the problem. Compute the per unit manufacturing cost of each job under the activity-based accounting system.

3. Compare the per unit cost figures for Job Orders 410 and 411 computed in requirements 1 and 2. Why do they differ? Why might these differences be important to Dalkey Products plc?

Question 6.9: Zebra Ltd.

The following data relates to costs, output volume and cost drivers of Zebra Ltd. for June 20x1.

	P	Q	R	TOTAL
1. Production and sales (units)	3,000	2,000	1,500	
2. Direct production costs	€	€	€	€
	PER UNIT	PER UNIT	PER UNIT	
Direct materials	12	11	8	70,000
Direct labour	3	6	2	24,000
	15	17	10	94,000

	P	Q	R	TOTAL
3. Labour hours per unit	0.5	1	0.3	
4. Machine hours per unit	2	1	2	
5. Number of production runs	8	2	10	20
6. Number of deliveries to customers	3	2	10	15
7. Number of production orders	30	5	15	50
8. Number of deliveries of materials into store	17	3	20	40
9. Production overhead costs:				
Machining				71,500
Set-up costs				10,500
Materials handling (receiving)				35,000
Packing costs (despatch)				22,500
Engineering (production)				25,500
				165,000

Indirect production overheads that are not driven by production volume are:

ITEM	COST DRIVER
Set-up costs	Production runs
Materials handling	Deliveries of materials (i.e. receipts)
Packing	Deliveries to customers
Engineering	Production orders

There were no opening stocks at the beginning of June.

REQUIREMENT

1. What would be the full production cost per unit of product R if overheads were absorbed on the basis of direct labour hours?

2. What would be the full production cost per unit of product R, using activity-based costing and the cost drivers described above, with overheads that are driven by production volume absorbed on a machine-hour basis?

Question 6.10: ABCD plc

ABCD plc manufactures four products — A, B, C and D — using the same plant and processes.

The following information relates to a production period:

	VOLUME	MATERIALS COST PER UNIT €	DIRECT LABOUR HOURS PER UNIT	MACHINE HOURS PER UNIT	LABOUR COST PER UNIT €
A	500	5	0.5	0.25	3
B	5,000	5	0.5	0.25	3
C	600	16	2.0	1.00	12
D	7,000	17	1.0	1.50	9

Total production overhead recorded by the cost accounting system is analysed under the following headings:

- Factory overhead applicable to machine-oriented activity is €37,425.
- Set-up costs are €4,355.
- The cost of ordering materials is €1,920.
- Handling materials costs €7,580.
- Administration for spare parts costs €8,600.

These overhead costs are absorbed by products on a machine hour rate of €4.80 per hour, giving an overhead cost per product of:

$$A= €1.20 \quad B = €1.20 \quad C = €4.80 \quad D = €7.20$$

However, investigation into the production overhead activities for the period reveals the following totals:

	NUMBER OF SET-UPS	NUMBER OF MATERIAL ORDERS	NUMBER OF TIMES MATERIAL WAS HANDLED	NUMBER OF SPARE PARTS
A	1	1	2	2
B	6	4	10	5
C	2	1	3	1
D	8	4	12	4

REQUIREMENT

1. Compute an overhead cost per product using activity-based costing, tracing overheads to production units by means of cost drivers.

2. Comment briefly on the differences disclosed between overheads traced by the present system and those traced by activity-based costing.

(*The Chartered Institute of Management Accountants*)

7

Decision-Making and Profit Planning

7.1 DECISION-MAKING

A decision represents a choice between alternatives. Without alternatives, there can be no decision. It is useful to characterise a decision as consisting of *five* separate stages, assuming a rational decision-maker. These stages are as follows:

1. **Define and agree objectives**: Know what result you want, for example, in terms of profit performance. A clear definition of what one is hoping to achieve is essential to enable possible solutions to be considered.

2. **Diagnose and define the problem**: What is wrong? This is probably the most important single stage in the decision-making process. Many decisions are either ineffective or totally wrong because they are directed at the wrong problem. The existence of a problem is normally inferred from a symptom. In many situations in management, the symptom of a problem is often a significant variance between the financial target and actual performance. It is important to establish the true cause of the symptom, which can only be achieved by a careful examination of the relevant facts including the history and build-up of the problem.

3. **Identify the alternatives**: What can we do? Once the problem has been correctly defined, it is necessary to decide what to do about it. Effective decision-making is only possible when all the relevant facts have been accumulated. Any similarities to previous problems should be highlighted and any possible relevance of their solutions noted. Information should be sought both from within the organisation and from appropriate external sources.

4. **Evaluate the alternatives**: What is likely to happen? In theory, there may be a vast number of alternatives. However, the range of solutions possible will often be limited by resource constraints particularly with respect to human, technological and financial resources. Unless these constraints are correctly recognised at the outset, managers may find that their final decision is only partially effective owing to a resource limitation.

   Few problems have only one solution. Managers must take care not to rush into accepting what might appear to be the obvious way to tackle the problem. The possible solutions should be evaluated against two criteria: (a) how realistic they are in the light of the available resources and objectives of the organisation, and (b) their cost-effectiveness An attempt should be made to quantify the benefits, costs and risks associated with each course of action.

5. **Select and implement the best solution**: The best solution will often represent a compromise between all the factors that have been considered and may sometimes be only a partial solution to the problem. Nonetheless, it might be better to accept a short-term partial solution pending the implementation of the preferred long-term solution. In any case, the manager will need to make a decision on his course of action. Effective implementation of the decision depends on preparing the necessary plans and schedules to ensure that those responsible are clear as to what is required of them. There should be a clear assignment of authority and responsibility to all concerned and any necessary co-ordinating mechanisms should be established at the outset.

When a decision is implemented, it is important to set up procedures for ensuring that plans are implemented as required at the appropriate times. A system for the regular, periodic reporting of results must also be set up so that these can be compared with what was expected. This will enable early detection of any deviations from expectations to allow appropriate corrective actions to be implemented.

Decision-Making and Rationality

It is frequently assumed that managers are rational in their decision-making — that they adopt the sequential method of making decisions outlined above. However, the rational model is inadequate in explaining the real decision-making processes of managers for several reasons:

1. Some decisions tend to be made quickly on the basis of previous experience or intuition and are often routine in nature.

2. In addition, because of time and other constraints, managers often

adopt an alternative that will provide a satisfactory rather than an optimal solution to a particular problem.

3. The rational approach cannot take into account the political and personality factors involved in decision-making. Many decisions are dominated by political considerations that override the rational process and, sometimes, management decisions are forced through by the manager with the strongest personality rather than the strongest argument.

4. The rational model assumes that the possible decisions can be evaluated with a high degree of certainty. Complete information is fairly rare and managerial intuition and judgment is necessary to evaluate incomplete data. There will always be an element of personal bias involved that can never be fully allowed for on a rational basis.

7.2   STRATEGIC MANAGEMENT ACCOUNTING

If accounting textbooks, course syllabi and examination papers are anything to go by, virtually all the relevant information produced by the management accountant is highly quantitative, introspective and geared towards the needs of financial reporting. Admittedly, this information is important in the context of operational planning and control. However, if this is the only information that is produced, executives will tend to concentrate mainly on operational issues rather than on overall policy and direction of the organisation. Advocates of change suggest that management accounting should broaden its range of relevant information to include data on the environment in which the company operates and on its competitors. In many ways, this new focus is intuitive. Writers on corporate strategy currently stress that the increased global competition favours pre-emptive strategic planning over management by reaction — the survival of the fastest. To survive, companies must have the capability to respond to changes in the market-place, to respond to technological changes and product innovations. Responsiveness is a matter of survival. Organisations must scan their environments, analyse their strengths and weaknesses and position themselves so as to minimise threats and maximise their ability to take advantage of opportunities.

This emerging discipline is referred to as Strategic Management Accounting (SMA). Being relatively new, its concepts and definitions are still being formulated and refined and many issues need to be resolved. However, one should note the fact that in its new syllabus, the Chartered Institute of Management Accountants (CIMA) has earmarked strategic management accounting as a major component of one of the four subject areas that will be examined in the final year (stage 4) examination.

It is useful to identify three main aspects of Strategic Management Accounting. These aspects are (a) Environmental Scanning, (b) Competitor Analysis, and (c) looking at certain internal data from a strategic rather than a purely operational perspective.

It should be appreciated that the thrust of strategic management accounting is to focus on areas that traditionally have been perceived as being outside the domain of the management accountant. However, the specialist skills of the management accountant in recording and summarising information can be harnessed to good effect in providing important information, especially in environmental scanning and competitor analysis.

Environmental Scanning

The essence of SMA is that it focuses managerial attention on the external environment of the company. Environmental scanning involves the monitoring of the environment for surprises (or reassurances that there are none). The surprises may be due to technological developments, changes in customer preferences or significant economic changes. Strategic information also includes general information relating to the demographic, social, legal and political environment in which the firm operates.

The major external environmental factors relevant to a company are highlighted in Exhibit 7.1.

Exhibit 7.1: External Environmental Factors

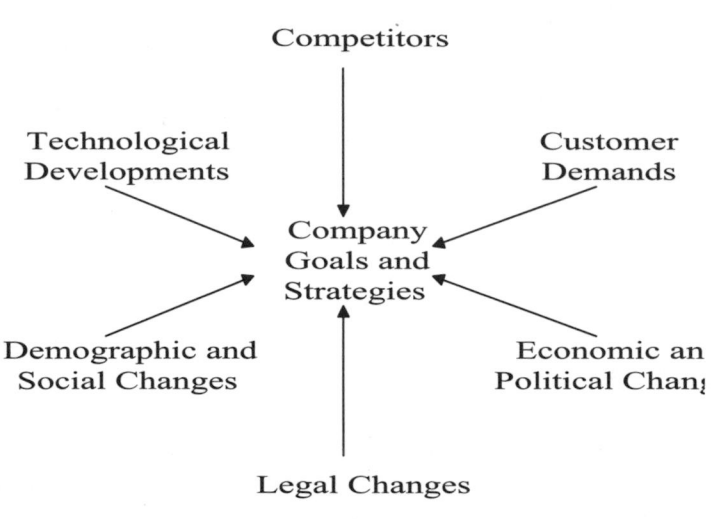

In the context of environmental scanning, the management accountant will need to collect and analyse market information, to assist in
strategy evaluation. The nature of this information relates, for example, to the stages of the product life cycle. Product life-cycle information is necessary since different phases (growth, maturity or decline)
can affect the success of different strategies (build, hold, harvest or
divest). For example, it may prove profitable to undertake a "build"
strategy in a growth market, though the same strategy in a declining
market may be disastrous.

Market share and relative market share are also useful as a sur-
rogate measure for assessing the success of corporate strategy. Actual
market share indicates how the company is performing against all
other competitors. Relative market share shows how well the company is performing in market share terms relative to its largest competitor. For example, a market penetration strategy may yield low
profits in initial years and, if judged on purely short-term financial
grounds, may appear to have failed. However, access to market data
may indicate the true position of increased market share.

By monitoring movements in market share, a company can identify whether it is gaining or losing position, and an examination of
relative market share will indicate the strengths of various competitors. Reporting market share data will improve the strategic relevance of management accounting reports. This type of information is
best generated in co-operation with the company's marketing department. This interdepartmental co-operation is fundamental if the
company's strategic position is to be fully recognised.

Competitor Analysis

It is also important to identify the company's competitive market position. The company can set objectives (or goals) and the resulting strategies only in the context of its position relative to its key competitors and the variety of external influences in the environment. After all, all companies (except a monopoly) compete in the market place. It is in this marketplace that customers have to be retained and new customers acquired from competitors. All the products available on the shared market compete not just on the basis of price but over a range of important variables. This perspective views products (goods or services) as a bundle of attributes or characteristics that are on offer to potential customers. All or some of these attributes appeal to customers and this provides goods with their value. Because of this, these attributes become crucial to the formulation of the company's strategies. These attributes include a variety of elements including quality, reliability, appearance, performance and after-sales service, including maintenance and spare parts. One can also include a time dimension such as response time to customers' orders.

Competitor analysis is also part of strategic management accounting and this involves a comprehensive analysis of competitors and is akin to setting up a competitor intelligence system. There are many possible sources of information in relation to competitors and these are detailed below. Although the list is not exhaustive, the table below indicates potential sources of information about competitors:

SOURCES OF COMPETITOR INFORMATION

Mutual customers
Own sales force
Mutual suppliers
Personnel hired from competitors
Industry trade journals and Government statistics
Advertising agencies and promotional literature
Trade exhibitions and physical analysis of competitors' products
Newspaper articles and press releases
Annual financial reports published by competitors
Industrial experts and consultants
Banks and financial markets

Although it is unrealistic to expect a competitor intelligence system to uncover full information concerning a competitor's activities, any information can provide useful input into the strategic analysis process.

Benchmarking

An increasingly popular method of competitive analysis is that of "benchmarking", which is simply the systematic process of discovery and examination for best practices that lead to superior performance. Benchmarks are measurements to gauge performance in various metrics of a company relative to others. Sales and profits are relatively measured but benchmarking also includes dimensions such as improving products, customer and employee satisfaction and many other measures of financial and non-financial performance.

This clear focus on best practices can provide the impetus for change, it can help identify what must change and can offer a vivid picture of the end-point after change. Benchmarking has become the starting point for process engineering efforts in many organisations. It is a technique of analysing best practices that can help an organisation avoid being ambushed by competitors.

The gaps between a company's performance relative to best practices can be stunning in magnitude for these important performance parameters. As a result, management's initial reaction to them may be one of denial or disbelief — senior managers may be unwilling to believe that any competitor could be so clearly advantaged. Alternatively, a large performance gap may be discouraging, causing managers to feel that they cannot possibly catch up to, let alone overtake, the performance of their best competitors. Nevertheless, benchmarking can be extremely useful in overcoming management complacency about the status quo and in exposing incorrect perceptions about the company's strengths and weaknesses.

Benchmarking (or the search for best practices) can be either internal or external to one's own company. To understand and imitate the world's best performance, a company will ultimately need some form of external benchmarking. However, many companies find that internal benchmarking can provide immediate opportunities for performance improvement. This is achieved by assessing whether a particular segment of the company is performing significantly better than others, by exploring the source of this relatively superior performance and by deciding how to translate this superior performance to other units within the company.

Benchmarking can be done by employees or external consultants. Companies that have been benchmarking for a number of years believe that a significant amount of money and time can be saved by training their own managers to perform benchmarking projects. More important, however, is that corporate experts believe an in-house effort is more likely to be of higher quality, better targeted and better translated into action. This is because, as the knowledge experts, consultants can take and drive the project. They become project managers rather than guides. This distracts from the company's own learning experience. Also, the external consultant may not fully understand the company's culture.

As part of the benchmarking process, information is accumulated that can be used in competitor cost analysis. An actual cost level is of limited value in helping management's strategic thinking even if honed to five decimal points. Without knowledge of relative competitor costs, the company does not know whom to attack or how strong a defence should be. In those circumstances, management must take strategic decisions in the dark.

Unfortunately, there are some barriers to benchmarking. First, developing relevant and accurate information can present legal, ethical and/or practical problems. For example, in highly competitive industries, peer companies are justifiably concerned that their important sources of competitive advantage could be compromised if they were to enter a benchmarking partnership with a direct competitor. This is one reason why successful benchmarking efforts often involve partnerships with world-class companies outside a company's own industry.

While benchmarks do reveal performance gaps, they are not truly useful without an analysis or explanation for why those gaps exist. Benchmarking requires a depth of understanding that generally can be developed only through an information agreement between participating companies.

Generic Strategies for Competitive Advantage

In order to implement and sustain successful performance, a company needs to gain and maintain at least one source of competitive advantage over its current and potential competitors. Corporate strategists acknowledge that there are three generic strategies that can be pursued to ensure sustainable competitive advantage.

First, the strategy of differentiation can be pursued where the company's product is perceived by customers as unique. Products are differentiated on the basis of their attributes. Consequently, it is logical to suggest that the company's market share will be determined by the product's attributes, consumer tastes and the attributes provided by competitors' products. The essential point here is that profit is determined not only by internal efficiency but also by the company's position relative to current competitors. Following this, a second generic strategy is to focus on a narrow segment of the market — a niche strategy.

The third generic strategy is that of cost leadership. Other things being equal, companies with a cost advantage (lower unit cost for a product of comparable specification) are strong and those with a cost disadvantage are weak. Thus, without knowledge of relative competitor costs, the company does not know what its relative strategic position is. Under such circumstances, strategic decisions may be based on insufficient information.

Strategic Perspective on Internal Data

In addition to the increased focus on external information, SMA also looks at the long-term implications of internally generated information. For example, it may be that a reduction in short-term profitability is due to actions undertaken to build market share and secure relative cost advantage, which will help ensure future improvements in profit performance. If the company places too great importance on its short-term profitability, it may be unwilling to invest either in improving its competitive position or in removing or minimising the potential impact of any adverse change in its environment. Conversely, in a strategic context, an increase in short-term profit may be associated with a deterioration in its strategic position. This is because the increased profits are due to selling prices being higher than before and above the competitive level, with a consequent reduction in market share.

Also, some aspects of capital expenditure evaluation should be viewed from a strategic perspective. In other words, capital investment proposals should not be treated as discrete projects that generate incremental but separate cash flows with no account taken of the company's competitive environment. Thus, cash flows are not generated from an individual investment *per se*, but from the company's overall competitive position. This broader, strategic view may allow the investment to proceed when it may have been rejected on purely financial grounds using criteria such as net present value (NPV). For example, an in-vestment in new technology that allows the company to claim market share from a competitor may not be justified on purely financial grounds. However, the effect on market share may ensure that it is undertaken.

Information Overload?

Top management will be concerned not only with internal performance but also external information. Inevitably the charge will be made that the addition of yet another layer of data creates a situation of information overload. According to Kaplan and Norton ("The Balanced Scorecard", *Harvard Business Review*, January/February, 1992), managers should not have to choose between financial and operational measures. Instead, managers want a balanced presentation of both financial and non-financial measures. By way of analogy, Kaplan and Norton refer to an aeroplane pilot who has a variety of dials and indicators in the cockpit that summarise the current and predicted environment. However, reliance on only one instrument can be fatal. They propose a "balanced scorecard" that allows managers to look at the business from four important perspectives as follows:

1. How do customers see us? (customer perspective).

2. What must we excel at? (internal business perspective).

3. Can we improve? (learning and growth perspective).

4. How do we look to shareholders? (financial perspective).

What needs to be done is to concentrate on the key performance indicators. By critical and innovative thinking, it should be possible to identify a limited number of key variables that reflect the critical success factors of the firm. These key variables (or key success factors) are the limited number of areas in which results, if they are satisfactory, will ensure successful competitive performance for the organisation. They are the few key areas where "things must go right" for the business to flourish. If results are not adequate, the organisation's efforts for the period will be less than desired. (This topic will be discussed in greater detail in Section 13.3.)

The following represents a general example of key variables:

GENERAL EXAMPLE OF KEY VARIABLES

Marketing and customers	Sales volume, growth and market share New products/ new customers
Production and delivery	Quality and on-time delivery Capacity utilisation
Asset management and profitability	Return on Investment (ROI) Management of working capital

An automatic side benefit of this critical thinking is the development of a deeper understanding of the various dimensions of the business and what activities the individuals within the company need to perform well if it is to achieve and maintain success. Indeed, by working closely with production, marketing, design and other staff to agree and obtain such information, the management accountant may help to bring together these disciplines and instil a sense of strategic purpose. If the management accountant can help to rid firms of interdepartmental rivalries and the focus on short-term results, he or she will facilitate smoother implementation of strategic plans.

The cost of acquiring this additional, strategic information must also be considered. The cost of information must be viewed in the context of its value to decision-makers. Since management generally can make, and has made, its most costly and fatal mistakes in formulating strategic plans, strategic information is potentially the most valuable! Alternatively stated, the lack of this information may generate significant opportunity costs.

Admittedly, some companies may capture some information about their external environment as a matter of routine. For example, the marketing department may generate a great deal of market information, in which case the role of the management accountant will be to "audit" the marketing figures to check that any underlying assumptions and accompanying data are reasonable and correct. In some companies, none of the tasks may be performed at present, in which case a major shift in emphasis in the method by which financial information is prepared and processed will be required.

However, this information gathering exercise is likely, at present, to be the responsibility of either the marketing department or production. It is reasonable to argue that the management accountant has not generally played a major part in this process. However, the importance of this information to the company coupled with the central role of the management accountant in the organisation suggest that he or she should become more involved with this information gathering process. The management accounting department should become the "information warehouse" of the organisation. Admittedly, there are important organisational and behavioural issues relating to this proposition that should first be addressed.

7.3   THE COST-VOLUME-PROFIT (CVP) MODEL

One of the more important analytical tools used in decision-making by management is cost-volume-profit analysis. Cost-volume-profit (CVP) analysis shows how costs, revenues and, therefore, profits behave in response to changes in the level of business activity. CVP analysis may be used by management to answer questions such as the following:

1. What level of sales must be reached to cover all expenses, that is, to break even?

2. How many units of a product (or service) must be sold to earn a given operating profit?

3. Is it worthwhile to spend more on advertising to increase units sold?

To apply CVP analysis, costs must be classified in relation to their behaviour following changes in output or volume. Ultimately, all costs can be classified into three categories:

1. **Variable costs**: A variable cost increases and decreases in total directly and proportionately with changes in volume. If, for example, volume increases by 5 per cent, a variable cost will also increase by 5 per cent. Petrol is an example of a variable cost for a car, since fuel consumption is directly related to miles driven.

2. **Fixed costs**: These are costs that remain unchanged in total with changes in volume. Usually such costs are incurred as a function of time, such as annual insurance or road tax for a car.

   The aggregate of fixed and variable costs represents total cost, which is usually depicted as follows:

Exhibit 7.2: Total Cost

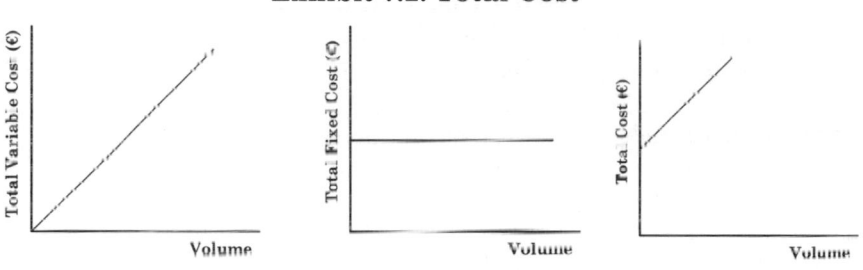

The importance of this classification lies in the fact that, when the financial impact of small changes in output is being studied, attention need only be concentrated on the variable costs, since fixed costs will remain unchanged for different levels of volume within a "relevant range". This classification is particularly appropriate in decision-making.

In relation to the fixed/variable classification, two points are important:

(a) The cost relationship is defined in terms of volume/output only. Yet fixed costs can change for a variety of non-volume reasons — for example, inflation.

(b) The cost/volume relationship is valid only within a relevant range of activity. Beyond the relevant range of activity, either fixed costs change due to the new level of output or variable cost changes due to, for example, economies of scale.

3. **Semi-fixed (or mixed) costs**: In reality, many costs are part fixed and part variable. These are referred to as semi-fixed costs

or mixed costs. For example, with a car, depreciation is a semi-fixed cost. Some depreciation will occur due to the passage of time, without regard to the miles driven and thus represents a fixed cost. However, the more miles a car is driven each year, the more it depreciates due to wear and tear, which is a variable cost. (There are various techniques for analysing semi-fixed costs into fixed and variable components and these techniques will be discussed later in the chapter).

Methods of Profit Planning

Once a cost-volume relationship has been established, it can be combined with volume-revenue relationships to evaluate alternatives in terms of profit impact. The study of profit-volume relationships is often referred to as Cost-Volume-Profit (CVP) analysis since it provides profit estimates at various levels of volume, given information on selling prices, fixed and variable costs. CVP analysis can use either a graphic approach or the CVP model. Both these approaches will be outlined using the following example:

ILLUSTRATION

Henry sells "widgets" for €8 each. His monthly operating data is as follows, based on monthly sales of 6,000 to 10,000 units:

HENRY'S SHOP
MONTHLY OPERATING DATA

	PER UNIT €
Average selling price	8.00
Cost of widgets	4.20
Sales commission	.40
Packaging costs	.40
Total variable costs per unit	5.00

Total fixed costs are estimated at €21,000 per month.

Graphic Analysis

A CVP graph of Henry's Shop is shown below in Exhibit 7.3. The horizontal axis shows the number of units sold per month, based on an upper limit of 10,000 units. The vertical axis is denominated in money terms, reflecting both total revenue and total costs. The graph is plotted as follows:

1. The sales revenue line is plotted running from €0 at zero volume of sales to €80,000, representing 10,000 units sold per month at €8 per unit.

2. The fixed monthly costs are plotted as a horizontal line at the level of €21,000 per month.

Exhibit 7.3: Henry's Shop — CVP Graph

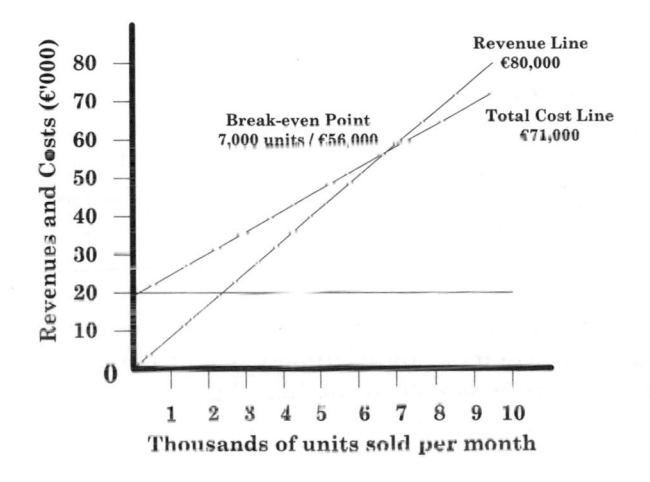

3. Starting at €21,000 on the vertical axis, the total costs are plotted. Therefore, total cost, at any given level of activity, represents a fixed cost element of €21,000 plus a variable cost of €5 per unit for each unit sold.

The operating profit expected at any sales level may be read from the CVP graph. One important level of activity is the break-even point. This is the level of activity at which total revenues equal total cost. It is important for planning purposes — in deciding whether to introduce a new product line or to build a new plant.

The monthly break-even point for Henry's business is 7,000 units or €56,000 in sales revenue. Sales below 7,000 units per month will result in a loss, and sales above this per month will result in profit.

Limitations of the Graphic Approach to Profit Planning

The graphic approach to profit planning and decision-making has two major limitations:

1. To be really useful, the graph must be drawn with proper accuracy, otherwise it will be difficult to determine precisely such information as break-even point, etc.

2. The graph represents a static situation. Thus, if, say, the selling price is changed, an additional line must be drawn on the graph. If several variables are changed — for example, selling price, variable cost and fixed costs — the graph will be covered with lines and will be virtually unreadable. So, the graphic approach does not readily lend itself to evaluating different alternatives.

The CVP Model

As an alternative to the graphic approach, profit planning calculations (including break-even point) can more easily be performed by way of a simple formula. The important concept is that of *contribution per unit* or contribution margin. Contribution per unit is the difference between sales revenue per unit and variable cost per unit. This contribution is the amount available to cover the company's fixed costs and, after all fixed costs have been covered, to provide an operating profit. Henry's contribution per unit is €3 (€8 less €5), and the total contribution is €30,000 at 10,000 units of output.

The CVP formula used in profit planning can be derived as follows:

$$\text{Profit} = \text{sales revenue - total costs}$$
$$= (\text{sales price x volume}) - \{\text{fixed costs} + (\text{variable unit cost x volume})\}$$
$$= (\text{sales price - variable unit cost}) \text{ x volume - fixed costs,}$$
$$\text{where volume represents units sold.}$$

Since contribution equals sales price per unit minus variable cost per unit, the above equation can be rearranged as follows:

$$\text{Profit} = (\text{unit contribution x volume}) - \text{fixed costs.}$$

CVP relationships are widely used in profit planning and decision-making situations. To illustrate, let us consider two ways in which cost-volume-profit relationships might be used by the management of Henry's Shop in planning marketing strategies:

ILLUSTRATION

To increase volume, Henry is considering a policy of reducing selling price (and, therefore, contribution) by €1 per unit. Sales are expected to increase from 10,000 to 12,000 units. What is the projected profit — in other words, is the price reduction worthwhile?

	€
The current contribution is: 10,000 units x €3	30,000
The revised contribution is: 12,000 units x €2	24,000
Profit reduction due to proposal	(6,000)

Thus, the revised pricing policy will cause contribution (and, therefore, profits) to fall by €6,000.

ILLUSTRATION

Henry is considering a proposal to reduce shop hours by opening two hours later each morning. It is estimated that this policy would reduce sales volume from 10,000 units to 9,000 units but would reduce fixed costs by €1,000 per month. What is the financial impact?

SOLUTION

	€
Revised contribution. 9,000 units x €3	27,000
Plus: Saving on fixed costs	1,000
	28,000
Less: Current contribution: 10,000 x €3	30,000
Profit reduction due to proposal	(2,000)

Clearly, this proposal is not worthwhile.

Break-even Point (BEP) and Target Volume

The CVP model can also be used to determine break-even point and target volume. The basic profit model is:

Profit = (unit contribution x volume) - fixed costs.

At break-even point, profit equals zero; therefore volume at break-even point in units can be found by re-arranging the equation as follows:

BEP (units) = $\dfrac{\text{Total fixed costs}}{\text{Contribution per unit}}$

At the break-even point, the shop must earn a contribution per unit large enough to cover all fixed costs. The monthly fixed costs amount to €21,000 and the contribution per unit is €3.00. Therefore:

BEP (units) = $\dfrac{€21,000}{€3.00}$ = 7,000 units per month.

When the contribution per unit is expressed as a percentage of sales, it is called the contribution/sales ratio (C/S ratio) and is defined as:

$$\text{C/S ratio} = \frac{\text{Unit contribution}}{\text{Unit sales price}}$$

The contribution/sales ratio at Henry's shop is:

$$\text{C/S ratio} = \frac{€8.00 - €5.00}{€8.00} = 0.375$$

The C/S ratio of 0.375 means that 37.5 per cent of the sales revenue earned in a Henry's shop is available to cover fixed costs.

The C/S ratio can be used to calculate the BEP in terms of sales revenue. The formula is derived by multiplying both sides of the BEP (units) equation by the sales price to provide:

$$\text{BEP (revenue)} = \frac{\text{Total fixed costs}}{\text{Unit contribution}} \times \text{Sales price}$$

$$= \frac{\text{Fixed costs}}{\text{C/S Ratio}}$$

This ratio can be very useful in the context of a multi-product business, a service company or where units of output are not available.

In Henry's example, the figures are:

$$\text{BEP (revenue)} = \frac{€21,000}{0.375} = €56,000$$

Target Volume

Frequently managers want to know not only BEP but the level of output that will produce a required profit target. This level of activity is called "target volume" and, intuitively, must be above BEP.

The two formulae above can be adapted to calculate a target volume — sales volume needed to achieve any desired level of operating profit — as follows:

$$\text{Target volume (units)} = \frac{\text{Total fixed costs plus required profit}}{\text{Contribution per unit}}$$

For example, how may units must be sold for Henry's Shop to earn a monthly operating profit of €6,000?

$$\text{Sales volume (units)} = \frac{€21,000 + €6,000}{€3.00} = 9,000 \text{ units per month}$$

Alternatively, compute the required sales revenue by substituting the contribution rate for the contribution per unit in our sales volume formula. The formula then becomes:

Target volume (revenue) = <u>Total fixed costs plus required profit</u>
C/S Ratio

To illustrate, compute the sales volume required for Henry's Shop to earn a monthly operating profit €6,000:

Sales volume (in €)   =   <u>€21,000 + €6,000</u>   =   €72,000 per month.
0.375

Margin of Safety

The amount by which actual sales volume exceeds the break-even sales volume is called the margin of safety. This is the amount by which sales could decline before the company incurs an operating loss. Henry's Shop has a break-even sales volume of 7,000 units. Therefore, with actual sales of 10,000 units, the shop has a margin of safety of 3,000 units. It is usual to express this as a percentage of anticipated volume — in this case, 30 per cent (3,000/10,000). This means that if forecast sales units fall by less than 30 per cent, an operating profit will still be generated.

7.4   ASSUMPTIONS UNDERLYING CVP ANALYSIS

The usefulness of any model in decision-making is restricted by the assumptions on which it is based. CVP analysis is based on a number of assumptions. These assumptions are that:

1. Sales price per unit remains constant, although economists point out that in order to sell additional units, selling price must usually be reduced.

2. Variable cost per unit of output remains constant, ignoring the impact of the learning curve, quantity discounts, etc., and assuming no economies or diseconomies of scale.

3. Fixed costs remain unchanged in respect to volume changes.

4. The ability to accurately segregate/classify fixed and variable costs.

5. Volume/output is the only factor influencing costs.

6. In a manufacturing business, sales equals production or, alternatively, stock is valued at variable cost of production.

7. If more than one product is sold, the proportion of the various products sold (sales mix) is assumed to be constant.

The Importance of Sales Mix in CVP Analysis

Most companies sell a variety of different products that generate different unit contributions. This applies just as much to a service company (an airline selling different priced tickets) as to a manufacturer producing small, medium and large versions of a product. For such cases, CVP analysis is based on the assumption of a constant product mix.

Assume a small business sells three types of product — Small, Medium and Large — as follows:

	SMALL	MEDIUM	LARGE
	€	€	€
Sales price per package	4.00	8.00	12.00
Less: Variable expense per package	2.80	5.00	6.00
Contribution per unit	1.20	3.00	6.00
Contribution/sales ratio	0.30	0.375	0.50
Fixed costs (apportioned)	€5,000	€7,000	€9,000

There are two ways of calculating BEP (and applying CVP analysis) for a multi-product business.

The first is to calculate the break-even point of each individual product and aggregate the answers to give an overall break-even point.

	SMALL	MEDIUM	LARGE
Fixed costs (above)	€5,000	€7,000	€9,000
Contribution/sales ratio	0.30	0.375	0.50
BEP (sales revenue)	€16,666	€18,666	€18,000

In the example above, the BEP for the company as a whole is €53,332. This approach assumes that the fixed costs can be accurately apportioned between the various products.

Alternatively, the overall BEP can be calculated from an "average" contribution/sales ratio, making the assumption of a constant product mix. Assume that the three products are sold in equal proportions, thus:

Average sales per unit (1:1:1)	€8.00
Average variable cost (1:1:1)	4.60
Average contribution (1:1:1)	3.40
Average C/S ratio	0.425
BEP (sales revenue) (€21,000/ 0.425)	€49,411

The difference in BEP under the two methods above stems from the different assumptions. In reality, it is difficult to correctly apportion all fixed costs to individual products. On the other hand, it may be difficult to identify the constant product mix.

7.5   COST RELATIONSHIPS AND PREDICTION

Since a decision represents a choice among alternatives, it can only affect the future. Thus, one of the important dimensions in decision-making is to estimate the financial consequences, in terms of cash inflows and outflows, of each alternative. This section is concerned with establishing valid cost relationships and estimates that can be used in decision-making. The purpose is to classify various types of costs into their fixed and variable components. Fixed costs in total do not, by definition, respond to output changes within a relevant range of activity; on the other hand, variable costs in total respond immediately to changes in output.

Cost behaviour patterns can be established by analysing historic data. This does not imply that historic cost data is relevant in decision-making since historic data relates to the past and, as such, cannot be relevant to the future. However, historic data can be useful in establishing relationships that can be used to estimate the future. It is the predictive ability of historic data that is relevant to decision-making rather than the historic data itself.

The following techniques are used to estimate cost relationships and each will be discussed in turn:

1. The high-low method.

2. The accounts classification method.

3. The scatter diagram.

4. Regression analysis.

The High-Low Method

The high-low method is also called the "two point" method. This is because two points are selected in a previous accounting period, corresponding to the periods of highest and lowest activity. Associated with these two points of extreme activity are the costs whose relationship is required to be determined. The difference between the total costs at these activity levels is explained by the behaviour of variable costs, which respond to changing levels of output.

ILLUSTRATION

The total overhead costs for a factory for the past four months are reported as follows:

MONTH	OVERHEADS	UNITS PRODUCED
	€	
January	€70,000	20,000
February	50,000	15,000
March	60,000	16,000
April	40,000	10,000

The months of highest and lowest activity are January and April respectively. Thus:

	HIGH JANUARY	LOW APRIL	CHANGE
Overhead costs	€70,000	€40,000	+ €30,000
Units of output	20,000	10,000	+10,000

The additional 10,000 units are associated with additional overhead costs of €30,000. But since variable costs are assumed to vary with output, the variable cost per unit can be estimated as follows:

Variable overhead (per unit) = €30,000 / 10,000 units = €3 per unit.

Estimated fixed costs per month can now be determined by using either the highest or lowest level of activity. For example, in January, 20,000 units were produced; thus, total variable costs can be estimated at €60,000. However, since total costs (fixed and variable) are reported to be €70,000 for that month, monthly fixed costs can be estimated at €10,000, being the difference between €70,000 and €60,000.

In summary, the overhead cost relationship can be stated in the form of a linear equation, $Y = A + BX$, where Y equals the total cost to be predicted, A is a constant (fixed cost), B is the rate of change between the two variables and X represents some measure of activity or volume. The cost model, based on the high-low method, is:

Y (Total overhead cost per month) = €10,000 + €3 X

where X equals the number of units produced per month, €10,000 represents the monthly fixed overhead costs, and €3 is the rate of change between the two variables. In this case, the variable unit cost is €3.

The advantage of the high-low method is its simplicity and ease of use. It also can provide a reasonable check on the estimates obtained by other methods.

The limitations of the high-low method are several. First, only two points are selected and a linear relationship is assumed even though this may not be representative of all other periods. Second, there may be ambiguity associated with this method since the month with the highest (lowest) activity may not be the month with the highest (lowest) cost. Third, this method does not provide any measures for the reliability of the relationship between cost and volume.

Accounts Classification Method

This method involves an analysis of each cost element and its subjective assessment into fixed or variable components. Where costs are considered semi-fixed, they are apportioned on an appropriate percentage basis.

While this method has the advantage of being reasonably quick and inexpensive, the subjectivity involved can result in significant inaccuracies. Moreover, there are no measures by which one can measure the reliability of the relationship.

ILLUSTRATION

The profit and loss account of the Downtown Supermarket Co. for the year 20x1 is expected to be as follows:

	€	%
Sales (at €1 each)	400,000	
Cost of goods sold	260,000	100
Gross profit	140,000	
Less: General expenses	29,400	25
Cleaning	2,400	10
Packing	4,600	100
Delivery	4,000	75
Depreciation	2,000	nil
Salaries and wages	10,000	nil
Rent, heating etc.	13,200	nil
Net profit	74,400	

The percentages on the right are estimates of the degree of variability of the items concerned in relation to sales volume.

REQUIREMENT

Calculate break-even point in terms of sales revenue for 20x1.

CLASSIFICATION BETWEEN FIXED AND VARIABLE COSTS

	VARIABLE	FIXED
Cost of goods sold	260,000	Nil
General expenses	7,350	22,050
Cleaning	240	2,160
Packing	4,600	Nil
Delivery	3,000	1,000
Depreciation	Nil	2,000
Salaries	Nil	10,000
Rent	Nil	13,200
	275,190	50,410

Contribution margin =	(€400,000 - €275,190) =	€124,810
Contribution/sales ratio =	€124,810/€400,000 =	0.31
BEP (sales) =	€50,410/0.31 =	€162,613.

The Scatter Diagram

This involves plotting both costs and output of previous periods on a graph and drawing a "line of best fit". While plotting the observations is a technical activity, drawing the line of best fit is very much a subjective exercise-based on the visual interpretation of the graph. It is realistic to argue that several individuals faced with the same set of observations will draw a different best fit line.

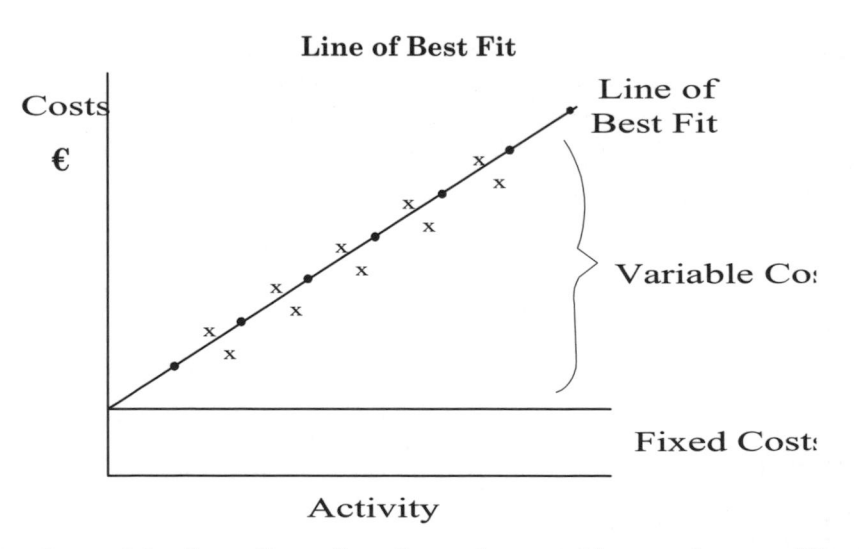

The slope of the line of best fit reflects the variable cost element. The intersection of the Y axis is the estimate of fixed costs.

This method is simple and convenient to use. Also, since it uses a set of data, it provides a good indication of whether a complete linear relationship exists, whether the relationship is in the form of a step function or whether a curvilinear relationship is more appropriate.

The disadvantage of the scatter diagram method is its subjectivity and that, like the previous methods, there are no measures with which to assess the reliability of the estimated relationship.

Regression Analysis

Linear regression analysis is a statistical technique that establishes an objective relationship between two variables. The precise workings are contained in the appendix to this chapter.

APPENDIX: LINEAR REGRESSION

In the case of simple linear regression, the objective is to model a relationship between two variables. Given the assumption of linearity, the equation showing the relationship between the X and Y variables is just a mathematical function for a straight line:

$$Y = A + Bx$$

Where: Y   = the dependent variable (the value to be predicted)

A   = the constant in the equation (fixed costs)

B (beta) = the amount of change in Y for each unit change in X

X   = the independent or explanatory variable.

(Where there are two or more explanatory variables, the analysis is referred to as multiple regression).

Based on a set of past observations for both the independent and dependent variables, one can estimate values for both A (Alpha) and B (Beta) using regression analysis.

Regression analysis serves three important purposes:

1. It provides a precise mathematical definition of the relationship.

2. It provides measures of reliability.

3. It provides the basis for establishing a range for the possible value of Y for a given X value, and also a range for the Beta values.

A frequently used method for determining the regression equation is the least squares method. This mathematical technique is entirely objective in that two or more persons, using the same data, will arrive at identical regression equations, barring arithmetical errors. The line determined by this technique is unique in that the sum of the squared deviations between the regression line and the observations is minimised, as in Exhibit 7.4.

Exhibit 7.4: Fitting a Regression Line

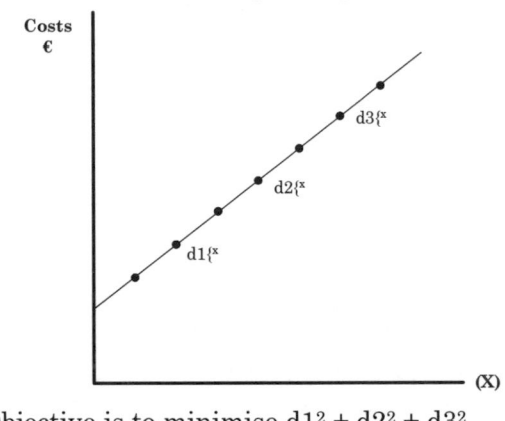

Objective is to minimise d1² + d2² + d3²

The immediate implication is that if extreme or outlying values are included in the set of observations on which the regression equation is determined, the resulting regression line may be distorted, in which case it is plausible to argue that such outlying values should be eliminated by the data set.

The regression equation Y = A + BX can be found from the following two equations and solving for A and B:

$$Ey = na + bEx$$
$$Exy = aEx + bEx^2$$

where:
N	=	number of observations	
Ex	=	the aggregate value of the independent variable;	
Ey	=	the aggregate value of the dependent variable	
a	=	constant (fixed cost) for range of observations	
b	=	rate of change between X and Y variables.	

Cheap and easy-to-use computer software now exists which performs these calculations very quickly and to a high degree of accuracy.

ILLUSTRATION

The following details are provided for the RD Company for a random sample where the number of units is the independent variable (X) and labour cost is the dependent variable (Y). The accountant presumes a linear relationship.

NO. OF UNITS (X)	LABOUR COSTS (Y) €	X^2	XY
15	180	225	2,700
12	140	144	1,680
20	230	400	4,600
17	190	289	3,230
12	160	144	1,920
25	300	625	7,500
22	270	484	5,940
9	110	81	990
18	240	324	4,320
30	320	900	9,600
E = 180	2,140	3,616	42,480

The two simultaneous equations are:

$$(1)\ Ey = Na + bEx$$

$$(2)\ Exy = aEx + bEx^2$$

Substituting the above into the two simultaneous equations, we obtain:

$$2,140 = 10A + 180B$$
$$42,480 = 180A + 3,616B$$

Solving the above simultaneous equations: b = 10.53 and a = 24.42, so that the estimating equation (Y = A + Bx) is: Y = 24.42 + 10.53X. This equation can be used to predict labour costs at different levels of output (units).

Measures of Reliability

The advantage of regression analysis is that measures are automatically provided (using computer software) to assess the reliability of the equation. There are two commonly used measures of reliability:

1. **The coefficient of determination (R^2)** can be used as a measure of the strength of the regression relationship. In mathematical terms, the coefficient of determination is constrained to lie between a value of zero and an absolute value of 1. A value of zero would indicate that there is no linear relationship between the independent and dependent variable. A value of "1" indicates perfect correlation between the two variables. The importance of the R^2 statistic is that, if the coefficient of determination is, say 0.90, this

indicates that 90 per cent of the variation in the dependent variable can be explained by the independent variable. Obviously, the higher the R^2 value, the higher the linear relationship.

However, a high R^2 value does not imply a cause-and-effect relationship. The coefficient of determination provides an estimate of the strength of the linear relationship between the independent and dependent variables. Both variables may be a function of another variable and no cause-and-effect relationship may exist. For example, there may be a high degree of correlation between advertising spend and wages expense; however we would not suggest that advertising spend causes wages. Rather both variables are linked to another (missing) variable, namely units sold. Thus, before performing regression analysis, it is important to establish the plausibility between the two selected variables. In other words, the relationship should make economic sense and be intuitive.

2. **t-value of the Beta coefficient**: The second test of reliability on the regression equation is to determine the statistical significance of the Beta coefficient. The Beta value for any regression equation is usually non-zero. This suggests some relationship between the X and Y values. The test is, in statistical terms, whether this non-zero Beta value could have occurred by chance.

The procedure is first to establish a "t-value" for the Beta coefficient. The "t-value" is computed as:

$$\text{t-value} \quad = \quad \frac{\text{Beta Coefficient}}{\text{Standard error of coefficient}}$$

say, t-value = 4.1.

To assess the significance of this computed t-value, consult the statistical tables of "t" for the appropriate degrees of freedom and required confidence level (usually 95 per cent). The appropriate degrees of freedom will be N - p, where N equals the number of observations and p equals the number of parameters in the estimating equation. In simple regression, there are always two parameters: the constant (A) and coefficient of the independent variable (B).

Using the table (Exhibit 7.5) for the t distribution with 10 (12 - 2) degrees of freedom, appropriate to 12 observations, t has a value of 2.228 at the 95 per cent confidence level. This means that there is a 5 per cent probability that the absolute value of t is greater or equal to 2.228. Thus, if the true value of beta is zero (which would indicate that there is no linear relationship), there is only a 5 per cent probability that the t value will be greater than 2.228.

Since the computed t value (4.1) greatly exceeds the value of 2.228 indicated above, reject the null hypothesis (B = O) at the 5 per cent level of significance. In other words, it is most unlikely that the computed Beta value could have arisen by chance, if the real Beta value was zero.

Exhibit 7.5: T-Values

DEGREES OF FREEDOM	95% CONFIDENCE INTERVAL
1	12.706
2	4.303
3	3.182
4	2.776
5	2.571
6	2.447
7	2.365
8	2.306
9	2.262
10	2.228
11	2.201
12	2.179
13	2.160
14	2.145
15	2.131
16	2.120
17	2.110
18	2.101

The table above shows that, in large samples, the statistical t-value approaches an absolute value of 2 (1.96). Accordingly, many accountants use "2" as a general rule of thumb in establishing statistical significance for Beta.

Establishing Confidence Intervals

Regression equations provide an estimated value of Y, given values for A, B and X. Thus, Y will represent the predicted level of total cost. However, it is only an estimate, with the actual value of Y being more or less than predicted from the regression equation. Use the statistical value, termed Standard Error of the Estimate (SEE) to establish a confidence interval for the actual value of Y.

The 95 per cent confidence interval for Y is calculated as:

$$Y +/- t95 (SEE)$$

It is not necessary to explain the calculation for standard errors since they are computed automatically using an appropriate computer programme. The following standard computer printout, based on the RD Company, was obtained:

Constant	24.42
SE of the Estimate (SEE)	15.80
R^2 (Coefficient of determination)	.94
SE of the beta coefficient (SEB)	.81
No. of observations	10
Degrees of freedom	8
Beta coefficient	10.53
t-value 8 degrees of freedom (95 per cent)	2.306

Conclusion: The overall regression equation is:

$$Y = 24.42 + 10.53x$$

where Y = predicted total labour cost; 24.42 = fixed labour cost per batch; 10.53 = the rate of change between X and Y; and X = number of units.

The R^2 statistic (co-efficient of determination) explains the percentage variation in Y explained by X (94 per cent). This indicates that there is a strong linear relationship between the X and Y variables.

A second test of linearity is to test the statistical significance of Beta. The computed t-value (10.53 / 0.81) equals 13, which greatly exceeds the statistical t-value (2.306), which corresponds to a 95 per cent confidence level at (N - 2) degrees of freedom.

The total predicted labour cost for a batch of 100 units is €1,077 {24.42 + (10.53 x 100)}. However, the actual value of Y, at a 95 per cent confidence level, will fall between: 1,077 +/- 2.306 (15.80) — between €1,113 and €1,041.

Finally, a 95 per cent confidence interval for Beta can also be established. The actual value of Beta is likely to fall between:

$$10.53 +/- 2.306 (0.81) — \text{between } 12.39 \text{ and } 8.67.$$

The above shows how computer-based regression analysis greatly improves the reliability of the linear cost model, Y = A + Bx.

7.6   END OF CHAPTER QUESTIONS

Question 7.1

The accountant of a medium-sized business attends regular meetings with his management colleagues. He is very careful to ensure that any information presented is interpreted by the meeting in the context in which it is supplied.

In relation to a break-even or cost-volume profit chart he declared: "The chart is a static analysis. If we increase our activity, we can move along the chart but beware of changes in capital expenditure or product mix".

REQUIREMENT

Assuming the meeting chose to discuss this issue further, explain and develop the points being made.

Question 7.2: Astra Company

The Astra Company produces and sells a single product. Price and cost data regarding this product for the current year 20x6 is as follows:

	€	€
Sales price per unit		40.00
Variable costs per unit:		
Direct materials	4.00	
Direct labour	9.00	
Variable overhead	3.00	
Selling expenses	3.00	19.00
Contribution per unit		21.00

Fixed costs for 20x6	€
Manufacturing overheads	20,000
Administrative expenses	75,000
Selling expenses	100,000
	195,000

Current tax rate	40%

REQUIREMENT

1. Calculate the break-even point, in units, for 20x6.

2. What is the projected net income (after tax) for 20x6, assuming an annual sales volume of €450,000?

3. How many units must be sold in 20x6 to earn a profit (*after* tax) of
   €15,000?

4. For 20x7, the following changes are anticipated: (a) Selling price
   will increase by 10 per cent; (b) Variable costs will increase by 20
   per cent and (c) Fixed costs will increase by €15,000. Calculate
   break-even point for 20x7.

Question 7.3

A manufacturer is engaged in the production and marketing of four
different products. The following information is provided:

	A	B	C	D
Quantity sold (units)	5,000	4,000	6,000	3,000
Sales price (€)	30	24	35	20
Material type No. 101 (Kg)	3	2	5	1
Material type No. 102 (Kg)	4	1	3	2
Skilled labour (var) (minutes)	10	30	40	20
Unskilled labour (var) (minutes)	30	30	15	15
Variable overhead (var)	50% of TOTAL labour cost			
Selling expenses (in cents) per unit	50	25	40	30
Commission	10% of sales price	5% of sales price	50c unit	20c unit
Specific fixed costs (annual) (€)	15,000	10,000	10,000	5,000

You are informed that the following rates applied:

Material type No. 101	€1 per kg.
Material type No. 102	€2 per kg.
Skilled labour	€15 per hour
Unskilled labour	€10 per hour

REQUIREMENT

1. Calculate contribution for each product (selling price less variable
   costs).

2. Which product, if any, should be discontinued? Why?

3. What is the break-even point in units for each product.

4. What is the margin of safety for each product?

5. Calculate a summarised profit and loss account, using the formula:

Profit = Contribution per unit x quantity — fixed costs

Question 7.4: Prints Ltd.

Prints Ltd. manufactures widgets that sell for €90 each and have a variable cost structure as follows:

	€
Material	40
Labour	10
Overhead	4

Sales during the current year (20x1) were €1,350,000 and fixed overhead was €140,000.

Under a wage agreement, an increase of 10 per cent is payable to all direct workers from the beginning of the forthcoming year (20x2), while material costs are expected to increase by 7.5 per cent, variable overhead costs by 5 per cent and fixed overheads by 3 per cent.

REQUIREMENT

1. Calculate the profit for the current year (20x1).

2. Calculate the break-even point (BEP) for the current year (20x1).

3. Calculate the margin of safety (MOS) for the current year (20x1).

4. Calculate the target volume (units) to be sold during the current year (20x1) to generate a profit of €30,000.

5. Calculate the current year's (20x1) C/S ratio

6. Calculate the break-even point next year (20x2) (incorporating cost increases) but assuming the selling price per unit remains at €90.

7. Calculate the quantity to be sold during the forthcoming year (20x2) to yield the same amount of profit as the current year, assuming the selling price is to remain at €90.

8. Calculate the new selling price (20x2) if the current contribution ratio is to be maintained.

Question 7.5: TV Company

The Managing Director of TV Company produces the following data based on the current year (20x1):

	€	€
Existing selling price (per unit)		80
Variable costs: Materials	30	
Labour	12	
Overhead	6	48
Contribution		32

	UNITS	€
Total capacity	5000	
Actual sales	2500	
Fixed costs		60,000

During the next year (20x2) materials, labour and overhead are expected to increase by 5 per cent, 10 per cent and 15 per cent respectively. Fixed costs will increase by €6,000.

REQUIREMENT

1. Calculate the profit earned during the current year (20x1).

2. Calculate the break-even point for the current year (20x1).

3. Identify the margin of safety for the current year (20x1).

4. Calculate break-even point for the forthcoming year (20x2), assuming that selling price remains unchanged at €80.

5. Calculate the level of activity next year (20x2) to earn the same profit as last year (20x1), assuming the selling price remains at €80.

6. Calculate the revised selling price for 20x2 if the current (20x1) contribution/sales (C/S) ratio is to be maintained.

7. For next year, management are evaluating three alternatives:

    (i) Increase sales price by €10 per unit, which would result in sales volume equivalent to 40 per cent capacity;

    (ii) Reduce sales price by €5 per unit, which would increase last year's sales by 500 units;

    (iii) Increase advertising (fixed costs) by €15,000, which would result in sales volume equivalent to 70 per cent capacity, assuming selling price remains unchanged at €80.

    Which alternative would you recommend? Why?

Question 7.6: CVP Company

CVP Company has experienced a steady growth in sales for the past five years. However, increased competition has led the Managing Director to believe that an aggressive advertising campaign will be necessary next year to maintain the company's present growth. To prepare for next year's advertising campaign, the company's accountant has prepared and presented the following data for 20x2:

Variable costs per unit:	**€**
Direct labour	8.00
Direct materials	3.25
Variable overhead	2.50
Total variable costs	13.75

Fixed costs:	**€**
Manufacturing	25,000
Selling	40,000
Administrative	70,000
Total fixed costs	135,000

Selling price, per unit	€25.00
Expected sales, 20x2 (20,000 units)	€500,000
Tax rate	40%

The sales target for 20x3 is €550,000 (or 22,000 units).

REQUIREMENT

1. What is the after-tax net profit for 20x2?

2. What is the break-even point in units for 20x2?

3. An additional selling expense of €11,250 for advertising in 20x3, with all other cost relationships remaining constant, will be necessary to attain the sales target. What will be the after-tax net profit for 20x3 if the additional €11,250 is spent?

4. What will be the break-even point in units for 20x3, if the additional €11,250 is spent for advertising?

5. If the additional €11,250 is spent for advertising in 20x3, what is the required sales level to equal the 20x2s after-tax net profit?

6. At a sales level of 22,000 units, what is the maximum amount that can be spent on advertising if an after-tax net profit of €60,000 is desired?

Question 7.7: Abbey's

Abbey's is a small family-owned fish and chip shop. During its most recent financial year, Abbey's made a profit of €26,300 as detailed below:

	€	€
Sales:		
Fried fish	40,000	
Chips	50,000	
Confectionery	10,000	100,000
Less: Expenses:		
Fish	28,000	
Potatoes	9,000	
Confectionery	8,000	
Frying oil	8,100	
Depreciation	5,000	
Wages	6,600	
Light and heat	9,000	73,700
Net profit		26,300

The following costs are considered *fixed*:

1. Depreciation, which is based on a straight line method.

2. Wages and a standing charge of €6,000 in respect of light and heat.

REQUIREMENT

1. Prepare a product profitability report based on the contribution format, clearly distinguishing between fixed and variable costs. Costs should be apportioned on the basis of sales revenue. Should sales of confectionery be discontinued? Why or why not?

2. Evaluate the following proposal: Close down the Confectionery line assuming that half of its sales would be transferred to Chips.

3. What is the additional profit if unit sales of Fish increase by 10 per cent?

4. What is the break-even point for the shop? Specify your assumptions.

Question 7.8: Newback Company

The Newback Company manufactures and sells three products. All products are sold and serviced by a single sales force; none has its own product manager or marketing staff. The company's manufacturing facilities are also general-purpose facilities, and all products require operations in every department of the factory. The company has products, for which you have the following data (all € figures are averages per unit):

	A	B	C
Annual sales (units)	200,000	1,000,000	500,000
	€	€	€
Variable costs	1.47	0.87	2.93
Fixed costs per unit	0.84	0 46	0.05
Sales price per unit	2.50	1.50	3.95

None of the fixed costs are traceable to a specific product. They have been apportioned to each product on the basis of annual sales units.

REQUIREMENT

1. Calculate the break-even volume for each product, in € gross sales, reflecting the fixed costs the company plans to assign to that product.

2. Calculate the break-even volume for the company as a whole, in € gross sales, at the present product mix. Why does this differ from the sum of the break-even volumes you calculated in answer to 1?

3. Prepare a forecast of the company's profit (loss) if the company's selling efforts produce the following product sales instead of those shown in the earlier table, all other factors remaining unchanged:

PRODUCT	UNIT SALES
A	250,000
B	800,000
C	600,000

Question 7.9: PEB Hotel

The PEB Hotel projects the following revenues and expenses for the forthcoming year:

		€
Sales:		
Rooms		10,000,000
Restaurant		18,000,000
Bar		22,000,000
		50,000,000
Expenses: Cost of sales:		
Food		10,000,000
Bar		13,000,000
		23,000,000
Fixed expenses		
Rooms		6,000,000
Restaurant		3,000,000
Bar		7,000,000
General fixed costs		8,000,000
		24,000,000
Projected net profit		3,000,000

You are informed that the hotel has 145 rooms available per day, 365 days per year. During the coming year, the anticipated room occupancy is 70 per cent.

REQUIREMENT

Using different methods, calculate the break-even point for the year. State the assumptions and the approach that you have used.

Question 7.10

A business that operates repair and maintenance services is examining a proposal to offer services for maintaining office equipment. Costs of operating the service have been broken down into three headings as shown below:

1. Fixed costs (administration).

2. Variable cost per visit (labour and fuel costs of average time taken to reach customers).

3. Variable cost per hour of service visit (labour costs while on customer's premises).

Estimates of the above are €20,000 fixed costs per month, €25 per visit and €12 per hour respectively. It is also expected that the average duration of a visit would be 20 minutes and that 800 service visits per month would be made.

REQUIREMENT

1. Calculate the price that would have to be charged for each visit if the management required a profit of €12,000 per month to be earned.

2. Prepare a chart which the management could use to see the impact on total profits of visit duration ranging between 20 and 100 minutes on the assumption of a charge of €50 per visit and 800 service visits per month. Indicate on the chart the maximum visit time to ensure that the scheme will still be profitable

3. Briefly identify any conclusions that may be drawn from your calculations, especially in relation to pricing policy.

(The Association of Chartered Certified Accountants)

Question 7.11: MOLE Company

The MOLE Company has produced the following information in relation to the budgeted results for the forthcoming year (20x1) when one product type is produced and sold:

	20x1	
Budget		
Units sold	45,000	
	€	%
Sales revenue	6,975,000	
Material costs	1,980,000	(100%)
Labour costs	1,000,000	(90%)
Production overhead	900,000	(N/A)
Administration	3,000,000	(0%)
Net profit	95,000	

The initial task for management in finalising plans for next year is to estimate cost-volume relationships. The bracketed figures beside the above costs indicate the percentage variability with respect to volume. However, no information is available in relation to production overhead. You are informed that overhead for last year (20x0) amounted to €850,000, based on an output of 40,000 units.

The planned level of production for 20x1 represents 90 per cent of practical operating capacity. Management is concerned about the low level of profitability. There is currently a request (not incorporated in the above figures) for a special order to produce 4,000 units at a price of €120 per unit. The product specifications for this special order allows the variable unit cost for this special product to be 10 per cent below the normal product cost. The marketing manager is not happy to accept this special offer since it involves lowering the normal selling price for this special customer.

As an alternative, the marketing manger has proposed that the selling price on the main product be reduced by 10 per cent, which would increase demand by 15 per cent. Fixed costs are expected to remain unchanged.

REQUIREMENT

1. Using the high-low and accounts classification methods of classifying fixed/variable costs, determine the normal variable cost per unit and the annual amount of fixed costs.

2. Indicate the impact on profitability if the special order is accepted.

3. Indicate the impact on profitability if the selling price on the existing product is reduced by 10 per cent stimulating a 15 per cent increase in demand.

4. Which alternative would you recommend? Why, and what non-quantifiable factors are relevant to your decision?

Question 7.12: Downtown Supermarket Co.

The profit and loss account of the Downtown Supermarket Co. for the year 20x1 is expected to be as follows:

	€	%
Sales (at €1 each)	400,000	
Cost of goods sold	260,000	100
Gross profit	140,000	
Less:		
General expenses	29,400	25
Cleaning	2,400	10
Packing	4,600	100
Delivery	4,000	75
Depreciation	2,000	nil
Salaries and wages	10,000	nil
Rent, heating etc.	13,200	nil
Net profit	74,400	

REQUIREMENT

For the coming year, market research suggests:

1. A reduction of 5 per cent in sales price will result in a 20 per cent increase in sales volume.

2. A reduction in the general level of prices of 8 per cent will result in an increase in sales volume of 50 per cent, provided that an additional €20,000 is spent on advertising.

You are required to prepare a statement showing the separate results of both the above alternatives 1. and 2.

The percentages above indicate the proportion of variable costs.

Question 7.13

The following data relates to production overheads for a recent accounting period:

	INDIRECT LABOUR €	POWER €	MAIN-TENANCE €	TOTAL MACHINE HOURS
January	347	677	1673	30
February	521	998	1876	63
March	398	985	1876	52
April	355	961	1564	38
May	245	821	1597	54

REQUIREMENT

Prepare a prediction model for each cost element, using the high-low method and assuming machine hours represents the explanatory variable.

Question 7.14: S.R. Ltd.

The directors of S.R. Ltd. have provided you with the following data in relation to total output (units) and factory overhead for the previous 12-month period.

MONTH NO.	OUTPUT UNITS	FACTORY OVERHEADS
1	4,500	9,000
2	3,500	8,000
3	4,000	9,000
4	3,000	8,000
5	3,500	9,000
6	4,500	10,000
7	4,000	9,000
8	4,000	9,000
9	3,000	8,000
10	5,000	9,000
11	5,000	10,000
12	2,000	8,000
	46,000	106,000

The following data was produced by a standard regression analysis programme:

Constant	6,340
S.E. of the estimate	442.8
R^2 (coefficient of determination)	0.65
S.E. of the Beta coefficient	0.15
Number of observations	12
Degrees of freedom	10
Beta coefficient	0.65
t-value - 10 degrees of freedom (95 per cent)	2.228

REQUIREMENT

1. What are the estimated total overheads for 4,200 units produced in a month?

2. Calculate a 95 per cent confidence for 1.

Question 7.15: Rambo Ltd.

The directors of Rambo are anxious to establish a relationship between labour hours and overhead costs. Using linear regression, the following data was obtained, based on 12 monthly observations.

No. of observations	12
Coefficient of determination (R^2)	0.91
Coefficients of regression equation:	
Constant	39,700
Beta (independent variable)	2.15
Standard error of the estimate	2,700
Standard error of the Beta coefficient	0.21
t-statistic for a 95 per cent confidence interval	2.228
(10 degrees of freedom)	

REQUIREMENT

1. Using the results of the regression analysis, estimate the overhead costs for 22,500 direct labour hours incurred during a month.

2. Apply two tests of linearity to the above regression equation.

3. Establish a 95 per cent confidence interval for (1) above.

4. What are the annual fixed overhead costs?

8

Accounting Information in Decision-Making

8.1 QUANTITATIVE AND QUALITATIVE CONSIDERATIONS IN DECISION-MAKING

Decisions require information even though some decisions are made purely on the basis of intuition or inspiration. Sometimes "hard" information is available but is ignored by the decision-maker. However, using, judiciously, the information at hand enhances the likelihood of making a good decision. The use of information is the primary focus of this chapter. Nevertheless, all information has its limitations — for example, information on future demand always has an element of uncertainty for the simple reason that the future is always uncertain.

There are different types of information available to decision-makers. One useful distinction is between "quantifiable" and "non-quantifiable" information. The former represents information that can be expressed in numbers (cost per unit, percentage defects, capacity utilisation, etc); non-quantifiable (or qualitative) information cannot be expressed in numbers and concerns such items as the state of staff morale and the image of a company. Although non-quantifiable, these factors are often highly relevant and important in decision-making. Decisions should not be taken solely on the basis of accounting numbers, because relevant accounting numbers may suffer from a degree of uncertainty and rarely take all the considerations into account. Failure to include all considerations may be attributable to genuine error; however, in many cases, some considerations cannot be adequately expressed in accounting numbers — for example, the impact on staff co-operation if a loss-making canteen is closed down in the factory.

Providing Cost Information

The role of the accountant in the decision-making process is to provide relevant *cost* information that must be constructed or revised to fit the specific problem. The focus of this chapter is on relevant costs in decision-making. In addition, the management accountant is responsible for providing information on revenue and a range of other performance measures.

8.2 RELEVANT COSTS IN DECISION-MAKING

In situations of choice, three categories of cost can usually be identified:

1. Historic and sunk costs.

2. Incremental cash costs.

3. Opportunity costs.

Historic and Sunk Costs

By definition, decisions affect future events — no event that has been completed can be altered by a subsequent decision. In the case of management decisions, decisions may affect either only a single event or all events subsequent to the decision.

During the initial stages of development of cost accounting, historical costing was the only method available for ascertaining and presenting cost data to management. Historical costs are post-mortem costs and, because they are ascertained after they have been incurred, they are *irrelevant* for decision-making. In many cases, they even fail to provide reliable guides for future performance, since it is not likely that conditions prevailing in one period will repeat themselves in another period. Changes in labour rates, material prices and other costs incurred in obtaining outside services may make historical costs relating to these resources irrelevant.

Nevertheless, historical cost data *can* play a role in decision-making. When past conditions are not expected to change significantly, historical costs are useful for predicting future costs. For example, if the product specification has not changed although the prices of raw materials have changed, the quantity used in the past is relevant in determining the raw material cost of product. In other words, although historical data may often be used as a guide to prediction, it is never relevant *per se* to the decision itself. Only the expected future data that is different is truly relevant.

Very similar to the concept of a historic cost is that of a *sunk* cost. Sunk costs are historical costs that cannot be changed, no matter what future action is taken. Costs that have already been incurred on design works are sunk or committed costs for purposes of considering whether to go ahead with the manufacture of a component — they cannot be changed by any decision that will be made in the future. Investments in plant and equipment or materials purchased are other good examples. In many instances, sunk costs will also be fixed costs and therefore *irrelevant* for decision-making. However, some fixed costs are relevant in decision-making when they are expected to be altered in the future, by the decision at hand.

Incremental Cash Costs

These are the portions of a total cost that involve cash payments and thus, they approximate *variable* or *marginal* costs. A useful definition of an incremental cost is a cash outlay that results from choosing one alternative instead of another. These out-of-pocket costs are relevant in decision-making because they are either incurred or avoidable and will have a significant effect on the decision.

Incremental cash costs and sunk costs are opposites. An incremental cash cost is a cash outlay either immediately or in the near future arising from a particular decision. Conversely, a sunk cost is a prior investment of cash resources of the company.

We shall see that there are *two* situations that require financial evaluation. It is important to recognise the difference in these situations since the financial evaluation techniques applied will differ.

The first situation is deciding between alternatives — to select option A or option B. A decision *between alternatives* should be made on the basis of *incremental cash inflows* and *incremental cash outflows*. (The illustration below ignores non-financial considerations and the time value of money.)

ILLUSTRATION

An oil company has paid a foreign government €15 million for the rights to explore for oil. If oil is found, the agreement calls for the Oil Company to pay the government €24 for every barrel produced.

The company has spent €9 million on the drilling operation and has just struck oil. Management estimates that it will be able to recover 10 million barrels of oil from the field. The oil can be sold for €30 a barrel and it will cost €3 a barrel to get it out of the ground.

However, the government has just imposed an additional fee of €2 a barrel, to pay for insurance against damages caused by oil spills that might take place in the future.

Should the company begin producing oil? Prepare a cost/revenue analysis to support your recommendation.

SOLUTION

Based on the accounting data alone, the decision to produce the oil should be taken only if the incremental cash inflows exceed the incremental cash outflows.

	€m
Incremental cash inflows	
Income (10 million barrels @ €30 each)	300
Incremental cash outflows	
Royalty to Government (10 million barrels @ €24)	240
Production costs (10 million barrels @ €3)	30
Insurance levy (10 million @ €2)	20
	290
Overall cash surplus	10

The €24 million already spent on exploration rights and drilling costs is irrelevant to the production decision. It represents sunk costs Based on the figures, production of oil should proceed.

This illustration shows the distinction between a good decision and a good outcome. The former consists of accumulating all the available information and using it in the decision context. However, a good decision can never be protected from the element of bad luck or uncertainty. Thus, if the Government had not recently imposed an insurance levy, the original decision might have been a good decision indeed. As things stand, the venture is set to lose a total of €114m, which includes sunk costs,

The Role of Opportunity Costs

The second situation that occurs in decision-making is that of evaluating a particular alternative, rather than choosing between alternatives. In other words, option A may be preferable to option B (based on incremental cash inflows compared with incremental cash outflows). However, what are the financial implications of selecting option B — that is, what are the financial implications of changing one's mind? In this second situation (evaluating one particular alternative), consider the opportunity cost involved. A useful definition of an opportunity cost is the cash benefit sacrificed in favour of an alternative course of action.

The relevant costs are the incremental cash costs (as before) plus any additional opportunity cost. In accounting terms, a particular alternative will not make sense unless the incremental revenues exceed the relevant costs, which represent the incremental cash costs plus opportunity cost.

Opportunity cost is always relevant *in evaluating the financial consequences* of an alternative. However, in most cases, it does not involve an immediate cash outlay and, thus, is subtler to identify and quantify in financial terms. It is important to stress that opportunity cost is not used in deciding *between* alternatives. Its relevance is in evaluating the financial consequences of a particular alternative.

ILLUSTRATION

Assume a company had to choose between only two alternatives — to continue with existing work or to undertake a special contract. The alternatives are mutually exclusive and the relevant cash flows are as follows:

	EXISTING WORK	SPECIAL CONTRACT
Incremental cash inflows	15,000	30,000
Less: Cash outflows	8,000	28,000
Cash surplus	7,000	2,000

The above decision is taken purely on the basis of net cash inflows (ignoring non-quantifiable factors). This results in the decision to continue with existing work. The offer of the special contract is rejected on financial grounds, using the information currently available. However, another way to look at the above situation is to ask the question "What is the minimum price (i.e. cash inflows) for the special contract to make it as attractive as the existing work? The answer is that the special contract will have to generate gross cash inflows of €35,000 to cover the incremental cash costs PLUS the opportunity cost involved. The opportunity cost is the cash contribution that would have been generated by opting for another alternative.

The incremental cash outflows amount to €28,000 in addition to the cash surplus foregone: €7,000 represented by the expected surplus from existing work that will be forfeited. The minimum revenue (gross cash inflow) required from the special contract is €35,000.

8.3   INTRODUCTION TO THE LEARNING CURVE

One of the fundamental assumptions underlying CVP analysis is a constant unit variable cost for a relevant range of activity. This implies, for example, that as output expands, direct workers will take the same time to produce each unit. In other words, the implicit assumption behind CVP analysis is that there is no learning curve. However, in some production processes, the average time taken to produce extra units will decline relative to the previous average time. Very simply, the more an activity is practised, the more operators become proficient at performing that activity. The learning curve theory is most applicable when (a) a high degree of manual skilled labour is required and (b) there is opportunity for repetition of the process. The learning curve allows costs to be predicted and is therefore extremely useful in standard costing and decision-making and control.

The fundamental principle of the learning curve can be described as follows: As the cumulative quantity of output doubles, the average time per unit will fall to a fixed percentage of the previous average time. It should be stressed that the learning curve may not apply to situations where quality is of utmost importance.

ILLUSTRATION

It is anticipated that an 80% learning curve applies to a specific assembly project. The first unit requires 100 hours to produce. Find the time required to produce 5 units.

NUMBER OF UNITS	AVERAGE TIME PER UNIT (MINS)	CUMULATIVE (TOTAL) TIME
1	100	100 for 1 unit
2	80	160 for 2 units
4	64	256 for 4 units
8	51.2	409 for 8 units

There are two ways by which to ascertain the average time per unit, given a specified, cumulative output. The first method is to prepare a table similar to the above and make a reasonable estimate of the average time involved. The above indicates that the average time for 4 units is 64 hours, which falls to 51.2 hours when cumulative output is doubled to 8 units. Accordingly, a reasonable estimate for 5 units is 60 hours, giving a total time for 5 units of 300 hours. (A graph would also provide a reasonable estimate).

The second method of calculating the average time is more precise and makes use of log tables. (The following discussion uses logs to the base 10). This method is to use a formula for the learning curve, based on an exponential expression:

$$Y = ax^b$$

Where: Y = average time per unit (or average cost per unit)
  a = number of hours (or cost) that the first unit requires
  x = cumulative number of units
  b = the index of learning, which represents a rate of increase productivity defined as:

$$b = \frac{\text{Log of learning curve}}{\text{Log 2}}$$

It is possible to convert the above exponential expression to a linear form using logs. Thus:

$$\text{Log } Y = \text{Log } A + b \times \text{Log } X$$

where   b =   Log 0.8 (80% curve)   = 0.322
                  Log 2 (Doubling effect)

Thus the average time to produce 5 units is as follows (using log table to the base 10) although natural logs could also be used:

$$\text{Log } Y \qquad = \text{Log } 100 + \frac{\text{Log } 0.8}{\text{Log } 2} \ (\text{Log } 5) = 1.775$$

$$Y = 59.57 \text{ hours}$$

Time required to produce 5 units = 5 x 59.57 = 297.85 hours

Learning Curve Applications

The learning curve generally applies to those situations where the labour input for an activity is large and where the activity is complex. Conditions conducive to the learning curve are to be found in the electronics, construction and shipbuilding areas, but industries that are capital-intensive may find the learning curve to be of little value.

Learning curves are not theoretical abstractions but are based on observations of past events. When new products have been made in previous periods, learning curve principles can be applied from the experience, which has been gained. In new situations where there is no historical data, the curves for previous products or processes with known improvement factors can be used if management can identify similarities with the new situation. Unfortunately, the true nature of the learning curve, which is associated with the new product or process, will never be known. However, a reasonable assumption of its shape is better than any assumption of no learning curve at all. The learning curve may be applied to the following situations:

1. Pricing decisions: The main impact of the learning curve is likely to be in providing better cost predictions to enable price quotations to be prepared for potential orders. The ability to forecast cost reductions and consequent selling price reductions may make the difference between landing and losing profitable orders. Indeed, a company could reduce its selling price (through the learning curve effect), which would further increase its volume and market share and eventually force some competitors out of the industry.

2. Work scheduling: Learning curves enable businesses to predict the required inputs more effectively, enabling them to produce more accurate delivery schedules. This in turn can lead to improved cus-

tomer relationships and, possibly, increased future sales. More accurate production scheduling should also reduce idle time.

3. Standard setting: If budgets and standards are set without considering the learning effect, meaningless variances are likely to occur. This is because budgets are established assuming constant efficiency whereas actual performance may capture efficiencies due to the learning curve. Significant favourable cost variances are likely to be reported simply because the original budgets were incorrect.

8.4   DECISION-MAKING WITH SCARCE RESOURCES

Another assumption implied by the CVP model is that there are no scarce resources. In the context of management accounting, these scarce resources are referred to as limiting factors. Limiting factors represent resource or input constraints that restrict the ability of the business to produce goods or services. Typical limiting factors are:

1. Shortage or raw materials.

2. Shortage of machine hours.

3. Shortage of labour.

Faced with limiting factors, managers must ration production capacity since they do not have the resources to satisfy demand. The basic CVP model can be adapted to decision situations involving scarce resources. The most important assumption to make in this type of decision-making situation is that of "profit maximisation". This will lead to the development of an optimal solution — a product mix that will generate an amount of profit that cannot be surpassed by any other combination of products. Thus, the focus will be on deriving an optimal plan, an optimal production mix or an optimal product mix.

There are a number of different techniques that can be used in the context of limiting factors. Exhibit 8.1 below suggests the appropriate technique, given the number of products that the company is producing and the number of limiting factors. Basically there are three techniques: Contribution per limiting factor, the graphic approach and linear programming. The first two techniques will be discussed below. The third technique (linear programming) deals with the most complicated situations. It involves describing and solving the problem in mathematical terms and is beyond the scope of this book. However, user-friendly computer software allows this technique to be applied easily to many situations.

Exhibit 8.1: Decision-Making with Scarce Resources

No. of limiting factors	Number of products	
	Two Only	*More Than Two*
Single	Contribution per limiting factor	Contribution per limiting factor
Two or more	Graphic Approach	Linear Programming

Contribution per Limiting Factor

In making capacity rationing decisions, management should always apply the general rule of ranking the products according to their "contribution per limiting factor". If this is done, the selected mix of products chosen will maximise profits. This means that no other product mix can provide a greater amount of profit. A four-step process can apply the general rule of maximising the contribution per limiting factor as follows:

1. Identify the contribution per unit. The contribution per unit is the unit sales price less the unit variable cost. In calculating contribution per unit, always exclude any fixed costs that may be provided in a total cost analysis.

2. Calculate the amount of scarce resource a unit of each product or service requires. The amount of scarce resource can be stated either in physical terms (machine hours) or in monetary terms (cost of raw materials required per product).

3. Calculate the contribution per limiting factor for each unit or service — by dividing contribution per unit by the amount of scarce resource required.

4. Rank the products (or services) in descending order of contribution per limiting factor. This ranking then forms the basis of selecting products to be produced by starting from the top of the list, working downwards until all capacity has been utilised.

ILLUSTRATION

The directors of Beetlenut are preparing a production schedule for the forthcoming quarter. Data relating to the four products produced are as follows:

	A	B	C	D
Selling price	20	40	30	25
Direct material	8	20	15	10
Direct labour	3	6	3	4
Fixed overhead	2	2	2	2
Profit	7	12	10	9

However, suppliers of raw materials have indicated to the company that they will be unable to deliver more than €80,000 worth of raw materials per quarter until conditions improve. Management accepts that this shortage of vital raw material will result in curtailment of production and sales. However, with a view to keeping the company's products in the minds of the public, they wish to produce a minimum of 1,000 units of each product during the forthcoming quarter. Any remaining materials should be used in the most profitable manner subject to maximum sales units of each product per quarter, as follows:

	Units
A	3,000
B	1,400
C	1,600
D	2,000

REQUIREMENT

Prepare a statement showing the quantities of each product that the company should produce in the forthcoming quarter, and show the forecast contribution for the period.

ANALYSIS AND SOLUTION

The first step in the process is to compute the contribution per unit. This is fairly evident from the above cost data per unit (above), provided care is taken to exclude the fixed cost per unit and one makes the assumption that direct labour is a variable cost. The unit contributions are €9, €14, €12 and €11 for products A, B, C, and D respectively as follows:

	A	B	C	D
Contribution per unit	€	€	€	€
Sales price	20	40	30	25
Variable costs	(11)	(26)	(18)	(14)
Unit contribution	9	14	12	11

The next step is to identify the input of scarce resource for each product and compute the contribution per limiting factor. Since raw materials are in scarce supply, management will want to produce the maximum contribution per input of raw material. The products will then be ranked according to their contribution per limiting factor. This is done as follows:

	A	B	C	D
Contribution per limiting factor	€	€	€	€
Unit contribution	9	14	12	11
Input (Limiting factor)	8	20	15	10
Contribution per limiting factor (ratio)	1.12	0.70	0.80	1.10

The final step in the decision process is to rank the products on the basis of contribution per limiting factor. The above calculation indicates that a unit of product A requires an input of €8 of raw materials and generates a contribution of €9; a unit of product B requires €20 input of raw materials and yields €14 in contribution; a unit of product C requires €15 input of raw materials and yields €12 in contribution margin; finally, product D requires a raw material input of €10 and provides a unit contribution of €11.

Thus, even though a unit of product B yields the highest contribution per unit, it is the least profitable product in terms of contribution per input of raw material. If sales of the other products do not depend on the sales of product B, and there are no operational problems involved in varying the production mix of the four products, the production of product B should be kept to a minimum. This is particularly appropriate since Beetlenut cannot meet the demand for all products because of limited supply of raw materials.

Contribution per limiting factor is used to assign production capacity to the four products. Product A makes the greatest use of the scarce raw materials, then product D, followed by product C, and finally product B. However, in assigning capacity to production, a minimum of 1,000 of each product is to be produced. This minimum production quota will require €53,000 of raw materials, leaving a balance of €27,000 to be used in the most profitable manner.

	Minimum Units	Material per unit	Total Materials
	€	€	€
A	1,000	8	8,000
B	1,000	20	20,000
C	1,000	15	15,000
D	1,000	10	10,000
			53,000

Balance of materials to be assigned: (€80,000 - €53,000) = €27,000.

This balance of raw materials will be used first in producing product A. However, since only 3,000 units of A can be sold (and 1,000 units are included in the minimum production quota), an additional 2,000 units of product A will be produced, which require an input of €16,000 of raw materials, as follows:

	€
Raw materials available	27,000
A: 2,000 units @ €8	16,000
Balance	11,000

The next most profitable product is D. However, a maximum of only 2,000 units can be sold. Since 1,000 units are already included in the minimum production quota, only 1,000 extra units of product D will be produced, requiring €10,000 of raw materials, as follows:

	€
Balance	11,000
D: 1,000 units @ €10	10,000
Balance	1,000

The remaining €1,000 of raw materials will be assigned to product C, the next most profitable product. Since each unit of C requires €15 of raw materials, only 66 units (€1,000/€15) can be produced, which uses up the balance of the remaining raw materials, as follows:

	€
Balance	1,000
C: 66 units @ €15	1,000
Raw materials available	Nil

Based on the analysis above, the optimal production plan and related contribution is produced below. The schedule indicates a total contribution of €75,792. This schedule is optimal in the sense that no other combination of products will generate a greater contribution.

OPTIMAL PRODUCTION/PROFIT STATEMENT

Product	Units	Unit Contribution	Total Contribution
A	3,000	9	27,000
B	1,000	14	14,000
C	1,066	12	12,792
D	2,000	11	22,000
			75,792

NOTE: Fixed costs have been ignored since they are irrelevant for decision-making.

The Graphic Approach

Having discussed how a single limiting factor can be incorporated in the decision model, now turn to a situation where there are several limiting factors but where only two products are manufactured. In such situations, the graphic approach is used, as explained below. However, the graphic approach can only be used where there are two products since there are only two axes on a graph: The horizontal and vertical axes.

ILLUSTRATION

Lindo aims to maximise its profits. In one factory, it manufactures two liquid products called Alpha and Beta. Each is a mix of readily available ingredients that passes through three successive processes of heating, blending and cooling. Lindo's management accountant has prepared the following up-to-date cost statement for the two products, expressed in €s per gallon of final product:

	Alpha €	Beta €
Selling Price	25	30
Materials	15	17
Variable Process Costs		
Heating process	4	1
Blending process	1	5
Cooling process	2	3
Contribution Margin	3	4

Each process is costed at €1 per hour of process time per gallon. Thus, product Alpha requires 4 hours in the heating department; 1 hour in blending, etc. However, based on existing information, the amount of processing time is limited to 3,000 hours in each of the three departments. These limits cannot be removed in the short term.

REQUIREMENT
Identify Lindo's optimal production plan and related contribution.

ANALYSIS AND SOLUTION
In mathematical terms the problem can be depicted as follows:

Maximise: 3 Alpha + 4 Beta

Subject to: 4 Alpha + 1 Beta $\leq$ 3,000 heating hours
1 Alpha + 5 Beta $\leq$ 3,000 blending hours
2 Alpha + 3 Beta $\leq$ 3,000 cooling hours

Where the number of Alphas and Betas to be produced is unknown but can be ascertained using the graphic approach. The graphic solution involves assigning one product (Alpha) to the vertical axis of the graph and the other product (Beta) to the horizontal axis.

There are three limiting factors, namely, processing hours in each of the heating, blending and cooling departments. Starting with the heating department, Lindo could produce either 750 units of Alpha (3,000/4) or 3,000 units of Beta (3,000/1). Alternatively, Lindo could produce any mix of products along a straight line starting with 750 units of Alpha and joining with 3,000 units of Beta. Secondly, the blending department is limited to 3,000 processing hours, Lindo could use all these hours to produce 3,000 units of Alpha (3,000/1) or 600 units of Beta (3,000/5). Alternatively, Lindo could produce any mix of products along a straight line starting with 3,000 units of Alpha and joining with 600 units of Beta. The same procedure applies to the cooling department with has only 3,000 processing hours available. Lindo could produce 1,500 units of Alpha (3,000/2) or 1,000 units of Beta (3,000/3). Alternatively, it could produce any mix of products along a straight line joining 1,500 units of Alpha with 1,000 units of Beta. The resulting graph appears below in Figure 8.2.

Figure 8.2: Graphic Solution

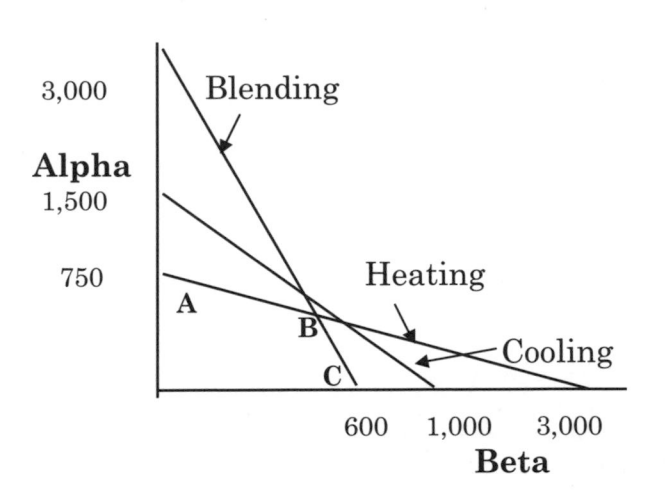

When all the constraints and limiting factors are plotted on the graph, the next stage is to identify the feasible region. This is the area within which the optimal solution must be found. This is because the feasible region satisfies simultaneously all the constraints imposed on the company.

Where a company intends to maximise its profits, the optimal solution will always be a corner point of the feasible region. This statement can be proved mathematically but it is not necessary here. In a minority of situations, it is possible that two corner points could provide the identical contribution and therefore, both would represent the optimal solution.

Perhaps the easiest way to identify the optimal solution is to calculate the number of units to be produced at each corner point and compute the related contribution. For example, with Lindo there are 3 corner points labelled A, B and C respectively. The units and contribution are as follows:

IDENTIFICATION OF OPTIMAL SOLUTION

	Point A		Point B		Point C	
A @ €3	750 =	2,250	632 =	1,896	Nil =	Nil
B @ €4	Nil =	Nil	473 =	1,892	600 =	2,400
		2250		3,788		2,400

It can be seen from the above that above that point B represents the optimal solution, since this generates a contribution of €3,778, which is higher than the contribution generated, by either point A or point C. In the context of management accounting we say that the value of the objective function is €3,778. The optimal production mix consists of 632 units of Alpha and 473 units of Beta.

In order to identify the precise quantities of Alpha and Beta at point B it is necessary to use simultaneous equations. At point B, two limiting factors exist, namely the heating and blending hours. These can be explained mathematically as follows:

   (i)   4 Alpha + 1 Beta ≤ 3,000

   (ii)   1 Alpha + 5 Beta ≤ 3,000

Equation (ii) can be rearranged by multiplying both sides of the equation by 4 as follows:

   (ii)   4 Alpha + 20 Beta ≤ 12,000

Therefore, equations (i) and (ii) can be manipulated as follows:

   (i)   4 Alpha + 1 Beta ≤ 3,000

   (ii)   4 Alpha + 20 Beta ≤ 12,000

By subtracting equation (i) from equation (ii) we obtain:

   19 Beta = 9,000

   1 Beta = 473 units

The value of Alpha can be determined by substituting 473 for Beta into either equation (i) or equation (ii) as follows:

   4 Alpha + 1 (473) = 3,000

   1 Alpha = 632 units

8.5   DECISION-MAKING UNDER CONDITIONS OF UNCERTAINTY

If this were a world of certainty, the decision-maker would know exactly what event was going to occur and would therefore select the alternative that provided the highest pay-off. This would represent decision-making by computation.

In a world of uncertainty, the decision-maker does not know which future event will occur. For example, demand could be for 100,000 or 200,000 units. Uncertainty can be defined as the possibility that a forecast amount will deviate from an actual amount. Uncertainty is inevitable because managerial decision-making is future-oriented.

It is useful to distinguish between several elements in an uncertain situation:

1. There will always be a number of alternatives available to the decision-maker. If there were no alternatives, there would be no de-

cision to make. One of these alternatives must be selected by the decision-maker.

2. There is likely to be a set of relevant events that can affect the ultimate outcome. In management accounting, these outcomes are referred to as "states of nature" and are usually outside the direct control of the decision-maker. Thus, the decision-maker has no choice over which state of nature will occur, in contrast to alternatives, which he can select. Examples of states of nature include sales demand, policy of competitors and Government action. The states of nature are assumed to be mutually exclusive. This means that no two events can happen simultaneously. For example, the result of a football match can be win, lose or draw. In addition, it is assumed that the list of states of nature is exhaustive — that only the events listed can happen.

3. There may be probabilities assigned to each state of nature. Strictly speaking, if probabilities are available, the decision situation is referred to as "uncertainty". Alternatively, if probabilities are not available, the situation is referred to as one of "risk". There is little benefit in distinguishing between risk and uncertainty and both situations are usually covered by the term uncertainty. Indeed, in many cases, the terms are used interchangeably.

4. Based on each alternative and states of nature, the decision-maker can construct a pay-off matrix or table. This represents the monetary value of each unique combination of managerial actions and particular states of nature. Thus, the action chosen and the state of nature determine the amount of the pay-off. The completed pay-off matrix represents the total range of experiences that can face the decision-maker.

The alternative selected by the decision-maker will depend on the attitude to risk. It is usual to distinguish between four fundamentally different attitudes to risk and therefore to three different decision criteria as follows:

1. Maximin: This is the most conservative approach to decision-making. In this case, the objective of the decision-maker is to maximise the minimum pay-off. It involves two stages:

   (a) Identify the worst or minimum pay-off associated with each alternative.

   (b) Select the best of these alternatives.

This approach avoids the best and worst pay-offs regardless of their probabilities. It is important to note that the maximin criterion does not make use of underlying probabilities.

2. Maximax: This is the most optimistic approach to decision-making. The decision-maker selects the alternative that offers the greatest pay-off. Again, like the maximin criterion, the under-lying probabilities are not used.

3. Expected Monetary Value (EMV): In many situations, the decision-maker can make meaningful estimates of the probabilities or likelihood of each state of nature occurring. In relation to these probabilities, a few points are worth stressing:

   (a) Probabilities only relate to states of nature and their probability (likelihood) of happening.

   (b) The sum of the probabilities of all the states of nature must equal 1, implying certainty that one of the states of nature will occur.

   (c) Each state of nature will be assigned a probability of between 0 and 1. A value close to 1 indicates that there is a good chance that an event will occur with a value near to zero indicating only a small likelihood.

4. The Least Regret criterion will be explained below.

The EMV of each alternative represents the weighted average pay-off for each alternative where the weights are the probabilities of each state of nature.

ILLUSTRATION

Bective Ltd. produces hamburgers. The directors are presently considering whether to produce hamburgers for the forthcoming Rugby International. Unfortunately, due to the location of the ground, the hamburgers must be produced prior to match day, and hamburgers unsold at the end of match day must be disposed of to charity. Each hamburger will sell for €1.00, and the variable cost is estimated at 45c per unit.

The Sales Manager is uncertain how many units can be sold at the forthcoming match, but is willing to place probabilities on his estimates as follows:

Estimated Unit Sales	Probability
10,000	0.1
20,000	0.4
30,000	0.3
40,000	0.2

REQUIREMENT

1. Prepare a payoff matrix to represent the four possible production strategies using variable costs and revenues.

2. What strategy should be selected using the following criteria?
   (a) Maximin.
   (b) Maximax.
   (c) Expected monetary value (EMV)
   (d) Least regret (opportunity cost)

ANALYSIS

The payoff matrix represents the monetary payoff associated with each possible alternative and each possible state of nature. There are four alternatives and four states of nature providing 16 different possible outcomes. They are presented in the following payoff matrix:

PAY-OFF MATRIX

<—STATES OF NATURE (DEMAND)—>

Production Units	10,000 units 0.1	20,000 units 0.4	30,000 units 0.3	40,000 units 0.2	EMV
10,000 units	5,500	5,500	5,500	5,500	5,500
20,000 units	1,000	11,000	11,000	11,000	10,000
30,000 units	(3,500)	6,500	16,500	16,500	10,500
40,000 units	(8,000)	2,000	12,000	22,000	8,000

Selection criteria

1. MAXIMIN: The worst that can happen under each alternative is €5,500 for 10,000 units produced, €1,000 for the production of 20,000 units; a loss of (€3,500) for a production of 30,000 units; a (€8,000) loss for the production of 40,000 units. The alternative chosen will be the production of 10,000 units.

2. MAXIMAX: The best that can happen under each alternative is a contribution of €5,500 for the production of 10,000 units increasing to a contribution of €22,000 for the production (and sale) of 40,000 units. The alternative selected is to produce 40,000 units.

3. EMV: This represents the weighted average payoff of each alternative. For the production of 10,000 units a payoff of €5,500 is guaranteed. The production of 20,000 units is estimated to produce a payoff of €10,000 (i.e. €1,000 x 0.1 + €11,000 x 0.4 + €11,000 x 0.3 + €11,000 x 0.2) etc.

   Using this criterion, 30,000 units would be produced (and sold).

   It is interesting to note that the most logical alternative to many persons is alternative 2 — produce 20,000 units — which is not selected using any of the above three criteria.

4. LEAST REGRET: This criterion is used when it is important to justify your choice afterwards in the context of accountability. Thus, you adopt a position of least regret. To apply this criterion another payoff matrix must be prepared in terms of opportunity cost. Thus, if the production strategy of 10,000 units were adopted but 40,000 units were demanded, then the regret amounts to €16,500 (the difference between €5,500 and the maximum contribution that could have been earned €22,000). For each alternative (production strategy of 10,000, 20,000, 30,000 or 40,000 units) the worst or largest opportunity cost is identified. Then the alternative, which provides the smallest of those opportunity costs, is selected. In this case alternative 3 is selected (30,000 units) which represents the minimum of the maximum regrets.

PAY-OFF MATRIX (LEAST REGRET)

<-STATES OF NATURE (DEMAND)
AND PROBABILITIES->

Production Units	10,000 units 0.1	20,000 units 0.4	30,000 units 0.3	40,000 units 0.2
10,000 units	0	5,500	11,000	16,500
20,000 units	4,500	0	5,500	11,000
30,000 units	* 9,000	4,500	0	5,500
40,000 units	13,500	9,000	4,500	0

* based on the actual loss of €3,500 per previous table. However, if we knew that demand was 10,000 units, we would have produced 10,000 units providing a contribution of €5,500. Therefore, the "regret" amounts to €9,000.

Limitations of EMV

Using EMV, the alternative selected may differ depending on the probabilities of the states of nature. This places extreme importance on how estimates of probabilities should be made. Two types of probabilities can be distinguished: Objective and subjective.

Objective probabilities are probabilities that can be determined without judgement — for example, tossing a coin or rolling a dice. They can be tested and proved either by logical reasoning or physical observations. Historical data may, or may not, be a valid method of calculating such probabilities.

Subjective probabilities are those probabilities determined by judgement of experienced people. They cannot be tested in the same way as objective probabilities but are usually formed on the basis of past experience. However, subjective probabilities can be very fallible. For example, it has been observed that higher probabilities are often assigned to those states of nature, which make sense and are understood than to more ambiguous situations. Also, subjective probabilities can be distorted by memory. If the probabilities are biased, the resulting decision will be biased.

Second, EMV represents the long-run pay-off of an alternative and is therefore appropriate to decisions that can be taken many times. However, in many situations, there is not the benefit of repetition especially since one bad experience could force the company out of business.

EMV is appropriate if the decision-maker is risk-neutral. This means that the decision-maker neither likes risk nor is afraid of it. Yet many decision-makers are risk-averse, especially when an alternative requires the commitment of a high percentage of the decision-maker's resources.

Finally, we have assumed that the states of nature are discretely distributed. This means that demand, for example, will be 10,000, 20,000 units, etc. In reality, most probability distributions are continuous rather than discrete.

8.6   END OF CHAPTER QUESTIONS

QUESTION 8.1

A 50 bedroom resort hotel operates its financial year from 1 November to the following 31 October. For the purposes of managing the seasonal features of this industry it is customary to consider May to October inclusive as the summer season and November to April inclusive as the winter season. The reported profit performance for the year ended October, 20x7, in which the hotel operated at 80% capacity, is as follows:

	SUMMER €000	WINTER €000	TOTAL €000
Sales - rooms	300	100	400
Sales - other	300	100	400
Variable costs	200	100	300
Fixed costs	100	100	200
Profit/(loss)	300	Nil	300

In late October 20x7 management is a little concerned about projections for the forthcoming winter season. For example, anticipated (room) bookings for the whole winter season are showing an expected sales level of €110,000. However, room sales for the subsequent summer season are estimated at €330,000. For the forthcoming year (20x7/x8) it is anticipated that the various cost and revenue relationships (except for fixed costs) will continue as in the previous year. Fixed costs are expected to increase by 20%, with effect from the start of the financial year. The managing director of the hotel has made two suggestions to improve the above situation:

1. Close the entire operations for the winter season and transfer all room bookings to nearby establishments. On average 20% commission would be received (on a one-off basis) for this based on existing room reservations. However, only one-quarter of the fixed costs would continue to be incurred.

2. With additional sales promotion costing €30,000, room sales for the winter season would increase from the projected €110,000 to €140,000. It is anticipated that other sales would rise in proportion to this.

REQUIREMENT

1. Calculate the break-even point for the CURRENT YEAR 20x6/x7 in terms of total sales revenue. What level of occupancy does this represent? (In your calculations, you may assume that the revenue per room is constant throughout the year and that existing cost and revenue relationships will continue as in the previous year).

2. Prepare a summarised profit budget for the forthcoming year (20x7/x8), based on existing projections: ignoring the proposal to close down the hotel during the winter months. (In your calculations, you may assume that the revenue per room is constant throughout the year and that existing cost and revenue relationships will continue as in the previous year).

3. Evaluate the two proposals put forward by preparing appropriate financial projections for the next six months. Your presentation should CLEARLY highlight the incremental, financial consequences.

4. Assuming that the €30,000 spent on advertising would affect winter trade only. What are the additional (total) sales in winter necessary to cover the additional advertising costs?

5. Comment on FOUR major matters which should be considered, and why they should be considered, by the hotel management before making a final decision.

QUESTION 8.2:

The Shanghai Theatre Company operates a theatre that is used by the local repertory company, other visiting groups and exhibitions. Management decisions are taken by a committee, which meets regularly to review the financial performance of the year to date and to plan the use of the facilities for the remaining part of the year. The theatre employs a full-time administrative staff and a number of performing artists at costs of €4,800 and €17,600 per month respectively. They mount a new production every month, which runs for 20 performances. Other monthly expenditure of the theatre is as follows:

	€
Costumes (variable)	2,800
Scenery (variable)	1,650
Heat and light	5,150
Insurance	8,000
Casual staff	1,760
Refreshments (cost of purchases)	1,180

On average the theatre is half full for the performances of the repertory company. The capacity and seat prices in the theatre are:

200 seats at €6 each
500 seats at €4 each
300 seats at €3 each

In addition, the theatre sells refreshments during the performances for €3,880 per month, programme sales cover their costs but advertising in the programme generates additional revenue of €3,360.

The management committee has recently been approached by a popular touring group to take over the theatre for one month (for 25 performances). This group is prepared to pay half of their ticket income as their booking fee. They expect to fill the theatre for 10 performances and achieve two-thirds full on the remaining 15 performances. The prices charged are 50c less than those normally charged in the theatre. The Shanghai Theatre Company will continue to pay for heat and light costs, insurance and will still honour the contracts of all performing artists and pay full-time administrative employees who will sell refreshments and programmes, etc. However, they will not be responsible for the monthly payment of costumes or scenery costs. The committee does not expect any change in the level of refreshments or programme sales if they agree to this booking.

REQUIREMENTS

1. For each of the two alternatives (to continue operations or subcontract to the touring company), prepare a schedule of total costs and revenues and highlight the resulting net surplus figure. Which alternative would you recommend?

2. Identify some of the non-financial considerations that would apply to a decision of this type.

(The Association of Chartered Certified Accountants)

QUESTION 8.3

"Outsourcing" represents a firm's decision to have a product or service traditionally provided by an internal support department supplied by an outside firm. List the advantages and disadvantages of outsourcing the management accounting function.

QUESTION 8.4

You are the director of the continuing professional education (CPE) division of a well-known business school. The business school offers a range of graduate programmes including MBA. The CPE courses for executives are especially popular, and you have developed an extensive menu of one-day and two-day courses that are presented in various locations throughout the country. The actual financial performance of these courses for the current fiscal year, which is almost ended, is:

	€
Tuition revenue	2,000,000
Direct costs of courses	800,000
General administrative expenses	300,000
Operating profit	900,000

The direct costs of the courses include fees for lecturers, rentals of classrooms, and advertising and other items, such as travel, that can be easily and exclusively identified as being caused by a particular course. The general administrative expenses represent administration salaries, institutional advertising and a share of university overhead.

The enrolment for your final (half-day) course of the year for executives in the manufacturing sector is 40 students, who have paid €200 each. The costs of this course represent €20 for lunches, €40 for copying of course materials and €2,100 for lecturer's fees. Four days before the course is to begin (in late November), you receive a telephone call from the Training Manager of the Department of Social Welfare. He enquires whether course discounts are available to participants from the public sector. During the course of the conversation, he indicates that he would like to select 10 participants from his Department for your course for a total fee of €1,000. You promise to consider his offer and respond quickly. The extra cost of including these ten participants would entail lunches at €20 each and course material at €40 each.

REQUIREMENTS

1. The *Mission Statement* of the CPE Division states that: "The mission of the School is to exercise leadership in business education in the country by aiming for the highest international standards in our research and scholarly publications and by communication of that knowledge to successive generations through excellence in learning". What non-financial performance measures are appropriate for the CPE Division? Why have you selected them?

2. What are the financial implications of the programme manager's offer to accept the 10 extra participants?

3. What other considerations are relevant to this decision?

QUESTION 8.5

A local hotel is preparing a detailed budget for residential accommodation for the high season, which consists of 20 weeks and runs from May through to September. Of this period only the months of July and August (8 weeks) are considered as the peak period. The remaining 12-week period is considered to be low peak. The hotel has 80 single rooms and 40 double rooms and it is hotel policy to charge double rooms at double the price of single rooms. Also, it is hotel policy to apply these room charges, irrespective of the number of occupants per room.

The following forecasts have been made for the forthcoming 20-week period:

Accommodation: Variable cost: €5 per single room per day; €7 per double room per day. Fixed costs are expected to amount to €170,000 for the 20-week period.

Bookings: All rooms are fully booked for the 8-week peak season. For the remainder of the high season occupancy is 60% in double rooms and 70% in single rooms.

REQUIREMENTS

1. If a profit of €100,000 is budgeted on the accommodation only, what is the required rate per single and double room?

2. What is the break-even rate occupancy rate for the 20-week period? You may assume that twice the number of single rooms are sold as compared to double rooms.

3. What factors other than cost should be taken into consideration by this hotel when making pricing decisions for the forthcoming period? Explain briefly your reasoning.

4. Assume that a tour operator was willing to book 10 double rooms for 5 days during the low period. In addition to the above costs, the hotel would be required to provide two tour guides. The cost of a tour guide is €200 each for 5 days. However, one guide can be recruited from existing hotel staff who would otherwise be idle. What is the minimum selling price per room that could be charged by the hotel?

QUESTION 8.6

A manufacturer has been offered a special contract to make equipment for a valued customer who is willing to pay €30,000 for the contract providing certain delivery requirements can be met. The following provisional costing has been made:

	€
Materials	15,000
Labour (1,000 hours)	8,000
Variable overhead	4,000
General fixed overhead	8,000
	35,000

However, the availability of labour is restricted. To enable this special contract to be accepted it will be necessary to forego some existing work which also takes 1,000 hours and is yielding a contribution of €5 per hour.

REQUIREMENT

1. Which alternative would you recommend: To continue with existing work or undertake the special project? Support your analysis with a financial evaluation.

2. What is the minimum fee management would require to undertake the special contact? Show your calculations.

QUESTION 8.7

A manufacturer has been offered a special contract to make equipment for a valued customer who is willing to pay €25,000 for the contract providing certain delivery requirements can be met.

The following provisional costing has been made:

	€
Materials	Note 1
Labour (1,600 hours)	8,000
Variable overhead	4,000
General fixed overhead	8,000

Notes

1. 3,000 kgs. of raw material are required for this special contract. These raw materials are used regularly by the company and there are ample supplies in stock, which cost €0.50 each. However, the current replacement cost is €1.00 per unit.

2. To enable this special contract to be accepted it will be necessary to forego some existing work which takes 1,600 hours and is yielding a contribution of €6.50 per hour.

REQUIREMENT

1. Which alternative would you recommend? Support your analysis in terms of a financial evaluation.

2. What is the minimum fee management would require to undertake the special contact? Show your calculations.

QUESTION 8.8

Jones Company has 2,000 kgs. of material on hand, purchased at €2 per kg. This material is surplus to the company's requirements and will shortly deteriorate. The net realisable value per year is €1.80 per kg.

However, some of the inventory of the material could be used to make product A. Each unit of product A would require one kg. of the material plus €3 in other incremental costs. A maximum of 500 units of product A could be sold at a price of €5.25 a unit.

The company is also thinking of manufacturing product B. Each unit of B would require one kg. of the material plus €4 in other incremental costs.

The Jones Company could buy additional quantities of this material, if required, for €2.40 a kilogram.

REQUIREMENT

1. A customer has offered to buy 2,000 units of product B in the next six weeks if the price is right and if Jones agrees to sell no product B to anyone else during that period. What relevant cost would you compare with the offer price in evaluating the desirability of accepting this order?

2. How would you answer to (1) differ if the offer was for 2,500 units of product B?

QUESTION 8.9

The directors of RELCAST Ltd. are considering whether to undertake a special contract for a new customer. The job specification requires 50,000 FLOPs to be produced during the forthcoming year for a fixed price of €35 each. An additional contract may be forthcoming at a later date.

The following information relates to client specifications and the company's operating capacity:

Raw materials: Each FLOP would require three different types of raw materials, designated X, Y and Z. Quantities required, current stock levels and cost of each raw material are as follows:-

Raw Material	Units Required per Flop	Current Stock Level (Units)	Original Cost €	Current Replacement Cost €	Current Realisable Value €
X	1	100,000	2.10	2.50	1.80
Y	2	60,000	3.30	2.80	1.10
Z	1/2	Nil	Nil	5.00	5.00
AA	3	100,000	1.00	0.80	Nil

Material X is used continuously by the company and stocks are always replenished. The current stock of Y is in excess to the company's requirements, and unless used to manufacture FLOPs, material Y would be sold. The company does not carry material Z in stock. The company has a stock of material AA in hand. If it is not used in the production of FLOPs, the material will have to be disposed at a cost of €2 per unit.

Labour: Production of each FLOP would require skilled and unskilled labour. Three hours of skilled labour are required per unit and current wage rates are €7 per hour. However, additional skilled labour can be obtained only by ceasing production of another product, details of which are set out below and by also incurring a penalty cost of €10,000 for non-delivery.

Another product:

	€
Selling price per unit	21
Material cost	3
Skilled labour	14
Fixed overhead	3

The production of FLOPs requires ½ hour of unskilled labour and unskilled labour is paid at the rate of €5 per hour. However, because of the cancellation of another contract requiring unskilled labour, RELCAST expects to have over 100,000 surplus unskilled labour hours available during the coming year. Because of the impact on staff morale, the directors have decided not to dismiss any workers in the foreseeable future.

Overheads: Fixed overheads for Relcast Ltd. are assigned to products on the basis of direct labour hours and the allocation for the coming year is €3.50 per labour hour. In addition, variable overhead costs for FLOPs are estimated at €1.20 per unit produced.

Packaging materials: The company has already committed to a contract to purchase 270,000 units of special packaging material at a unit cost of €5 per unit. However, this order will have to be increased by 50,000 units to accommodate the production of FLOPs. The supplier offers a discount of €1 per unit (on all units) whenever the total purchase size exceeds 300,000 units per annum.

Packaging equipment: Specialised packaging machines, purchased by the company some years ago would have to be used for the FLOPs contract. While the machinery has an estimated useful life of two years, it is unlikely to be used in any other contract. Its current book value is €40,000 and its estimated realisable value is currently €24,000. It is estimated that these values would be €30,000 and €10,000 respectively at the end of the contract.

REQUIREMENT

1. Prepare a schedule of relevant costs indicating whether FLOPs should be produced. Your schedule should distinguish between incremental, out-of-pocket cash costs and opportunity costs.

2. What non-financial considerations are relevant to this decision and how are they relevant?

QUESTION 8.10

Technologies Ltd. manufactures products that incorporate advanced technological features. Each new product is virtually unique, and the effect of learning on cost is very pronounced.

A customer has asked for a price quotation on an order for 512 sensometers. They would be produced in series, one at a time. Technologics' engineers estimate that the production labour costs of the first unit would amount to €4,000, and an 80 percent cumulative learning curve would apply to production labour costs.

REQUIREMENT

1. What is the labour cost if the learning curve is overlooked?

2. Using the learning curve, estimate the labour cost of the order.

3. The customer feels that the bid based on your estimate in (a) is too high. You are unwilling to reduce your bid for this quantity, but the customer has suggested that you rebid on the basis of a total production run of 750 units. Prepare a new cost estimate.

QUESTION 8.11

The Burns Company is manufacturing a special part for the Rathgar Company. The first batch produced the following costs:

	€
Direct materials 1,000 pounds (@ €2/pound)	2,000
Direct labour 2,000 hours (@ €5/hour)	10,000
Variable overhead 160% of direct labour cost	16,000
Fixed manufacturing expenses (special dies)	10,000
Total cost (first batch)	38,000

The Rathgar Company would like the Burns Company to produce an additional 3 batches and has asked them to prepare a bid for the additional units. In analysing the situation, Burns would like to prepare a bid that would ensure a €20,000 contribution margin on the new order. Burns feels that the special dies used for the first batch will be usable for the additional 3 batches. Based on previous experience, Burns estimates that the employees should experience an 80% learning curve for this job.

REQUIREMENT

Prepare an estimate of the bid that Burns should submit to the Rathgar Company for the additional three batches.

QUESTION 8.12

The LC Company builds leisure boats. As part of its research program, it completes the assembly of the first of a new model. The LC Company will keep the first model, costed at €725,000, as a demonstration model for other potential purchasers.

A potential client is impressed with the new model and they request that LC submit a proposal on the cost of producing SEVEN models. The accounting department at LC reports the following cost information for the first model assembled by the LC Company.

	€
Direct materials	100,000
Direct labour (10,000 hours @ €30)	300,000
Tooling cost*	50,000
Variable overhead**	200,000
Fixed overhead***	75,000
	725,000

*   Tooling can be reused, even though all of its costs were assigned to the first unit.
**   Variable-overhead is directly affected by direct-labour hours; a rate of €20 per hour is used for purposes of bidding on contracts.
***   Fixed overhead is assigned at a flat rate of 25% of direct-labour cost for purposes of bidding on contracts.

The LC Company uses an 80% cumulative average-time learning curve as a basis for forecasting direct-labour hours on its assembling operations.

REQUIREMENT

Prepare a detailed prediction of the expected cash outflows for producing the seven units for the potential client.

QUESTION 8.13

Ivor Ltd., a small business that specialises in manufacturing electronic equipment, has just received an order for the production of 256 identical units. These units will be made in the company's premises using the existing labour force who have agreed to work overtime on this project. The cost and estimating department has provided you with the following product specification:

Product Specifications

Component X	2 kg. per unit
Component Y	1 kg. per unit
Component Z	3 kg. per unit
Labour (first unit, subject to learning curve)	2 hours
Variable overhead	€2 per unit
Fixed Overhead (inspection)	€20 per direct labour hour worked

You are also provided with the following additional information:

1. Component X is used regularly by the company. There are 80 kgs. in stock, costing €10 per kg. but the regular supplier has announced a price increase of 30% effective immediately.

2. Component Y has no alternative use by the company. There are 300 kgs. in stock due to a cancelled order following the bankruptcy of a customer. The stock originally cost €9,000. However, due to market shortages the realisable value is estimated at €35 per unit. The company can sell all or portion of its stock of material Y on the market.

3. Component Z is used regularly by the company. There is none in stock. The supplier charges €5 per kg.

4. The production director has indicated that due to an 80% learning curve the cumulative average labour requirements will fall by 20% every time output is doubled from the initial requirement of 2 hours per unit.

5. The basic labour rate is €10 per hour. The overtime premium is €5 per hour.

6. Research costs already incurred in respect of this special job amount to €2,000.

7. The suggested price for the contract is €15,000.

REQUIREMENT

1. Prepare a schedule clearly indicating the incremental cash costs (out-of-pocket costs) associated with this project and compare this with the revenue from the project.

2. What are the opportunity costs (if any) associated with acceptance of the contract?

3. What is the minimum price that should be accepted for this contract?

QUESTION 8.14

Ben Johnson Ltd. produces four different types of products whose contribution is made up as follows:

	A	B	C	D
	€	€	€	€
Direct materials (variable)	7	20	15	15
Direct labour (variable)	3	6	3	4
Variable overheads	2	4	3	2
Contribution per unit	8	10	9	14
Unit selling price	20	40	30	35

Fixed costs per month amount to €30,000.

Suppliers of raw material have warned the company that they will be unable to deliver more than €77,000 worth of materials per month. Management realises this will result in curtailment of production and sales. However, with a view to keeping the company's products in the minds of the public management wishes, if possible, to produce a minimum of 1,000 of each product per month, and to use any materials which remain, in the most profitable manner.

REQUIREMENT

You are required to prepare statements showing the quantities of each product which the company should produce each month, bearing in mind the restricted supply of raw materials together with the revised budgeted profit.

QUESTION 8.15

The PSV Company Limited is engaged in the manufacture of three products, namely, P, S, and V for the household consumer market. They are considered to be complementary products in the sense that the level of sales of one product is closely related to the sales of another. Production and sale of 5,000 units of each are forecast during the following budget period (January-December 20X1). The unit prices (excluding VAT) at which the products will be sold to customers are €26, €37 and €22 respectively for P, S and V. The estimated costs per product are estimated as follows, based on an annual output of 5,000 units of each product:

	P	S	V
	€	€	€
Direct materials	6	8	3
Direct labour (variable)	4	7	5
Production overhead costs	8	14	10
Variable selling and admin. costs	2	1	3
Fixed selling and admin. costs	1	2	1

The direct material cost is based on a single raw material that is used in all three products. In addition, production overhead costs are absorbed at the rate of 200% of direct labour cost, based on an expected volume of 5,000 units of each product. Half of this production overhead is considered variable in relation to changes in volume. The variable selling and administration costs represent commission per unit paid to sales agents.

Before finalising the budget plan for next year, two factors emerge and should be taken into consideration. First, the raw material is imported and the company now faces a problem of quotas imposed by the sole supplier and a long lead-time for delivery. Orders for raw materials are placed about one year in advance and the supply of raw materials cannot be increased for the current year (20x1). The forecast production plan for 20X1 of 5,000 of each of the three units uses to the full the present quota of 42,500 kgs.

Second, the marketing director has determined that, because of a sudden and positive change in forecast conditions, it would be possible to expand the sales of any or all of the products by 20%.

REQUIREMENTS

1. Compute the original contribution and related profit, based on 5,000 units of each product.

2. As the management accountant, assuming profit maximisation, prepare the optimal production plan and related profit. Compare you resulting net profit figure with (1) above. Why is there a difference between these two figures?

3. What is the maximum price the company could pay to acquire an extra 30 kgs. of raw material? Explain your reasoning.

4. Briefly discuss the role of "sensitivity analysis" (the study of the effect of changes of assumptions on the results of a decision model) in the context of the above decision.

5. Briefly discuss the use of profit maximisation as a criterion in managerial decision making in general.

6. Suggest reasons why the sales agents in this situation may be happy to comply with your optimal production plan in (2) above.

(The Association of Chartered Certified Accountants)

QUESTION 8.16

Crocus Ltd., a small manufacturing company, produces three products, referred to as Products 1,2 and 3 respectively. It has forecasted its trading results for the year ended 31 December, 20x1 as follows:

	Product			
	1	2	3	
	€	€	€	Total
Unit selling price	10	12	8	
Forecast sales revenue	100,000	96,000	32,000	228,000
Forecast variable costs	60,000	56,000	24,000	140,000
Share of general fixed costs	30,000	27,000	10,000	67,000
Profit/(Loss)	10,000	13,000	(2,000)	21,000

REQUIREMENT

1. Explain how the company's forecasted profits would be affected if product 3 were discontinued, assuming sales of the remaining products would not be affected; any other assumptions made should be clearly stated.

2. The marketing manager is considering an advertising campaign for product 2 at an additional cost of €8,000 (not included in the above forecast). Calculate the minimum additional sales of Product 2, in units, required to cover this cost.

3. Assume product line 1 is discontinued. What are the additional sales for BOTH product lines 2 and 3 combined necessary to compensate?

4. The suppliers of a material used in the manufacture of each of the three products has just informed the production manager that next year's supply of this material will be restricted to 92,000 kgs. Advertising or price adjustments are not possible at such short notice and no stocks can be carried. There is no substitute material available and the estimated consumption of this material, per unit of each product, is:

1	8 kg.
2	4 kg.
3	1 kg.

The sales manager regards the forecast demand for the year ended 31 December, 20x1 to be the maximum demand. What is the optimum production plan to maximise profits?

QUESTION 8.17

Superstores sell a wide range of goods in its city-centre location. Managers are given discretion over the items offered for sale in their store, which are drawn from a range, which is purchased centrally. The manager of one small store is planning his counter arrangements for the coming month. There are only seven counters available in his store, each counter will hold only one product group for the month and each counter is of similar size. Monthly fixed overhead for the store amounts to €20,000. The manager is anxious to maximise profits each month and he has provided you with the following estimates of product turnover (in terms of sales per counter) and the respective contribution/sales (C/S) ratios. These figures are based on the annual figures for each product, divided by 12.

	Sales expected from ordinary counters €	C/S ratio per counter (%)
Sweets	18,000	20%
Stationery	4,000	40%
Clothes	7,200	40%
Records	6,000	50%
Food	5,000	40%
Toys	8,000	55%
Hardware	4,000	40%
Gardening	5,000	35%

However, two of the seven counters available can be situated at the entrance to the store. Products placed on entrance counters have a greater opportunity of attracting chance business and it is estimated that products placed on these counters in any one month will experience double their expected turnover in that month.

The manager is not compelled to offer all product groups, and it is within the company policy to offer the same product on two different counters, but not more than two. If the same product is offered on two counters, sales from the second counter, regardless of its location, are only 50% of those shown in the above table.

REQUIREMENTS

1. Identify **financial** performance measures that may be used to evaluate the performance of each store manager and describe how he or she can be distorted and/or generate inappropriate behaviour.

2. Determine the product range, which the manager should offer in order to maximise his profit for the coming month and the amount of such profit. Explain briefly the process you follow to achieve this.

3. What other factors should be considered before deciding on a counter layout based strictly on such a programmed approach to decision making?

(The Association of Chartered Certified Accountants)

QUESTION 8.18

A Chinese farmer owns 560 acres of land on which he grows spinach, potatoes, lettuce and beans. Of the total, half is suitable for all four vegetables, but the other half is suitable only for potatoes and lettuce. Labour for all kinds of farm work is plentiful.

Government restrictions require that all four types of vegetable must be produced with a minimum of 10,000 boxes of any one line. The farmer has decided that the area devoted to any crop should be in terms of complete acres and not in fractions of an acre. Also, only one crop can be grown on each plot of land per annum. Data concerning production, market prices and costs are as follows:

	SPINACH	POTATOES	LETTUCE	BEANS
Annual yield (boxes per acre)	350	100	70	180
	€	€	€	€
Direct costs:				
Raw materials per acre	1,300	1,000	500	900
Harvesting, packing and transport, per box	8.00	9.00	7.00	13.00
Market price, per box	16.00	17.00	19.00	22.00

The fixed overheads per annum are estimated at €400,000.

REQUIREMENTS

1. You are required to advise the farmer, within the given constraints, the area to be cultivated with each crop if he is to achieve the largest total profit, and the amount of this total profit.

2. What are the limitations of using this approach to decision making?

QUESTION 8.19

Henrico is operating from a small restaurant serving two pizza products that are known as Fasta Pizza and Suppa Pizza, and both are baked on the premises immediately the customer places his order. He has consulted you for your advice in selecting the most profitable product, which should receive greater emphasis in his promotion material.

The Fasta Pizza can be cooked quickly and will suit the lunchtime customer. The Suppa Pizza is a more elaborate product, a larger serving, although using the same imported topping, cooked a little differently taking more time and served with a garnish. The topping is a special recipe and is imported by Henrico. Customers are very complimentary about the taste and he is keen to use this to increase demand. The following information on the two products is provided:

	FASTA PIZZA	SUPPA PIZZA
Variable costs	€	€
Ingredients: Base	0.50	1.00
Topping:		
100 grams	0.50	
160 grams		0.80
Cooking time for variable labour and overhead at €8 per hour:		
7.5 minutes	1.00	
15 minutes		2.00
Selling price	2.50	4.50

Cooking time is limited and he estimates that in any one month he will have 3,000 hours of cooking time available on the range of equipment at his disposal. Henrico is confident that a market exists for both the basic and elaborate product in any quantities. He wants to keep both products circulating within the restaurant and has stated that 3,000 Fasta Pizzas and 1,500 Suppa Pizzas should be produced monthly as a minimum.

REQUIREMENT

1. Taking note of the minimum quantity of each product calculate the product mix and maximum possible contribution assuming he can sell any quantity produced.

2. Further investigation reveals that the supplier of pizza topping is deliberately limiting quantities available such that monthly quantities would not exceed 2,000 kgs (2,000,000 grams). This constraint is in addition to the limited cooking time available.

Present the problem graphically, make recommendations to Henrico and explain them, stating any qualifications you may have.

(The Association of Chartered Certified Accountants)

QUESTION 8.20

A small business manufactures pre-packed windows and doors for the building trade. There has recently been unprecedented expansion and some attractive orders have been received. Unfortunately there is little opportunity to accept all of the orders because of the lead time required in ordering machines for two vital processes, cutting and joining. The company has no way of increasing, in the next planning period, the time available beyond 4,800 hours from each machine in both the cutting and joining departments.

Windows are sold for €100 each and material costs amount to €45. Doors sell for €180 each, their material content amounts to €80.

The cost accounting system recovers (absorbs) conversion costs (labour and overheads) into machine hour rates, which are focused on the two critical processes. Overhead rates are €10 per machine hour in cutting and €15 per machine hour in joining. As a rough guide 40% of the overhead is fixed in relation to throughput. The specifications for the manufacture of windows and doors state that windows require one and a half-hours cutting and one hour for joining. Doors are expected to involve two hours cutting and three hours joining.

REQUIREMENTS

1. Recommend the mix of window and door manufacture, which will be most beneficial to this business, explain briefly your approach to the problem and demonstrate that the machines are fully utilised.

2. What limitations and assumptions apply to the approach you have adopted?

3. Identify the main critical success factors (the limited number of areas in which performance must excel for the firm to be successful) for this business and any related performance measures.

(Association of Chartered Certified Accountants)

QUESTION 8.21

The Wing Manufacturing Company produces a chemical compound, product X, which deteriorates and must be discarded if it is not sold by the end of the month during which it is produced. The total variable cost of the manufactured compound, product X, is €50 per unit, and its selling price is €80 per unit. Wing can purchase the same compound from a competing company at €80 per unit plus €10 freight per unit. It is management policy to fill orders, either from own production or by external purchase. This is because failure to fulfil orders would result in the loss of customers.

Wing has manufactured and sold product X for the past 20 months. Demand for the product has been irregular, and at present there is no consistent sales trend. During this period monthly sales have been as follows:

Units Sold per month	Number of months
8,000	5
9,000	12
10,000	3

REQUIREMENTS

1. Compute the probability of sales of product X of 8,000, 9,000 or 10,000 units in any month. What is the expected level of sales?

2. Prepare a payoff matrix, reflecting the three levels of demand and the three production alternatives of the firm: Produce 8,000, 9,000 or 10,000 units.

3. What is the appropriate strategy using the maximax, maximin and EMV criteria?

4. Specify some of the problems associated with using probabilities in decision-making. It may be useful to distinguish between subjective and objective probabilities in framing your answer.

(The Association of Chartered Certified Accountants)

QUESTION 8.22

A Company is developing a new product that will have a life cycle of one year. This selling price is €13 per unit. The company estimates it will be able to sell 30,000 units of this product. A pessimistic view suggests 24,000 units may be sold whilst an absolute maximum of 36,000 units is considered possible. Unsold units can be retained in closing stock without financial penalty. Cost estimates have revealed the following:

	per unit €	per annum €
Material cost	2.50	
Specific fixed costs		40,000
General fixed costs		45,000

In addition, there are semi-variable costs that are attributable to the product in relation to the percentage of normal capacity as follows:

Percentage of normal capacity (24,000 units)	Cost per annum €
80	50,000
90	53,750
100	57,500
110	61,250
120	65,000

Resources diverted to this product could continue to be employed earning an annual net profit of €60,000. This profit is fairly certain as it is from selling an existing product to established customers.

REQUIREMENTS

1. Calculate the net profit attributable to the new product for the three volume levels indicated.

2. Upon further investigation it is agreed that probabilities may be subjectively applied to the three volume levels thus:

Unit sales	Probability
24,000	0.3
30,000	0.5
36,000	0.2

Additionally, though the material price quoted is the most likely value (probability 0.7), a higher price of €3 (probability 0.3) may also occur. The probabilities quoted are independent.

Using the probabilities provided extend, as you think appropriate, the profit projections in (1) above and draw some conclusions about the new product development.

3. What are your views on the use of probabilities in this sort of decision?

QUESTION 8.23

The sales manager of the Black Company has been asked to submit a price quotation for 100,000 units of a product used by a customer. The out-of-pocket cost of filling the order, if it can be obtained, is €90,000. Three possible prices are being considered: €1, €1.25, and €1.50.

The sales manager is not certain how busy competitors' factories are, but in the light of their bids on recent jobs she thinks that the chance of their operating at a rate as high as 80 percent of capacity or higher is only 20 percent. Similarly, she believes that the probability that those competitors are operating at 60 percent of capacity or less is 30 percent.

She estimates that if competitors' operating rates are 80 percent or higher, she can secure the order at any bid up to and including €1.50. If competitors are operating between 61 and 79 percent of capacity, a price of €1.25 or less will secure the bid, but if competitors' operating rates are 60 percent or less it will take a bid of €1 to land the order.

REQUIREMENTS

1. Prepare a payoff table to reflect this data.

2. Assuming that the decision rule is to maximise the expected value of the monetary return, which bid should be submitted?

QUESTION 8.24

Marathon Ltd. is a shoe manufacturer that makes shoes for multiple stores to be sold under the store's 'own label'. The management at Marathon has been approached by a multiple store to tender for the supply of 10,000 or 14,000 pairs of these 'own label' products. With a minimum of re-arrangement the company could increase capacity to cope with this possible order. It is the company's policy to prepare cost estimates based on full cost plus profit formula. Manufacturing overhead recovery is based on 400% of direct labour cost and administration based on 40% of the manufacturing cost. For this tender the raw material for a pair of shoes is estimated at €8 and the direct wages €2 per pair. Sales commission and packaging variable costs amount to €4.80 per pair. To set the tender price, management has decided to mark up the full cost by 30% for the higher volume (i.e. 14,000 units) and 40% for the lower volume (10,000 units).

Before Marathon plc submits its tender, an enquiry is received from Nibock for the supply of 12,000 pairs of shoes at €50 per pair. An examination of the direct costs of their design specification reveals raw material costs of €10, labour costs of €3.50 and sales commission and packaging of €5.50 per pair. If Marathon plc accepts this order from Nibock they cannot take the order from the multiple store.

The incremental cost element of the manufacturing and administration overhead, in order to create the capacity of 10,000 extra pairs, is €60,000. For a capacity in excess of this, costs of €65,000 would be incurred.

REQUIREMENTS

1. Evaluate the alternatives of selling to the multiple store or to Nibock using relevant costs and revenues.

2. The marketing department estimates that there is only a 60% chance that Marathon will get the Nibock border. Additionally, they predict that there is an 80% chance of the multiple store accepting their prices and placing an order. If the multiple accepts, there is 70% probability that this order will be for 14,000 pairs and 30% probability it will be for 10,000 pairs. Adapt your answer to (1) for this information, incorporating the calculation of the expected values of meeting each order. The probabilities are independent.

3. Discuss how the probabilities provided in (2) assist management in its evaluation and point out any difficulties with the use of these.

(The Association of Chartered Certified Accountants)

QUESTION 8.25

In preparing its 20x4 budget, the EMV Company conducted a market research study to estimate demand and unit sales. The demand for the product is not very responsive to price changes and the price for the forthcoming year (20x4) has already been agreed and decided. The company's management accountant received a memo from the head of market research with the following summary:

> It is impossible to predict 20x4 sales with certainty. If the economy continues as it is, unit sales will be 400,000. But if the economy falters, we expect 300,000 units to be sold this year and if it is unexpectedly robust, annual sales will reach 500,000 units. Our economist predicts a 40% probability of a stable economy, a 40% chance of a faltering economy, and a 20% chance of an unexpectedly robust economy.

REQUIREMENTS

1. How could the company use all three estimates of sales demand in the budgeting process for next year?

2. What sales estimate would an optimist (maximax) and a pessimist (maximin) make?

3. Prepare a single-value estimate of 20x4 sales units. Use the concept of expected value.

4. What are the benefits of using the EMV calculation? What are its limitations?

9

Capital Investment Decisions

9.1 CAPITAL INVESTMENT EVALUATION

Some of the most significant decisions made by management involve capital expenditure, e.g. the acquisition of plant and machinery. The process of planning and evaluating such proposals is called capital investment evaluation or capital budgeting.

Capital investment decisions are characterised by an immediate and significant outlay of cash in order to generate inflows of cash in future time periods. Not only are large amounts of cash involved in relation to overall company size but many such decisions are difficult or impossible to reverse once the funds have been committed and the project has begun. To complicate the issue, these decisions must be made from estimates of future operating cash flows, which by their nature involve a considerable degree of uncertainty. These decisions are often crucial to the financial health of a business enterprise. Capital expenditure decisions will impact on an enterprise's growth and its ability to attract new capital. Companies benefit from good capital budgeting decisions and suffer from poor ones.

Capital budgeting decisions are based on the ability of estimated future cash inflows to exceed current investment. Without this (excess) return, the company will not be able to generate sufficient internal funds for future investment projects. Yet, non-financial factors must also be considered — for example, staff morale and pollution control. There are many techniques for evaluating the financial considerations in such situations. The most common techniques are:

1. Simple payback period.

2. Net present value (NPV).

3. Internal rate of return (IRR).

One major difference between the simple payback period method and the other two is that the payback method does not consider the time value of money.

9.2   TIME VALUE OF MONEY

These techniques all involve analysis of the estimated annual net cash flows pertaining to the investment. Annual net cash flow is the excess of cash receipts over cash payments in a given year. Because the time span of a project will extend over a number of years, one might want to take into consideration the *timing* of the future cash flows, since receiving money today is preferable to receiving money at some later date. The concept of *present value* (PV) is based upon the "time value" of money. The present value of a future cash receipt is the amount that a knowledgeable investor would pay today for the right to receive that future receipt. The advantage of using present values is that all future cash flows, regardless of when they occur, can be translated to a common base (present value), which facilitates the comparison of alternatives. The present value will always be less than the future amount because cash received today can be invested to earn interest and thereby becomes equivalent to a larger amount in the future.

The exact amount of the present value depends upon:

1. The amount of the future receipt.

2. The length of time until the receipt will be received.

3. The rate of return required (called the discount rate).

The required rate of return will approximate the going *market rate* of interest. This rate of interest can then be used in evaluating capital investment decisions. The technique that takes into account the timing of cash flows is called *discounting* future cash flows (DCF). In other words, discounting is the process of determining the present value of future cash flows.

The relationship between present values and future values is depicted in the following example.

ILLUSTRATION

An investment of €100 is made at a 7 per cent rate of interest:

	€
Amount to be invested	100
Interest: Year 1 (€100 x 7 per cent)	7
Amount to be received in one year (future value)	107
Interest: Year 2 (€107 x 7 per cent)	8
Amount to be received in two years (future value)	115

If €115 will be received two years in the future, the investor would pay only €100 for the investment today. In other words, the future value (FV) of €115 at the end of two years has a present value of €100.

The relationship between present and future values can be expressed by the following equation:

$$PV = \frac{FV}{(1+R)^n}$$

where PV = Present value; FV = Future value; 1= Unity (or 1); R= Rate of interest (return); and, N= Number of years.

Present Value Tables

When calculating the present value of future cash flows, use tables of present values or discount tables to find the appropriate discount factor and multiply that value by the future amount. For example, using Exhibit 9.1 below, the present value of €107 to be received in one year, discounted at 7 per cent per annum, is €100 (€107 x 0.935). The present value of €115 to be received in two years, at 7 per cent, is also €100 (€115 x 0.873).

Exhibit 9.1: Present Values of €1 Due in N Periods

NO. OF YEARS	7%	10%	DISCOUNT 12%	15%	20%
1	.935	.909	.893	.870	.833
2	.873	.826	.797	.756	.694
3	.816	.751	.712	.658	.579
4	.763	.683	.636	.572	.482
5	.713	.621	.567	.497	.402
6	.666	.564	.507	.432	.335
7	.623	.513	.452	.376	.279
8	.582	.467	.404	.327	.233
9	.544	.424	.360	.284	.194
10	.508	.386	.322	.247	.162

[*NOTE*: An extract of discount tables appears in Appendix 1].

ILLUSTRATION

The application of all three methods to a capital investment decision will be illustrated using the example of Ohio Ltd. below.

Ohio Ltd. is considering the purchase of equipment for €21,000 that has a four year life, with an estimated salvage value of €1,000. The additional income from this investment will be €2,000 per annum, as follows:

	€	€
Additional sales		17,000
Additional depreciation: (€21,000 - €1,000)/4 years	5,000	
Additional cash costs	10,000	15,000
Additional income		2,000

REQUIREMENT

Calculate the payback period, the NPV and IRR for this proposal.

Before working through the calculations for Ohio Ltd., it is worthwhile making a few important points regarding capital investment decisions in general:

1. The initial cash outlay is assumed to take place immediately, sometimes designated t_0 representing time period zero. All other cash flows are assumed to take place at the end of the accounting period.

2. Capital investment proposals frequently require investment in additional working capital — for example, stock and debtors — to support the additional volume of sales. Such investment will involve a cash outlay and should be treated accordingly. Remember to reverse this investment in working capital at the end of the project's life.

3. In evaluating capital investment decisions, concentrate only on future cash flows rather than accounting profits or income, because cash is the only resource that is available for reinvestment or discharging liabilities. Ignore depreciation of fixed assets, since it is a non-cash item of expenditure. In making short-term decisions earlier, the fact that there is a difference between accounting profits and cash flows was ignored; it now must be acknowledged since capital expenditure decisions have long-term implications.

4. Some fixed assets have an eventual salvage value at the end of the project's life. If this item is significant, it should be included as a cash inflow at the end of the asset's useful life.

5. Some proposals involve an opportunity cost — for example, the proposal to process scrap material further may involve forfeiting the possibility of selling that scrap material in its unprocessed state. The loss of such cash inflow represents an opportunity cost. Opportunity cost is equivalent to a cash outflow and should be included in the calculations.

Simple Payback Period

The payback period is the length of time necessary to recover the initial investment from future net cash flows. If all sales are received in cash and all expenses other than depreciation are paid for in cash, the expected annual net cash flow from this project is €7,000. Note that annual net cash flow exceeds estimated income by the amount of the depreciation expense, since depreciation is purely a book-keeping exercise and does not represent a cash flow.

$$\frac{\text{Amount invested}}{\text{Estimated annual net cash flow}} = \frac{€21,000}{€7,000} = 3 \text{ years.}$$

In selecting between alternative investment opportunities, a short payback period is desirable since it reduces the risk associated with changes in future economic conditions. In addition, the sooner the amount of the investment is recovered, the sooner the funds may be put to another use. The principal advantage of the payback period is the caution it introduces to the investment decision and, thus, generally it produces satisfactory results. Also, it is simple to apply and understand.

The payback period ignores the total life and, therefore, the total profitability of the investment. It also disregards the time value of money although a discounted payback period could be computed.

Net Present Value (NPV)

The objective of the NPV technique is to find out whether a given proposal promises a rate of return at least equal to the minimum acceptable rate. If the discount rate is set equal to the cost of capital and the NPV of a proposal is positive, the benefits from the expenditure will exceed its costs. In other words, the NPV of a proposal is the difference between the total present value of future cash flows and the cost of the investment as follows:

TIME	CASH FLOWS €	DISCOUNT FACTOR	PRESENT VALUE €
End of year 1	7,000	.909	6,363
End of year 2	7,000	.826	5,782
End of year 3	7,000	.751	5,257
End of year 4	7,000	.683	4,781
End of year 4 (sale of asset)	1,000	.683	683
			22,866
less: Amount to be invested (payable in advance)			(21,000)
Net Present Value (positive)			1,866

The advantage of the NPV technique is that it is concerned with the total lifespan of the proposal and the timing of all cash flows. As a result, it allows management to compare proposals that differ in the timing of their cash flows.

NPV suffers from the disadvantage that it is very sensitive to the choice of discount rate used. The greater the discount rate, the smaller the present value of a given stream of cash flows. In addition, for computational purposes, restrictive assumptions must be made such as that all cash flows, apart from the initial investment, are deemed to take place on the last day of the accounting period.

The Internal Rate of Return

The Internal Rate of Return (IRR) can be defined as the discount rate at which the net present value of a proposal is zero. The calculation of IRR is a trial-and-error process involving the selection of discount rates at random and applying them to future cash flows until one gets two rates, one of which gives a negative NPV and the other a positive NPV, in order to pinpoint the actual IRR.

Using the earlier example of Ohio Ltd., at a discount rate of 10 per cent, the NPV was +€1,866. At a discount rate of 14 per cent, the NPV is -€17. The IRR must therefore lie between 10 per cent and 14 per cent and very close to 14 per cent. The IRR is the discount rate at which NPV equals zero and this can be approximated by interpolating between two points as follows:

$$4\% \left[\begin{array}{ll} 10\% & PV = €1,866 \\ \\ 14\% & PV = €-17 \end{array} \right] €1,883$$

Approximate IRR = 10% + $\dfrac{€1,866}{€1,883}$ X (4%) = 13.96%

Speeding up Calculations

Discounting future cash flows can be a time-consuming exercise. Fortunately, the calculations can be considerably speeded up using annuity tables. An annuity represents the receipt of a constant amount of cash for a specified amount of time — for example, €1,000 to be received over each of the next four years. The PV of this inflow can be calculated as follows (assuming 10 per cent interest):

	FUTURE CASH FLOWS	DISCOUNT FACTOR	PRESENT VALUE
	€		€
Year 1	1,000	.909	909
Year 2	1,000	.826	826
Year 3	1,000	.751	751
Year 4	1,000	.683	683
			3,169

The PV of €1,000 to be received at the end of each of the next 4 years is €3,169, based on a 10 per cent return. This calculation can be performed more quickly using annuity tables but such tables can only be used for *constant* cash flows. A partial annuity table is provided below in Exhibit 9.2.

Exhibit 9.2: Present Value of an Annuity of €1 per Period for N Periods

YEARS	10%	14%	15%	20%
1	.909	.877	.870	.833
2	1.736	1.646	1.626	1.528
3	2.487	2.320	2.283	2.106
4	3.170	2.912	2.854	2.589

[*NOTE*: An extract of annuity tables appears in Appendix 2.]

Annuity tables are compiled by aggregating the individual discount factors in the PV table for the appropriate number of years — for example, the discount factors for 10 per cent on the Present Value table for 4 years amount to 3.170 which corresponds to the factor equivalent to 4 years and 10 per cent in the annuity table. Thus the PV of an annuity of €7,000 for each of four years can be quickly ascertained as:

Present value = €7,000 x 3.170 = €22,190

Annuity tables can be used in the computation of Internal Rate of Return (IRR) by applying the following steps:

1. Calculate the payback period of the project (assume 3 years).

2. Ascertain the project's life (assume 4 years) and consult the annuity tables corresponding to 4 years (the life of the project).

3. The annuity table indicates that the factor nearest to 3 (the payback period), based on 4 years, is found under the 14 per cent column. Thus, the IRR on this project is 14 per cent approximately.

9.3 THE COST OF CAPITAL

Discounted cash flow calculations (NPV and IRR) require as an input the required rate of return, which is the minimum required rate of return on an investment. This rate is also called the discount rate, hurdle rate or cost of capital. The overall cost of capital can be defined as the discount rate which, when applied to the company's future cash flows, leaves the company's value unchanged. For debt (Kd), it is the annual rate of interest (net of tax) charged by the lender, based on the current market value of the debt. For example, if a company raises €800,000 debt for ten years at 12 per cent per annum, the gross rate of interest is 12 per cent. However, interest paid on debt finance is tax-deductible and so the after tax cost of debt finance must be calculated and used. Assuming a tax rate of 40 per cent, then the after-tax cost of debt is 7.2 per cent.

The calculation of the cost of equity capital (Ke) is more complicated. The owner of equity shares can either sell the shares or retain them. It is logical to suggest that the shareholder will sell his shares unless they provide him with an "adequate" return based on the risk free interest rate plus a premium for risk. The level of the premium will depend on the investor's perception of the riskiness of the project under review. How do we measure the return expected by shareholders?

One approach is to look at the growth in dividends in past years. It is reasonable to assume that shareholders will expect this growth in dividends in future years. If we assume that dividends in the future will grow at a constant rate of G per cent, the rate of return expected by the market will be:

$$Ke = \frac{D}{P} + G$$

Where: D = Expected dividend (although the current dividend is sometimes used)
P = Current market price
G = Expected growth in dividends.

If the share receives a return of Ke per cent in the following period, the value of the share should remain unchanged. This formula can be used to determine the cost of equity capital and is referred to as Gordon's growth model.

It is important for companies to assess carefully the cost of capital relevant to a project, since this is the figure at which it should discount the project's cash flows to determine its profitability. Projects that have positive net present values at the appropriate cost of capital are likely to increase a company's share price. Those with negative net present values will decrease a company's share price and should not be undertaken.

ILLUSTRATION
The capital structure of a company is:

	€000
Equity	6,000
Debt (7 per cent)	4,000

The current level of dividend is 10p per share and this has been growing at 6 per cent per annum in recent years. The market price of equity is 200c. The market value of debt is equal to its par value. The tax rate is 50 per cent.

REQUIREMENT
Compute the weighted average cost of capital to be used as a discount rate in project appraisal.

Using Gordon's growth model, the cost of equity capital (Ke) is given by:

$$Ke = \frac{D}{P} + G$$

where D = expected dividend per share; P = market price per share and G = dividend growth per annum.

Since the current dividend is 10c per share, which is expected to grow by 6 per cent per annum, then the expected dividend is 10.6c. Thus:

$$Ke = \frac{10.6}{200} + 0.06 = 0.113 = 11.3\%$$

The weighted average cost of capital (WACC) is based on the capital structure:

	€000	COST	€000
Equity	6,000	11% (rounded)	660
Debt	4,000	3.5% net	140
	10,000		800

$$\text{Weighted average cost of capital} = \frac{€800}{€10,000} \times 100 = 8\%$$

The Weighted Average Cost of Capital (WACC)

The illustration above used the weighted average cost of capital. There are a number of advantages associated with the WACC:

1. A weighted cost gives recognition to the fact that a company's capital structure has both debt and equity elements. It is suggested that all projects should be appraised at this composite rate thus enjoying some benefit from cheaper debt finance, even though a particular project may be entirely equity financed.

2. The WACC reflects the long-term future capital structure — that over time, the company finances capital expenditure proposals in the proportions specified.

3. The capital structure changes slowly over time. Therefore the marginal cost of new capital should be roughly equal to the WACC.

One of the difficulties in applying the Gordon growth model is the prediction of future dividends. It is usual to predict future growth rates in dividend payments from an analysis of the historic growth rates in dividends over the past few years. For example, assume that in year 1 a company paid dividends of €150,000 and in year 5 they amounted to €262,350. Thus the growth over *four* years can be modelled as:

$$(1+G)^4 = \frac{€262,350}{€150,000} = 1.749$$

$$(1 + G) = \sqrt[4]{1.749}$$
$$1 + G = 1.15$$
$$G = 0.15 = 15\%.$$

9.4   IMPACT OF TAXATION

In most Western economies, the tax rate on corporate profits typically ranges between 30 and 45 per cent. These high tax rates mean that the payment of tax liabilities is a most important component of cash flow and should be taken into consideration in evaluating capital investment proposals.

There are two separate considerations. First is the actual rate of tax to be paid on profits and the timing of the payment. Obviously, the actual tax rate in force should be used but, for the purposes of this book, we will typically use rates of 40 or 50 per cent. It should be noted that in some circumstances — for example, manufacturing enterprises — the actual tax rate could be as low as 12.5 per cent. Corporate tax liabilities are usually paid within one year of the end of the accounting period but, more often, within six months. However, one of the working assumptions of capital expenditure evaluations is that cash flows always occur at the end of the accounting period. Therefore, one must decide whether mid-year cash flows are deemed to take place at the end of the year to which they relate (six months early) or are discharged at the end of the following year (six months late).

The second issue is the different treatment of capital expenditure — for example, the purchase of fixed assets for taxation and accounting purposes. For accounting purposes, capital expenditure is recorded under the heading of fixed assets on the balance sheet and expenditure is written off by way of depreciation to the profit and loss account over the estimated useful life of the asset. However, the taxation authorities do not allow deduction of accounting depreciation in computing profits for taxation purposes. Instead, "capital allowances", or "tax depreciation", are granted on the cost of qualifying fixed assets. Not all fixed assets, however, qualify for tax depreciation. Those that do qualify normally attract capital allowances at specific rates. Generally speaking, most fixed assets will qualify for an annual tax allowance of 15 per cent of cost for the first six years on a straight line method, followed by 10 per cent in the seventh year.

This system differs fundamentally from a previous system that granted capital allowances on an accelerated basis. With accelerated capital allowances, a company could write off the entire cost of the qualifying fixed asset immediately on purchase against taxable profits. The general result of this treatment was that a company would not have any tax liabilities in the early years of capital investment programmes. The tax liabilities would be effectively postponed to later years when the present value of those cash payments would be much less severe. In effect, companies would use the investment in fixed assets to postpone (but not eliminate) the payment of tax liabilities to future time periods.

When estimating the impact of taxation liabilities on capital expenditure proposals, two separate sets of calculations are recommended. First, calculate the amount of taxable profits for each year using normal accounting conventions such as the accruals concept. However, depreciation expense should not be included since it is not an allowable expense for taxation purposes; instead, the appropriate capital allowances should be deducted. The purpose of this calculation is to determine the amount of the tax liability, if any, for each accounting period.

The second set of calculations is to determine the overall cash flows for each accounting period, which will include the payment of any tax liability. It is these cash flows that are discounted under the NPV technique to determine present values. These cash flows should also include any cash received on the eventual disposal of the fixed asset. However, such disposal may attract an additional tax liability, referred to as a balancing charge and representing the excess of the sales price of the fixed asset over the tax written down value at date of disposal. The opposite of a balancing charge is a balancing allowance and represents a tax loss on sale. This balancing allowance is also granted in year of disposal and represents the difference between the tax written down value of the fixed assets and the cash proceeds on disposal.

ILLUSTRATION

The Holly Company is evaluating a capital expenditure proposal that will allow the introduction of a new product that will increase profits by €40,000 (before depreciation) over the next three years. The proposal requires an immediate investment in new plant and machinery costing €90,000. This machinery has an estimated life of three years with an estimated scrap value of €20,000. Accelerated capital allowances are available.

The current rate of taxation is 40 per cent and is payable in the year to which it relates.

REQUIREMENT

Is the proposed expansion worthwhile, assuming the firm's cost of capital is 10 per cent (after tax)?

1. COMPUTATION OF TAX PAYABLE

	YEAR 1	YEAR 2	YEAR 3
Additional profit	40,000	40,000	40,000
Less: Capital allowances	(90,000)		* 20,000
	(50,000)	(50,000)	
Taxable profit		(10,000)	(10,000)
			50,000
Tax @ 40 per cent	Nil	Nil	20,000

*   The balancing charge represents the excess of sales proceeds
       (€20,000) over the tax written down value at date of sale (Nil). In ef-
       fect, the company has claimed capital allowances in total of €90,000,
       whereas the actual depreciation suffered was only €70,000 (€90,000–
       €20,000). This excess claim is now being clawed back by the taxation
       authorities as a taxable item.

2. COMPUTATION OF NPV OF FUTURE CASH FLOWS

	INVESTMENT	CASH-FLOW	TAX	NET FLOWS	PV FACTOR	PV
	€	€	€	€		€
Now	(90,000)			(90,000)	1.0	(90,000)
Year 1		40,000		40,000	.909	36,360
Year 2		40,000		40,000	.826	33,040
Year 3	20,000	40,000	(20,000)	40,000	.751	30,040
NPV						9,440

Based on the after-tax cost of capital (10 per cent), this proposal
should be accepted due to its positive NPV. It is important to note
that under current legislation (under which capital allowances are
granted on a straight line rather than an accelerated basis), the proposal would be less attractive.

Sensitivity Analysis

In formulating the NPV decision model, one assumes the accuracy of
all estimates. In reality, however, estimates are rarely perfect and
decision-makers must never lose sight of the uncertainty inherent in
the decision process. Sensitivity analysis is the study of the effect on
a plan due to changes or errors in any of the variables in a decision
model. It is usually carried out because nobody can forecast with
complete accuracy.

   If, by changing any variable in the decision model, the new outcome is significantly different from the original forecast, management

is forewarned that the original solution is extremely sensitive to certain changes in the parameters of the model. Decision-makers are well advised to use sensitivity analysis to test their original solution before committing their economic resources. The important point is that sensitivity analysis enables decision-makers to appreciate the uncertainty existing in any decision process.

A Strategic Focus?

It is important to remember that DCF analysis can give only a general feel as to the possible economic outturn of an investment project — the imponderables are far too great to do any more. And, this being so, there is really no justification for indulging in mathematical fine-tuning. Indeed, it could well be improper since usually it can only result in spurious accuracy and so mislead management as to the reliability of any ultimate figures. It is far better to examine the project in terms of overall commercial strategy and long-term financial plans. It should be clear that "measuring the financial benefit of projects" — as DCF or payback methods attempt to do   is only one step in the investment decision-making process.

Consequently, management should spend its time improving the quality of the assumptions and ascertaining that the strategic questions have been asked, rather than being concerned with more refined capital budgeting techniques. Explicit attention to the major assumptions, together with use of sensitivity analysis, is strongly recommended.

Capital expenditure proposals do not begin life in a filing cabinet awaiting only the collection of the information necessary for their evaluation. Such proposals must be created, and so the capital investment process within the firm should be regarded as a socio-political, as well as a financial, process. Yet some of the literature on such decisions tacitly assumes that proposals already exist and await evaluation.

We have erred too long by exaggerating the "improvement in decision-making" that might result from the adoption of DCF or other refined evaluation techniques. What is needed are approximate answers to the precise problem rather than precise answers to the approximate problem. There is little value in refining an analysis that does not utilise sound assumptions and ask strategic questions. In some capital expenditure analyses, the major assumptions are either not provided or are buried in the supporting detail. More attention should be directed toward improved use of sensitivity analysis and the communication of its results to top management. This would enable executives to demand more detailed justification of crucial assumptions.

9.6   END OF CHAPTER QUESTIONS

Question 9.1

Discuss the procedures a business should adopt for approving and reviewing large capital expenditure projects.

(*The Association of Chartered Certified Accountants*)

Question 9.2

The following data is available for a particular project:

	Case A	Case B
Initial cost of a certain machine	€60,000	€70,000
Predicted useful life	10 years	8 years
Expected terminal residual (scrap) value	€7,000	€8,000
Expected increase in annual cash operating income (because of annual savings in cash operating expenses)	€12,000	€15,000
Present value of €1:		
Due 10 years from now	0.27	
Due 8 years from now		0.35
Present value of an annuity of €1 per year:		
Due 10 years from now	5.20	
Due 8 years from now		4.64

REQUIREMENT

Compute both the payback period and NPV based on the above data.

Question 9.3

Presented below is the information pertaining to three investment proposals:

PROJECT	INITIAL INVESTMENT €	LIFE OF PROJECT	ANNUAL CASH INFLOW AT END OF THE YEAR €
A	380,000	10	80,000
B	80,000	10	20,000
C	80,000	5	30,000

The present value of an annuity of €1 in arrears is given below:

YEARS	10	12	14	16	18	20	22	24
			DISCOUNT RATE					
5	3.79	3.60	3.43	3.27	3.13	2.9	2.86	2.75
10	6.14	5.65	5.22	4.83	4.4	4.1	3.92	3.68

REQUIREMENT

1. Rank these three projects according to their internal rates of return and pay-back period.

2. Rank these three projects according to their net present values if the required rate is 12 per cent.

Question 9.4: AMT plc

AMT plc is increasing the level of automation of a production line dedicated to a single product. The options available are total automation or partial automation. The company works on a planning horizon of five years and either option will produce the 10,000 units that can be sold annually.

Total automation will involve a total capital cost of €1m. Material costs will be €12 and labour and variable overhead will be €18 per unit with this method.

Partial automation will result in higher material wastage and an average cost of €14 per unit. Labour and variable overhead are expected to cost €41 per unit. The capital cost of this alternative is €250,000.

The products sell for €75 each whichever method of production is adopted.

The scrap value of the automated production line, in five years time, will be €100,000 while the line that is partially automated will be worthless. The management uses straight-line depreciation and the required rate of return on capital investment is 16 per cent per annum. Depreciation is considered to be the only incremental fixed cost.

In analysing investment opportunities of this type the company calculates the average total cost per unit, annual net profit, the break-even volume per year and the discounted net present value.

REQUIREMENT

1. Determine the various figures that would be circulated to the management of AMT plc in order to assist the investment analysis. Ignore taxation.

2. Comment on the figures produced and make a recommendation with any qualifications you think appropriate.

(*The Association of Chartered Certified Accountants*)

Question 9.5: Moore Company

The Moore Company manufactures and sells a wide range of durable products. Currently it is evaluating the possible introduction of a new product, the Alpha. It is anticipated that sales and costs of Alpha over the next four years will be as follows:

Year	UNIT SALES	UNIT SELLING PRICE €	UNIT VARIABLE COST €
1	20,000	44	40
2	26,000	45	39
3	21,000	50	39
4	20,000	50	40

Production of Alpha requires an immediate investment in new plant and machinery costing €200,000. This machinery has an estimated life of four years with an estimated scrap value of €10,000. Accelerated capital allowances can be claimed on this item for tax purposes.

In addition, a special advertising campaign would cost €250,000 and be launched immediately. Additional investment in working capital would also be required in the amount of €80,000, which would be disinvested at the end of year four.

The current rate of taxation is 40 per cent and is payable one year in arrears.

REQUIREMENT

Is the proposed expansion worthwhile, assuming the company's cost of capital is 10 per cent (after tax)?

Question 9.6: Lochinvar Company

Lochinvar Company has an opportunity to manufacture 100,000 custom-designed units on contract for Greeley Corporation.

Under the terms of the contract, Greeley would pay Lochinvar €100,000 immediately to help Lochinvar tool up for this special order. It would then pay €8 for each of the first 50,000 units delivered plus €10 for each of the next 50,000 units. Deliveries would be 15,000 units this year, 45,000 units next year, and 40,000 units in the third year. Greely's payments for these units would be made at the time of delivery.

Lochinvar would need to buy special equipment for €110,000 immediately and pay €50,000 in cash for the initial materials inventory. Manufacturing costs would be as follows:

Materials	€2 a unit
Labour	€3 a unit
Overhead	€70,000 a year

The annual overhead costs would include €30,000 in depreciation on the new equipment. Total overhead would be only €60,000 for the first year because the new facilities would not be in operation for the whole year. A full year's depreciation would be taken, however. No allocations of divisional or corporate overhead costs are included in these figures.

Materials inventories would remain constant until early in the third year. They would be completely used up by the time work on the contract was completed. There would be no work in process at the end of any year.

Additional selling and administrative costs of €45,000 would be incurred in each of the next three years.

Lochinvar's management estimates that the new equipment would have a €10,000 market value at the end of the third year. It seems very unlikely to have any usefulness to Lochinvar after that time. Lochinvar's management evaluates all capital expenditure proposals by discounting the after-tax cash flows to their present value at 8 percent. The tax rate is 40 per cent. Use accelerated capital allowances on new equipment for tax purposes. Tax would be paid at the end of the year in which it is accrued.

REQUIREMENT

Calculate the net present value of this proposal. Should the contract be signed?

Question 9.7: LA Group

The American plant in Boston had been a trouble spot in the group for a few years, thought George Frost, the managing director of LA Group, which was a large international company, based in France. Some years ago, as part of its corporate strategy, it had begun to diversify into packaging, pharmaceutical and consumer products. One of its packaging plants was situated in Boston but, based on the monthly returns, it was an inefficient operation. The monthly operating report contained sales figures, production figures and overall profit and return on investment.

Frost would visit the packaging plant once a year for a day, usually unannounced. However, this usually coincided with a "home" game of the Boston Celtics and many of the plant's senior managers were not available to brief Frost fully on developments. Frost grew very critical of the Boston operation. In addition to being inefficient, Frost felt that many managers did not have the commitment for the job and many had lost their technical curiosity. Resulting from his most recent visit, Frost set out rigid guidelines on future capital expenditure requests from the Boston plant. Frost thought that he might not be able to improve the efficiency of the Boston plant but he could veto future capital expenditure requests that did not make economic sense.

According to Frost's directive, most proposals for capital expenditure would have to be personally sanctioned by him or one of his assistants. The procedures to be followed were contained in considerable detail in a Capital Expenditure manual that was distributed to the key financial personnel at the Boston plant. The Capital Expenditure manual contained an explicit set of requirements including, inter alia, a minimum payback period of less than 3 years and that all proposals would earn at least 10 per cent.

The Capital Expenditure manual also contained an explicit categorisation of capital expenditure requests such as Cost Reduction schemes (Code C). There was also a distinction drawn between New Capital Expenditures (NCEs) and Regular Capital Budgets (RCBs).

One of the assistant managers in the Boston plant, Frank Ross, had recently submitted a capital expenditure proposal. Frost looked at the summary sheet (below) requiring a choice between two alternatives to implement a cost reduction scheme by investing in new equipment. However, Frost quickly realised that the capital expenditure analysis was really incomplete. The proposal had simply included a detail of cash flows with no further analysis except a recommendation to accept "Project L" rather than "Project S".

Since Frost was busy that evening, he has provided you with the summarised data.

OPERATING DATA FOR CAPITAL EXPENDITURE PROPOSALS

	PROJECT S €000	PROJECT L €000
Initial cash outlay	(1,000)	(1,000)
Future cash savings		
At end of year 1	500	100
At end of year 2	400	300
At end of year 3	300	400
At end of year 4	100	600
Cumulative total savings	300	400

REQUIREMENT

Analyse the data and advise George Frost on which alternative to accept. Use payback period, NPV and IRR.

Question 9.8: Riseley Chemicals Ltd.

Riseley Chemicals Limited is considering installing a new reactor unit in one of its major chemical plants. The unit is of a revolutionary new design which has been developed and patented by the company and it is expected to give greatly improved raw material conversion efficiencies and lower manning levels. Riseley is planning to finance the purchase of this plant by a €14,000,000 bank loan. Interest on the loan will be payable at 3 per cent above bank base rate, currently standing at 10 per cent. Riseley's existing capital structure is:

	€000
Share capital	60,000
Reserves	40,000
	100,000
Loans (long-term)	6,000
Total	106,000

It has a number of projects awaiting approval and it aims to increase the amount of its debt to 60 per cent of its equity within the next 3 years.

At present, it is considering the cost of capital to use in its evaluation of the profitability of the new reactor. The finance director has discovered that various members of the management team have different ideas on this. The production director argues for using the rate of interest on bank borrowings as this is the rate that the company will have to pay. The marketing director had claimed that in his discussions with a competitor he had learned that they required a rate of 35 per cent. "We should attempt to make at least 5 per cent more than them, if we are to expand and become one of the largest chemical companies."

Riseley's shares are at present valued at 300c on the stock market. Its current dividend is 15c per share and this has been growing at 12 per cent per annum compound over recent years. The current rate of corporation tax is 35 per cent.

REQUIREMENT

1. Explain what you understand the term "cost of capital" to mean. Why is it important for companies to try to estimate this figure carefully? Explain the difference between the cost of capital in real terms and the cost of capital in money terms.

2. Comment on the remarks of the two directors.

3. Compute the weighted average cost of capital for Riseley.

(The Association of Chartered Certified Accountants)

Question 9.9

You have been told that the financial director in your company has identified a capital structure that he believes will minimise the long-run average cost of capital. This structure is:

	€000
Equity	6,000
Debt (@ 7 per cent)	4,000

The current level of dividend is 10c per share and this has been growing at 6 per cent per annum in recent years. The market price of equity is 200c. The market value of debt is equal to its par value.

The company is profitable and a 50 per cent Corporation Tax rate is relevant.

You are senior member of the engineering capital section, and with your team you have been examining a problem in the crimping department. The PX73 machine was purchased 5 years ago for €20,000, and was given a depreciation life of 8 years with no residual value. However, for tax purposes, the entire cost of this machine had been written off.

Although the PX73 machine could be used for 3 more years, it has been showing significant signs of wear, with a consequent adverse effect upon material and operating costs. Having regard to the rapid deterioration in the condition of the machine, your team has estimated costs for the next 3 years:

YEAR	1	2	3
Material and operating costs	19,500	24,500	29,000
Depreciation	2,500	2,500	2,500
	22,000	27,000	31,500

Your team has suggested that a modified crimping machine would be purchased for use over the next 3 years. The modified machine would cost €28,500, but would have no market value in 3 years' time. The existing machine has no current sale value. The use of the modified machine will, your team believes, give rise to the following costs:

YEAR	1	2	3
Material and operating costs	13,500	14,500	16,000
Depreciation	9,500	9,500	9,500
	23,000	24,000	25,500

A 100 per cent first year tax allowance is available for the modified machine, and will be taken if it is purchased.

REQUIREMENT

Having some appreciation of capital investment techniques, you decide to make an initial assessment of the data produced by your team, before submitting the proposal to divisional management.

1. Compute the weighted average cost of capital to be used as a discount rate in project appraisal. Explain the rationale underlying the use of an average.

2. Present your appraisal of the proposal to purchase a modified machine. Taxation benefits and charges can be assumed to give rise to cash flows in the year in which they occur.

(The Association of Chartered Certified Accountants)

Question 9.10: Trexon plc

Trexon plc is a major oil and gas exploration company that has most of its operations in the Middle East and South East Asia. Recently, the company acquired rights to explore for oil and gas in the Gulf of Mexico. Trexon plc proposes to finance the new operations from the issue of equity shares. At present, the company is financed by a combination of equity capital and loan capital. The equity shares have a nominal value of €0.50 and a current market value of €2.60. The current level of dividend is €0.16 per share and this has been growing at a compound rate of 6 per cent per annum in recent years. Interest on the loan capital is at the rate of 12 per cent and interest due at the year end has recently been paid. At present, the company expects 60 per cent of its finance to come from equity capital and the rest from loan capital. In the future, however, the company will aim to finance 70 per cent of its operations from equity capital.

When the proposal to finance the new operations via the rights issue of shares was announced at the annual general meeting of the company, objections were raised by two shareholders present. Corporation tax is at the rate of 35 per cent.

REQUIREMENT

1. Explain the term "cost of capital" and state why a company should calculate its cost of capital with care.

2. Calculate the weighted average cost of capital of Trexon plc that should be used in future investment decisions.

(*The Association of Chartered Certified Accountants*)

10

Financial Control through Budgets

10.1 THE CONCEPT OF CONTROL

Unfortunately, there are many different definitions of the term "control" in the English language, having a wide range of nuances ranging from "prohibit" to "manipulate". Within this variety are two major themes. First, there is the idea of control as domination; the person "in control" is the one who has the power to enforce or influence his or her will on subordinates. Second, there is the idea of control in the context of regulation, here, the controller detects whether there is a significant difference between "what is" and "what ought to be" and this difference acts as a stimulus for corrective action.

In the context of management accounting, the term "control" has been discussed in different ways. The traditional approach to control can be regarded as an *ex post* exercise — monitoring the outcome of activity, comparing it with standards and, if necessary, taking corrective action. Recently, the term control has taken on a broader nature and is regarded as an *ex ante* exercise to direct managerial activity in the light of knowledge or anticipation of future circumstances. This wider definition integrates planning and control. Planning and control are two sides of the same coin. Without planning, there cannot be control. Similarly, planning is virtually useless unless there is a control mechanism in place. One can therefore look at control as a process by which managers assure that resources are obtained and used efficiently and effectively in the accomplishment of the organisation's objectives.

A distinction must be drawn between effectiveness and efficiency, as they are essential concepts in the control process. *Effectiveness* is concerned with the attainment of objectives; an action is effective to the extent that it achieves what it was intended to achieve. Effectiveness is therefore concerned with doing the right thing. *Efficiency* is used in the engineering sense — the output achieved for a given level of inputs. Efficiency is concerned with the resources consumed by an organisation. An efficient machine is one that produces a given output from a minimum consumption of inputs or produces a maximum output from given inputs. Efficiency is concerned with doing the thing "right". Therefore, an action may be effective, but inefficient in that the result could have been achieved more economically. Alternatively, an action may be efficient but not effective.

It is also useful to make a distinction between "control" and "controls". Controls are a means that lead towards the condition of overall "control". However, overall control is not necessarily achieved by a proliferation of controls. In other words, an organisation littered with rules and procedures for many possible eventualities may be less likely to be successful because it becomes so concerned with detail that it does not see much greater changes that threaten its long-term future. Thus "control" is more than a matter of generating "controls"; it involves a continual monitoring of the position of the enterprise with where it is intended to be.

10.2 ELEMENTS OF A CONTROL SYSTEM

A number of important elements of a control system can be specified.

1. The first element is the goal or objective to be achieved. Goals are sometimes differentiated from objectives. Goals are timeless and broad and exist until they are changed — though this is infrequent. Objectives are stated in more specific terms, preferably in such a way that there is some way of determining whether the objective is being achieved. For example, a company might have profitability as its goal though its objective for the next accounting year might be to achieve a return of 10 per cent on sales. Objectives are "operational", in the sense that the control system can measure their degree of attainment.

   This chapter is devoted mainly to financial accounting controls. The process of financial control involves setting financial targets that reflect the desired state or condition. These financial targets then become the reference point for evaluation of actual performance. In the modern, complex world of business, a business is more likely to be successful and survive if some form of financial planning and control is carried out. Nevertheless, plans do not guarantee success, though the absence of planning (and control) is often characterised by:

   (a) Responding to crisis positions that were not anticipated.

   (b) Failure to grasp opportunities in the marketplace.

   (c) Too many products, due to failure to eliminate out-of-date products, perhaps due to lack of understanding of market needs and/or lack of precise information on product costs.

(d) No new products being introduced, especially ones that could compete in the market on the basis of price and quality.

(e) Expansion of sales volume without regard to underlying financial implications, such as additional investment in working capital and fixed assets, even though additional profits may be reported.

Enterprises *per se* do not have goals or objectives; instead, goals/objectives are set *for* the organisation by the dominant individuals or groups within the enterprise. Financial objectives can be described as "end" objectives and, typically, are stated in terms of profitability. A more modern description of historical financial numbers is that of "lagging indicators". Although lagging indicators represent the aggregate financial outcome of all the activities within an organisation, they measure the results too late. In contrast, "leading indicators" reflect factors that are crucial to the long term success of the business. For example, leading indicators of success in customer retention may predict future sales and overall profitability In the long run, a business cannot survive without earning a commercial rate of profit. Most textbooks assume profit maximisation as the objective of any commercial business, yet there is little, if any, evidence that this is so. In many cases, managers are prepared to accept satisfactory profits, usually based on previous year's figures.

In order to achieve financial objectives, a company must do a number of things right. It must concentrate on certain key variables – those areas of achievement that are critical to the success of a business. Market share is one such key variable. In order to achieve market share, a company needs a *competitive edge*. This can be achieved by:

(a) Cost leadership which can be achieved by high volume which, in turn, lowers unit cost and allows the company to set lower prices. Direct labour may also experience a learning curve as output increases. This is the most sustainable source of competitive advantage since it represents a formidable entry barrier for potential competitors. Cost leadership status can also be achieved by research and technology, preferential access to raw materials, and diversification into producing inputs that would otherwise be purchased externally by the company.

(b) Product differentiation that allows the company to charge a high price — a premium. This premium may be attributable to the reliability or quality of the product, friendliness of staff or cleanliness of premises. However, product differentiation is not necessarily a sustainable form of competitive advantage. The product sold in the market place can be considered a bundle of characteristics; those that provide product differentiation can, in time, be copied by competitors.

(c) Niche marketing, which involves the company focusing on a market not currently catered for by other companies. In other words, the company tries to avoid competition.

2. The second element in the control system is to monitor actual performance. This compares actual performance against original plans — typically, the financial targets set in the planning stage. The reports doing so should be relevant, where relevance is determined by the user of the reports rather than the preparer of the report. To be relevant, reports should focus on those aspects that are the responsibility of the individual recipient. Different levels of management have different needs for performance information — for example, production supervisors require daily information about operations under their control whereas a production director may require only monthly performance reports. Also, the reports must be timely in order to allow corrective action to be taken during the budget period. Reports should be accurate and cost-effective, though there is an inevitable trade-off between timely, accurate and cost-effective information. If information is not relevant, not timely, or not understandable, then it ceases to be useful for control purposes.

It is also important to compare like with like. For example, there is little benefit obtained by comparing the budgeted cost of producing 10,000 units with the actual costs of producing 9,000 units. Thus, to compare like with like, the budget must be "flexed" (this will be discussed later in this chapter).

Performance reports must be sound from a human behaviour point of view. In making this judgment, a number of criteria can be used:

(a) Targets must be understood by those affected and be within their aspirations or capabilities.

(b) Employees should feel they have some influence over targets established.

(c) Individuals should feel that they will not be unfairly penalised or blamed for variances outside their control.

3. The third element in the control process is the comparison of actual with budget. The difference between "budget" and "actual" is a variance, and can be positive or negative, favourable or adverse.

In many respects, this is the most important part of the control system since the manager must decide what variances are significant. In other words, the manager must exercise his judgment on whether the system is or is not in control. This is referred to as the *control decision point*. The crucial consideration is whether the variance is "significant". There is no easy way to determine what is "significant". Many managers determine significance in terms of the percentage variation. Other criteria that can be used relate to the absolute amount of the variance under consideration; the trend in the variance or the nature of the process. It may be company practice to be concerned with, say, only adverse variances. In other cases, managers may be concerned if the variance occurs very infrequently. The key issue is that of judgment. In some companies, statistical techniques, such as control charts are used to determine the significance of the variance and this will be discussed in the next chapter.

4. The final element in the control system is the "control action" — what is the most appropriate action to take in relation to the significant variance? First, the cause of the variance must be determined. In some cases, the variance may be entirely random and would not be expected to occur again. In other cases, the cause of the variance may be permanent — a price increase in raw materials. In other cases, the variance may be due to incorrect standards in the first place — the calculation of the required input of direct labour hours may have been incorrect. However, if the variance is due to operational causes (malfunctioning of machines or labour inefficiency, for example), corrective action should be taken, subject to cost/benefit considerations. The appropriate response is still a matter of judgment. This is the *control action point*. The corrective action to be taken may not be obvious — for example, costs may be too high, but there may be no obvious or easy method of reducing them. Indeed, there may be several methods and management must exercise judgment as to what corrective action is most appropriate.

Before looking at detailed accounting control systems (budgets and standard costing), there are two points worth stressing:

1. Variances only represent *signals* that the system is in or out of control. The control system requires a managerial response to

those variances. Without managerial response, there can be no control.

2. Control is a short-term concept. By this is meant that one can only control an event that is in the process of happening. This involves regular and periodic monitoring of actual performance against budget. One cannot control an event that has already occurred though one can learn from experiences. Thus, a variance can be included in discussing and agreeing targets for the following accounting period.

There are a number of different ways in which control can be achieved. For example, there may be "stop/go" controls that regulate activities *before* they happen. The purpose of this control system is to prevent a situation happening. Typical examples of such control systems are passport and visa controls designed to prevent illegal immigration; a central heating thermostat designed to keep a room within certain temperature ranges; traffic lights intended to regulate traffic flow. Also, in the context of an organisation, spending authorisation limits (spending above a certain amount must have prior sanction) come under this heading. Such controls are usually driven by routine and procedures. However, it is difficult to control human behaviour. Different individuals behave in different ways — look at how different drivers react to orange traffic lights! Even our own behaviour to such situations differs from time to time. Some companies try to rely on social controls whereby individuals, because of the corporate culture and codes of conduct will behave in a particular way. However, most organisations use accounting or "results" control.

Any planning and control system involves two key characteristics:

1. **Technical**: This is concerned with a flow of appropriate information, mainly accounting information. To facilitate this planning and control process, there must be a formal management accounting and information system (MAIS) that communicates relevant information throughout the organisation. In many cases, the accounting system is often the only source of quantitative information that combines the results of the activities of all the different parts of an enterprise. There are two basic reasons for this:

   (a) Accounting information is the only way of assessing the results of the diverse activities in terms of a single dimension. In other words, money is capable of summarising the impact of a wide variety of activities. Accounting information both integrates diverse activities within the organisation and acts as a measure of overall performance and position.

(b) Profitable performance is one of the prime interests of those who have invested their funds in the enterprise. Even if profitability is not necessarily the sole objective of the enterprise, it is an important consideration, for without adequate profitability, it may be impossible to raise additional funds for development or to discharge financial obligations.

However, accounting information in no way reflects the totality of activities that take place within the organisation and its interaction with the wider environment. Thus, there is a danger inherent in the use of accounting information. Because it is often the only quantitative measure of the activities, it can become treated as if it represented the only important aspect of organisational activity. This tendency has often been reinforced by the dominant concern with financial return, but it must be recognised that there are non-financial aspects of performance. These other measures of performance ultimately affect the accounting measures adversely, if not given appropriate attention. Also, accounting measures too often focus on short-term measures of performance. This phenomenon, called "short-termism" is now the increased focus of accounting research both in financial and management accounting.

2. **Behavioural**: The essence of control is behaviour – the interaction of managers with one another and with subordinates. It is a people-oriented process, so psychological considerations are dominant in management control. Activities such as communicating, persuading, influencing and criticising are an important part of the process.

It is useful to note that any control action generally has adverse effects on some individuals or groups. Tighter credit control implies that some customers will have to pay their bills sooner than they otherwise would; improved stock control may lead to greater fluctuations in the production demanded of the factory. In general, although a control action may serve the good of the overall organisation, some participants are likely to be adversely affected. Thus, control actions are often seen as unpleasant and unpopular, by some participants at least. For example, a new manufacturing process may require a smaller workforce, yet offer improved wages and increased job security for those who remain. The implementation of control actions by managers is a complex process, involving the resolution of conflict between groups who will be affected in different ways.

Feedback and Feedforward

The basic financial control model described above is essentially error-based. A significant variance between the actual result and the target set for a process causes a control action to be implemented. This is described as negative feedback control, and it is evident that one objection to its use is that errors are allowed to occur. This is particularly important in systems where time lags occur between the occurrence of an error, its reporting and the implementation of corrective action. In such cases, there is a need for anticipatory or feedforward control.

In feedforward control, instead of actual outputs being compared with targets, predictions are made of what outputs are expected to be at some future time. If these expectations differ from what is desired at that time, control actions are implemented that will minimise these differences. To the extent that the actions are effective, control is achieved before any deviation from the objective actually occurs. The difference between feedback and feedforward control is that the measurement of actual output is replaced by a *prediction* of expected output at some future time. Arguably the time lags that occur in human organisations make feedforward control equally, if not more, important than feedback control. Indeed, the activity of planning is an example of feedforward control. Planning is essentially a process in which expected outcomes of current actions are compared with aspirations; to the extent that the outcomes fall short of the aspirations, alternative actions are considered until a plan is produced that is expected to result in a satisfactory set of outcomes.

A distinction can therefore be made between programmed and non-programmed decisions in the control process. A programmed decision is defined as one where the decision situation is sufficiently well understood for a reliable prediction of the decision outcome to be made. A non-programmed decision is one that has to rely upon the judgment of managers because there is no formal mechanism available for predicting likely outcomes. In programmed decisions, the means-end relationships involved are sufficiently well understood for instructions to be confidently given as to how activities should be carried out in order to achieve a given objective. In non-programmed decisions, the causal relationships are less well understood so that it is possible only to instruct a manager as to what he is expected to achieve; the means of achievement have to be left largely to his or her judgment.

In decision situations, the objectives must also be known. However, frequently, decisions are made in the context of a group situation and different individuals within the group may have different objectives. Consequently, a two-by-two matrix of decision situations can be constructed. The top of the matrix represents the relative agreement on objectives; the horizontal indicates the degree of uncertainty regarding possible outcomes.

In Exhibit 10.1, the top left-hand box shows objectives that are known and where the cause-effect relationships are well-understood. Thus, decisions are programmable and the accounting system enables a clear and optimal decision to be made. Alternatively, objectives may be clear but predictive models may be poor so that we do not know which courses of action are most likely to yield the optimum results. Here, it is important to learn from past actions that have not always led to the desired consequences. The accounting system is often the only formal record of the effectiveness of past decisions and therefore can serve as an important source for learning. In this situation, decisions must be based on the judgment of participants.

Exhibit 10.1: Objectives and Uncertainty in Decision-Making

	AGREEMENT ON OBJECTIVES	
	Agreement	**Disagreement**
Certainty of cause and effect relationship	Decision-making by computation	Decision-making by compromise
Uncertainty of cause and effect relationship	Decision-making by judgment	Decision-making by inspiration

When objectives have not been agreed (and different individuals sometimes have different objectives), decisions emerge by a process of negotiation and compromise. The accounting information may be used to justify or support certain arguments. Finally, when objectives are ambiguous and predictive models are poor, decisions must be made on the basis of inspiration with, perhaps, accounting information playing a very minor role.

Even if one does not fully accept the above matrix, it is plausible to argue that accounting information systems often appear to have been designed as if they were operating in the top left-hand box, under conditions of absolute certainty. In reality, objectives are usually conflicting and ambiguous, and predictive models imperfect. This suggests that accounting systems should be used in a flexible manner, with users conscious of the fact that accounting information always suffers from limitations and that non-financial measures are also important.

10.3 BUDGETARY CONTROL

A budget is a comprehensive financial and/or quantitative plan for a defined, future period of time, setting out the expected route for achieving the financial and operational goals of an organisation.

Budgeting is an essential step in effective financial planning. Budgetary control is a technique whereby actual results are compared with budgets, and any differences (variances) arising are made the responsibility of key individuals who either take corrective action or revise the original budget. Budgetary control covers both the planning and control functions of the management accountant. Virtually all organisations engage in some form of budgeting. The extent to which plans are formalised in written budgets varies from one business to another. Large well-managed companies generally have carefully managed budgets for every aspect of their operations. Smaller business may prepare only a sales budget. To appreciate fully the budgeting process in the context of financial planning, consider the benefits.

Advantages of Budgeting and Budgetary Control

1. **Provides an enhanced managerial perspective**: In preparing a meaningful budget, managers are forced to make estimates of and anticipate future economic conditions, including interest rates, demand for the company's product and level of competition. Thus, budgeting increases management's awareness of the company's position and external economic environment.

2. **Provides advance warning of internal problems**: Since a budget shows expected results, management is forewarned of impending financial or operational problems. If, for example, the cash budget shows the company will exceed its overdraft limit in future months, management has advance warning of the need to hold down expenditure or to obtain additional financing. Budgeting, thus, reduces the need for crisis management. Allied to this is improved internal co-ordination and communication, because the preparation of a budget provides management with an opportunity to co-ordinate the activities of the various departments within the organisation. For example, the production department will be aware of the quantities required by the sales department.

3. **Provides a yardstick for evaluating actual performance**: Once the budget has been prepared, it provides a yardstick against which to measure performance. Variances can be identified and corrective action can be taken if deemed necessary. Usually, variance reports operate on the principle of management by exception, in that only significant variances are reported.

4. **Motivation**: A budget indicates in quantitative terms exactly what is expected of managers and that they will be held responsible for performance. Successful performance leads to rewards and so managers are motivated to achieve results. In addition, participation in the budgetary process can improve motivation. In order

to motivate employees, *three* ingredients must be present in the budgeting process:

(a)　The target (budget) must be perceived as achievable.

(b)　There must be reward promised, contingent on successful performance.

(c)　These rewards must be attractive to the individual. Some financial rewards may be attractive, although after tax, they become less so. Alternatively, non-financial rewards (promotion or titles) can be desirable.

Types of Budgets Prepared

The type of budget prepared will depend on the organisation. For example, a university would not prepare a production budget, which is designed to determine the number of units to be produced. The preparation of other budgets, such as a research and development budget may depend on the overall size of the organisation. As a useful guide to budgetary activities, Exhibit 10.2 represents budgets that may be prepared for different types of organisations.

Budget Preparation

When preparing budgets, it is customary to start with the sales budget. This is because sales ultimately determine production levels, materials purchases and many expense budgets. In other words, most budgets are sales-driven. A typical budget preparation sequence (for a manufacturing business) is as follows:

1.　**Operating budgets**
    (a) Sales budget.
    (b) Production budget.
    (c) Raw materials and purchasing budget.
    (d) Various expense budgets.

2.　**Master budgets**
    (a) Cash budget.
    (b) Budgeted profit and loss account.
    (c) Budgeted balance sheet.

Exhibit 10.2: Budgets

TYPE OF BUDGET	PRODUCTION BUSINESS	RETAIL BUSINESS	SERVICE BUSINESS
Sales Budget (Sales quantity and price)	Yes	Yes	Yes
Production Budget (Number of finished goods to be produced)	Yes	No	No
Raw materials purchase budget (Quantity and cost price of raw materials)	Yes	Purchase of finished goods only	No
Labour cost budget (Labour hours required and rate per hour)	Yes	Yes	Yes
Overhead cost budget (A range of budgets: advertising, administration)	Yes	Yes	Yes
Cash budget (Projected cash flows)	Yes	Yes	Yes
Forecast Profit and loss account (Projected revenue from sales budget less projected expenses)	Yes	Yes	Yes
Projected Balance sheet (Projected assets, liabilities and shareholders' funds)	Yes	Yes	Yes

Operating Budget

Sales Budget

The sales budget will be based upon estimates of general business and economic conditions, expected levels of competition and consumer demand. The sales budget is a prediction of expected sales by product, market and price for a defined future period. It is, therefore, the major key to internal planning since it is the predictor of future revenues, cash flows and profit. The business plans of the organisation, including major capital expenditure decisions, will be determined by future, expected sales levels. However, for operational purposes, one year's sales figures will be adequate. For strategic (long-term) purposes, projected sales figures for several years will be required.

In some instances, product demand is fairly stable and easily predictable but this is unusual. More normally, product demand varies widely depending on many factors external to the organisation and hence beyond its direct control. The need for a sound sales forecasting system is now accepted by almost all businesses. There are several distinct approaches to sales forecasting as follows:

1. **Surveys of users' buying intentions**: In this method, the organisation bases its sales forecast on a survey of buyers' intentions — it asks its major customers for a schedule of their expected future purchases by product and price. Clearly, if this information is reliable and complete, its own sales forecast can be estimated fairly accurately. Obviously, this method could not be applied where there is a large number of small customers; it tends to be most useful where there is a relatively small number of larger, industrial customers who must be co-operative and are able to forecast their own demand with reasonable accuracy.

2. **Salesforce composite method**: With this method, the various sales personnel are asked to forecast the future product sales for their own particular areas; these are successively collated and reviewed as they pass up the sales management hierarchy towards a full composite forecast. This method is based on the belief that the person nearest to the customer is best placed to judge market conditions. However, it suffers from the possible optimism of sales personnel and resulting potential overstatement of demand.

3. **Statistical method**: This involves projecting the sales patterns of previous periods according to various mathematical relationships. It has the advantage that cyclical trends and seasonal variations can be more easily identified and allowed for. In some more sophisticated instances, businesses have attempted with limited success to build into their forecasts variables such as consumers' disposable incomes, sales of inter-related products and economic forecasts of national and international growth rates. Usually statistical methods are used in combination with one or more of the other methods.

4. **Market research method**: Some businesses attempt to forecast demand for specific products by trying to estimate, from market and consumer surveys, the total market demand and their own

market share. This method is often combined with the salesforce composite method to provide a more balanced estimate.

While the above methods can, and are used, to forecast sales, one must remember that ultimately it is the "product" which is being sold. A "product" can be viewed as a bundle of characteristics — in other words a car, for example, has a physical dimension but it also provides one with comfort, security, status, reliability, economy etc. Every product competes on the basis of its characteristics. Consequently, many companies look not only at their own products but also at the products offered by competitors. A frequently used term to describe this process is *benchmarking*.

The importance of the sales forecast as the basis for future operational planning ensures that businesses will continue to seek better methods for estimating future sales demands. However, increasing competition, both nationally and internationally, will inevitably complicate the background against which such forecasts are made. Organisations must recognise that sales forecasts are at best reasoned estimates of future demands and operational plans must be as flexible as possible to allow for errors.

Production Budget (units)

The purpose of the production budget is to determine the number of finished goods that must be produced during the forthcoming accounting period. This budget is prepared only for a manufacturing enterprise, and is based on the sales forecast. It is prepared in terms of finished units only and one must be careful to adjust for opening and closing stocks of finished goods to identify the number of completed units that must be produced.

If production requirements exceed capacity, the company has to decide whether to subcontract, plan for overtime or hire additional capacity. If requirements are less than capacity, any spare capacity may be used for other profitable purposes by management.

Raw Materials and Purchasing Budget

This budget identifies the raw materials to be used in production (from the production budget) and adjusts this figure for any opening or closing stocks of raw materials. Such stock holdings are influenced by storage space and costs, trends of materials prices etc.

Expense Budgets

These include labour, overhead and other expense budgets. Since these expenses relate mainly to either production output or sales, many are driven by either the production or sales budget. For example, the labour budget depends on the number of units to be produced. Based on projected output, the number of labour hours can be estimated. The total number of hours multiplied by the anticipated wage rate provides a budget for labour cost.

Many of the expense budgets are organised around responsibility centres. If the accounting system measures the expenses (the costs) incurred by a responsibility centre but does *not* measure its outputs in terms of revenues, the responsibility centre is called an expense centre. Every responsibility centre has outputs, that is, it does something. In many cases, however, it is neither feasible nor necessary to measure these outputs in terms of revenues. For example, it would be extremely difficult to measure the monetary value of the accounting department's outputs. For this reason, most individual production departments and most staff units are expense centres.

However, there are two types of *expense* responsibility centre — engineered and discretionary. Engineered costs are costs for which the right or proper amount of costs that should be incurred can be estimated with a degree of reliability for the output achieved. Consequently, the relationship between input and output is a measure of efficiency. Engineered cost centres have three characteristics:

1. Their inputs can be measured in monetary terms.

2. Their outputs can be measured in physical terms.

3. An acceptable level of efficiency can be determined.

Discretionary costs (also called "managed" costs) are those for which no such engineered estimate is feasible; the amount of costs depends on management's judgment about the amount that is appropriate under the circumstances. Discretionary cost centres produce outputs that are much more difficult to observe and more difficult to model — for example, a personnel department. In many companies, the budgeted amount of discretionary costs is based on the previous year's figure adjusted for inflation and for the cost of any changes in operations contained in the budget proposals. This approach is described as incrementalism.

The distinction between discretionary and engineered cost centres has implications for budget preparation, type of financial control and measurement of performance. In an engineered cost centre, management will be concerned with efficiency whereas the manager of a discretionary expense centre will be concerned with the magnitude of the task — based on judgment. In terms of financial control, engineered cost centres will be evaluated in terms of efficiency; on the other hand, discretionary cost centres should be evaluated on the basis of non-financial measures of performance such as the quality of service provided. However, in many cases, they are evaluated simply by their ability to stay within budget!

Master Budgets

Cash Budget

The cash budget summarises (monthly) cash receipts and cash payments. Cash receipts depend upon the sales forecast and the company's experience in collecting amounts receivable from customers. Cash payments depend upon the budgeted levels of materials purchases, capital expenditures and operating expenses, as well as credit terms offered by suppliers. Anticipated borrowing, debt repayments, dividends paid and capital raised are also reflected in the cash budget. Depreciation of fixed assets should never be included in the cash budget since it does not represent either an inflow or outflow of cash funds.

Budgeted Profit and Loss Account

This budget is based upon the sales revenue forecast and estimates of the cost of goods sold and various operating expenses. It is prepared on the normal accruals basis of accounting and does not require estimates of the timing of cash receipts and cash payments.

Budgeted Balance Sheet

The final budget to be prepared is the forecast balance sheet at the end of the budget period. All assets (both fixed and current) will be disclosed together with all liabilities and shareholders' funds. The closing bank balance will be the closing balance as per the forecast cash budget. The profit for the period (to be included in shareholders' funds) will be the same figure that appears in the forecast profit and loss account for the period.

The various budgets mentioned above, together with workings, are illustrated using the following example:

ILLUSTRATION

The management of Digby Ltd. is anxious to expand into manufacture of widgets that will be sold for €30 each. A new limited company has been incorporated and you are provided with the following information regarding sales and production requirements for the manufacture of widgets.

1. The following capital expenditure will be required during January 20x9:

	€
Factory premises	100,000
Plant and equipment	100,000
Motor vehicles	20,000
	220,000

2. The factory will commence production on 1 March 20x9 and the following cost structure per unit of output is anticipated:

	€
Direct material (2 kg per unit @ €4 per kg).	8
Direct labour	2
Variable factory overhead	3

3. The initial purchase of raw material will take place during February 20x9. Closing stock of raw material will be maintained at 5,000 kg throughout the period. Suppliers will give three months' credit to the new company. It is intended to hold 1,000 finished units in stock at the end of each quarter. The normal level of production is 10,000 units per annum.

4. The forecast fixed production overheads amount to €10,000 in quarter 1 with €12,000 being paid in each of the remaining three quarters. Depreciation of fixed assets has not been included in these figures. Direct labour and variable overheads will be paid in the quarter in which they are incurred. Administration overheads amount to €10,000 per quarter and will be paid as incurred. The only distribution expense is represented by the depreciation of motor vehicles.

5. The sales forecast for 20x9 is as follows:

QUARTER	SALES UNITS
1	Nil
2	2,000
3	3,000
4	4,000
	9,000

6. It is anticipated that 20 per cent of total sales will be for cash and the remainder will receive three months' credit.

7. The new company will have an issued share capital of €100,000 which will be subscribed for in full during Quarter 1, 20x9. In addition, the parent company will advance €50,000 per quarter by way of an interest-free loan.

8. Accounting policies:

(a) Stocks: (i) raw materials are valued at cost of purchase; (ii) finished goods are valued at variable cost of production.

(b) Depreciation: (i) plant and equipment at 20 per cent on cost per annum; (ii) motor vehicles at 25 per cent on cost per annum; (iii) premises at 2 per cent on cost per annum.

REQUIREMENT

You are required to prepare a comprehensive set of budgets to reflect the financial performance and position for the forthcoming year.

SOLUTION

The first budget to be prepared is the sales revenue budget:

SALES REVENUE BUDGET

	QUARTER			
	1	2	3	4
Units	Nil	2,000	3,000	4,000
Revenue @ €30 each	Nil	€60,000	€90,000	€120,000

The amount to be collected in cash each quarter can now be estimated from the expected collection period. It is anticipated that 20 per cent of total sales will be for cash and the remainder will receive three months' credit. Thus, cash collections in quarter 2 will amount to €12,000 (20 per cent x €60,000). Debtors or accounts receivable at the end of the final quarter amounts to €96,000 (80 per cent x €120,000).

The sales budget determines the number of finished goods to be produced, taking the stock holding policy into consideration. The company intends to hold 1,000 finished units in stock at the end of each quarter. The production budget appears as follows:

PRODUCTION BUDGET (FINISHED UNITS)

	QUARTER			
	1	2	3	4
Units sold	Nil	2,000	3,000	4,000
Add: Closing stock	1,000	1,000	1,000	1,000
Less: Opening stock	Nil	(1,000)	(1,000)	(1,000)
Units to be produced	1,000	2,000	3,000	4,000

Once the production budget is agreed, the amount of raw materials to be purchased (in kilograms) must be ascertained. This will be based on each quarter's production requirements, adjusted for any stock-holding policy on raw materials. It is company policy to hold 5,000 kilograms of raw materials at the end of each quarter. The raw material purchase budget is as follows:

RAW MATERIAL PURCHASE BUDGET

	QUARTER			
	1	2	3	4
Units produced each quarter	1,000	2,000	3,000	4,000
Materials required (kg)	2,000	4,000	6,000	8,000
Add: Closing stock (kg)	5,000	5,000	5,000	5,000
Less: Opening stock (kg)	Nil	(5,000)	(5,000)	(5,000)
Purchases (kg)	7,000	4,000	6,000	8,000
Total purchases	€28,000	€16,000	€24,000	€32,000

The cash consequences of purchasing depend on the length of credit received from suppliers. Since three months' credit is received, the first payment (€28,000) takes place in quarter 2. At the end of the year, €32,000 will be owing to suppliers and this will be listed on the balance sheet at that date.

The remaining budgets to be prepared concern the various expense headings. For convenience, the direct labour and variable overhead figures are combined since they both relate to the number of units produced. The combined direct labour and variable overhead budget is as follows:

DIRECT LABOUR AND VARIABLE OVERHEAD BUDGET

	QUARTER			
	1	2	3	4
Units produced	1,000	2,000	3,000	4,000
Total cost of labour and variable overhead (€5)	€5,000	€10,000	€15,000	€20,000

These amounts will be paid for in cash as incurred and this will be reflected in the cash budget. Likewise, administration expenses are paid in the amount of €10,000, in each quarter. In addition, fixed production overheads are paid amounting to €10,000 in quarter 1 and €12,000 in each of the remaining three quarters.

The depreciation budget is based on the cost of the assets and the relevant depreciation policy as follows:

DEPRECIATION BUDGET

		€	
Premises	2% x €100,000	2,000	
Plant	20% x €100,000	20,000	
		22,000	(production overhead)
Motor vehicles	25% x €20,000	€5,000	(distribution overhead)

Once all the operating budgets have been prepared, they can be co-ordinated into a set of master budgets consisting of a cash budget (quarterly), forecast profit and loss account (for the year) together with a projected balance sheet at the end of the financial year.

The cash budget is as follows:

CASH BUDGET
FOR YEAR ENDED 31 DECEMBER 20x9

	QUARTER			
	1	2	3	4
	€	€	€	€
Cash collections from sales				
Cash (20%)	Nil	12,000	18,000	24,000
Credit (80%)	Nil	Nil	48,000	72,000
	Nil	12,000	66,000	96,000
Capital invested	100,000	Nil	Nil	Nil
Loan	50,000	50,000	50,000	50,000
Total [€474,000]	150,000	62,000	116,000	146,000
Cash outflows				
Fixed assets	220,000	Nil	Nil	Nil
Purchases	Nil	28,000	16,000	24,000
Labour and variable overhead	5,000	10,000	15,000	20,000
Fixed production costs	10,000	12,000	12,000	12,000
Administration	10,000	10,000	10,000	10,000
Total [€424,000]	245,000	60,000	53,000	66,000

The total cash inflows for the year amount to €474,000 compared with total cash outflows of €424,000. Thus, the projected bank balance at the end of the financial year amounts to €50,000. This will be shown on the balance sheet under the heading of current assets.

The forecast profit and loss account for the year summarises sales revenue, cost of goods sold, and expenses. The residual will either be a net profit or a net loss. It is useful to calculate the cost of goods sold (9,000 units) from the budgeted unit cost as follows:

COMPUTATION OF UNIT COST (VARIABLE COSTING)

	€
Direct materials (per unit)	8
Direct labour (per unit)	2
Variable overhead (per unit)	3
Total unit cost	13

Since the number of units sold was 9,000, the cost of goods sold amounts to €117,000 (9,000 x €13). However, 10,000 units will be produced, leaving an estimated 1,000 units in stock at the end of the accounting period. These will be valued at €13,000 (€13 x 1,000) and shown on the closing balance sheet under the heading of Current assets.

The budgeted profit and loss account for the year is as follows:

PROFIT AND LOSS ACCOUNT
FOR YEAR ENDED 31 DECEMBER 20x9

	€
Sales (9000 units @ €30)	270,000
Less: Cost of sales (9000 units @ €13)	(117,000)
	153,000
Depreciation of premises and plant	(22,000)
Fixed production overheads	(46,000)
Distribution expense (depreciation of vehicle)	(5,000)
Administration overhead	(40,000)
Net profit for year	40,000

Finally, the projected balance sheet can be presented, showing the assets, liabilities and shareholders' funds. The advantage of preparing this statement is twofold. First, it highlights the overall financial position. Second, a properly balanced balance sheet proves the arithmetical accuracy of the budgeting process.

BALANCE SHEET
AT 31 DECEMBER 20x9

	€	€	€
		ACCUM.	
	COST	DEPN.	NET
Fixed assets			
Premises	100,000	2,000	98,000
Plant	100,000	20,000	80,000
Vehicles	20,000	5,000	15,000
	220,000	27,000	193,000
Current assets			
Stocks:			
Raw materials		20,000	
Finished goods		13,000	
Debtors (80% x €120,000)		96,000	
Bank		50,000	
		179,000	
Current liabilities			
Trade creditors		(32,000)	
			147,000
			340,000
Financed by			
Invested share capital			100,000
Add: Projected profit for year			40,000
			140,000
Interest-free loan			200,000
			340,000

The budget above has been prepared on the assumption of a direct or variable costing system, which means that finished goods are valued at variable cost of production rather than full cost of production. This contrasts with absorption costing, which automatically assigns a portion of fixed production overhead to stock valuation. (This issue was earlier discussed in section 5.5). The difference between these two methods will impact on stock valuation in the balance sheet and also overall profitability.

The difference can be reconciled by the following formula:

$$Pd - Pa = \frac{F\ (Y - X)}{N}$$

Where: Pd = Profit under direct costing
         Pa = Profit under absorption costing

F   =   Fixed production overhead (€)
N   =   Normal production volume for overhead recovery
Y   =   Sales volume (in units)
X   =   Production volume (in units).

Applying the formula to Digby, the figures are:

$$€40,000 — Pa = \frac{€22,000 + €46,000}{10,000} \quad x \quad (9,000 — 10,000)$$

Effectively, under absorption costing, closing stock will be valued at €13 per unit (variable cost) plus €6.80 representing fixed production overheads. The €6.80 per unit reflects the level of fixed production overheads (€68,000), divided by the normal production level (10,000 units). Thus, closing stock will be valued at €19,800 under absorption costings compared with €13,000 under variable costing. The additional stock value under absorption costing means that the projected profit is increased to €46,800 and the value of finished goods stock is increased in the closing balance sheet. However, the cash position is unchanged.

10.4 FLEXIBLE BUDGETING

In the Digby Ltd. example, a master budget was prepared based on certain assumptions about the level of sales at specific prices and other operating data. This is a static budget. However, it is unlikely that these expectations will be exactly met and so it is important, in the control process, to compare like with like. For example, it would not be realistic to compare budgeted cost for 10,000 units of output with actual costs of an output of 12,000 units, especially where many costs are considered variable with respect to volume. Thus, for control purposes, we need to determine actual and budgeted revenue and costs for the same level of activity. This is the essence of flexible budgeting. Flexible budgets are budgets that are constructed for various levels of sales and production volume. Generally, they are relatively straightforward to prepare, provided one distinguishes between fixed and variable costs. They are prepared for control and evaluation purposes rather than for planning purposes.

ILLUSTRATION

The Casey Company produces one uniform product. The assembly department encounters wide fluctuations in volume (activity) levels from month to month. However, the following department overhead budget depicts expected costs for a normal level of activity of 20,000 units of production per month and the actual costs incurred in the month of June.

	BUDGET NORMAL MONTH €	ACTUAL COSTS INCURRED JUNE €
Supplies-variable	21,000	20,000
Power-variable	1,000	980
Repairs-variable	3,000	2,680
Depreciation-fixed	10,000	10,000
Other fixed overhead	5,000	6,000
	40,000	39,660

REQUIREMENT

In June, the department operated at a 17,600-unit level of volume. Prepare a performance report, comparing actual performance with the flexed budget.

SOLUTION

COMPARISON OF ACTUAL WITH FLEXED BUDGET

	ACTUAL COSTS €	FLEXED BUDGET 17,600 UNITS €	VARIANCE €
Supplies-variable	20,000	18,480	1,520 A
Power-variable	980	880	100 A
Repairs-variable	2,680	2,640	40 A
Depreciation-fixed	10,000	10,000	Nil
Other fixed overhead	6,000	5,000	1,000 A
	39,660	37,000	2,660 A

Comparison between actual performance and the flexed budget highlights an overall adverse cost performance of €2,660.

Flexed budgets enable more accurate assessments of performance to be made. The notion of the flexed budget should be used as the basis for all variance analysis. It is based on the simple concept that, for evaluation between budget and actual, one should compare like with like and this assumes an ability to identify fixed and variable costs and other input/output relationships. The next chapter explains that flexible budgeting is the basis for computing standard cost variances.

10.5 BEYOND BUDGETING?

The technique of budgeting in business organisations became popularised at the start of the twentieth century and its main use was as a method of cost control. The era also saw the emergence of the earliest comprehensive texts on budgeting and managerial accounting. For many people, budgeting was a technical issue and a favourite topic on management accounting examinations was to "prepare a budget" given a range of operating and financial data about a business.

In Ireland, current evidence indicates that most Irish firms "make some use of budgets", although one may query how extensive their use and role is within organisations. The situation is similar in, for example, the UK, where recent surveys indicate that budgets were and will continue to be the most important tool for management accountants in fulfilling their organisational role. The same can be said to be true of other countries in the world. In simple terms, most organisations make some use of budgetary control techniques.

However, in a pioneering and highly influential study in 1952 Chris Argyris illustrated the behavioural effects of budgeting in organisations. The findings of his study highlighted that the use of budgets could cause dysfunctional behaviour in subordinates, regardless of the degree of technical sophistication of the budgetary system. Since then there has been numerous articles identifying and investigating the "behavioural" aspects of the budgetary process. Many of these articles stress the negative, behavioural side of budgets. While not exhaustive, some of the main criticisms of the annual budgeting process are presented below:

1. Budgets are typically prepared without regard to company strategy. In such circumstances the agreed budget does not communicate strategy within the organisation. Thus, the implementation of strategy is the preserve of top management rather than every person in the organisation.

2. The focus of the budgetary process is on financial numbers only for a short period of time, usually 12 months. They typically exclude all other metrics such as performance measures relating to key success factors and promote a climate of "short-termism".

3. Since the business environment is changing so rapidly, realistic budgets for the future cannot be prepared.

4. The annual budgeting process becomes an incremental activity within organisations. It involves justifying annual increases/decreases based on the out-turn of the previous year. Such

an approach rarely encourages innovative thinking within organisations.

5. The cost of budget preparation is enormous in terms of managerial time, effort and monetary resources consumed. The exercise is protracted and is characterised by substantial delays and the need for regular reworking associated with changed assumptions. A recent benchmarking survey of some 1,500 organisations by one of the "Big Five" Accountancy firms revealed that companies would typically take from 60 – 90 days to complete the annual budget process and can typically consume about 20% of management's time. Indeed, much of this time is spent on putting the figures together rather than analysis.

6. People play "games" with budgets such as setting targets that are easily achieved or overspending budget allocations in case the budget is reduced for next year. Also, budget evaluation and rewards create tension and anxiety among employees which, in turn, can lead to a range of inappropriate behaviour, e.g., reducing spending in critical areas in order to achieve profit targets or manipulate the data etc.

7. Budgeting can create conflict between superiors and subordinates, for example, in agreeing targets for next year, especially where superior performance in one year becomes the target performance in the following year (the ratchet effect). In other words, can a budget be used simultaneously for motivation and accurate forecasting purposes?

8. Budgets can create a climate of "by the book" within organisations whereby achieving budget target is all that matters and is all that will be rewarded.

There is a recent and alternative viewpoint on the importance of the annual budgeting process for corporate success. Some argue that the annual budget is a barrier to effective management in today's competitive environment and that companies can gain substantial benefits from managing without budgets. Strong support for this controversial argument comes from a number of sources but particularly from CAM – I (Consortium for Advanced Manufacturing – International). CAM–I is an international research consortium of companies, management consultants and academics and, is perhaps, best know for its development of Activity-Based Costing, which has already been covered in this text. In 1998, CAM–I Europe initiated a research project known as the Beyond Budgeting Round Table (BBRT) which investigates how companies can manage without budgets. Some impressive theoretical arguments have been advanced together with case studies of a number of big European and American companies that have successfully abandoned their traditional budgeting practice. It is appropriate that we pay some attention to these developments. What does *Beyond Budgeting* imply for companies?

1. Traditionally budgets were used to control costs, and at the start of the 20th century they were supplemented by standard costing systems in large manufacturing companies. Cost control is still important in most businesses and underpins the "cost leadership" strategy suggested by Porter in his book entitled *Competitive Strategy*. Unfortunately, "cost leadership" is capable of being eroded, especially with the rapid diffusion of best practices within an industry. Perhaps, less capable of being imitated is the "differentiation" strategy whereby companies create a perception among consumers that the company's product or service is unique in some important way. Approaches to product differentiation include an emphasis on product quality and features, superior customer service and brand loyalty, yet these considerations are rarely made explicit in traditional budgets. In simple terms, the application of strategy is about competition and being different; in contrast, budgets are about control. *Beyond Budgeting* companies continuously review their strategic position. The new emphasis is on continuously looking for opportunities and threats in the future rather than continuously looking backwards at historical performance.

2. Related to strategy and the success of organisations is the performance in critical success factors. Critical or key success factors are those few, key areas that are most important in determining long-run profitability for the company. Such factors include quality, service, lead time and on-time delivery, customer satisfaction and loyalty, production flexibility and product innovation. Facilitating performance in these areas will be the knowledge, initiative and judgement of employees. Thus, we can distinguish between lagging and leading indicators of performance; the former represent the end result (in financial terms) and the latter provide insights relating to the process and means of achieving financial targets. To be effective, management control systems should not only be concerned with the ends, but also with the means by which goals will be achieved. In *Beyond Budgeting* companies, measure-

ment and reporting are confined to a few key performance indicators rather than a mass of detail. The quality of the information is more important than the quantity of the information.

3. The *Beyond Budgeting* approach assumes that effective organisational performance is likely to be associated with giving employees the training and authority to make decisions, and rewarding them accordingly. Frequently, traditional budgets act as a form of "control by constraint" in the sense that they restrict certain types of behaviour and may suppress employee creativity and innovation. Therefore, in order to be successful, modern organisations need to replace a system that constrains employee behaviour with a system that empowers and facilitates actions based on value propositions of the firm. Some readers will equate this as being similar to the notion of extensive decentralisation and empowerment.

4. *Beyond Budgeting* companies have changed both the target and reward systems associated with traditional budgets. Rewards are now based on group or unit rather than individual performance. Also, rewards are structured around beating the competition – a term that is widely defined and includes comparable sections within the company. Thus, the focus is on relative, competitive performance and not comparative performance in relation to previously agreed budget targets. Thus, no matter how well one is doing, in terms of rewards it is always advantageous to do better.

5. Budgets, as we currently understand the term, will still be important in terms of forecasting and planning. For example no one would suggest that cash flow forecasts should be abandoned and, indeed, rolling forecasts will be increasingly used. Also, cost forecasts will be required, for example, in setting predetermined overhead absorption rates in manufacturing firms using normal costing systems.

Conclusion

It may be difficult for managers and management accountants to accept the proposition that the traditional budgeting process should be abandoned. Personally, this author is sympathetic to the argument that, in order to survive, companies will have to plan and control their operations in a different way in the future. Albert Einstein said, "We cannot solve problems with the same thinking we used when we created the problem". At a minimum, the current criticisms of traditional budgeting practices should prompt us to question the efficiency and effectiveness of current management control systems within organisations. Better budgeting practices should allow us to move forward with constantly improving methods of management accounting. The result should be a better alignment of accurate forecasting with corporate strategy which, in turn, should be integrated with attempts to motivate managers in a positive manner.

10.6 END OF CHAPTER QUESTIONS

Question 10.1

At a management development seminar, a case study on budgeting and budgetary control was presented. When a small discussion group was formed, it emerged that different members of the group had perceived quite separate and distinctive roles for budgets within organisations, particularly:

◊ Planning.

◊ Motivation.

◊ Evaluation.

The objective of the seminar was to stimulate discussion about the conflict between these roles and practical ways of reducing this role conflict.

REQUIREMENT

1. Elaborate briefly on the three different roles that the separate managers identified.

2. Describe potential conflicts in these roles and make some practical suggestions that may help to reduce or eliminate such conflicts.

(*The Association of Chartered Certified Accountants*)

Question 10.2

The annual budget is the basis of much internal management information. What is the relationship of the annual budget process to:

1. Strategic planning?

2. A comparison of periodic forecast and actual results?

(*The Association of Chartered Certified Accountants*)

Question 10.3

Fixed budgets and flexible budgets are different types of budgets in everyday use for management planning and control.

REQUIREMENT

1. Explain the meanings of the terms fixed budget and flexible budget.

2. Discuss the reasons for and the advantages and disadvantages of each of the three types of budget from the viewpoint of an operating manager.

(The Association of Chartered Certified Accountants)

Question 10.4

The manager of an established transport fleet has consulted you regarding the preparation of a flexible budget for the department under his control. One purpose of the budget is to compile an average cost per mile for charging to user departments.

The fleet consists of eight similar vehicles costing €45,000 each with an estimated residual value of €9,000 and an estimated useful life of four years.

Typical maintenance costs for each vehicle consist of a service every six months or 10,000 miles (whichever occurs first) costing €250 and spare parts costing €50 in the first year.

On consulting other records, the manager is able to establish that annual licence and insurance costs €300 per vehicle. Tyres costing €80 each are changed every 20,000 miles on these four-wheeled vehicles. Fuel is estimated at €1.80 per gallon and each vehicle can achieve 20 miles per gallon.

The annual administration cost of the transport department is part fixed and part variable in relation to the annual mileage covered by all vehicles. The following table shows the prediction of this cost taken from a study recently undertaken:

MILEAGE TRAVELLED	TOTAL ADMIN. COST PA €
175,000	55,000
200,000	60,000
250,000	70,000

The manager is undecided about the annual workload of his department and for purposes of budget discussion has put forward three possible levels: 20,000, 25,000 and 30,000 miles per vehicle. These are average miles per vehicle, which means that some of the vehicles will do less mileage and others will do more.

REQUIREMENT

Prepare flexible budgets for the transport department covering one year, taking account of the possible range of vehicle mileage. Provide explanations or workings where you consider it appropriate and comment where you consider further information would improve the accuracy of budget preparation.

(The Association of Chartered Certified Accountants)

Question 10.5

An engineering company is developing a reporting system for cost-centre managers relating to both direct costs and overheads. The budget for period 7 of a typical production department contains the following overhead costs:

	€
Rent and rates (fixed)	16,000
Supervision (fixed)	14,400
Indirect materials (variable)	5,200
Power (variable)	10,800
Depreciation of machinery (fixed)	8,000

The budgeted machine hours, which are considered realistic for the establishment of overhead cost rates, were 8,000 hours.

However, 8,800 machine hours were actually worked and actual output of the department was in line with the machine hours worked.

The *actual* expenditure was as follows: Rent and rates €16,800, supervision €14,000, depreciation as budgeted, indirect materials €5,800 and power €12,880.

REQUIREMENT

1. Establish the budgeted fixed and variable overhead rate for period 7 from the information given, stating any assumptions necessary.

2. Design a performance report, completed so far as information permits, for presentation to the manager of the cost centre providing appropriate feedback on her/his responsibilities. You should try to segregate controllable from non-controllable variances. Comment on significant features of the report and any assumptions made.

(The Association of Chartered Certified Accountants)

Question 10.6: Monet Company

The Monet Company has estimated sales of product W for the next four months as follows:

	UNITS
January 20x1	60,000
February 20x1	80,000
March 20x1	70,000
April 20x1	80,000

The stock on hand of product W on 31 December 20x0 is 12,000 units. The management of the Monet Company has decided that at the end of each month the stock of product W should be sufficient to satisfy 20 per cent of the next month's estimated sales units.

The production of product W requires two different direct materials: No. 1056 and No. 1057. One unit of product W requires 2 kg of direct materials No. 1056 and 1 kg. of direct materials No. 1057. Because of the time required to obtain both direct materials, management maintains closing stock of direct materials sufficient to produce the following month's production of product W. The 31 December 20x0 stock of direct materials No. 1056 is 128,000 kg and direct materials No. 1057 is 64,000 kg.

REQUIREMENT

1. Based on the budgeted sales quantities prepare a production budget for January, February, and March.

2. Prepare a raw materials usage and purchases budget for January and February.

Question 10.7: Manacco Company

Manacco Company, a company that is to be formed with an issued share capital of €105,000, is expecting a period of rapid growth, and the estimated sales in units are as follows:

	UNITS
January	4,000
February	6,500
March	8,500
April	11,000
May	14,000

The sales price per unit is €30. Twenty per cent of sales will be paid for in cash and the remainder will be received in the month following sale. There were no debtors (accounts receivable) on 1 January.

The stock of finished goods and raw materials at 1 January was Nil and the company has now decided to institute a stocking policy of having in hand 80 per cent of next month's sales of finished goods and 100 per cent of next month's raw materials required for production. The production process is very rapid and there is no "work in progress"; units are started and completed in the same day. Production of one unit requires 2 kilos of material at €3.50 per kilo and 2.5 hours of labour at €5 per hour. Material is purchased one month before production and is paid for in cash. Labour is paid for in the month in which it is used. Administration costs amount to €10,000 per month and variable production overheads amount to €1 per unit. There are no fixed production overheads.

REQUIREMENT

Prepare the following monthly budgets for the period January to March.

1. Sales and cash collections.

2. Production.

3. Material purchases and payments.

4. Labour.

5. Profit and loss for the quarter.

6. Cash budget.

7. Balance Sheet at 31 March.

QUESTION 10.8: Somerton Ltd.

Somerton Ltd. produces and sells two products: Y and Z. Its balance sheet at 31 December 20x8 is attached. On the basis of sales forecasts, it is anticipated that 40,000 units of Y and 12,500 units of Z will be sold (all on credit) in the coming year at selling prices of €10 and €16 respectively.

At the end of the year, management requires 1,200 units of Y and 800 units of Z to be held in stock. In addition, 7,000 kg of raw material is also to be held.

The production inputs and costs of each product are as follows:

	Y	Z
Raw materials	2 kg	3 kg
Cost of raw material	€1/kg	€1/kg
Direct labour	3 hours	2 hours
Rate per hour	€1.50	€1.50
Other production overheads (variable)	50p/unit	€1/unit

The following costs are anticipated during the year:

	€
Selling expenses	65,000
Light and heat	3,600
Administration	22,000
Rent and rates	25,000

Depreciation is calculated at the rate of 10 per cent on book value of assets in existence at end of year.

During the year, €35,000 of new fixed assets will be purchased. In addition, 60,000 new shares will be issued at €1 each.

Strict credit limits will be imposed on customers. It is agreed that the average period of credit allowed to customers will be 45 days (based on a 360-day year) and this figure is to be used in budget calculations. Creditors are anticipated to increase by 20 per cent on the opening balance.

SOMERTON LTD.
BALANCE SHEET
AT 31 DECEMBER 20x8

	€	€
Fixed assets		
(at cost less aggregate depreciation)		260,000
Current assets		
Stocks of finished goods:		
500 units of product Y at €7	3,500	
500 units of product Z at €7	3,500	
Raw materials at cost:		
5,000 kg. at €1.00	5,000	
Debtors (accounts receivable)	24,000	
Cash/Bank	29,500	
	65,500	
Less: Current liabilities (Creditors)	(12,000)	53,500
Total net assets		313,500
Financed by:		
Issued share capital of 50p each		240,000
Retained profits		73,500
		313,500

REQUIREMENT

1. Prepare a cash budget for the year to 31 December 20x9 (monthly figures are not required).

2. Prepare a budgeted profit and loss account for the year and a closing balance sheet, assuming stock is valued at variable cost of production.

Question 10.9: Kildare Ltd.

Kildare Ltd. has recently been incorporated and will commence its retail operation on 1 July 20x8. The issued share capital consists of 500,000 €1 ordinary shares.

1. The selling price per unit is €6 and it is estimated that 20,000 units will be sold in each of the first three months and 30,000 units per month thereafter.

2. It is anticipated that all sales will be paid for in the month following sale.

3. The company's policy is to purchase one unit of stock for each unit of sale. Stocks are to be maintained at a level equal to the planned unit sales of the following month. There was no opening stock.

4. The purchase price per unit of stock is €3 but is anticipated to increase by 10 per cent on 1 September. Purchases are paid for in the month following purchase.

5. Fixed assets require to be purchased and paid for as follows:

	€
1 July	75,000
1 October	25,000
1 November	19,000

6. Administration overheads are expected to be €2,000 per month.

7. It requires one employee to sell 10,000 units. The current salary is €800 per month for each worker. Assume that new employees can be hired as needed.

REQUIREMENT
You are required to prepare:

1. Appropriate operating budgets — sales, purchases, etc — for July to December on a monthly basis.

2. A cash budget for July to December, on a monthly basis.

3. A budgeted profit and loss account for the six months ended 31 December and a balance sheet at that date.

Question 10.10: P and G Management Services Group
P and G Management Services Group offers consultancy services to a range of clients. The following information relates to May's activities:

	ACTUAL CONSULT.	BUDGET CONSULT.
Revenues (€)	96,000	99,000
Staff hours	1,200	900
Salaries (€)	38,400	32,400
Marketing expenses (€)	10,500	12,600

Clients are charged at an hourly rate for all hours that staff work on their projects. Hourly rates were budgeted at €110 per hour for consultancy. The group employs both full-time and part-time staff and this renders the salary costs sufficiently flexible to be considered variable. Marketing costs are discretionary fixed costs, which are directly identifiable to the individual divisions.

REQUIREMENT

In relation to the consultancy division only:

1. Prepare a financial statement and brief commentary that will provide an overview of the performance of the division.

2. From this statement and any other supporting information which you care to present comment on:
   (i)   the sales performance, noting that the actual revenue almost meets the budget,
   (ii) the adequacy of control over salary costs,
   (iii) the meaning of discretionary fixed costs and how the division should approach the control of these marketing expenses.

(The Association of Chartered Certified Accountants)

Question 10.11: Baygong Ltd.

Baygong Ltd. plans to produce a new product for which the standard marginal cost per unit is as follows:

	€
Direct material	3
Direct wages	2
Variable overhead	1
	6

Fixed overheads are budgeted at €96,000 for the year commencing 1 July 20x9. These will be incurred and paid in equal amounts during each month.

Production is to commence in July and sales from 1 August 20x9.
The sales budget for the period to 30 November 20x9 is as follows:

	UNITS	SALES VALUE €
August	2,000	20,000
September	4,000	40,000
October	6,000	60,000
November	11,000	110,000

The following data is available:

1. Direct wages are paid in the month in which they are incurred.

2. Direct materials: Starting in July, 100 per cent of direct materials required for each month's production are purchased as required. These are paid for in the month of purchase.

3. Variable overhead: Paid as and when incurred.

4. Stock: It is company policy to hold closing stocks of finished goods equivalent to the following month's sales.

5. All sales will be on credit and will be received as follows: 10 per cent received in the month of sale, and 90 per cent received in the following month. There are no bad debts or sales discounts.

REQUIREMENT

Prepare a detailed monthly cash budget for the new product, for the four month period from 1 July to 31 October 20x9.

Question 10.12: Fitzroy Ltd.

John Fitzgerald has been employed in a senior position in the electrical appliance industry. Through his contacts, he has obtained the agency for a well-established product, manufactured by a US company. In order to exploit this agency on a full-time basis, he has formed a company, Fitzroy Limited, with a close friend and colleague, Michael Royston. John Fitzgerald and Michael Royston are the two directors of the company. They have found suitable premises that will be available on 1 January 20x9, from which date the company will commence business.

Royston has made the following calculations:

1. Capital expenditure on plant and machinery will total €15,000 and will be paid in January 20x9.

2. In 20x9, the company's fixed costs will amount to €24,000, excluding directors' salaries. With the exception of €12,000 annual rent, which is payable half-yearly in advance on 1 January and 1 July, the fixed costs will be incurred evenly throughout the year and payable when incurred.

3. Variable expenses will amount to 12.5 per cent of monthly sales, and will be paid one month in arrears.

4. Sales from January to June are estimated at €70,000 monthly.

5. The gross margin will be 20 per cent on sales.

6. It will be necessary to carry stocks at all times at the level of 2 months' forecast sales. The January stock purchases will be paid

for in January, 20x9: thereafter there will be monthly payments one month in arrears.

7. Fitzroy Ltd. allows one month's credit to all customers.

8. The two directors will draw a salary of €2,000 per month each from the company.

REQUIREMENT

You are required to calculate, on the basis of the above forecasts, the cash requirements that may arise for Fitzroy Ltd., for the first four months of trading.

11

Standard Costing and Variance Analysis

11.1 INTRODUCTION

Standard costing is part of a budgetary control system, although a company may operate a budgetary control system without having a standard costing system. Standard costing involves the setting of detailed predetermined *unit* cost estimates, in order to provide a basis for comparison with actual cost performance. The term "standard cost" is therefore a unit concept — for example, the standard cost of material is €1 per unit. However, the term "budgeted cost" is a total concept — for example, the budgeted cost of material is €10,000 if 10,000 units are produced.

Before looking at the issue of standard costing in greater detail, remember the distinction between direct (variable) and absorption costing. The difference between these two methods is the accounting treatment of fixed production overheads. Under direct costing, these fixed costs are written off in full to the profit and loss account in the period in which they are incurred. No attempt is made to include them in stock valuation. On the other hand, absorption costing includes a portion of these fixed costs as part of the closing stock valuation. Thus, the profit impact of these two methods is generally different. This has implications for calculating standard cost variances. This chapter initially examines variances in the context of direct costing and devotes a separate section to highlighting the differences under a standard absorption costing system.

One of the keys in understanding the technique of standard costing is to relate it to the different levels of budgetary control that may exist in a company. The most basic level is to compare budgeted costs and revenues with actual performance on a line-by-line basis. This is the simplest but crudest level of variance analysis and is referred to here as level 1 analysis. Thus, individual cost and revenue variances can be ascertained as follows:

LEVEL 1 ANALYSIS: LINE-BY-LINE

	BUDGET €	ACTUAL €	VARIANCE €
Sales	60,000	70,000	+ 10,000
Materials	(30,000)	(40,000)	(-10,000)
Fixed overheads	(20,000)	(25,000)	(-5,000)
Net profit	10,000	5,000	(-5,000)

This analysis shows that, in the example, the favourable revenue/sales variance was more than offset by the adverse material and overhead variances. However, a second level of analysis is both possible and desirable. This involves eliminating the distorting effects of changes in output when comparing budget with actual. To generate meaningful variances in terms of both revenue and costs, one needs to adjust for output changes. This is done by way of flexible budgeting and was mentioned in the previous chapter.

A flexed budget is the budget that would have been prepared if one had known in advance what the actual output would be. In some sense, it is a retrospective calculation. However, from a control point of view, as distinct from a planning point of view, it allows one to isolate the effects of changes in the level of business activity from changes in selling prices, costs and/or operating efficiencies. Level 2 analysis involves taking the static budget (say 10,000 units) and flexing it with actual output (say 14,000 units). The variance figures reported below are the differences between flexed budget and actual performance. However, one can also report a variance between the static and flexed budget, amounting to €12,000. This is referred to as a sales volume variance and reflects the difference between the anticipated profit figure in the different budgets.

LEVEL 2 ANALYSIS: FLEXED BUDGET ANALYSIS

	STATIC	FLEXED	ACTUAL	VARIANCE
Unit sales	10,000	14,000	14,000	
	€	€	€	€
Sales revenue	60,000	84,000	70,000	(-14,000)
Materials	(30,000)	(42,000)	(40,000)	+2,000
Fixed overheads	(20,000)	(20,000)	(25,000)	(-5,000)
Net profit	10,000	22,000	5,000	(-17,000)

Sales volume variance	+12,000

Level 2 analysis indicates that there are really two different kinds of variances. The first variance arises from comparing flexed budget figures with actual performance. This comparison reveals a total cost/revenue variance in the amount of €17,000 (adverse). This total variance reflects two factors: A change in sales price per unit and a change in operating costs. For convenience, refer to these as *operating variances*.

The second type of variance reported above arises by comparing the profit figure per the original (static) budget with the flexed budget. There is a favourable variance of €12,000 relating to *sales volume*, which is simply described as the sales volume variance. The sales volume variance can be proved (under direct costing) in relation to the budgeted unit contribution (€3) — selling price minus variable unit cost and the additional units sold. Since 4,000 additional units were sold, the anticipated profit impact was favourable in the amount of €12,000. Refer to this as a *planning variance* to contrast it with the operating variances disclosed earlier.

The purpose of level 2 analysis (flexed budget analysis) is to segregate variances that arise due to volume changes (the sales volume variance) and the cost/price related variances arising from operating conditions. Such a separation is fundamental to variance analysis.

11.2 SALES REVENUE VARIANCES

The previous section shows that sales revenue variances can be divided into a sales price variance and a sales volume variance. These are highlighted below.

ILLUSTRATION

Brown Ltd., a retail company, sells two products, J and E, each in two different areas and the following represents the budget for 20x1:

	BUDGET UNITS	BUDGET SALE PRICE €	BUDGET UNIT COST €
J	5,000	32	24
E	10,000	24	20

During 20x1, the following represented the actual performance:

	ACTUAL UNITS	ACTUAL SALE PRICE €	ACTUAL UNIT COST €
J: Area 1	4,000	32	24
J: Area 2	2,000	33	24
E: Area 1	6,000	24	20
E: Area 2	3,000	23	20

REQUIREMENT
Calculate appropriate sales revenue variances.

SOLUTION
In order to concentrate only on the sales revenue variances, actual cost figures are exactly in line with budget. Also, fixed costs are ignored as they are assumed to be insignificant.

The first working is to prepare static and flexed budgets and report actual performance as follows:

SALES REVENUE	STATIC €	FLEXED €	ACTUAL €
Total for product J	160,000	192,000	194,000
Total for product E	240,000	216,000	213,000
Total sales revenue	400,000	408,000	407,000

BUDGET COSTS	STATIC €	FLEXED €	ACTUAL €
Total for product J	120,000	144,000	144,000
Total for product E	200,000	180,000	180,000
Total costs	320,000	324,000	324,000
Budget net profit	80,000	84,000	83,000

The presentation above displays two important features, when comparing budget with actual:

1. There is a sales volume variance due to selling more (less) than anticipated. The impact of the sales volume variance can be calculated by comparing the profit figures from the static and flexed budgets. This amounts to €4,000 and is favourable.

2. There is a sales price variance caused by selling at a price higher (lower) than budget. These sales price variances amount to €1,000 (€84,000 – €83,000) and are adverse. There are no cost variances.

Sales revenue variances are due to changes in sales volume — sales volume variances. Sales volume variance can be calculated by using the following formula:

Sales volume variance:
(Actual volume – budgeted volume) x budgeted contribution per unit.

The purpose of this calculation is to reveal the extent of the planning variance, which is equal to the difference between the profit figures in the static and flexed budgets. The figures are as follows:

		€
J: Area 1 and 2	(6000 - 5000) x €8	8,000 F
E: Area 1 and 2	(9000 - 10,000) x €4	(4,000)A
		4,000 F

Sales revenue variances are also due to changes in selling price – sales price variances.

The sales price variance can be calculated by way of formula:

Sales price variance:
(Actual price – budget price) x number of units sold.

The calculation for each product and area is:

		€
J: Area 1	(32 - 32) x 4000	Nil
J: Area 2	(33 - 32) x 2000	2,000F
E: Area 1	(24 - 24) x 6000	Nil
E: Area 2	(23 - 24) x 3000	(3,000)A
		(1,000)A

The analysis above indicates that there was a €1 per unit price increase in product J in area 2, providing additional profits of €2,000, based on the actual number of units sold. There was a price reduction of product E in area 2, reducing profits by €3,000.

To summarise, the different profit figures can be reconciled as shown in Exhibit 11.1.

Exhibit 11.1: Reconciliation of Profit Figures

	€
Static budget profit	80,000
Add: Sales volume variances	4,000
Flexed budget profit	84,000
Less: Sales price variances	(1,000)
Actual profit	83,000

Based on these variances, management may want to find why there were price changes and also why sales targets were exceeded for product J but were not achieved for product E. The purpose of the analysis is to highlight the issues to which managerial attention should be focused.

11.3 MATERIAL AND LABOUR COST VARIANCES

There is a third and more detailed level of analysis referred hereunder as standard cost variances. It involves calculating the cost variances between flexed budget and actual (level 2 analysis) and dividing each cost variance into two component parts: A price variance and a usage variance. Again, it is important to remember that a standard direct costing system is assumed.

Standard costing involves the setting of predetermined cost estimates for a *unit of output*. It is usual to set a *unit cost* for all three cost elements: Standard material cost, standard labour cost and standard overhead cost. Standard costs do not apply to non production costs because they are not part of the stock valuation process; many of them are fixed costs and no meaningful input-output relationship can be established. A standard cost is initially determined with reference to:

1. A standard physical input — input of labour hours or kilograms of raw materials, for each unit of output, and

2. A standard price for each physical unit of input.

For example, if a unit of output requires 2 kg of raw materials (Qs), and each kg costs €3 per kg. (Ps), the standard material cost per unit is €6 (Qs x Ps). This is pictured below in Exhibit 11.2.

Exhibit 11.2: Standard Material Cost per Unit

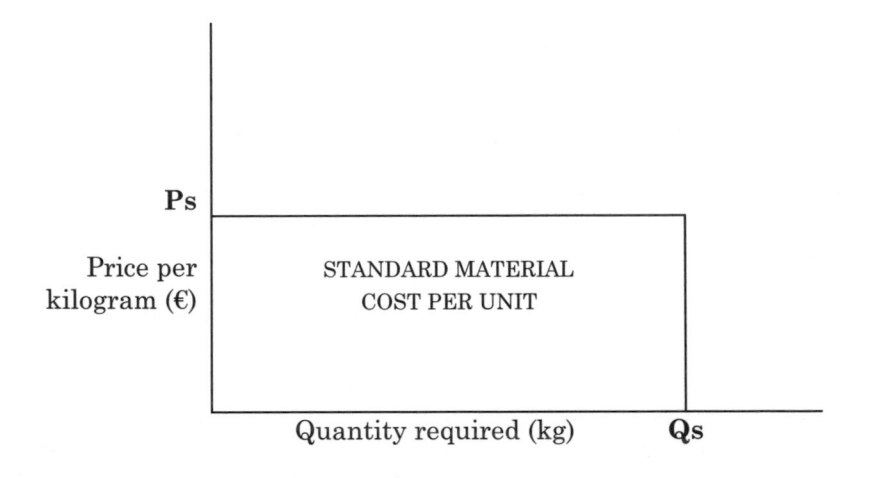

If the standard cost is compared with actual, *two* important variances can be isolated: A *price* variance and the *usage* variance. The price variance is due to the actual price (Pa) of a physical input being higher (or lower) than anticipated. Moreover, the actual amount of kilograms consumed (Qa) may have been more or less than anticipated. Thus, a company may have consumed, say, an average of 3 kg compared with an expected, standard average of 2 kg.

The variances are depicted in Exhibit 11.3.

Exhibit 11.3: Standard Material Cost Variances

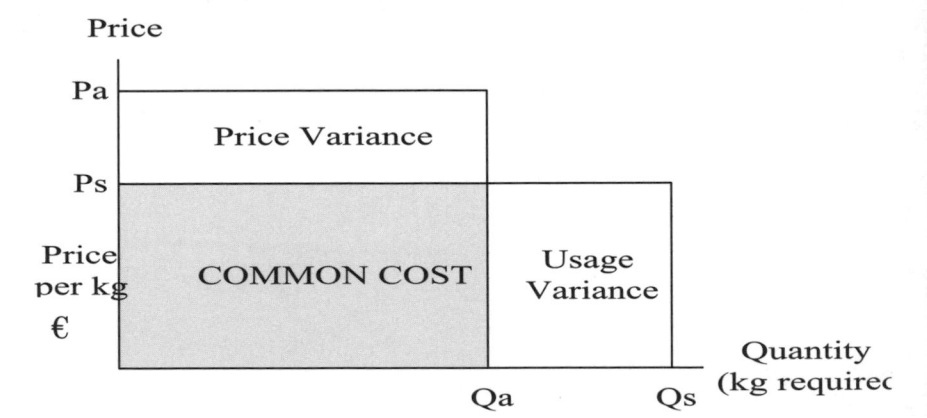

Using the diagram above for reference, the price variance can be computed as follows:

Price variance:
(Actual unit price – budget unit price) x actual quantity purchased.

This indicates whether the average unit purchase price was more or less than budget and the magnitude of the overall resulting discrepancy.

Usage variance:
(Actual quantity used – budget quantity for actual production) x standard unit price.

This indicates whether the amount of materials (or labour) consumed for the actual output produced was more or less than anticipated and the overall magnitude of the resulting discrepancy.

The calculation of standard cost variances will be illustrated below. Before that, it may be useful to summarise the range of variances that can be calculated for a standard direct costing system — see Exhibit 11.4. The sales revenue variances — the sales price variance and the sales volume variance — have already been covered and correspond to variances (A) and (B) below.

Exhibit 11.4: Profit Variance Chart for Direct Costing

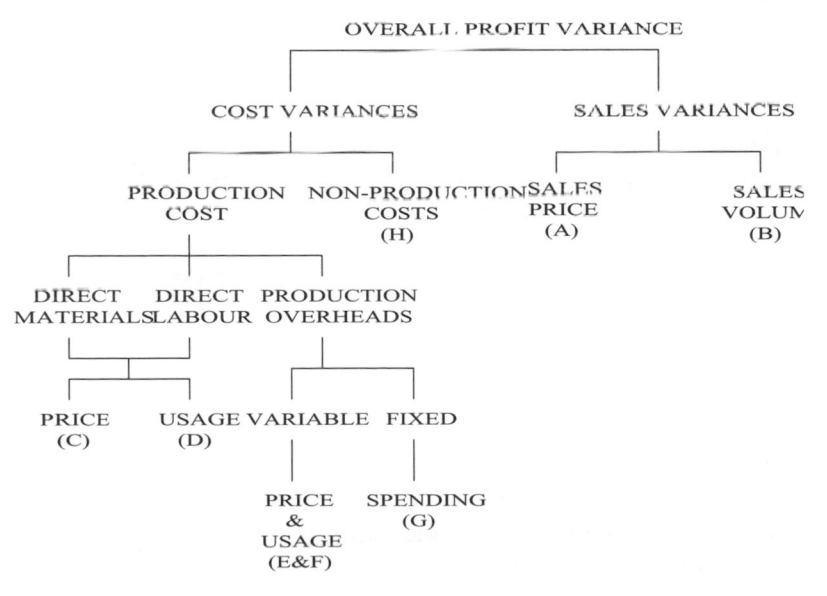

Example of Direct Material and Direct Labour Variances

The variances for both direct materials and direct labour will now be computed. The variance for each cost element will be divided into a price variance and a usage variance, which correspond to variances (C) and (D) in Exhibit 11.4. Note that the labour price variance is more commonly referred to as the labour rate variance and the labour usage variance as the labour efficiency variance.

ILLUSTRATION

The Direct Cost Company plans to produce 40,000 units of a single product during the coming year. The material and labour cost figures are budgeted as follows:

		€
Material	3 kg @ €2 each	6.00
Labour	1 hour @ €3 each	3.00

However, only 36,000 units were produced and sold during the year. The purchased and used materials amounted to €196,000, involving 112,000 kg at €1.75 per metre. The total labour cost was €142,600 representing 46,000 direct labour hours at €3.10 per hour.

For the purpose of variance reporting, the company ignores overhead costs.

REQUIREMENT

Calculate appropriate standard cost variances.

SOLUTION

	STATIC BUDGET	FLEXED BUDGET	ACTUAL	VARIANCE
Units	40,000	36,000	36,000	
	€	€	€	€
Material	240,000	216,000	196,000	20,000F
Labour	120,000	108,000	142,600	(34,600)A

According to the above, the total material cost variance amounts to €20,000 favourable and the labour variance is €34,600 adverse. The purpose of the standard costing system is to divide both these variances into a price and usage component.

The material and labour price variances can be calculated according to the following formulae:

Price variance:
(Actual unit price – budget unit price) x actual quantity purchased.

Usage variance:
(Actual quantity used – budget quantity for actual production) x standard unit price.

		€
Material price	(€1.75 – €2.00) x 112,000	28,000 F
Material usage	(112,000 – 108,000) x €2	(8,000) A
Total material cost variances		20,000 F

The same type of calculations are performed for labour:

		€
Labour rate	(€3.10 – €3.00) x 46,000	(4,600) A
Labour efficiency	(46,000 – 36,000) x €3	(30,000) A
Total labour cost variance		(34,600) A

In some manufacturing businesses, the calculation of variances is done by way of accounting entries rather than by formulae. A "T-account" is prepared for each cost element. The left hand side of the account reflects actual expenditure and the right-hand side reflects the actual output, recorded in standard cost. Each side of the account records both the physical flow of resources and the monetary amounts. Using the data above, the material and labour records are as follows:

DIRECT MATERIALS

	Kg	€		Kg	€
Actual input (36,000 units)	112,000	196,000	Standard output	108,000	216,000

The T-account records that 112,000 kg were purchased at a total cost of €196,000, and 36,000 units were produced. In standard costing terms, each unit should have used 3 kg of materials — 108,000 in total. The standard cost per kilogram was €2, giving an overall standard cost of €216,000.

At this stage, one looks for a discrepancy in relation to the physical amounts involved. There is an obvious discrepancy between the physical amounts –112,000 kg and 108,000 kg. Alternatively, stated, the company used 4,000 more kilograms than anticipated. This is an adverse usage variance and can be recorded as:

DIRECT MATERIALS

	Kg	€		Kg	€
Actual input	112,000	196,000	Standard output	108,000	216,000
			Usage variance	4,000	8,000
	112,000			112,000	

The final discrepancy can be found in the money columns. Simply, the total of the left hand side column must be compared with the total of the right hand side column. The final calculation completes the direct materials account as follows:

DIRECT MATERIALS

	Kg	€		Kg	€
Actual input	112,000	196,000	Standard output	108,000	216,000
Price variance	Nil	28,000	Usage variance	4,000	8,000
	112,000	224,000		112,000	224,000

The same T-account method can be used to calculate the direct labour cost. The direct labour cost account appears as follows:

DIRECT MATERIALS

	HOURS	€		HOURS	€
Actual input	46,000	142,600	Standard output	36,000	108,000
			Usage variance	10,000	30,000
			Price variance	Nil	4,600
	46,000	142,600		46,000	142,600

This indicates that 10,000 more hours were used than should have been. This labour *inefficiency* variance cost €30,000. Finally the price variance was €4,600 adverse, indicating that the company spent more money on direct labour than it should have for the actual level of output.

11.4 OVERHEAD COST VARIANCES

Before presenting the calculation of overhead cost variances, one must distinguish between production and non-production overheads. Because of the production orientation of standard costing systems, variances similar to the above can be calculated in relation to production overheads. One must also distinguish between fixed and variable overheads: Fixed production overheads are assumed to remain unchanged in total with changes in output; conversely, variable production overheads are expected to change with changes in output. Bearing this distinction in mind when computing production overhead variances, it is recommended that both fixed and variable calculations be performed separately.

Chapter 5 discussed how overheads are assigned to cost units. Since, by definition, production overheads cannot be traced directly to a specific unit, accountants use the technique of overhead absorption. Production overheads are typically assigned to units using activity bases such as direct labour or machine hours. For example, assume that variable production overheads are assigned to units on the basis of €3 per labour hours. Obviously, the amount of labour hours worked can be greater or less than expected. Also, the amount paid for overhead resources can be more or less than anticipated. Therefore, the total variable production overhead can be subdivided into price and usage components, corresponding to variances (E) and (F) in Exhibit 11.4.

ILLUSTRATION

The S Company has budgeted to produce 1,000 units during the coming period. Each unit will require 2 hours of labour processing time. The variable production overhead absorption rate is €20 per labour hour.

During the relevant period, 900 units were produced in 2,000 hours. The actual variable overhead incurred amounted to €43,000.

REQUIREMENT

Calculate the variable production overhead variances for the period.

SOLUTION

During the period, variable overheads amounting to €43,000 were incurred in producing 900 units. The variable overheads that should have been incurred amount to €36,000 (900 x 2 x €20). Clearly, the amount of the variable overhead variance is €7,000 adverse, which can be subdivided into price and usage (efficiency) variances based on the following formulae:

Rate variance:
(Actual hourly rate – budget hourly rate) x actual hours worked.

Efficiency variance:
(Actual hours worked – budget hours for actual production) x budget hourly rate.

The actual rate per hour for variable overheads amounted to €21.50 compared with a standard rate of €20. Thus, for every hour worked (2,000), there was a rate variance of €1.50. The rate variance is computed as follows:

Variable overhead rate variance:
(€21.50 – €20.00) x 2,000 = €3,000 A.

Since variable overheads are absorbed on the basis of labour hours, calculations must be performed on the basis of labour hours rather than on the basis of units produced. The 900 units produced are equivalent to 1,800 hours (the standard allowance for actual output). Since 2,000 hours were worked, there is an adverse efficiency variance of 200 hours. The efficiency variance is computed as follows:

Variable overhead efficiency variance:
(2,000 – 1,800) x €20= €4,000 A.

Rather than using formulae, the variances can be computed by way of a T-account. The left-hand side always records the actual amounts expended and the right-hand side records actual output in terms of standard hours and standard cost. This account appears as follows:

VARIABLE OVERHEADS

	HOURS	€		HOURS	€
Actual input	2,000	43,000	Standard output (900 units)	1,800	36,000

The T-account records that 2,000 hours were worked at a total cost of €43,000 and 900 units were produced. In standard costing terms each unit should have used 2 hours of labour — 1,800 in total. The standard cost per hour was €20, giving an overall standard cost of €36,000.

Initially, one always looks for a discrepancy in relation to the physical amounts involved. There is an obvious discrepancy between the physical amounts — 2,000 hours and 1,800 hours. Alternatively, stated, the company used 200 more hours than anticipated. This is an adverse usage variance and can be recorded as:

VARIABLE OVERHEADS

	HOURS	€		HOURS	€
Actual input	2,000	43,000	Standard output	1,800	36,000
			Efficiency variance	200	4,000

The final discrepancy can be found in the money columns. Simply, the total of the left hand side column must be compared with the total of the right hand side column. The final calculation completes the variable overhead account as follows:

VARIABLE OVERHEADS

	HOURS	€		HOURS	€
Actual input	2,000	43,000	Standard output	1,800	36,000
			Efficiency variance	200	4,000
			Rate variance	Nil	3,000
	2,000	43,000		2,000	43,000

Fixed Production Overhead and Non-production Overheads

The final set of variances that are usually calculated concern fixed production overheads (G in Exhibit 11.4) and non-production overheads (H in Exhibit 11.4). Since both these cost items are essentially fixed, the only meaningful variance is that of a spending variance. Simply, the spending variance is the difference between the budgeted amount of the spend compared with the actual expenditure. It is not necessary to calculate sub variances, although this is sometimes done. Since fixed costs do not respond to changes in output, the amount in the static budget will be the same as the amount in the flexed budget.

11.5 VARIANCES UNDER ABSORPTION COSTING

In the previous section, variances were computed for sales revenue and costs on the basis of direct costing. In many cases, manufacturing companies operate an absorption costing system whereby a portion of fixed production overheads are assigned to the valuation of finished goods and this impacts on profit calculations. This means that the calculation of the sales volume variance must be changed.

The sales volume variance is intended to highlight the impact on profit as a result of a change in sales volume. Under absorption costing, this variance is calculated as the difference between the static budget units and actual units sold, multiplied by a "margin" per unit. The margin is the contribution per unit less the unit fixed production overhead. (Remember that, under direct costing, the term "contribution" per unit is used, rather than "margin" per unit. The difference between the two systems is the accounting treatment of fixed production overhead).

The absorption of fixed production overheads is based on estimated activity. This inevitably means that there will be a prediction error in the calculations. In other words, there will probably be a difference between the amount of fixed production overhead absorbed during the period and the amount of fixed production overhead budgeted. To cater for this eventuality, compute an additional cost variance, referred to as the fixed production overhead volume variance. This variance will only occur with absorption costing. It does not occur under direct costing because all fixed overheads are written off immediately to the profit and loss account rather than being included in stock valuation. These two variances are the only differences between variances computed under standard direct and standard absorption costing.

ILLUSTRATION

Cod Limited produces widgets. Fixed production overheads are estimated at €6,000. The company anticipates production of 100 units per period and each unit requires 10 hours of machine time. Fixed production overheads are absorbed on the basis of machine hours.

During the recent period, 90 units were produced and actual overhead amounted to €7,000. Machine running hours amounted to 900.

The predetermined recovery rate is:

$$\frac{€6,000}{1,000} = €6 \text{ per machine hour.}$$

Thus, for each unit produced, €6 by way of fixed production overhead is assigned to production cost. The total amount absorbed during the period amounts to €5,400 (90 units x 10 hours x €6). However, this leaves two variances.

The first is the spending variance of €1,000, which is the difference between budget and actual spending and is identical to that calculated under direct costing.

The second variance reflects the discrepancy between the amount of fixed overhead absorbed and the budgeted amount, due to a volume variance. It is calculated as the difference between standard hours for the actual output and *budget* hours multiplied by the overhead rate per hour. The reason that budget hours is used in the calculation is that the absorption rate is based on budget hours. This calculation is as follows:

Fixed overhead volume variance:
(900 – 1,000) x €6 = (€600) Adverse.

This volume variance does not mean that costs were €600 more than anticipated. It simply means that no production was available to absorb €600 of fixed overheads that were expected to occur. The volume variance can also be favourable. This occurs when actual production volume is greater than expected. Therefore, production volume will absorb more fixed overheads than the company expects to incur.

The production manger does not establish his production schedule in isolation. Instead, the volume of production is determined elsewhere on the basis of customers' orders and other factors. This being so, the fixed overhead volume variance is not really controllable by the production manager and should not be attributed to him. It is simply a variance that can help explain the total overhead variance to top management, where a company operates a standard absorption costing system.

Alternatively, the T-account can be used to perform the calculations as follows:

FIXED PRODUCTION OVERHEADS
(AT €6 PER MACHINE HOUR)

	* HOURS	€		HOURS	€
Actual input	1,000	7,000	Standard output	900	5,400
			Volume variance	100	600
			Spending variance	Nil	1,000
	1,000	7,000		1,000	7,000

^ *Budgeted hours are used, rather than actual hours, in this instance, because the absorption rate is based on budgeted hours.*

11.6 PROFIT ANALYSIS

The distinction between standard direct and standard absorption costing is illustrated by the example of Mike Baker, who produces widgets and operates a standard costing system. His budget for the first quarter of 20x8 is as follows:

	€	€
Sales (5,000 units at €12 each)		60,000
less: Cost of production		
Materials (5,000 kg at €3 each)	15,000	
Labour (5,000 hours at €6 per hour)	30,000	
Variable overhead (at €1 per hour)	5,000	
Fixed overhead	5,000	
		55,000
Production surplus		5,000
Administration costs		2,500
Budgeted profit		2,500

1. 6,000 kg of raw materials were purchased at a cost of €18,600 during the quarter of which 700 kg remain in stock at the end of the period.

2. The total hours worked was 3,900 hours at a total cost of €29,250.

3. Variable overheads incurred amounted to €4,800. Fixed production overheads incurred during the quarter amounted to €5,100. Production overheads are absorbed on the basis of labour hours. Administration costs amounted to €2,560.

4. Actual unit sales during the quarter were 5,200 units, which realised €61,880. 5,200 widgets were produced during the period. There were no opening stocks of finished goods.

REQUIREMENT
Calculate appropriate variances from budgeted profit using standard direct costing. Calculate appropriate variances from budgeted profit using standard absorption costing.

SOLUTION
The solution below is presented by way of T-accounts. The sequence to be followed will always be:

1. Record the actual physical and monetary inputs on the left-hand side of the account, with fixed costs being treated as explained above.

2. Record the actual physical and monetary outputs in terms of standard on the right-hand side of the account.

3. Record any closing (or opening) stock at standard, in the appropriate account. This will mainly refer to stock of raw materials.

4. Identify the discrepancy in the physical columns. This will correspond to the usage (efficiency) variance, which is multiplied by the standard cost.

5. Finally, the remaining discrepancy in the account can only be explained by the price (rate) variance.

Each of the cost elements of Mike Baker's production is treated below.

DIRECT MATERIALS
AT €3 PER KILOGRAM

	Kg	€		Kg	€
Actual input	6,000	18,600	Standard output	5,200	15,600
			Usage variance	100	300
			Price variance	Nil	600
			Balance	700	2,100
	6,000	18,600		6,000	18,600

DIRECT LABOUR COST
AT €6 PER HOUR

	HOURS	€		HOURS	€
Actual input	3,900	29,250	Standard output	5,200	31,200
Efficiency variance	1,300	7,800	Price variance	Nil	5,850
	5,200	37,050		5,200	37,050

VARIABLE OVERHEADS
(ABSORBED AT €1 PER LABOUR HOUR)

	HOURS	€		HOURS	€
Actual input	3,900	4,800	Standard output	5,200	5,200
Efficiency variance	1,300	1,300	Rate variance	Nil	900
	5,200	6,100		5,200	6,100

In this example, variable overheads are absorbed on the basis of direct labour hours. Therefore, since there is an adverse efficiency variance in labour hours, there must also be an adverse efficiency variance in relation to variable overheads.

The only other cost variances relate to fixed production overheads and administration costs. Since both are fixed in relation to changes in volume, the only meaningful variance is a spending variance, calculated as the difference between budget and actual. The spending variances are:

Fixed production spending variance:
(€5,100 – €5,000) = (€100) Adverse.

Administration spending variance:
(2,560 – €2,500) = (€60) Adverse.

The sales price variance is computed as the difference between average actual price and standard price multiplied by the number of units sold and is as follows:

Sales price variance:
(€11.90 – €12.00) x 5,200 = (€520) Adverse.

The sales volume variance is computed with reference to the profit impact of the change in volume and is as follows:

Sales volume variance:
(5,000 units – 5,200 units) x €2 = €400 favourable.

Thus, an additional 200 units were sold and each unit was anticipated to generate a contribution (sales price less variable costs) of €2.

All the variances calculated above can be combined to prepare a comprehensive performance report to management. Start with a flexed budget report prepared under direct costing for illustration purposes, although this is not really necessary.

FLEXED BUDGET REPORT

	STATIC	FLEXED	ACTUAL	VARIANCE
Sales units	5,000	5,200	5,200	
	€	€	€	€
Sales revenue	60,000	62,400	61,880	520 A
Materials	15,000	15,600	* 16,500	900 A
Labour	30,000	31,200	29,250	1,950 F
Variable overhead	5,000	5,200	4,800	400 F
Fixed overhead	5,000	5,000	5,100	100 A
Administration	2,500	2,500	2,560	60 A
Net profit	2,500	2,900	3,670	770 F

*   *Actual purchases less closing stock valued at standard. Since closing stock is valued at standard, this has the effect of isolating the full material purchase price variance at time of sale. This is a logical treatment since the price variance has been incurred. Alternatively, closing stock could be valued at actual rather than standard cost. This would have the impact of isolating the price variance only when the materials were used rather than when they were purchased. The former treatment is recommended.*

The cost and revenue variances can be used to reconcile budget with actual profit figures as follows:

RECONCILIATION OF BUDGETED TO ACTUAL PROFIT: DIRECT COSTING

	€	€
Net profit per static budget		2,500
Add: Sales volume variance		400 F
Net profit per flexed budget		2,900
Sales price variance	520 A	
Materials price variance	600 A	
Materials usage variance	300 A	
Labour rate variance	5,850 A	
Labour usage variance	7,800 F	
Variable overhead rate variance	900 A	
Variable overhead efficiency variance	1,300 F	
Fixed overhead expenditure variance	100 A	
Administration expense variance	60 A	770 F
Actual profit		3,670

The reported net profit under absorption costing will also be €3,670 since there is no increase or decrease of finished goods. However, there will be two changes to the schedule of variances above: The sales volume variance will change and an additional variance (the fixed overhead volume variance) will be calculated.

Under absorption costing, the sales volume variance will be calculated as actual sales volume less budgeted sales volume multiplied by the margin per unit (5,200 − 5,000) x €1 = €200. The margin per unit is the unit selling price (€12) less, all variable costs and unit fixed production overhead (€11). In addition, under absorption costing, there is likely to be a prediction error associated with the number of hours worked. The budgeted fixed production overhead absorption rate is €1 per labour hour (€5,000 / 5,000 hours). However, the equivalent of 5,200 hours were worked, based on the output of 5,200 units. Thus, (fixed) production overheads were over-absorbed amounting to €200 (budget less absorbed). This is a favourable cost variance.

The profit reconciliation under absorption costing appears as follows:

RECONCILIATION OF BUDGETED TO ACTUAL PROFIT: ABSORPTION COSTING

	€	€
Net profit per static budget		2,500
Add: Sales volume variance		200 F
Fixed overhead volume variance		200 F
Net profit per flexed budget		2,900
Sales price variance	520 A	
Materials price variance	600 A	
Materials usage variance	300 A	
Labour rate variance	5,850 A	
Labour usage variance	7,800 F	
Variable overhead rate variance	900 A	
Variable overhead efficiency variance	1,300 F	
Fixed overhead expenditure variance	100 A	
Administration expense variance	60 A	770 F
Actual profit		3,670

Interdependency of Variances

One of the difficulties of operating a standard costing system is the interdependency of variances, where a variance is caused by one manager but is reported in another manager's performance report. A typical example is where inferior but cheap materials are purchased. A favourable price variance may be reported for the purchasing manager but the inferior materials lead to adverse efficiency variances and extra materials are consumed in production. Alternatively, workers may require additional time as a result of the poor materials quality. Standard costing systems do not reveal the causes of variances. Instead, by helping managers understand how those causes have manifested themselves in financial terms, they reveal areas in which important questions should be asked.

Setting Standard Costs

A crucial part of the management control system is setting standards against which actual performance can be measured. There are three aspects that need to be considered:

1. **System variability**: In establishing standards, it is important to recognise that performance does not remain constant over a period of time. Some degree of variability should be expected and anticipated. A machine operator might be expected to produce 100 units per day, yet actual performance might normally be expected to range between 90 and 110 per day, depending on various factors. Thus, in developing standards, one must define not only desired levels of performance but also acceptable degrees of variation.

   These variations can be positive or negative. In some cases, both are considered unacceptable if their magnitude is large; in other cases, any variation is unacceptable — for example, in producing pharmaceutical products; in still other cases, a manager's primary concern might be to avoid negative variances while welcoming positive variances — for example, where a worker exceeds the required number of units to be produced in a period. However, extreme positive variations may be indicative of organisational problems requiring corrective action. Some reasons for this are:

   (a) Standards are set too low.

   (b) Trade-off against some other objective. For example, a department may be showing profits by cutting back on staff training, research and development, advertising or quality control. All these four factors influence the long-term position of the firm.

   (c) Good performance may have been caused by incorrect reporting. For example, cases have been reported of supervisors failing to report minor accidents in their department in order to make their accident reports look better than they actually are.

2. **Behavioural considerations**: In performing different tasks, different individuals will have different degrees of ability, motivation and perhaps, different working conditions. Standards can have a crucial impact on motivation. Most individuals have an aspiration level — that is, a level of future performance towards which they strive. Ideally, standards should be roughly equivalent to aspiration levels. If standards are perceived to be unfair, workers may not be motivated to achieve them. There are a number of points that can be mentioned regarding the behavioural implications of standards, including:

   (a) Success generally increases the level of aspiration whereas failure generally lowers the level of aspiration.

   (b) Employees become very conscious of the "ratchet effect" whereby standards are continually adjusted upwards, based on successful performance.

3. **Setting standards**: There are two main types of performance standards:

   (a) Ideal standards assume perfect conditions. In other words, it is assumed that material and labour can be acquired at the cheapest cost, and there is no inefficiency, wastage, nor machine breakdowns. Such standards are often unrealistic and tend to have an adverse motivational effect on the workforce. On the other hand, standards that are too loose may have little motivational impact on workers. Therefore tight standards should be set so that operators of the system will consider the achievement of standard performance to be worthwhile. However, it is important that standards are not too tight as they may be perceived as been unrealistic (that is, unattainable).

   (b) Expected (currently attainable) standards: These are realistic and do allow for some normal loss, machine breakdowns, and efficiency. However, an expected standard is still high enough to have a motivational effect on employees, and tends to be commonly used. In many cases, expected standards are based on historic performance. But, for standards based on historic performance to be valid, it is necessary that the factors influencing the particular performance are stable. The main limitation of historic standards is that historic performance may not have been what it should have been. In other words, inefficiencies are being compounded in the standard cost system.

Investigation of Variances

This chapter has discussed standard costing systems and the computation of variances. Both cost and revenue variances indicate deviations between actual performance and the results that would have occurred if the standards were exactly met. Since any standard is only an estimate of what is likely to be achieved in reality, variances in virtually all cost elements can be expected to occur. Therefore, a manager could receive a performance report showing a variance for every material, labour and overhead item under his responsibility for which a standard had been established.

Management by exception helps managers focus their attention on those operations where there are significant deviations between planned and actual results. These variances or exceptions represent potential problem areas and as such it is worthwhile for management to investigate the cause of these variances. If the variance is not significant, then it suggests that actual performance approximates planned performance. Variables that are "in control" are not reported.

The problem with management by exception is that it indicates *when* corrective action should be taken but not *what* specific action should be taken. Variances are only signals. Corrective action can only come about after investigation and analysis has been undertaken to find out why the performance was inadequate.

It should not be inferred that control actions are taken *only* when the performance becomes unacceptable. In many cases management may note that, while performance is within satisfactory levels, negative trends toward unacceptability are occurring. Corrective action may be taken in an effort to reverse the trend. For example, it might be noted that sales, while satisfactory, are declining; steps may be taken to reverse this decline before it becomes a serious problem.

Also, favourable variances from budget may offer potential since better ways of doing things may have been found which might be applied to other activities of the department or firm. Alternatively a favourable variance may indicate that the original budget was too easy. This has implications for the formulation of budgets for the coming period.

While most companies operate on the basis of exception reporting, its disadvantages include:

1. It is perceived as emphasising failures and exceptional success, thereby ignoring the solid but unspectacular performance of most staff. Only the significant variances are reported.

2. Employees may perceive the system as punitive rather than informative.

3. It may promote a cautious attitude among staff towards innova tive behaviour.

However, the alternatives to exception reporting are not very attractive. These include reporting everything, which would quickly lead to the problem of information overload; report nothing, which would result in the absence of feedback; or report performance without standards, which would provide no measure of effectiveness.

Between the two extremes — of investigating every deviation that is reported and of investigating none of them — lies the optimal policy. Somehow, the manager with or without the aid of a decision support system must selectively decide which variances are the most significant and which will probably yield benefits from investigation. There are a number of techniques, ranging from simple rules of thumb to statistical decision models, which are useful in deciding which variances should be reported and investigated.

1. **Percentage variation**: This involves setting a predetermined limit — say, 10 per cent — and investigating all variances in excess of this limit. The advantage of this approach is its simplicity and ease of implementation. One could simply implement this

method by adding an additional column to the performance report in which the percentage variation is reported. Perhaps all variances in excess of the specified limit could be reported in a different colour.

There are a number of disadvantages with this approach. For example, it does not take into consideration the costs of investigation and the possible resulting benefits. Also, some small accounts may have severe fluctuations that are not significant in company terms though well in excess of the predetermined limit — for example, a 100 per cent variation in a budgeted expense item of €1,000 would not be deemed significant by most managers. Thus, the percentage rule needs to be supplemented by a rule specifying absolute monetary amounts. What tends to happen is that small percentage variations are used for large monetary amounts and large percentage variations allowed for small monetary amounts. However, the use of any percentage is always arbitrary.

2. **Frequency of variance**: Some managers investigate a variance, based on the infrequency of its occurrence. Thus, a very rare variance may be deemed sufficiently important to warrant investigation in comparison to a variance that occurs on a regular basis.

3. **Trend of variance**: Some variances may be small in percentage terms, but increasing over successive accounting periods. This trend, especially if it is adverse, could signal a variance investigation decision, to try to prevent a significant variance occurring in a future time period.

4. **Control charts**: These are a more formal method of investigation and involve setting limits within which deviations are deemed to be "in control". The approach recognises that standards represent average performance and not a single measure. Thus, one can expect a normal pattern of variability from any particular process under observation. Any measurement outside this acceptable pattern of variability is considered a signal that the process is "out of control" and that the cause should be investigated. If the actual performance remains within these limits, the variance is assumed to be insignificant and no investigation is deemed necessary.

The acceptable limits are referred to as the upper control limit (UCL) and lower control limit (LCL). Usually samples from the process are taken daily (or hourly). The mean (average) of the sample observations are plotted on a control chart. Upper and lower statistical confidence limits are also placed on the chart. For example, assuming normally distributed means, 95 per cent confidence limits are obtained by setting the control limits at 1.96 standard deviations from the mean. An observation falling outside such confidence limits would have less than a 5 per cent probability of arising in an in-control process. It is also possible to establish a 99 per cent confidence limit by using 2.58 standard deviations. A typical control chart is displayed in Exhibit 11.5 based on a mean (average) value of 10 and a standard deviation of 1. The upper and lower control limits, for 95 per cent confidence, are set at 11.96 and 8.04 respectively. Successive observations have been plotted on the control chart, with only observation 5 falling outside the control limits.

Exhibit 11.5: Control Chart

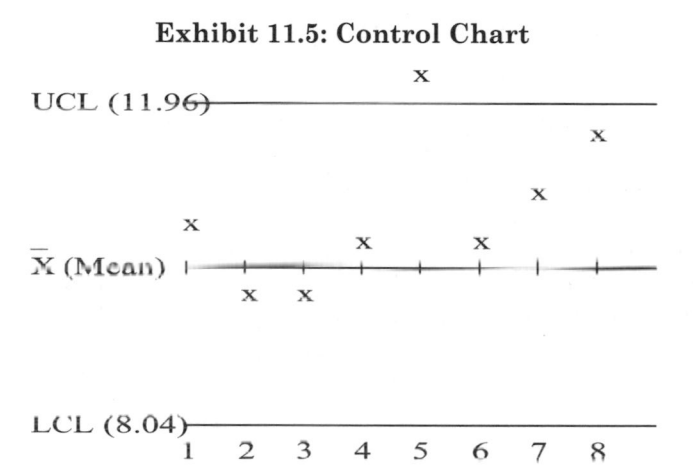

Control charts have a number of advantages:

(a) They avoid the unrealistic assumption of a single standard and therefore allow some variability in performance.

(b) They are simple, cheap and quick to operate.

(c) The graphic format of control charts is an excellent way of communicating trends for ready interpretation by the human eye. In Exhibit 11.5, one can see a pattern of increasing variances in observations 6, 7 and 8 without hitting the upper control limit. This pattern indicates a shift away from standard operations, but no significance is given by a mechanical rule applied only to the most recent observation.

The main limitation of control charts is the use of an arbitrary rule — for example, investigate if an observation is beyond the specified control limits. Should one use 95 or 99 per cent confidence limits? Associated with the control limits is the possibility of type 1 and type 2 errors. A type 1 error results when an in-control process is investigated. The cost of the investigation is wasted because no benefits accrue from investigation. Type 2 errors result when an out of control process is not investigated. The opportunity cost of type 2 errors is the savings that could have been obtained by investigation. Thus, the wider the control limits, the lower the possibility of a type 1 error but the higher the probability of a type 2 error.

The second limitation of control charts is that there is no attempt to associate the cost of investigation with potential savings.

11.7 END OF CHAPTER QUESTIONS

Question 11.1: Global Ltd.

Global Ltd. manufactures and sells its products to a wide range of retailers. Each product in its range is the responsibility of a product manager. The company has recently introduced a rolling budget system with your assistance in which budgets are prepared at least three months in advance of four quarter-year periods beginning on 1 January. The budget for the three months ended 31 March 20x4 and the actual results for Mint, one of the range, is shown below:

THREE MONTHS ENDED 31 MARCH 20x4

	BUDGET	ACTUAL
Sales units	32,500	37,700
	€	€
Sales revenue	110,500	118,755
Variable costs:		
Cost of goods sold	27,625	33,300
Transport to customers	5,525	6,420
Sales commissions	2,275	2,375
Fixed costs:		
Marketing	29,900	35,200
Administration	14,500	15,150

REQUIREMENT

1. Calculate the budgeted contribution per unit.

2. Prepare a schedule for management clearly distinguishing between a planning (volume) variance and operating variances due to cost/price changes.

(*The Association of Chartered Certified Accountants*)

Question 11.2

A private sector college has recently been established in Dublin. Amongst its plans is a course in computer literacy. It is a short but intensive course and the price originally proposed is €100 per member. The price is to include a copy of the course manual, currently in production, which is also to be marketed separately. A cost of €15 per copy has been estimated to be relevant for this manual.

The cost of lecturers' fees and travelling expenses has been estimated at €1,020 for the course. For the purpose of planning and costing the course, 40 student members per course are predicted.

REQUIREMENT

1. Determine the budgeted operating profit and break-even number of students for the course as shown above.

2. Assume that the course was ultimately offered at €95 per member and it attracted only 30 members for the current session. The course manual, when completed, had a cost of €15. Lecturers' costs totalled €950. Calculate the actual profit achieved for the course.

3. Calculate the profit per flexed budget

4. Reconcile the actual profits with the budgeted profit by computing the following variances:

   (a) Sales price variance.

   (b) Sales volume variance.

   (c) Cost variances.

5. Comment briefly on the implications of your figures.

Question 11.3

The management of a retailing business recently set up to sell personal computers to small businesses has been reviewing its profit performance for the last quarter year. One of the partners, Irene Hardcastle, has specific responsibility for sales of computer hardware of which two well-known brands are stocked and sold. These are the "Brand 1" and the "Brand 2". The original budget for the most recent quarter year showed that total budgeted sales units were 480 over both brands, split 25 per cent for "Brand 1" and 75 per cent for "Brand 2".

Budgeted price and variable cost information is shown below:

PER UNIT	BRAND 1 €	BRAND 2 €
Price	3,000	1,400
Variable cost	1,200	1,000

The actual results for the most recent quarter showed the following:

	BRAND 1	BRAND 2
Units sold	81	459
	€	€
Revenue	243,000	550,800
Variable costs	97,200	459,000

Irene felt that the business had not been as profitable as expected particularly as total unit sales had exceeded budget by 12.5 per cent and costs were unchanged.

REQUIREMENT

1. Prepare a financial statement for Irene Hardcastle covering the most recent quarter that identifies:

   (a) The (static) budgeted contribution.

   (b) The (flexed) budget contribution.

   (c) The actual contribution.

   (d) The variance in contribution due to changes in selling prices and quantity.

2. Comment on the implications of your figures for planning and control.

(The Association of Chartered Certified Accountants)

Question 11.4: Rod Company

The Rod Company produces "widgets" and operates a standard costing system in relation to raw material inputs.

The material requirements specifies the following material requirements and the standard product includes the following:

MATERIAL TYPE	QUANTITY	PRICE
Brass rod	0.5 kg	€20 per kg
Sheet steel	3 sq. metres	€50 per sq. mtr.

During the accounting period in question, purchases (received into store) of brass rod were 500 kg at a price of €22 per kg of which 200 kg were unused at the year end. Purchases of sheet steel during the same period amounted to 2,450 sq. metres of sheet steel at an overall cost of €110,250 of which 800 sq. metres was held in stock at the end of the accounting period.

In the accounting period just completed, 500 units of these products were manufactured.

REQUIREMENT

1. Indicate whether closing stock of raw materials should be valued at standard or actual cost. Explain your reasoning.

2. Calculate the actual cost of raw materials consumed during the accounting period.

3. Calculate the standard material cost of finished goods produced during the period.

4. Calculate the material usage variances for the period together with the material price variance.

5. A sophisticated planning system using standard specifications will work in a mass production environment. What is your opinion of applying this in a company that also manufactures one-off products? How, if at all, could this be made to work in such a company?

Question 11.5: MINITAX Ltd.

The manager of MINITAX, a small taxi service, is in the process of improving the management control of his operation. There are expansion plans in prospect, but the potential sources of finance are unwilling to advance further cash until modern management methods are introduced.

At a first stage in this process, the manager decided to introduce controls on fuel costs. A standard cost of fuel of 9p per mile was established on 1 November 20x0, based on a cost of 40p per litre of fuel. All fuel purchases are from a local garage.

The account for fuel for November 20x0 showed that 8,250 litres had been purchased at a total cost of €3,135. Readings taken from the taxi fleet mileage recorders showed 34,400 miles covered, of which the drivers reported covering 1,800 miles for personal use. The business employment regulations state that all fuel used for private purposes is to be replaced by drivers from their own funds before the end of any month. Thus, you may assume that the 8,250 litres above relates only to *business* mileage.

REQUIREMENT

1. Since the output of this business is "miles driven", calculate the anticipated miles per litre.

2. Prepare a report for the manager that analyses the cost data for November 20x0, and comment briefly on your data.

3. Identify what benefits you consider your report will bring to the business.

(*The Association of Chartered Certified Accountants*)

Question 11.6: Jones Furniture Company

The Jones Furniture Company uses a standard direct cost system in accounting for labour and material costs.

The standard cost of a unit of furniture based on normal production output of 1,000 units is as follows:

	€
Timber, 100 feet @ 15p per foot	15.00
Direct labour, 4 hours @ €2.50 per hour	10.00

In addition, variable overheads are budgeted to be €6 per unit and fixed overheads are budgeted to be €3,000.

The following actual costs for the month of December were incurred in producing 1,200 units:

	€
Timber used (132,000 feet @ 12p per foot)	15,840
Direct labour (5,100 hours @ €2.60 per hour)	13,260
Manufacturing overhead (variable)	7,650
Manufacturing overhead (fixed)	2,910

REQUIREMENT
Prepare an analysis of the material, labour and overhead variances.

Question 11.7: Flex Company

The Flex Company controls its operations by means of a range of short-term performance measures. These measures are supplemented on a four-weekly period basis by a statement reconciling the fixed budget profit with actual profit using a flexible budget.

The fixed budget and variances for Period 7 is shown below:

	FIXED BUDGET	VARIANCES
	€	€
Sales	250,000	7,500 A
Direct material	80,000	5,000 A
Variable overhead	95,000	19,500 A
Fixed overhead	35,000	2,000 A
Profit	40,000	34,000 A

NOTE: Variable overhead includes all labour costs.

A review of actual results for Period 7 shows that the overall level of business was 10 per cent lower than expected, the value of actual sales was €225,000. Direct material purchased and used amounted to €77,000. The variable overhead paid was €102,000, additionally €3,000 of indirect labour was accrued in this period but not yet paid. The total fixed overhead was €40,000 but this included €3,000 for lease payments in advance.

You are approached by a new manager of this company, who is keen to know the meaning and significance of these variances, their possible causes and how they have been calculated.

REQUIREMENT

1. Determine the actual profit for Period 7.

2. Explain how the cost variances and the sales variance shown have been computed.

3. Give two possible reasons each for the direct material and sales variances.

4. Recommend possible action for the management of this company in relation to the variable overhead and sales variances.
    Ignore stock levels.

Question 11.8

A company operates standard absorption costing for reporting purposes, as follows:

	€ PER UNIT
Material	6
Direct labour	3
Variable manufacturing overhead	5
Fixed manufacturing overhead	10
Total manufacturing cost	24
Variable selling overhead	2
Fixed selling overhead	2
	28

This is based on an assumption of an even quarterly pattern of 2,000 units produced and sold. The product sells for €40 per unit.
    Quarter three has just ended and 1,800 units were produced whilst only 1,300 were sold. The routine report in relation to this product is shown below:

QUARTER THREE: ACTUAL RESULTS

Units produced	1,800
Units sold	1,300

	€	€
Sales (1,300 x €40)		52,000
Standard manufacturing cost of sales (1,300 x €24)		31,200
		20,800
Fixed manufacturing overhead:		
Volume variance (Adverse)	2,000	
Expenditure variance (Adverse)	300	
Actual variable selling overhead	2,600	
Actual fixed selling overhead	4,500	
		9,400
Actual net profit (on a full cost basis)		11,400

There are no cost or efficiency variances other than those that can be determined from the above. Variable manufacturing and selling costs are assumed to vary with volume produced and sold respectively.

The marketing department has become interested in variable or direct costing, break-even analysis and the use of this in reporting results.

REQUIREMENT

1. From the budgeted information provided, using the variable (direct) costing approach, determine the break-even number of units of product and the profit based on the actual sales in quarter three.

2. Explain the fixed manufacturing overhead volume variance and demonstrate how the value shown has been calculated.

3. Explain and calculate any variance that exists between the actual and expected costs in relation to variable and fixed selling overheads.

4. Reconcile the variable costing profit from part (1) with profit under absorption costing.

(The Association of Chartered Certified Accountants)

Question 11.9

A variance indicates a deviation from a plan, but not all variances should be investigated.

REQUIREMENT

Elaborate on this comment, in order to explain to your colleague what you mean.

Question 11.10: Longford Ltd.

Longford Ltd. uses a standard direct costing system for budgetary and control purposes and values all finished goods at standard. The following figures represent the budget for the variable costs involved in the production of 6,000 units of the company's single product during April 20x8, 800 of those units representing a planned increase in finished goods levels:

	€
Direct material cost	15,600
Direct labour costs	18,000
Variable overheads	7,200
	40,800

The company actually produced 6,200 units and sold 5,300. The variable costs incurred were as follows:

	€
Direct material costs (6,400 units)	17,280
Direct labour costs	18,600
Variable overheads	7,688
	43,568

You are given the following additional information:

1. The budgeted sales price per unit was €10.00; in fact, the company was able to implement a price increase to €10.50 per unit throughout the month.

2. One unit of material is used for each unit of production and material is purchased as required for processing. All units purchased were effectively used in production. The cost per unit of material was €0.10 in excess of standard.

3. Each unit of output requires two standard hours of direct labour; the actual rate of pay was €1.55 per hour during April.

4. The standard for variable overheads is calculated in terms of cent per direct labour hour.

5. The company originally expected to spend €15,000 on fixed costs during the month; in fact, a total of €17,100 was paid. During the year, fixed costs are expected to total €162,000.

REQUIREMENT

1. Calculate the standard variable cost per unit of production.

2. Reconcile the actual profit with the budgeted profit of €3,140.

Question 11.11: TOD Ltd.

You have recently been appointed as management accountant to TOD Ltd., which manufactures aluminium windows for the construction industry. The company has just finished its initial three months of operations and your first major assignment is to compare actual performance with budget.

Prior to commencing business, the company's financial advisors had prepared the following standard costs and projections:

	€	€
Sales price (per unit)		25
Variable costs:		
Direct labour (4 hours at €2 per hour)	8	
Direct material (10 feet at 0.60 per foot)	6	
Variable production overheads		
(4 hours at €1)	4	
Variable administration costs	2	
		20
Budgeted unit contribution		5
Fixed costs per annum:		
Production overhead	€120,000	
Administration	€80,000	

Based on these figures, the company planned to reach break-even point of 10,000 units for the first quarter.

The draft profit and loss account for the first quarter was presented to you as follows:

PROFIT AND LOSS ACCOUNT
QUARTER 1

	€	€
Sales (9,500 units at €26)		247,000
Less: Production costs		
Direct labour (40,000 hours)	72,000	
Direct materials (100,000 feet)	61,000	
Variable overheads	40,000	
Fixed overheads	18,000	
		191,000
Manufacturing surplus		56,000
Administration costs (variable)	24,000	
Administration (fixed)	22,000	
		46,000
Actual profit for quarter		10,000

The managing director of TOD Ltd., who has little knowledge of accounting, is pleased to have recorded a profit during the quarter even though the break-even production target was not achieved. He has asked you to prepare a statement showing the variances from budget.

REQUIREMENT

1. Prepare a static and flexed budget profit for the first quarter, on direct cost principles.

2. Prepare a schedule of variances, reconciling budget with actual profit.

3. How would your figures change, if absorption costing were used?

12

Performance Evaluation and Structure

12.1 INTRODUCTION

Decision-making and control are meaningful concepts only when an objective exists. Individuals have objectives but enterprises do not! Instead, there are objectives *for* enterprises. In the context of a business enterprise, each participant is interested in his own economic welfare and it is logical to assume that the interests of different individuals are conflicting. Shareholders are interested in earning a return on their investment; employees are interested in secure and well-paid employment; customers are interested in a quality product at low cost that provides high customer value. These interests are not necessarily mutually exclusive. There is likely to be some basic level of agreement since it usually in the interest of all participants if the business continues to exist. This book assumes that consensus on objectives can be reached.

In pursuit of corporate objectives, a technical and behavioural element has been stressed. The technical element represents the flow of information, some of which concerns the internal operations of the firm while other information relates to the environment in which the company operates. This information may be obtained routinely or on an *ad hoc* basis and may be communicated formally or informally to participants. The behavioural element represents the decisions taken by managers in response to this information. The information relates to current performance and forms the basis for future plans. It is true to say that information is power.

Previous chapters of this book have examined different types of decision situations. For each situation, the essential information that would be useful to managers was identified. This approach was helpful in understanding decision-making and control in relatively small organisations where all important decisions can be made by one individual. However, as an organisation grows and becomes more complex, it is difficult and undesirable for one individual to make all the important decisions. There are too many decisions to be made and no single person can control all functions.

It follows that, in an organisation of substantial size, there must be an organisational structure. Traditionally, this structure is formal and hierarchical. The objectives of the business are established by top management and are communicated to members of the organisation. There are clear lines of responsibility. Managers must decide on the tasks that are to be performed in order to achieve these objectives and on the resources that are to be used. In turn, progress toward the objectives must be monitored and corrective action taken when the need arises. Thus, control is a process of activity in response to information but activity must take place within a *structure*. If managers are to be held accountable for their performance, they must have clearly defined areas of responsibility based on an organisational structure. In other words, if decisions have to be taken to progress towards objectives, there must be a structure to ensure that decisions are taken by appropriate individuals (or groups). Finally, there must be a monitoring system to measure performance and evaluate the decision-makers. The situation is depicted in Exhibit 12.1

Exhibit 12.1: Context of Performance Evaluation

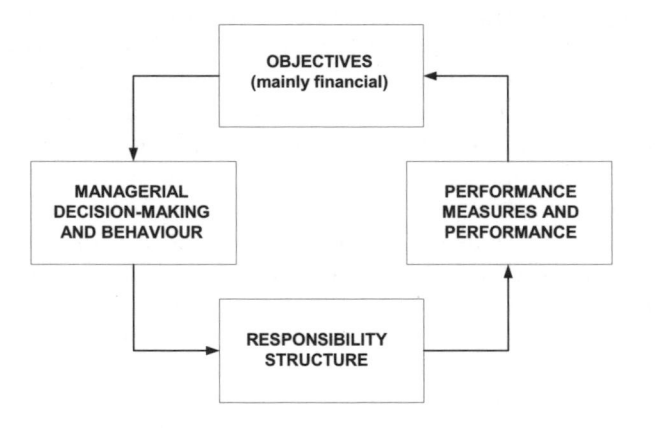

12.2 DECENTRALISATION AND STRUCTURE

As the organisation grows in size, successful management of it by a small group of people becomes more difficult. In order to overcome this problem, the modern trend is towards decentralisation — that is, the breaking down of the organisation into sub-units where individual managers have the freedom to make their own decisions. The essence of decentralisation is the freedom to make decisions.

The following advantages of decentralisation should be noted:

1. It frees top management from everyday decision-making, thereby enabling it to concentrate on strategic planning, policy formulation, and providing overall direction for the company.

2. It improves the decision-making within the company by ensuring that those personnel thoroughly acquainted with an aspect of the firm make decisions concerning it. In other words, local decision-makers have the benefit of local knowledge.

3. There is a more rapid response to environmental changes and opportunities by eliminating cumbersome and slow communications that would be required in a centralised firm.

4. It provides additional motivation for managers, due to their increased status within the company, and more control over the factors that determine good performance.

The disadvantages of decentralisation must also be noted. Primarily, there is the possibility of dysfunctional decision-making, where a manager makes a decision that is beneficial to his own unit, but which is not in the interests of the organisation as a whole. For example, a manager may postpone essential machine repairs in order to "beat" his expense budget. However, there are long-term, adverse consequences of this action. Such decisions are likely when there is a lack of motivation or where the accounting measurement system is geared towards short-term results. Managers are likely to maximise profits in the short-term to the detriment of long-term performance. This situation represents a lack of goal congruency.

However, decentralisation also creates two issues not specifically addressed in previous chapters:

1. What is the appropriate corporate structure and how can autonomous managers be evaluated? (This is discussed below).

2. What is the appropriate price to be charged for transfers between units of the same company? This is the issue of transfer pricing and is discussed in section 12.3 below.

Types of Responsibility Centre

Responsibility centres are based on the fundamental principle of "controllability". For example, every cost is a direct cost to one responsibility centre in the business. If one looks at the business as a whole, then all costs are direct costs of the business.

Alternatively, for an individual department, only a small amount of costs may be considered direct. Admittedly, some common or overhead costs will be charged to each small department for costing purposes. However, for evaluation purposes, a manager should be held responsible only for those costs (and revenues) under his control. To do otherwise will demotivate the manager and thus may affect his performance in the areas which are under his direct control.

A responsibility centre is any unit within an organisation that is headed by a responsible manager. All responsibility centres have some form of inputs. These may be physical goods, services or simply cash. With these resources, certain activities are performed, which can be referred to as outputs in the form of goods or services. All responsibility centres have outputs — that is, they do something. These goods or services go either to other responsibility centres within the organisation or to customers in the outside world.

For decision-making and control purposes, it is usually necessary to translate the inputs into monetary amounts. Money (accounting information) provides a common denominator that permits physically unlike elements of resources to be combined in terms of cost. If the outputs of a responsibility centre are sold to an outside customer, the accounting system measures these outputs in terms of revenue. If, they are not sold, then non-financial measures such as the number of service units provided can be used.

There are four types of responsibility centre, classified according to the nature of the monetary inputs or outputs, or both, that are measured in a decentralised organisation.

Expense Centres

If the accounting system measures the level of operating costs incurred by a responsibility centre but does *not* measure the value of its output in terms of revenues, the responsibility centre is called an expense centre. The production department, for example, is required to produce goods. It is not required to generate revenues. If a reliable relationship can be determined in relation to inputs and outputs, this department is referred to as an engineered expense centre. Consequently, the comparison between actual input spending and physical output is a measure of efficiency — cost per unit. Such expense centres can also be evaluated in terms of overall effectiveness — whether the production centre produced the required level of goods.

Thus, engineered cost centres have two important characteristics:

1. Their inputs can be measured in monetary terms.

2. Their outputs can be measured in physical terms.

For other expense centres, especially of a service nature, it is not possible to measure actual outputs or the relationship between inputs and outputs are much more difficult to model — for example, the administration department. These are referred to as discretionary cost centres.

However, since operating costs (inputs) can be easily determined for both engineered and discretionary expense centres, they may be evaluated simply on their ability to stay within budget. This budget-constrained focus can lead to various forms of dysfunctional behaviour. The example of postponing essential repairs has already been cited. There is also the situation of deliberate overspending of budget on the assumption that, if the budget is not spent, it will be cut in the forthcoming year.

Revenue Centres

If a responsibility centre manager is held accountable for the output of the centre as measured in monetary terms (revenues) but is not responsible for the costs of producing the goods or services that the centre sells, then the responsibility centre is a revenue centre. Most sales departments are considered as revenue centres.

Profit Centres

Revenue is a monetary measure of outputs, and expense (or cost) is a monetary measure of resources consumed. Profit is the difference between revenue and expense. If performance in a responsibility centre is measured in terms of the difference between the revenue it earns and the expense it incurs, the responsibility centre is a profit centre.

A profit centre resembles a business in miniature. Like a separate company, it has a profit and loss account that shows revenue, expense, and profit. Most of the decisions made by the profit centre manager affect the numbers on the profit and loss account, which becomes the basic management control document. As a result, managers are motivated to make decisions that increase overall profits. Typical measures of performance include the absolute amount of profits generated, profits as a percentage of sales and overall cost levels. These performance measures relate both to budget and actual performance.

Investment Centres

Where a manager has responsibility for the investment of assets as well as revenues and costs, his part of the business will be evaluated as an investment centre. An alternative expression is that of a division or business unit. In such cases, managers will be evaluated on their ability to generate a sufficiently high return on investment. There are many definitions of exactly what is "investment". This section defines the term in relation to the total assets of the investment centre. There are two favoured evaluation measures: Return on investment and Residual income. Unfortunately, return on investment means different things to different people. To avoid confusion, this section uses the term "return on total assets" (ROTA), which is less ambiguous than "return on investment".

1. Return on total assets (ROTA) is calculated as the profit before interest and tax (PBIT) divided by the assets invested in the company. It will always be expressed as a percentage (%).

ILLUSTRATION

Division A and Division B provide the following summarised results for a recent accounting period:

	DIVISION A	DIVISION B
Operating profits (a)	€100,000	€200,000
Investment in total assets (b)	€600,000	€900,000
Return on total assets (a)/(b)	16.6%	22.2%

ROTA is commonly used in the context of performance evaluation. It has a number of advantages, including:

(a) It uses financial accounting measurements that should be readily understood by management.

(b) It can be used as a basis for calculating additional ratios that are used for identifying financial strengths and weaknesses. For example, the overall return on total assets can be divided between the profitability of sales multiplied by the investment intensity. In turn, these ratios can be broken down further. Thus:

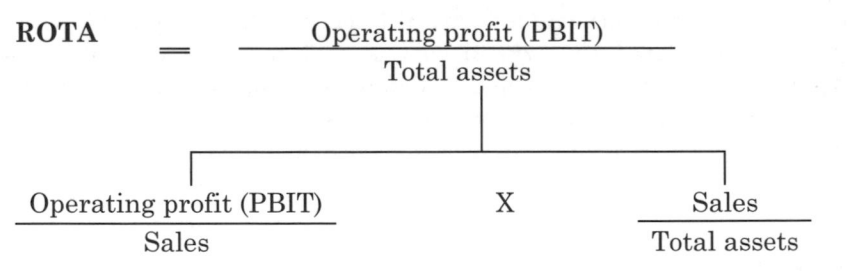

$$\textbf{ROTA} = \frac{\text{Operating profit (PBIT)}}{\text{Total assets}}$$

$$\frac{\text{Operating profit (PBIT)}}{\text{Sales}} \quad \text{X} \quad \frac{\text{Sales}}{\text{Total assets}}$$

(c) It may be used in inter-company comparisons, provided that the companies whose results are being compared are of comparable size and of the same industry.

There are several disadvantages associated with ROTA. Typically:

(a) It is difficult to establish a satisfactory definition of "investment". Should it be the net or gross value of fixed assets? If net book values are used, then, as these tend to decline over time, the

ROTA will tend to increase over time, other things being equal. There are no definitive answers to these questions. Various research studies indicate that different companies use different definitions. The important point, therefore, is consistency of application.

(b) When comparing ratios of different divisions (or companies), ensure that similar accounting policies are used in valuing stocks, fixed assets and the treatment of research and development expenditure. Different accounting treatments of these items will result in different profit figures.

2. An alternative measurement is that of Residual income (RI), which is the operating profit (PBIT) of a division less the "imputed" interest on the assets used by the division. Residual income is used rather than residual profit, since this measurement was popularised in the United States where the term "income" is generally used instead of "profit". Unlike ROTA, it will always be an absolute monetary amount rather than a percentage. It can be positive or negative.

ILLUSTRATION
Division A has an investment in total assets of €50,000, which generates an operating profit of €15,000. The minimum acceptable rate of return is 14 per cent. Residual income is computed as:

	€
Operating profit	15,000
Imputed interest (14% of €50,000)	(7,000)
Residual income	8,000

This compares with a ROTA of 30 per cent.

The main advantage of Residual income is that it avoids the possible dysfunctional decision-making associated with ROTA. The use of ROTA may influence divisional management to select only investments with high rates of return and to reject opportunities that might increase the value of the business. This point is clarified in the following illustration of Division X and Division Y.

ILLUSTRATION
Division X and Division Y of the same company are both currently considering an outlay on new investment projects, referred to as projects X and Y respectively. The required return on total assets for both divisions is currently 13 per cent, based on total assets of €1 million and this is used to evaluate the performance of each di-

vision. The current ROTA is 18% for Division X and 9% for Division Y.

PROJECTS	DIVISION X	DIVISION Y
Investment outlay	€100,000	€100,000
Profit return	€ 16,000	€ 11,000

The ROTA for the projects is 16 per cent for X and 11 per cent for Y. Clearly, project X should be sanctioned whereas project Y should be rejected. However, it is possible that project X may also be rejected because the manager of Division X does not want his projected ROTA to fall from its existing level of 18 per cent. This is because the proposal is above the minimum return but below what the division is currently earning. Because a comparison of old and new returns would imply that performance had worsened, the investment centre's manager might hesitate to make such an investment, even though the investment would have a positive benefit for the company as a whole. Conversely, the manager of Division Y may accept the project submitted to him since its acceptance will increase his projected ROTA from its existing level of 9 per cent.

This inappropriate behaviour will not occur if residual income is used. The residual income calculations before and after the proposal are as follows:

PROJECTS	DIVISION X €	DIVISION Y €
Existing residual income		
Operating profit	180,000	90,000
Less: Capital charge (13%)	(130,000)	(130,000)
Residual income	50,000	(40,000)

The revised residual income, if both projects are accepted will be:

PROJECTS	DIVISION X €	DIVISION Y €
Operating profit	196,000	101,000
Less: capital charge (13%)	(143,000)	(143,000)
Residual income	53,000	(42,000)

Using residual income, the manager of division X is motivated to accept project X since residual income increases. On the other hand, project Y should be rejected since the negative residual income increases from €40,000 to €42,000. This indicates that project Y does not earn its required rate of return.

Another advantage of using residual income is that divisional managers are continually made aware of the opportunity cost of funds.

Nevertheless, residual income has some disadvantages. Chiefly, there is the difficulty in identifying the appropriate percentage to use in computing the capital charge and also in identifying the appropriate value of assets on which the capital charge should be based. Second, residual income is not as commonly understood as ROTA or ROI.

Economic Value Added (EVA®)

The term "Economic Value Added" was coined (and trademarked) by Stern Stewart and Co., a US consulting firm. It can be defined as a business unit's income after tax and after deducting a notional capital charge. This capital charge is linked to the capital invested in the unit multiplied by the cost of capital. The idea is not new and it has many similarities with "Residual Income". However, there are important differences and these will be explained later. The objective of EVA is to measure the residual wealth created by a business unit during an accounting period. This residual wealth is obtained by deducting all operating costs, taxes and the cost of capital from operating revenues.

If EVA is positive, the company is creating wealth. Over the long term, only those companies creating wealth can survive. EVA is used to focus managers' attention on creating wealth for shareholders by earning profits greater than the unit's cost of capital. If it is negative, then the company is destroying capital. EVA can be enhanced if earnings can be increased more rapidly than invested capital, or if activities generating negative EVA (destroying value) can be discontinued.

EVA and Residual Income

The concept of EVA is similar to that of Residual Income. Indeed, some textbooks do not differentiate between the two terms since, in reality, Residual Income is a simplified form of EVA. Residual income has been recommended as a measure of business performance since at least the 1920s, when it was adopted by General Motors. Yet, EVA, as a measure of performance, has been part of the economist's toolkit for more than 200 years. In a minority of cases, both calculations of both residual Income and EVA will produce identical figures. However, there are likely to be differences for two reasons:

1. In contrast to Residual Income, EVA uses the firm's cost of capital instead of a minimum rate of return. The cost of capital is usually obtained by calculating a weighted average of the cost of the firm's two sources of funds – debt and equity. For many business units, the minimum desired rate of return and the cost of capital are very nearly the same, with small differences due to adjustments for risk and for strategic goals such as the desired growth rate of the firm.

2. Another difference is that users of EVA do not follow conventional, conservative accounting policies. For example, expenses that contribute to the long-term value of the business unit are capitalised. These expenses include research and development costs, certain types of advertising, training and employee development. Thus, in calculating EVA, we use the terms 'adjusted earnings' and 'adjusted capital'. EVA is always a monetary amount (positive or negative) rather than a percentage as the following presentation shows:

Adjusted (operating) earnings after tax	xx
Less Adjusted capital x cost of capital	(x)
EVA	x

   It is important to note that the figures for adjusted earnings and adjusted capital used to calculate EVA will generally not be those appearing in the financial statements. This is because EVA focuses on economic earnings and economic capital rather than accounting earnings and capital. In essence, the EVA adjustments attempt to transform accounting earnings (revenue minus expenses) into a financial number that more closely approximates economic income (cash flows in excess of the opportunity cost of capital).

Adjustments to Eliminate the Distortions of Accrual Accounting
Generally accepted accounting principles require managers to account for transactions on an accrual basis. Accrual accounting adjustments transfer costs and revenues between accounting periods. Thus, a cost incurred for, say, advertising, in one accounting period might be expensed (written off to the profit and loss account) in a subsequent accounting period. Alternatively, other costs, such as research costs, may be written off in the period in which they are incurred. This accounting treatment is done for two reasons: (1) to match costs with revenues better and (2) to ensure a conservative cal-

culation of profit when there is uncertainty about the timing of future revenues. For some events – such as recording accounts payable for unpaid invoices – there is little dispute about the desirability of shifting costs to the correct accounting period. However, there are other adjustments that accountants make for matching purposes or for prudence purposes that can potentially distort the economic income of a business. EVA calculations attempt to undo these adjustments to (1) generate a profit number that more closely represents economic cash flows and (2) restate the balance sheet to reflect the true value of resources used to generate income.

Stern Stewart, the consultancy firm that registered the term EVA, has 164 adjustments to the accounting numbers. In reality, companies use only a few adjustments. The main adjustments are:

1. Capitalise expenditures on Research and Development.

2. Do not amortise goodwill.

3. Adjust current year's tax expense to eliminate deferred taxation.

4. Restate closing stock valuation to replacement cost.

5. Capitalise expenditures on customer development and staff training.

6. Use gross book values to reflect the actual economic value of the fixed assets.

7. Capitalise operating leases.

The first four items will now be discussed in greater detail.

Research and Development Expense
Any asset, by definition, represents the future cash flows. If a resource cannot generate future cash flows for its owners, it cannot be classified as an asset. One of the hotly debated issues in accounting over the years is how to account for R & D expenditures. Are they assets or expenses? Some argue that managers invest in research and development for the sole purpose of developing new products and processes that will generate future cash flows. According to this reasoning, R & D expenditures should be capitalised as an asset and expensed against revenues of future periods. Accountants, however, are suspicious that the amounts spent on R & D may not be fully recoverable in future periods. They argue that some R & D expenditures are inevitably wasted, because experimentation by nature implies trial and error. Therefore, rather than permitting managers to record R & D expenditures as assets – and amortise them over the lives of new

products and processes – accounting standards require managers to write off to the profit and loss account all R & D expenditures in the period in which the expenditure takes place.

The EVA calculation reverses this thinking. R & D expenditures are put back on the balance sheet as assets and amortised over some estimated life (typically five or 10 years). This has the effect of increasing profit (earnings) by the amount of the R & D expense (less any amount associated with its amortisation over time) and increasing the value of the asset and the associated capital base recorded on the balance sheet.

Amortisation of Goodwill

Accountants account for the difference between the purchase price of a company and its identifiable net assets as goodwill. For example, if Company A purchased Company B for £40 million, and the net assets of Company B (assets minus liabilities) were valued at £30 million, the balance of £10 million would be shown on the purchaser's balance sheet as an asset – "goodwill". In turn, this sum would be amortised over some period up to 20 years. Over each of the future 20 years, some portion of the goodwill would be amortised against income, thereby reducing it. For EVA purposes, the goodwill accrual must be adjusted in two ways.

First, the reduction in income due to the amortisation of goodwill in the current period is added back to income. Second, to the extent that accumulated amortisation has eroded goodwill, the balance sheet is restated to reflect the full purchase price of the acquisition so that managers are held accountable for generating returns on the full value of the assets employed.

Deferred Tax Expense

Many people think that "tax expenses" on a company's profit and loss account shows the amount of taxes a company is required to pay on its profits to the government. This is only partially true. First we must distinguish between a company's accounting and taxable income. The former is the amount of income reported on the profit and loss account presented to shareholders. This is sometimes referred to as "book income" and is prepared under generally accepted accounting principles. Taxable income, on the other hand, is the amount of income that is taxable. Because of the complexities of the taxation code, it is a rarity that these two figures will correspond. In some extreme cases, a company may have considerable accounting or book income but no taxable income.

Generally accepted accounting practice requires companies to record a tax expense based on the reported accounting rather than taxable income. The difference between what a company records on its profit and loss account as tax expense and what it actually pays the tax authorities reflects a *timing difference*. The most common timing difference is due to the difference between depreciation for accounting and taxation purposes. For example, many companies choose a straight-line method of depreciation for their bookkeeping to best match revenues with expenses; however, for the calculation of taxable income, companies often adopt some method of accelerated depreciation to minimise taxable income and reduce current tax liabilities. Thus, accounting income and taxable income will differ.

Accountants believe that the taxes saved today because of accelerated depreciation for tax purposes will have to be paid tomorrow. The difference between the taxes actually paid and the amount that would have been paid using the company's accounting (or book) income is recorded as an additional tax expense in the firm's profit and loss account. In addition, a corresponding liability (referred to as a deferred tax liability) is reported on the balance sheet. For EVA calculations, the current year's income tax expense attributable to the accrual of deferred taxes is added back to income. Similarly, deferred taxes payable on the balance sheet are considered part of the capital of the firm, since it doesn't really exist under EVA.

Stock Valuation
In accordance with generally accepted accounting principles, closing stock (inventory) is valued at the 'lower of cost or net realisable value'. For EVA purposes, the value of stock in the financial statements is valued at replacement cost to more accurately reflect operating cash flow. This is because stock needs to be replaced if the company requires to stay in business. This is in keeping with the notion of maintaining the operating capability of the organisation. However, with low levels of inflation, coupled with the falling cost of replacing stock, this adjustment is rarely used.

Benefits of EVA
It is certainly a priority for commercial organisations to generate returns for shareholders. EVA focuses managers on generating returns in excess of the cost of capital entrusted to them. An important ingredient in this return is the overall movement in share price (for listed companies). The first proclaimed advantage of EVA is that its proponents argue that a strong correlation exists between EVA and share price movement. In fact, share prices follow EVA better than other

accounting measures of return, such as earnings per share or return on equity. However, it shall be interesting to see whether this correlation continues, as stock markets in recent years remain decidedly sluggish.

Secondly, EVA can be, and is increasingly, linked to managerial compensation. In this way, managerial compensation is closely linked with wealth creation. While accounting numbers used in external financial statements must comply with generally accepted accounting principles (GAAP), those in incentive compensation plans need not comply with GAAP. Designers of incentive plans should examine desired behaviour to ascertain how to modify the accounting numbers to provide incentives for desired behaviour. For example, suppose top management of a software development company wishes to encourage the company to make substantial investment in research and development. Under GAAP, much, if not all, of that investment will have to be written off as an expense in the period in which the expenditure is incurred. Yet, this company wants to encourage managers to invest in R&D. Consequently, the Board of Directors will probably elect to capitalise these expenditures for the purpose of its incentive compensation plan.

Thirdly, EVA can be used in making decisions regarding various strategic business units because it highlights those units where shareholder wealth is being created or destroyed. Thus, it can be used in deciding which business units can be expanded or reduced.

Fourthly, EVA highlights the cost of capital of a business unit. A number of companies have discovered that EVA helps to encourage the right kind of behaviour from their business units in a way that emphasis on operating income alone cannot. It appears to some managers that investment seems free to the business units and, of course they want more. Moreover, this focus may encourage senior management to examine the capital structure of the business unit more carefully. In many small and medium-sized businesses, the capital structure is often accepted as a 'given' and rarely receives serious scrutiny. In other words, making the cost of capital explicit may concentrate managers' attention on financing the business in a cost-effective manner.

Finally, it is, in theory, relatively simple for a company to incorporate EVA into the Balanced Scorecard by including it one of the financial measures in the financial perspective category. The Balanced Scorecard looks at performance measures relating to factors such as market share, customer complaints, and personnel turnover rates and is discussed in Chapter 13.

Limitations of EVA

There are a number of limitations associated with the use of EVA. First of all, it is a single measure of financial performance and should not be used in isolation for evaluation purposes. The recent literature on management accounting is in agreement that performance measurement and evaluation should not exclusively focus on a single metric – financial or non-financial. Moreover, any metric is capable of distortion and promoting dysfunctional consequences.

In common with other financial measures of performance, EVA does not explicitly attempt to place a value on all the assets of an organisation. This remains problematic for knowledge-intensive businesses or any business with intangible resources that do not appear on the balance sheet. The result of this is that EVA is not a complete measure of the manager's stewardship of the shareholders' investment and may therefore overstate the wealth generated during an individual accounting period.

In large multi-product organisations the difficulties in calculating EVA will multiply. Common assets and costs will need to be apportioned between divisions and/or products to enable calculation of divisional and or product EVA. Of course, such problems do not solely arise in the calculation of EVA and already exist in the calculation of divisional/product ROIs.

A major practical issue that arises in the calculation of EVA is how earnings and capital should be defined. Stern Stewart have identified in excess of 164 alterations that might be required to adjust accounting earnings. Adjustments such as the capitalisation of R & D costs and the determination of the optimal period of amortisation of Goodwill will involve subjective judgements. Ultimately it would be more correct to consider EVA as a "range" of possible EVAs rather than a single unambiguous figure (of course, the same could be said of accounting earnings!). It may be difficult for investors or analysts to make all the suggested adjustments because they will only have access to the information disclosed in the published accounts.

Conclusion

One might ask why EVA took hold in the 1990s, when accountants have made little progress previously in successfully selling the idea of residual income. Part of the answer may be in EVA's ability to bring accrual accounting closer to economic cash flows. EVA is unlikely to be a passing fad, because it is based on the fundamental concept of economic profit, which is the profit generated after considering all costs, including the cost of capital. The notion that companies earning an economic profit will add wealth to their owners is well-grounded in economic theory and in practice. Thus, EVA is an attempt to operationalise the concept of economic profit.

12.3 TRANSFER PRICING

Transfer prices are the prices at which transactions are recorded between divisions of a large company. They contrast with market prices, which measure exchanges between a company and the outside world. Internal exchanges that are measured by transfer prices result in revenue for the responsibility centre supplying the goods (or services) and represent a cost for the responsibility centre buying the goods. In addition, transfer prices can either be international transfer prices for international trade or domestic prices for trade within the one country.

In international trade, the bulk of such trade is conducted by multinational corporations, referred to as MNEs (multinational enterprises). An MNE is defined as an enterprise that owns and controls value-adding activities in more than one country. This acknowledges the geographical dispersion of their activities. This definition also recognises that such companies may produce both goods and services. Indeed, an increasing amount of transfer pricing relates to the provision of services.

There are a number of reasons why MNEs developed. Originally, some MNEs needed to gain access to the natural resources of certain countries — the resource seeking MNEs. For example, aluminium-processing companies will tend to have bauxite mines in other countries, and rubber or tyre companies will tend to own plantations in other countries. The basic motivation is to secure a supply of raw materials. In most cases, the MNE's superior access to capital, technology and global markets put it in a stronger position to develop these resources more efficiently than local enterprises.

Other MNEs developed in order to seek additional markets. In this case, the MNE, rather than exporting to a country, establishes a local manufacturing base in that country due, for example, to transport costs or trade restrictions. For example, EU regulations resulted in many US and Japanese companies setting up in Ireland to supply the EU market. Because the goods are produced in Ireland and exported to the EU no restrictions (tariffs) applied.

Finally, MNEs developed in order to allow a particular overseas division to specialise in a particular product or a specific stage of a production process — product specialisation or process specialisation. The purpose is to make optimal use of the locations suitable for the production of the particular products or to maximise the economies of scale in the manufacture of individual products. This is typically the case with production or assembly in low labour-cost countries. Alternatively, there may be government incentives on offer such as investment incentives and generous tax concessions.

It is generally desirable from the *group's* viewpoint that companies within the same group should trade with each other. However, the concept of decentralisation is that the respective managers are free to make their own decisions. Transfer prices represent revenue for the selling division and associated costs for the purchasing division. This can create dysfunctional behaviour and this is illustrated in the Blade division example below.

ILLUSTRATION

The Blade Division of Dana Group produces steel blades. One third of the Blade Division's output (10,000 blades out of 30,000) is sold to the Lawn Products Division of Dana; the remainder is sold to outside customers.

The Blade Division's estimated sales and cost data for the coming year is as follows:

	LAWN PRODUCTS	OUTSIDERS	TOTAL
	€	€	€
Sales revenues	15,000	40,000	55,000
Variable cost of goods	(10,000)	(20,000)	(30,000)
Fixed costs	(3,000)	(6,000)	(9,000)
Net profit	2,000	14,000	16,000

The Lawn Products Division now has an opportunity to buy 10,000 blades of identical quality from an outside supplier on a continuing basis at a delivered cost of €1.25. The Blade Division cannot sell any additional products to outside customers and therefore will curtail its production if Lawn Products buys its blades from an outside supplier. As a result of this loss of trade and reduced production output, the total fixed costs will decrease in total from €9,000 to €8,000.

REQUIREMENT

1. What is the impact on Blade's annual profit if trade with Lawn products is discontinued and Blade is unable to find an alternative market or customer?

2. What is the financial impact on Lawn Products if it acquires the goods from the external supplier?

3. By how much will Dana Group's profit before tax increase or decrease if Lawn Products buys the blades from the outside supplier?

SOLUTION

The impact on Blade's profit can be highlighted by preparing a sum-marised profit and loss account on the basis of trade with external customers only, as follows:

REVISED PROFIT AND LOSS ACCOUNT FOR BLADE

	€
Sales to external customers only	40,000
Less: variable costs	(20,000)
Less: fixed costs	(8,000)
Revised net profit	12,000
Original net profit (given)	16,000
Reduction in Blade's profit	4,000

The reduction of €4,000 in Blade's profit can be explained alternatively by the lost contribution from internal sales of €5,000 (€15,000 – €10,000), offset by a small saving of €1,000 on fixed costs.

The financial impact on Lawn Products will be positive since it is buying units at €1.25 each compared with €1.50 previously. Its profits will increase by €2,500 [(€1.50 - €1.25) x 10,000].

This means that the overall profit of the group will be reduced by €1,500 — the impact on both divisions combined. This reduction can be proved as follows:

	€
Additional cash outflow on purchases	(12,500)
Saving on cost of production	10,000
Saving on fixed costs	1,000
Overall reduction in group's profits	(1,500)

Methods of Transfer Pricing

Because of the profit impact of transfer prices on individual divisions and the group as a whole, some method of determining transfer prices should be established. At this stage, note that transfer prices do not impact on the *pre*-tax profit of the group. Transfer prices simply shift pre-tax profits from one division to another. However, the *post*-tax profits of the group can be significantly changed with transfer prices. Ignoring tax considerations, there are two main methods to determine transfer prices — those based on internal costs and those based on external market prices.

Market Price

This approach usually starts with an established market price and puts the selling and the buying divisions on the same footing as independent contractors. It satisfies the criteria of goal congruence and autonomy. The buying responsibility centre should ordinarily not be expected to pay more internally than it would have to pay if it purchased from the outside world, nor should the selling division ordinarily be entitled to more revenue than it could obtain by selling to the outside world. The use of market-based transfer prices has a number of advantages.

Competition of the marketplace sets an upward limit to the transfer price. This should generate economic efficiency within the transferor division and prevent excessive costs from being passed on. Also, market based transfer prices have the benefit of being relatively objective, rather than being a function of the relative negotiating skills of the selling and buying profit centres' managers. In practice, however, it is sometimes not clear what "the" market price is because different suppliers may set different prices on essentially identical items. Also, if the goods are highly specialised or represent work-in-progress, a market price may not exist. In addition, market prices can fluctuate considerably and the problem arises as to whether long-run average or existing (current) prices should be used. Current prices are normally chosen as it is considered better to evaluate managerial performance in the light of prevailing conditions, be they good or bad. Finally, it can be expensive to continually acquire up-to-date market prices in a complex market-place.

Cost-Based Transfer Prices

In a great many situations, there is no reliable market price that can be used as a basis for the transfer price. In these situations, a cost-based transfer price is used. If feasible, the cost should be a standard cost. If it is an actual cost, the selling responsibility centre has little incentive to control efficiency because any cost increases or decreases will be automatically passed on to the buying centre in the transfer price.

The method of computing cost and the amount of profit to be included in the transfer price may be specified by top management in order to lessen arguments that may otherwise arise. To avoid disputes, any policy statement as to what costs should be used, allowable profit margin, etc. must be unambiguously worded. In particular, short-term per unit costs may be different from longer-term costs. There can also be questions as to whether all of the cost elements normally included in the seller's definition of full cost should be included in the definition of cost used to determine transfer prices.

If the profit margin allowed on transfer prices is severely restricted by group policy, there is a strong argument that the respective divisions should no longer be evaluated as an investment (or profit) centre. Since divisions are no longer autonomous, traditional measures of performance (e.g., ROTA) no longer apply.

Negotiation and Arbitration

Because of the potential areas for disagreement in both market-based and cost-based transfer prices, transfer prices sometimes are negotiated between buyer and seller. In some cases, the selling division may be willing to depart from the normal company transfer pricing policy. For example, the selling responsibility centre may be willing to sell below the normal market price rather than lose the business, which could happen if the buying responsibility centre took advantage of a temporarily low outside price. Also, the selling division may have spare capacity. In such circumstances, the two parties negotiate a "deal".

Unless both responsibility centre managers have complete freedom to act, these negotiations will not always lead to an equitable result because the parties may have unequal bargaining powers. That is, the prospective buyer may not have the power of threatening to take its business elsewhere, and the prospective seller may not have the power of refusing to do the work. Unfortunately, negotiation can be a very time consuming exercise that is capable of generating friction between the two divisions rather than co-operation.

Profit-Switching Transfer Prices

It is frequently alleged in the media that transfer prices can be used to manipulate group profits. In reality, transfer prices can be used to do many other things but we shall initially concentrate on the issue of taxation.

Throughout the world, corporate profits are liable to tax. A minority of countries tax the profits of companies, regardless where the profits were generated (at home or abroad). However, the majority of countries only tax corporate profits generated by companies within their jurisdiction. While the issue of international taxation is very complex, it is fair to say that, as a result of double taxation agreements (DTAs), tax is generally paid only in the country in which the profits are generated. Thus, using transfer prices, profits can be shifted from a high-tax regime to a low-tax regime. While the pre-tax profit of the group is unchanged (ignoring import/export duties), the post-tax profit of the group will be improved.

ILLUSTRATION

An American company produces 100,000 units per annum at a cost of €5 each. These units are sold on the European market at €9 each. The corporate tax rate is 40 per cent.

The directors are now considering setting up a manufacturing plant in Ireland that will produce the goods for €5 each. These will be sold by the Irish company for €9 each. The corporate tax rate in Ireland is 10 per cent.

Highlight the financial impact of this proposal.

SOLUTION

The profits generated in the United States amount to €400,000 of which €240,000 remains after tax. Thus, the post tax profit of the "group" is €240,000. If the proposal to set up a manufacturing facility in Ireland goes ahead, all the profit will be shifted to the Irish subsidiary company, whose profits are liable to tax at 10 per cent. The after-tax profit of the group will be €360,000.

Global after-tax profits are affected simply because tax rates differ between countries. The tax rates can vary from 0 to 50 per cent. As a result, an MNE may choose to make an investment in a particular country in order to take advantage of that country's lower tax rates, and thereby increase its global after-tax income. Using transfer prices, profits can be taken out of a high-tax country and into a low-tax country. Exhibit 13.2 below shows how profit-switching transfer prices can operate.

Transfer prices can also be used to by-pass anti-dumping laws or to penetrate a foreign market using penetration pricing. Companies can underprice goods sold to foreign subsidiaries and the affiliates can then sell them for prices that local competition cannot match. If anti-dumping laws exist on final products, a company can underprice components and semi-finished products to its affiliates. The affiliates can then assemble or finish the product at prices that would have been classified as dumping prices had they been imported directly into the country rather than being produced inside.

Exhibit 12.2: Profit-Switching Transfer Prices

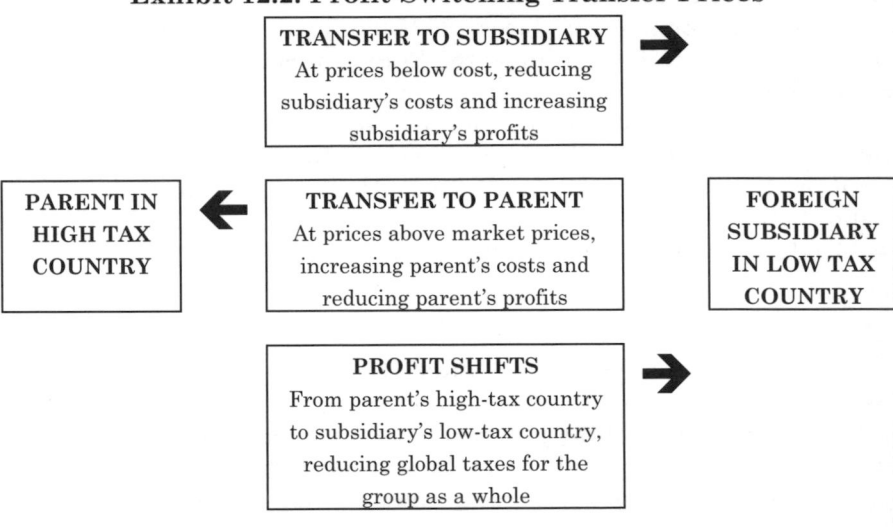

Transfer prices can also be used to effectively reduce tariffs. *Ad valorem* duties are based on the imported value as reported by the transfer price. Although no company can do much about the tariff itself, its effect can be lessened if the selling company underprices the goods it exports to the buying company. This can also be used to get more products into a country that is rationing its foreign currency by limiting the value of goods that can be imported. A subsidiary company can import twice as many products if they can be bought at half price.

In other cases, high transfer prices can be used to circumvent or significantly lessen the impact of national controls. A government prohibition on dividend remittances to foreign owners can restrict the ability of a firm to repatriate profits. However, overpricing the goods shipped to a subsidiary in such a country effectively takes the funds out. (Alternatively, goods may be invoiced to head office from that subsidiary at a cheap price). High transfer prices can also be a benefit to a company if it is paid a subsidy or earns a tax credit based on the value of goods it exports. The higher the transfer price of exported goods, the greater the subsidy received or the value of the tax credit.

High transfer prices on goods shipped to subsidiaries can also be desirable when a parent wishes to lessen the reported profitability of its subsidiary. This may be because of demands by the subsidiary's workers for higher wages, or because of political pressure to expropriate high-profit and foreign-owned operations. Alternatively, profits are kept deliberately low so that new competitors will not be lured into the industry by high profits. There may also be inducements for having high-priced transfers to the subsidiary when a joint venture is involved, the inducement being that the increase in the parent company profits will not have to be split with the subsidiary's joint venture partner. High transfer prices may also be desired when price controls in the subsidiary's country are based on production costs (costs that include high transfer prices for purchases).

Exhibits 12.3 and 12.4 summarise particular conditions that make it advantageous for companies to use a specific level of transfer price.

In Exhibit 12.3, the parent sells at low prices to the subsidiary and buys from it at high prices. Thus, profits are shifted to the subsidiary, reducing the global tax burden and increasing global after-tax profits. At the same time, the impact of the high *ad valorem* duty (tariffs) in the subsidiary's country is lessened and the financial appearance of the subsidiary is enhanced for local borrowing purposes. In addition, the impact of foreign exchange rationing on imports from the parent and dividend payments to the parent are lessened, the subsidiary's ability to penetrate its local market is enhanced, the parent is less affected by its government's restrictions on capital outflows, and so on.

Under this set of conditions, the subsidiary's country gains more than the parent's: More funds, more taxable income, greater economic growth of the subsidiary, and more export revenues. It loses somewhat in other areas, however: Local competitors may suffer adversely, have lower profits, pay less taxes and lay off its workers, if the foreign subsidiary actively adopts a market penetration strategy. The government also pays greater subsidies and gives more tax credits because of the subsidiary's artificially high value of exports and, like the government of the other country, has its national control lessened.

Exhibit 12.3: Profit-Boosting Transfer Prices

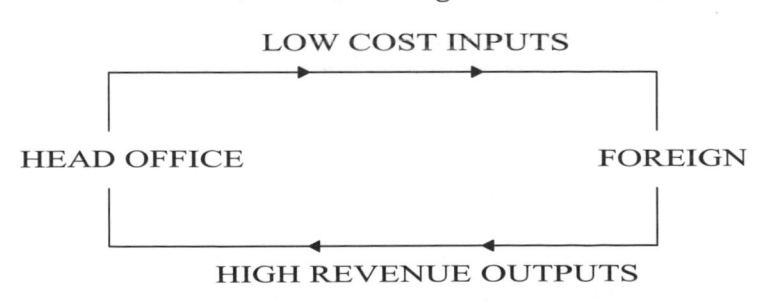

Profit-boosting transfer prices may be due to a number of factors, including:

1. Corporate tax rate lower than in parent's country.

2. High *ad valorem* import tariffs.

3. Significant competition in economy in which subsidiary operates.

4. Local loans based on the financial profit and profitability of subsidiary.

5. Export subsidy or tax credit based on value of exports.

6. Restrictions on value of goods that can be imported in local economy.

Exhibit 12.4: Profit-Depressing Transfer Prices

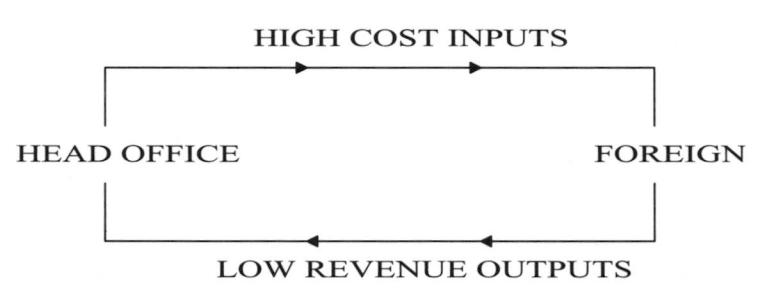

The policy of depressing the profits of the subsidiary company may be due to:

1. Local partners in joint ventures.

2. Pressure from workers for greater share in profits.

3. Desire to reduce reported profits to keep competitors out.

4. Political instability in local country.

5. Restrictions on profit or dividend remittances to head office.

However, seldom do the conditions line up as nicely as depicted in the above exhibits. It is far more likely that a country will simultaneously have conditions taken from both exhibits. For example, a country experiencing balance of payments difficulties typically would be restricting dividend payments or profit repatriations and the amount of imports. A company using high transfer prices on sales to its subsidiaries in such a country would gain in terms in taking out more money than it might have been able otherwise, but would lose by having to decrease the quantity of imported materials its affiliate needs. Alternatively, a country may have high *ad valorem* tariffs and high corporate tax rates. Underpricing goods shipped to an affiliate in such a country lessens the tariffs duties but also increases subsidiary profits due to lower input costs, resulting in higher taxes for the subsidiary.

Exhibits 12.3 and 12.4 are based on a two-country model. In reality, several countries may be involved and this greatly increases the complexity of using transfer prices to increase global after-tax profits. Some companies use deterministic models to determine optimum transfer prices. This means that all the data are included in a model, usually in the form of an algebraic equation, to determine the optimum price. For example, the after-tax profits of a company can be modelled as $(R - C)$ multiplied by $(1 - T)$ where R equals revenue, C equals costs and T represents the corporate tax rate. In conclusion, the presence of profit-switching prices complicates the performance evaluation of divisions, especially overseas divisions since reported profit may be largely determined by centralised policy on transfer prices.

12.4 EVALUATION OF PUBLIC SECTOR PROGRAMMES

Earlier sections stressed that no proper evaluation of any activity can take place unless there is objective and specific conditions under which the activity or programme may be considered a success.

It is frequently assumed that, in the private sector, the dominant objective is to maximise the long-term profitability of the business while maintaining adequate liquidity of the enterprise subject to good ethical practices. Although this objective may be difficult to achieve in reality, it has the advantage of being highly specific and is a well-established criterion for measuring how well a private sector company is performing. Evaluation of the company's activities is undertaken with reference to profits so that unexpected losses produce a chain reaction of investigation and correction. Because the original objective is quantifiable and measurable in money terms, the information and reporting system is dominated by financial data. The link between a specific objective and the evaluation of various alternatives in achieving that objective is obvious.

In the public sector, the dissimilarity between objectives becomes apparent. In the public sector, there may not be a single dominant objective of a particular programme. For example, a motorway project may have simultaneous objectives such as reducing transport costs, reducing accidents or encouraging people to change their residence. This presents a problem for performance evaluation in the public sector. In addition, many government programmes involve the provision of a service whose accomplishments are difficult to measure. These services seek to achieve political, social and economic objectives. The economic and social obligations, by their very nature, place constraints on any element of government expenditure being evaluated solely on commercial or financial considerations. Thus, a contrast between the public and private sectors can be traced to differences in their fundamental objectives.

The essence of any public sector activity is the influence or impact that it has on a particular subject matter. This desired impact is the end product of policy formation and implementation. The fundamental issue therefore in the evaluation of public sector activity is to provide information on the intended and actual impact of a particular subject matter (effectiveness) and the relative efficiency with which the task is carried out. In this regard, it is obvious that achieving effectiveness and efficiency is nothing more than good management and conceptually there is no difference at this level between management in the public sector and management in the private sector. Any manager ought to manage the operation for which he is responsible so that he maximises his outputs in relation to his inputs and ought to achieve the objectives that are clearly identified.

Evaluation, however, can be viewed in two different but interrelated ways. The first is concerned with the evaluation of future activities and the subsequent allocation of resources (that is planning). The second is concerned with the control and evaluation of actual outcomes. Although this dichotomy provides a convenient basis for analysis, the two processes of evaluation cannot be divorced in practice. Once plans have been formulated, management must ensure an appropriate conversion into actual results. Thus actual results are monitored against plans. Based on this feedback information, subsequent plans may need to be modified. In this way, decision-makers will be able to learn about their performance and about the environment in which they operate. *Ex post* and *ex ante* analysis should be viewed as a continuous and interactive process.

In the ideal world, activity is preceded by the setting of goals that are then defined more narrowly in terms of specific targets. This process also applies to the public sector. For example, if the postal authorities have a goal of providing "a reliable and efficient mail service to meet the needs of the country", how can the achievement of this goal be evaluated? An operational objective must be set, such as delivering mail between particular zones within a particular time and with a certain percentage of loss or damage to the mail. (The only advantage of setting broad objectives is that since everybody agrees with them, general consensus is quickly reached without conflict.) The major task is, therefore, to translate goals into objectives or targets that are more specific and operational.

Performance Indicators

The specification of operational objectives is a preliminary stage in the evaluation process. It is essential to obtain information on the effectiveness and efficiency of a programme. Effectiveness may be broadly defined as the degree of success of a programme in achieving what it is supposed to achieve — in other words, the impact achieved in relation to output. Efficiency, on the other hand, seeks to measure unit costs in carrying out the prescribed tasks; in other words, it expresses the relationship between the monetary inputs required to carry out the task and the actual output in terms of goods and services. In many cases, output can be measured in physical terms — for instance, the number of housing units or motorway miles constructed. In other cases, it must be acknowledged that outputs will be almost incapable of quantification — for instance, the work of the Department of Foreign Affairs. The distinction between these two concepts, effectiveness and efficiency, is important, since it is possible to have programmes which are extremely efficient but are ineffective in achieving objectives and vice versa. Ideally, therefore, evaluation of public sector programmes should encompass these two concepts which combined are equivalent to "value for money", which describes the impact in relation to the inputs involves. This is highlighted in Exhibit 12.5 below.

Exhibit 12.5: Value for Money in the Public Sector

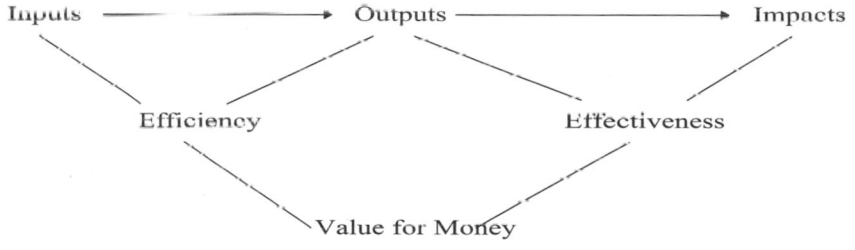

Information on effectiveness and efficiency (value for money) represents a major element of public sector evaluation. In addition, it is important to assess the availability of the service provided to the intended recipients and the public's awareness of that service. For example, there would seem to be little logic in providing a certain service if the intended beneficiaries are unaware of its existence. In addition, the service provided should be acceptable and satisfactory to users. This is an important element because of the potential conflict between standards of service and financial targets. It is therefore important from the point of view of consumers and the public to see whether financial results are being achieved at the expense of quality of service (or even whether services are being improved at the expense of financial performance). Finally, one can list the measure of extensiveness, highlighting the amount or quantity of service provided in relation to the underlying problem. These six dimensions (there are probably others) suggest that evaluation of public sector programmes should encompass an appropriate range of performance indicators. The objectives and examples of these performance indicators are presented in Exhibit 12.6. They are not an alternative to financial data. Rather they are both an extension and application of financial data in the evaluation process, and ideally they should be used by the organisation for its own management purposes. We shall see in the next chapter how various performance measures are incorporated in the Balanced Scorecard.

Exhibit 12.6: Properties of Performance Indicators

MEASURE	CONCEPTUAL CONTENT	EXAMPLES
Efficiency	Compares resource inputs with outputs	• Staff/student ratio • Cost per patient
Effectiveness	Compares accomplishment with objective (what was intended)	• Number of patients cured • Number of trainees in permanent employment • Incidence of disease in cattle herd
Availability	Amount and type of service provided	• Waiting lists • Number of visits
Awareness	Knowledge of users, population and other agencies (especially referral agencies) of existence; Range and conditions for which services are appropriate	• Percentage of user group using service • Number of referrals from other agencies
Extensiveness	Compares quantity of services rendered relative to extent of problem	• Number of outpatients • Number of enrolments • Number of users
Acceptability (standards of service)	Assesses service provided to preference of users	• Number of complaints • Punctuality of trains • Postal delays

The preparation and use of an appropriate range of performance indicators for various public sector programmes would greatly enhance the evaluation process. This process would then be essentially a task of comparative analysis of which three main types can be distinguished:

1. Analysis against present targets that reflect desired objectives and obligations, or comparison with what could reasonably have been achieved in the circumstances. This may or may not be the same thing as a target figure, depending upon how recent and relevant the target is as a measure of what is reasonably attainable.

2. Analysis against the performance of other organisations, including where appropriate, relevant international comparisons. This is the essence of "benchmarking" or the search for best practices. However, the validity of these comparisons may be affected by several factors such as the rates used for converting foreign currencies and different accounting policies. The problem, therefore, is to find strictly comparable organisations.

3. Comparison with what the organisation has achieved in the past — trend analysis. Where performance is expressed entirely in quantitative terms (unit of output per employee), indicators will not be affected by inflation. However, where indicators are expressed in financial terms, some adjustment should be made, with financial indicators being expressed in terms of constant purchasing power. The limitation of this measure is that one would normally expect efficiency and other measures of performance to improve over time in any event.

A multitude of performance indicators can conceivably be developed for various dimensions of public sector activity and therefore it is desirable to determine what criteria should apply to their selection. Since the purpose of these performance indicators is to supply information to enable a more meaningful evaluation of programmes to be undertaken they can be tested against the following four criteria: Relevance, timeliness, consistency and institutional acceptability.

Relevance can be defined as information's capacity "to make a difference" in making a decision either by helping to form predictions about the future or by confirming or correcting current expectations. Relevance is the dominant criterion since, if information is not relevant in a particular context, it has no decision value.

The second characteristic, timeliness, is important because unless information is up-to-date at the time of making a decision it cannot be useful. The preparation of performance indicators in accordance with the third criterion, consistency, is to facilitate comparisons with performance at other times, thus reinforcing the notion that it is the trend of data which is often more informative than point estimates. However, where indicators are used to compare the relative efficiency of two or more units, it is important to establish not only that the system of measurement is valid but also that the similarities between the units are sufficiently strong to make comparisons justified. Sometimes the similarities are superficial and so an over-enthusiastic and uncritical application of this technique must be guarded against. However, this danger can be reduced if several indicators are used.

The final criteria of institutional acceptability means that measures of performance adopted may not themselves be the most reliable indicators of effectiveness or even efficiency. Nevertheless they could be justified if they lead to improved performance or discussion. What is vital is that the people using the indicators should accept them and the basis on which they are devised as relevant and fair. One is thus recognising the important behavioural dimension whereby accounting information affects individuals and individuals affect accounting information.

Conclusion

Public sector expenditure is intended to achieve certain objectives so that the evaluation of such expenditure should be undertaken with reference to these objectives. However, traditional accounting procedures within the public sector were developed as a vehicle for authorisation and accountability. As a result, they focus only on financial inputs. The unfortunate consequence is that it is difficult to imagine how reasoned judgements can be formed as to whether an activity supported by public funds should be granted additional support, have its activities modified or be closed down completely. In such an environment, the annual budget inevitably becomes a routine and incremental process in which last year's expenditure becomes the basis on which to negotiate next year's allocations.

What is needed is information on the objectives for public sector programmes and what they are actually achieving: Their efficiency, their availability; the public's awareness of and satisfaction with them. It is this type of information that all managers need, whether they are in the public or private sector. In the absence of relevant information on these measures of performance, management becomes a task beyond the capabilities of all but the most inspired or lucky individual!

12.5 END OF CHAPTER QUESTIONS

Question 12.1

A supermarket group is organised on regional lines. There is a management group that takes responsibility for about 40 stores in each region.

Each store manager, while having some freedom within his or her own store, is responsible to the regional management group, which in turn reports to the head office.

The head office delegates capital expenditure decisions to the regions up to a limit of €50,000 per project. Store managers have no authority to undertake capital expenditure above €1,000.

Each store offers a wide range of goods including food products, clothing and hardware. There is an in-store cafeteria and a warehouse attached, from which the shelves are regularly stocked.

The group has an arrangement to buy some products centrally and undertake national promotions. However, the quantities stocked, all local purchases and many in-store promotions and most selling prices are decisions that are delegated to the individual store managers.

Reporting to each store manager are three or four departmental managers who are responsible for running their own departments or sections, involving decisions on product ranges and management of staff.

The responsibility accounting control system of the group makes use of cost centres, profit centres and investment centres.

REQUIREMENT

1. Distinguish between cost centres, profit centres and investment centres, illustrating your answer by reference to the supermarket group.

   For each of the managerial levels mentioned, department, store and region, suggest two possible performance measures, one financial, the other non-financial.

2. Discuss the potential problems in using cost, profit and investment centres for management accounting and control.

Question 12.2

"In any divisionalised organisation, complete autonomy of action is impossible when a substantial level of interdivisional transfers take place."

REQUIREMENT

1. In this context, what is a divisionalised organisation and autonomy of action?

2. Is this autonomy good? If so, why?

3. Are there any dangers from permitting autonomy of action and in what ways do interdivisional transfers make complete autonomy impossible?

Question 12.3

The following information applies to the budgeted operation of Goodman, a division of the Telling Group International.

	€
Sales (50,000 units)	375,000
Variable costs @ €6 per unit	(300,000)
Contribution margin	75,000
Less: Fixed costs (excluding interest)	(50,000)
Divisional profit	25,000
Divisional investment	150,000

The minimum desired rate of return is the cost of capital of 20 per cent.

REQUIREMENT

1. Calculate the:

   (a) Divisional expected ROI.

   (b) Divisional expected RI.

2. The manager of Goodman has the opportunity to sell an additional 10,000 units at €7.50 to an external customer, but fixed costs would increase by €5,000. Additional investment of €20,000 would also be required in fixed assets. If the manager accepted this special order, by how much would RI change?

   (NOTE: Requirement 3 below is independent of requirement 2.)

3. Included in Goodman's budget is the sale of 10,000 units to Sharp, another division in the Telling Group. A company external to the group has promised to supply Sharp with the same number of units at €7.20 each. Since this is 30c *less* than the price being charged by Goodman, the manager of Sharp wants Goodman to reduce his price, otherwise Sharp will purchase from the external supplier.

(a) Calculate the effect on the total profit of the Telling Group if Goodman meets the €7.20 price and supplies Sharp with 10,000 units.

(b) Calculate the effect on the total profit of the Telling Group if Goodman does *not* lower his price and Sharp purchases the 10,000 units externally. It is not possible for Goodman to acquire another customer for the 10,000 units in the current accounting period.

(The Association of Chartered Certified Accountants)

Question 12.4: Glasnost plc

Glasnost plc is a large group organised on divisional lines. Two typical divisions are East and West. They are engaged in broadly similar activities and, therefore, central management compares their results in order to make judgements on managerial performance. Both divisions are regarded as investment centres.

A summary of the current year's return of the two divisions is as follows:

	WEST		EAST	
	€000	€000	€000	€000
Total Investment		2,500		500
Sales		1,000		400
Manufacturing cost:				
Direct	300		212	
Indirect	220		48	
Selling and distribution cost	180		40	
		700		300
Divisional profit		300		100
Allocation of uncontrollable				
central overhead costs		50		20
Net profit		250		80

West division has recently incurred substantial expenditure on automated production lines and new equipment. East has old plant. Approximately 50 per cent of the sales of East are inter-company transfers to other divisions within the group. These transfers are based on an unadjusted prevailing market price. The inter-company transfers of West are minimal.

Management of the group focuses on return on investment as a major performance indicator. Their required minimum corporate rate of return and cost of capital is 10 per cent.

REQUIREMENT

Compute both ROI and RI to help in an assessment of the costs and performance of the two divisions. Comment upon this performance making reference to any matters that give cause for concern when comparing the divisions or in divisional performance generally.

(*The Association of Chartered Certified Accountants*)

Question 12.5: Motorgo

A major motor dealership called Motorgo offers the usual range of garage services including new and used car sales, repairs and servicing. The general manager is keen to achieve a high level of co-operation and incentive in his managers' actions so a profit centre reporting system has recently been established. In addition to a basic salary, managers are paid a commission based on their performance against target profit levels.

A recent event has, however, caused some friction between the three profit centre managers and cast doubt in the general manager's mind. He provides you with the following information:

A new car, which had a list price of €8,000, was in stock at a cost of €5,000. It had proved to be a difficult car to sell. A customer had approached the dealer about this car with a vehicle to trade in. The value of this vehicle according to a trade-in guide was €2,800. It would then retail from the used car section with a warranty for about €3,600.

The service department had carried out a brief inspection and estimated that repairs and servicing costing €600 would be required to prepare the vehicle for their own showroom. The service manager added that, if similar repairs were to be carried out for an external customer, the charge would be €900. Being aware of the above information, the new car sales manager had authorised a trade-in price of €3,500 against the new car.

REQUIREMENT

1. If all the transactions envisaged were completed at the values indicated, within one trading period, determine their impact on the profit of Motorgo and each of the three profit centres of the company.

2. Explain how the results would change if the company elected to send the vehicle that was traded in to a cut-price auction for €1,700 without any warranty or repair work undertaken.

3. Is the system of profit centres good for the company? Should it be preserved? Make some recommendations.

(*The Association of Chartered Certified Accountants*)

Question 12.6: Nugget Group plc

Nugget Group plc, your employer, operates two divisions, one in food production, the other in catering and leisure. You do not yet have full information in relation to last year's performance of the two divisions.

From various memoranda and conversations, you have been able to extract the following:

- The food production division made a profit (PBIT) of €12 m. This represented an average margin of operating profit to sales of 10 per cent. The rate of turnover of investment to sales during the last year was two.

- The catering and leisure division achieved sales of €80m, the return on investment of the division was 32 per cent achieved with an operating profit (PBIT) to sales ratio of 20 per cent.

- Nugget Group uses a cost of capital of 18 per cent in all its calculations.

The in-tray of a colleague who deals with group purchases contains a letter, the abbreviated contents of which are:

"Included in the reported profit of the food production division is €4m made from interdivisional sales of €22m to the catering and leisure division. An outside supplier is offering to undertake this supply in the future. Its price for supplies equivalent to the above would be €19m. Funds invested would not be affected significantly by such an event."

REQUIREMENT

1. From the information on last year's performance, calculate other appropriate measures or ratios in order to determine which division you consider to be more profitable. Give your reasons and any qualifications you may have. For the purpose of this part, *ignore* all reference to the outside supplier.

2. Briefly examine the implications for each division and the group of the outside supplier's offer. For any numerical illustration, you should use the figures relating to last year assuming such a situation would otherwise be repeated in the current year.

(*The Association of Chartered Certified Accountants*)

Question 12.7: Butte Company

The Brown Group is divided into a number of operating companies. The Butte Company is one division within the group that manufactures "widgets" in the Sudan for sale on the domestic market but a significant proportion (20 per cent) of its output is sold to an American company in the Brown Group. The unit selling price is €10.

The Butte Division's estimated sales and cost data for the coming year are as follows:

	TOTAL €
Sales revenues (100,000 units @ €10)	1,000,000
Raw material costs	(200,000)
Direct labour costs (assume variable)	(100,000)
Variable production overheads	(100,000)
Fixed production overheads	(200,000)
Administration costs (fixed)	(200,000)
Net profit	200,000

Having prepared the above forecasts for the coming year, the Sudanese company now discovers that its sister division in America is unwilling to purchase the anticipated quota of goods. The problem is that the American company now has an opportunity to buy 20,000 widgets of identical quality from another supplier (not in the Brown Group) on a continuing basis at a delivered cost of €8.

The Butte Company cannot sell any additional products on the local Sudanese market and it is not possible to get new customers at such short notice.

REQUIREMENT

1. Prepare a revised statement in contribution format, showing the impact on Butte's annual profit if trade with its American sister company is discontinued and Butte is unable to find alternative markets.

2. By how much will Brown Group's profit before tax increase or decrease, if the American company obtains the 20,000 units from the external supplier?

Question 12.8: PG Group

The PG Group operates with two divisions: S, which operates with spare capacity, and F, which operates at full capacity. Division F only makes two products, the Alpha and Beta and details regarding each product are as follows:

	ALPHA	BETA
Direct material	€30 per unit	€25 per unit
Production time	3 hours	2 hours
Budgeted production	3,000 units	4,000 units
Selling price	€120.00	€86.25

The labour costs of division F are classified as conversion costs and treated as overheads which amount to €374,000 for the period in question, of which €119,000 are estimated to be variable overheads. The pricing method adopted by division F is to add 25 per cent onto the total product cost to arrive at a selling price for external sales.

Since division S has slack capacity, it intends to request 500 units of product Beta from division F, in order to adapt it into a new product Gamma. Division S expects to sell the 500 units of this new product (Gamma) for €110 each. Direct costs incurred by division S will be €12 per unit, additionally there are variable overhead costs of €6 for each unit of Gamma manufactured.

A meeting is to be convened shortly to discuss the possibility of transfer of Beta from division F to division S.

REQUIREMENT

1. Identify four possible prices (or ranges) that could be used to determine a transfer price between the F and S divisions.

2. State any other points that should be borne in mind in relation to the possible transfer of Beta to division S.

Question 12.9

An American corporation produces "widgets" which it sells on the US market. Profits in the US are liable to a corporate tax rate of 40 per cent but this is levied only on American income or foreign profits repatriated.

The American company is keen to expand into the European market and, towards this end, it has established a wholly owned assembly plant in Ireland. This assembly plant qualifies for a corporate tax rate of 10 per cent on goods manufactured in Ireland. Because of its location in the EU, the goods exported to Europe from Ireland are not liable for any import or export tariff. However, the cost of assembly in

Ireland and export to Europe is estimated at 20 per cent of final selling price.

The management of the American company is anxious to determine in advance a transfer pricing strategy — a low- or high-cost transfer price.

REQUIREMENT

1. Develop a deterministic (mathematical) model suitable for predicting cash flows to the American company; the Irish company and finally, the overall group, assuming the existence of the American and Irish companies only.

2. Prove your answer assuming an Irish selling price (ISP) of €100, a transfer price of €50 and the cost in the US of €20.

Question 12.10: Lotus Electronics, Inc.

The amplifier division of Lotus Electronics, Inc., a diversified international company headquartered in New York, sells amplifier kits in the United States and several foreign countries.

The selling price for these kits is €40 in the United States, where the income tax rate is 50 per cent.

The Brazilian market is one of the foreign markets in which the amplifier division is active. Lotus Electronics has a 60 per cent owned subsidiary in Brazil, which buys the amplifier kits from the amplifier division and sells them to local wholesalers.

Brazilian tariffs on amplifiers are 40 per cent of declared value. These duties are paid by the Brazilian subsidiary.

The applicable income tax rate in Brazil is 35 per cent. There are no other restrictions or taxes affecting the transfer of funds from Brazil to the United States.

REQUIREMENT

Develop a deterministic model suitable for predicting cash flows to Head Office.

NOTE: The operational costs in Brazil can be ignored.

Question 12.11: GT Company

GT Company is a computer bureau and a management consultancy practice. Each division offers its services separately, although a considerable proportion of work is undertaken in collaboration.

The services of the computer bureau centre are the preparation and analysis of the final accounts of the clients, usually small businesses. The management consultancy offers advice and consultancy, which can be based on the final accounts produced by the bureau.

Charges to clients are standardised as follows:

(i)   final accounts preparation only — €200 per client

(ii) final accounts preparation and subsequent consultancy service — €300 per client billed by the consultancy division.

An analysis of variable costs of each operation involving machine time, management time and special stationery reveals:

(i)   final accounts preparation — €120 per client;

(ii) consultancy service (not including final accounts preparation) — €150 per client.

The owners, while keen to promote the profitability of the business as a whole, are seeking to focus also on the contribution made by each division. When a client has received both the final accounts and consultancy, it has been practice for the computer bureau management to charge the consultancy division with the full market rate for the final accounts preparation — €200 per client. The manager of the consultancy service objects to this charge, asserting "when the two divisions collaborate, I can never be profitable".

REQUIREMENT

1. Summarise the data in a form that will either refute or confirm the assertion made by the manager of the consultancy division, and make brief comments.

2. If the computer bureau is fully occupied, should it undertake work for the consultancy division in preference to its own "outside" work? What transfer charge per client should be adopted in such circumstances? Explain your reasoning.

3. If the computer bureau is not fully occupied, should it undertake work for the consultancy division? What transfer charge would be appropriate in such circumstances? Explain your reasoning.

(The Association of Chartered Certified Accountants)

Question 12.12: ABC plc

ABC plc is organised into autonomous divisions. For the purposes of evaluating managerial performance, a return on investment (ROI) is calculated. The company interprets investment as current assets plus fixed assets.

Extracts from the budgeted results of Divisions A and B for the coming year are:

	DIVISION A €	DIVISION B €
Profit	200,000	64,000
Current assets	200,000	150,000
Fixed assets	800,000	650,000

There are two projects that are now being considered but neither of them is included in the above figures.

1. Project Alpha, in which Division A has the opportunity to increase annual sales by €200,000 by undertaking a special advertising campaign that will cost €15,000. The sales increase will improve the division's contribution by €30,000 (excluding advertising costs) but will require an additional investment in stocks of €100,000 per annum.

2. Project Beta, in which Division B can purchase some new equipment costing €200,000, which will improve annual profits by €20,000 due to increased efficiency.

REQUIREMENT

1. Determine the budgeted ROI for each division:

   (i) before the two projects are incorporated;

   (ii) assuming the managers adopt the projects available to their division and incorporate them into their respective budgets.

2. Determine the budgeted Residual Income (RI) for each division before and after the incorporation of the respective projects. The company has a cost of capital of 12 per cent per annum.

3. Contrast the results under 1. and 2. and consider to what extent they encourage the divisional managers to pursue corporate profit objectives whilst acting in their own best interests.

13

Current Developments and Reflection

Even the most casual reader of management accounting journals must be aware of the great deal of criticism during the past decade or so concerning the current state of cost/management accounting. For convenience, it is useful to group the many criticisms of management accounting into three broad areas.

The first relates to the current preoccupation with accounting numbers and the consequent failure to adapt to a world class manufacturing philosophy with its focus on quality and customers' needs. The second relates to the distortion of product costs in multi-product companies by using simplistic definitions of fixed and variable costs, and by inappropriate methods of overhead absorption, based on volume only considerations. It has been suggested that product costs should be determined using an Activity-Based Costing (ABC) system. The third criticism is that accounting information concentrates mainly on internal data. It is argued that management accounting should broaden its focus to encompass the external environment — the enterprise's competitive position. In other words, accounting information should reflect a strategic focus — an emerging discipline referred to as strategic management accounting.

In earlier sections of this book, we have looked at the concept and technique of activity-based costing and also the topic of strategic management accounting. We now look at some of the management accounting implications of a world-class manufacturing philosophy.

13.1 MANAGEMENT ACCOUNTING IN WORLD CLASS MANUFACTURING

World Class Manufacturing (WCM) is a convenient label to describe the manufacture of high-quality products reaching customers quickly (or delivery of a prompt and quality service) at a low cost to provide customer value through performance and service. It is a customer-oriented philosophy. In a WCM system, costs are obviously important but one must also consider the other factors that consumers want from the product. Modern consumers, faced with a greater range of choices, have other requirements other than just a low price. Consumers are concerned about quality, levels of service, lead times and product flexibility. In other words, a product should be considered as a bundle of characteristics. If a company is to be successful in the marketplace, it must match its competitors in each of these relevant characteristics. For example, one rarely chooses a restaurant only on the basis of menu prices or an airline on the basis of ticket price.

Advanced Manufacturing Technology

There have been a number of technological advances in recent years that can lead to World Class Manufacturing performance. These advances are often referred to under the label of "Advanced Manufacturing Technology" (AMT). For example, Computer-Aided Engineering (CAE) represents computer software for designing, analysing, testing and modelling parts and components. Engineers enter their assumptions about new ideas for better designs and immediately watch their computer adjust the computer model and see the consequences of their assumptions. Enough information can be obtained through computer modelling to eliminate most design flaws and problems. Computer-Aided Design (CAD) represents a system that automates the drafting process. The final output of CAD is electronic drawings and specifications that are used in manufacturing. Computer-Aided Manufacturing (CAM) uses the information produced from the CAD process and allows computers to control and direct the manufacture and assembly of a product with very little input from direct labour.

Just-in-Time

Just-in-time (JIT) systems are also part of the process leading to world class manufacturing. JIT systems can be either purchasing and/or production. The objective behind JIT is to eliminate the lead time from the delivery of raw materials to production and the lead time from the production line to the delivery to the customer. Non-value-added activities represent waste; these activities can be reduced or eliminated without decreasing the enterprise's ability to compete and meet customer demands. Inspection of incoming raw materials is a non-value-added activity that can be eliminated without diminishing the value received by the enterprise or its customers. Customers do not value inspection; they value high quality. If a vendor of raw materials commits to supplying high-quality materials, then inspection is no longer required, and buying testing equipment and hiring more people to inspect the incoming raw materials would waste time and money.

ILLUSTRATION

The following activities occur in manufacturing a product. Identify the value added and non-value added activities:

1. Quality inspection of materials on arrival.
2. Storage of material in warehouse.
3. Machining of raw materials in process 1.
4. Moving work in progress from process 1 to process 2.
5. Machining of work in progress in process 2.
6. Inspection of finished goods.
7. Packaging of goods with instruction leaflet.

The only activities that add value are:

3. Machining of raw materials in process 1.
5. Machining of work in progress in process 2.
7. Packaging of goods with instruction leaflet.

A relationship between WCM, AMT, JIT and Activity-Based Costing (ABC) is shown in Exhibit 13.1.

Underlying the entire process is the measurement system. If accountants are to remain as the information specialists within the organisation, they must first realise what they are supposed to measure. It is important to stress that "financial performance is the result of operational actions, and financial success should be the logical consequence of doing the fundamentals well". However, the measurement system must focus on the goal of continuous improvement. Employees, for example, must learn to do things better and to do better things. The measurement yardstick is dynamic, not static.

Exhibit 13.1: Elements of WCM

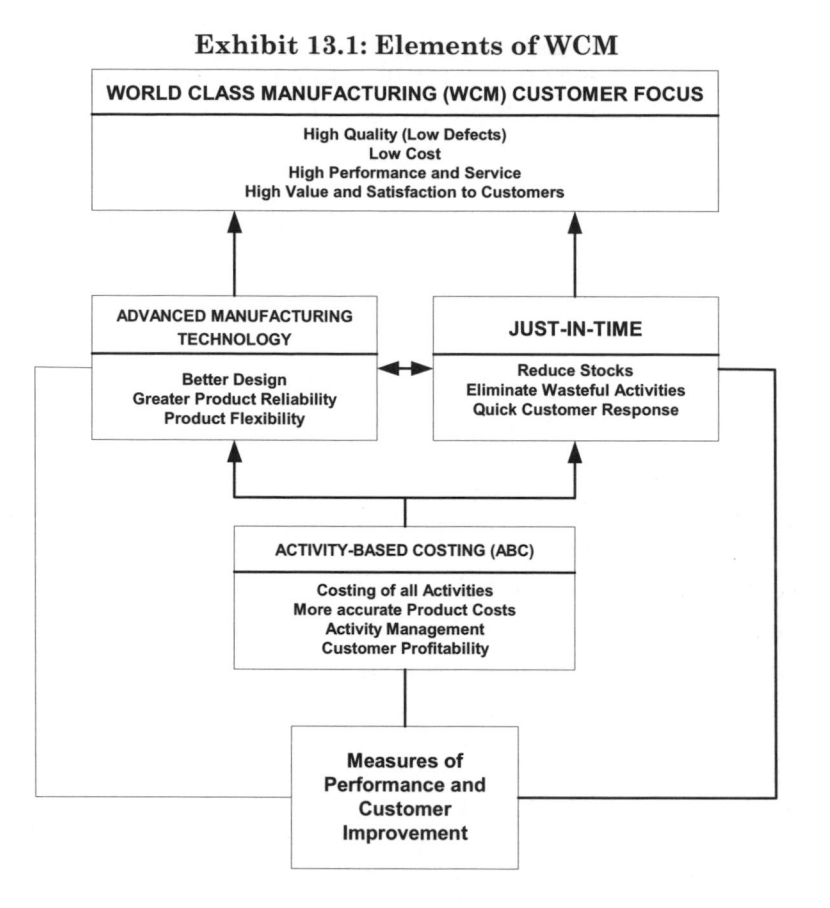

The Accounting Implications of WCM/AMT/JIT

Management accounting in the new manufacturing environment needs to change its current orientation. The factory of the future will see the increased use of high-technology production methods using machines rather than human labour. Not only does the automated equipment reduce labour cost but it also contributes to the objectives of high quality, product reliability, fast and flexible manufacturing and lower stocks. Some of the major accounting implications are as follows:

1. **Employee involvement in data collection**: One change will be that personal observation and therefore reaction by production-line workers will play an increasing role in cost control. This contrasts with the traditional system of cost accounting based on month end reports. There are a number of reasons for this. First, the dramatic reductions in production-cycle time due to small

batches mean that weekly/monthly cost-control reports arrive too late to be of value in controlling production operations except as a guide to identify trends that are not apparent on the spot.

Second, production workers directly observe non-financial variables such as quality on the factory floor. These non-financial variables are intuitive, easily understood and more relevant to factory personnel. Greater emphasis will be placed on in-process control mechanisms that require operating personnel to quickly isolate a quality problem, stop production and remedy the situation before it results in significant scrap, rework or other effects of poor quality. The failure of in-process checks results in a number of customer complaints and warranty claims and these should also be monitored.

It may be necessary to reorganise workers into cells and staff training will be required. In addition, vendor approval costs will be incurred in association with increased quality of supplies. These additional costs should be covered by the increased cost savings due to improved quality of production. Training employees to be more flexible and to work in cells with their colleagues should lead to greater job satisfaction. There may be increased levels of motivation due to higher pay in the form of bonuses.

2. **Changes in cost patterns and cost behaviour**: The shift from labour to machines changes both the proportion and characteristics of manufacturing costs. Labour and variable costs decrease, overhead and fixed costs (traditionally defined) increase.

In some manufacturing companies direct labour is as low as 10 per cent of all costs (or even lower) and it is treated as a sub-part of overhead. In some companies, the term "direct worker" has little relevance especially in a plant that uses robots extensively. In such circumstances, labour accounting will not necessarily require time clocks, work tickets, or other source documents, thus reducing significantly the costs of accounting for labour.

Coupled with the decline in direct labour costs will be a dramatic increase in overhead costs resulting from expensive machines and skilled indirect labour. Most overhead costs will be fixed. With the new technology, variable costs may virtually disappear except for raw materials and the energy needed to operate equipment. As companies automate, they find that they are being hit twice: First, overheads grow in percentage terms as direct labour costs fall and second, overheads grow in real terms because of the increased support costs associated with maintaining and running automated equipment. This reduces to an absurdity the practice of recovering overhead as a percentage of direct labour cost.

There will also be a change in emphasis from the traditional fixed/variable classification towards cost planning. In today's manufacturing environment, only raw materials, power, sales commission and perhaps sub-contract labour are likely to be variable costs in the short term. The switch towards automation inevitably leads to a higher proportion of fixed costs. Increasingly, costs will be committed at the planning and design stage and greater emphasis will therefore be placed on the control of costs at the planning stage. In other words, the emphasis will be on cost containment. Cost reduction at the planning stage is now one of the most urgent problems facing cost accountants. The explanation lies in the fact that almost 100 per cent of product cost is determined at the planning and design stages. By the time it comes to production, it is too late to control the costs. Budgets will have an important role to play in the planning stage but control reports are less important when the majority of the costs are committed at the planning stage.

3. **A new definition of product cost?** Product cost determination is another area where changes and, in some cases re-orientation, needs to take place. The very definition of what constitutes a product cost is becoming problematic. Due to the impact of financial reporting requirements, only production expenses are absorbed into product cost. Yet, if a company is in business to produce and sell products, then all costs are really product costs. Thus marketing, general management and research and development costs also relate to the products being produced and need to be brought into the product-cost computation.

4. **Reduced inventory and inventory accounting**: Since inventories are minimised under JIT, the need for detailed accounting for inventories of raw materials, work in progress and finished goods is reduced. The reduction in the amount of stock (inventory) saves on interest costs associated with investing in working capital. There should be related cost savings in lighting and heat expenses, insurance, handling, pilferage, and clerical costs. In addition, obsolescence costs should be reduced.

If a high degree of trust has developed between the customer and supplier, inspection and the goods receiving process is eliminated. Indeed, if goods were paid for when received, the creditors (accounts payable) ledger could be virtually eliminated! Furthermore, if completed goods are shipped immediately to customers, there is no need for finished goods inventory records.

Finally, since levels of inventory are very low, then inventory valuation becomes a less important issue and should be more quickly and accurately obtained.

5. **Standard costing systems**: Virtually all large Western manufacturing companies use standard costing systems in planning and cost control. But standard costing systems are suited to the large-scale production of homogeneous units. Standard costs for planning and authorisation purposes still will be important but their use for control will lessen. The new technology will facilitate the production of non-homogeneous units. For example, companies must acknowledge that customers' needs are diversified, resulting in a demand for the production of a large variety of products with numerous characteristics. This leads to greater difficulty in setting the standards calling into question the notion of variance analysis for performance evaluation. Indeed, if the manufacturing process is of the high quality level intended, actual costs incurred should approximate the standard costs estimated for planning purposes. Variances should be small and therefore unnecessary to track, at least from an accounting sense.

   Today's vast array of products is subject to rapid obsolescence. As standard cost systems cannot be revised quickly enough for many products in this environment, the usefulness of variance reports is open to question.

6. **Material and labour cost variances**: The advent of the new technology and JIT methods will lead to fewer defects and less spoilage, which in turn lessens the importance of traditional *usage* variances. Purchase *price* variances are no longer as important since the key issues are supplier reliability and component quality. To judge the purchasing manager's performance on the basis of purchase price variance may generate inappropriate behaviour and/or focus attention *away* from quality and reliability.

   Direct labour cost is becoming increasingly fixed and less important in terms of the overall cost structure. Consequently, labour variances are becoming less significant. Labour efficiency variances are likely to be meaningless in the new manufacturing environment because labour utilisation varies with each new batch produced. A labour variance in this environment may simply reflect the current machine process rather than employee efficiency or inefficiency.

   It is also important to remember that JIT takes a non-traditional approach to labour efficiency. The traditional approach to labour efficiency is that it is desirable to keep employees as productive as possible. However, under JIT it is better for a person to be idle than to be producing goods that are not immediately required.

13.2 COST MANAGEMENT

The issue of "costs" has always been an important consideration in the affairs of business organisations. Indeed, it is likely that with increased competition and globalisation, the cost issue will become more dominant for all organisations during the forthcoming decade. In simple terms, if costs are too high, the business is likely to be uncompetitive and unprofitable. Recent evidence suggests that many management accountants spend a great deal of their time "counting costs", and this information is used for product-costing purposes. In such an environment, it is possible that companies find it difficult to manage their costs. Two reasons explain this. First, the annual budgeting exercise within companies is likely based on incremental activity. In other words, the starting point for next year's budget was the actual cost out-turn last year. Managers, thus, have the incentive to always overspend in a given year. Unspent budgets meant that budgets would be cut the following year! The only budget items that received scrutiny are those that are "incremental" to last year either in the form of increases for inflation or new spending proposals. Possibly, more than 80 percent of the budget escapes serious scrutiny. Secondly, the emphasis on "counting costs" frequently meant that cost accountants were at a loss to explain WHY the costs were incurred. (Keeping the score in a match does not explain why the goals were scored!). This is particularly relevant in the case of overhead costs. Overheads refer to general costs that are not directly traceable to any individual product and can typically comprise as much as 50 per cent of the overall cost structure in a manufacturing company.

It became obvious some years ago, that merely identifying and counting costs would not provide sufficient information to managers to enable them to make important strategic and operating decisions. By definition, strategic decision-making requires information in relation to factors that are external to the firm and, in such a context, internal cost data may have limited relevance. In addition, many costs are incurred in, for example, providing non-value added activities. Recognising the limitations of merely "counting costs" has led to the development of what now is commonly referred to as cost management. In simple terms, cost management helps organisations to use their resources efficiently to provide products and services that customers value. The main focus of cost management is to continually reduce costs while providing customer satisfaction. This cost management orientation differs from the traditional cost control in a number of ways.

Firstly, the management accountant does not monopolise cost management. Successful cost management is everyone's responsibility and is an interdisciplinary and multi-functional activity. Certainly, the management accountant will be involved but will be influenced by the insights of production managers and engineers, design experts and others. The management accountant will act more like a facilitator rather than a leader or source of inspiration. The cost management project team should identify and influence those factors that can radically affect costs. Secondly, there is an external focus in the sense that it is acknowledged that costs should be incurred within organisations in order to provide customer value and satisfaction. Thirdly, cost management does not accept that the cost structure in an organisation is an inflexible baseline. Rather, managers and employees are encouraged and expected to manage costs in a proactive way. Cost management is about ways of transforming and managing the cost structure within the organisation. Indeed, formal staff suggestion scheme programmes can be useful in this regard. Finally, there is growing acceptance that a significant proportion of costs is determined at the design rather than the production stage of manufacturing. For example, the number of features included in a product together with the type of material used will significantly impact on the overall cost of that product. The design of the manufacturing process also impacts on costs. For example, some Japanese manufacturers operate on the basis that over 70 per cent of their production costs are determined at the design stage. As a result, Japanese managers prefer to spend a great deal of time getting the design stage right and spend considerably less time trying to control or reduce cost at the operational stage.

Techniques for Cost Management

How does an organisation implement cost management? Only three techniques will now be briefly revisited since they have been previously mentioned in this book. Regrettably, these techniques do not seem to be used in organisations as widely as the academic proponents would expect.

1. Identify value and non-value added activities: It is rather simplistic to note that organisations consist of a myriad of activities. The important thing about activities, in the context of cost management, is to query whether these activities are necessary? One way to answer this question is to segregate activities into two categories i.e. value added or non-value added activities. The feature of a value added activity is that it enhances the value of the product or service in the eyes of the customer. It is rather basic but nevertheless important to stress that a customer will only pay for an activity (or related feature) if it provides him with value and satisfaction. If organisations undertake even a crude inventory of activi-

ties they will discover many activities that do not add value to customers. In essence, they are wasteful and should be reduced or eliminated.

2. Activity-based costing systems: Related to the previous point is the technique of activity-based costing (ABC). It will be recalled that, in brief, ABC acknowledges that products require activities and these activities consume resources. These activities are costed using either actual and/or budgeted data. Usually, some activities are highlighted as being ridiculously expensive. Obviously, the potential for cost reduction, highlighted by an ABC system, is enormous. However, before taking action, managers first need ABC cost information. The arguments in favour of an ABC system have already been outlined elsewhere in this book. The arguments in the opinion of this author are very convincing. Thus, it is surprising to note that evidence suggests that the vast majority of firms do not place significant emphasis on activity based costing systems in any form!

3. Cost of quality reports: Many activities that do not add value are associated with inferior quality. That inferior quality production exists in the first place is unacceptable given that quality products and services enhance competitive advantage. Reporting a range of performance measures can highlight inferior quality. Typical measures include the number of defective products produced, the number of customer complaints, the amount spent on warranties. But a better way to get attention is to present the information in the form of a financially orientated Cost of Quality (COQ) report. This normally condenses activities into four categories – Prevention, Appraisal, Internal Failure and External Failure – and highlights the spending under each heading. The overall total is usually expressed as a percentage of sales turnover and this COQ report can provide the necessary impetus for a focus on cost management.

The cost management ideas presented above are relatively simple. They have been circulating for some time and have gained credibility and acceptance in companies in other countries. Increasing customer satisfaction, competition and globalisation require management accountants to progress from merely counting costs to a more proactive process of actively managing costs. If management accountants adopt this new approach they will play an important role in adding value to their organisation.

13.3 PERFORMANCE MEASUREMENT, INCLUDING THE BALANCED SCORECARD

The generally accepted role of management accounting is to provide relevant information to managers in order to facilitate their planning and control decisions. These decisions should be taken in the context of corporate objectives. Decisions should relate to a particular objective. Profit is usually stated to be the primary objective of all commercial organisations. There is an inherent weakness in attempting to evaluate an organisation's performance toward its goals based on this criterion alone. The most significant drawback of measuring profit is that it is a lagging indicator. Profit is a measure of *past* performance: it represents a result rather than a determinant. Thus, in the context of performance measurement, one can distinguish between "leading" and "lagging" measures of performance. Leading measures alert managers to the likely results of operations; lagging indicators point to results of past decisions. In brief, the management accounting system should report a range of measures of performance, both financial and non-financial. In turn, these performance measures should be supported by performance standards, and should be reinforced by reward mechanisms within the organisation.

In today's competitive environment, this pure financial orientation is deficient in four main respects:

1. Financial measures are always *incomplete* because they cannot tell the full story of an event or transaction. For example, goods returned as defective will be recorded as "sales returns". However, the possible loss of customer goodwill will not be recorded. Admittedly, loss of goodwill may be reflected in subsequent financial reports in the form of declining sales and profitability. In many situations, the accounting information comes too late for corrective action. One can also suggest that traditional accounting measurement systems can cause a variety of inappropriate actions, some of which are highlighted below.

Financial measurement	Managerial response	Overall result
Material purchase price variance	Buy cheap goods	Excess material usage
Sales targets	Grant excessive credit	Bad debts
Cost centre reporting	Focus on spending but ignore output	Incremental approach to budgeting

The first two actions, namely the purchase of cheap goods and the granting of excessive credit in order to meet sales targets do not require clarification. With cost centre reporting the focus is very much on overall spending limits especially for discretionary cost centres. Consequently, the focus is often on the amount spent (compared with budget) and the quality of service provided is overlooked. Also, the annual budgeting process seeks to only justify incremental or marginal spending each year rather than questioning the whole budget allocation.

1. Traditional management accounting reports can be described as scorecard reports in that they report the "result" rather than the "means". In other words, they focus on the result rather than explain how the result was achieved or, more importantly, what should be done differently in the future. Generally speaking, traditional accounting reports are not directly related to the company's strategy and, therefore, are not powerful enough on their own to push corporate change. Traditionally, there appears to be little recognition that financial results cannot be DIRECTLY managed, but instead are caused by the level of performance in various areas. To succeed today in a growing competitive marketplace, companies must perform well on a number of dimensions such as market share, cost, quality and customer care, delivery time and product innovation. Identifying these non-financial performance indicators is the first step in achieving a strategic advantage and gives a more meaningful picture of organisational performance than do financial figures used alone.

2. Accounting reports are often concerned with internal cost data. While this is important in its own right, it has limited relevance in, say, pricing decisions in which case, managers need to know the selling prices of competitors' products.

3. Companies and their managers are increasingly being judged by their performance in the short-term especially in relation to sales and profit growth. However, this short-term focus may result in inappropriate behaviour to the detriment of the long-term advantage of the company - a phenomenon referred to as short-termism. If the firm places too great importance on its short-term profitability, it may be unwilling to invest in improving its competitive position, or in reducing the potential impact of any adverse change in its environment. For example, when sluggish sales or rising costs make near-term profit targets hard to achieve, managers often try to boost profits by cutting spending on research and development,

marketing, quality improvements and customer care - all of which, are of course, vital to a company's long-term performance. The immediate effect of such reductions is the increase in reported profitability, but at the expense of the company's long-term competitive position.

The above limitations of accounting numbers and reports should stimulate management accountants to review their performance measurement systems. Management gurus like to stress: "What gets measured, gets done". However, although measurement is critical to improved performance, organisations don't always get what they measure. If measurement, by itself, had that much impact on human behaviour, anyone who had a weighing scale would never get fat! In other words, measurement only provides one with data. If the data are not used to make good managerial decisions and to drive improvement efforts, a good measurement system is of little value. Thus, the ideal performance measurement system is one that energises people in an organisation to focus on things that really matter.

Establishing a performance measurement system can be viewed as consisting of five related steps as follows:

1. Choosing the critical dimensions of performance that must be measured — what areas to measure?

2. Selecting the performance metrics that will be used for those dimensions — how to measure it?

3. Establishing and communicating clear targets or standards for each metric.

4. Implementing an evaluation-reward system to reinforce positive performance and to modify negative performance.

5. Designing an information system to collect the information necessary for measurement and to facilitate the feedback that measurement generates.

Choosing the Critical Dimensions of Performance

Recent discussion on the area of performance measurement has indicated that a broad set of dimensions should be employed to assess performance and these performance metrics should be linked in a cause-and-effect chain from mission through objectives and strategy to action. Thus, the starting point to any well-constructed performance measurement system must therefore be a clear exposition of the organisation's mission and objectives and resultant strategy. An organisation's mission is its basic function in society. Mission statements should identify the following:

1. It explains the stakeholders that it intends to serve and its level of commitment to each stakeholder group. In other words, it specifies who matters to the organisation.

2. It also communicates to employees its guiding principles, beliefs, values and standards of behaviour. It helps organisation members identify what is important, thereby guiding employees as they formulate business strategies and make the decisions that help the organisation achieve its stated purpose. Communicating to all employees what the organisation stands for and what it needs to do to be successful provides the foundation for organisational control.

3. It also outlines the corporate strategy. There is no single universally accepted definition of the word "strategy". The term comes from the Greek "strategia" which means the "art or science of being a general". Basically a strategy is a shared understanding about how the vision/mission (and resulting short-term objectives) are to be achieved. Strategy concerns the matching between what a company can do (given organisational strengths and weaknesses) with what it might do (within the context of environmental opportunities and threats). Thus, an organisation's strategy is the plan of competitive action to reach a destination represented by its objectives. Strategy should be driven through the organisation by way of performance measures so that all people in the organisation understand what the strategy is and how their performance is linked to that overall strategy.

The relationship between Mission, Objectives, Strategy and Performance Measures is depicted below in Exhibit 13.2.

Exhibit 13.2: Mission, Objectives, Strategy and Performance Measures

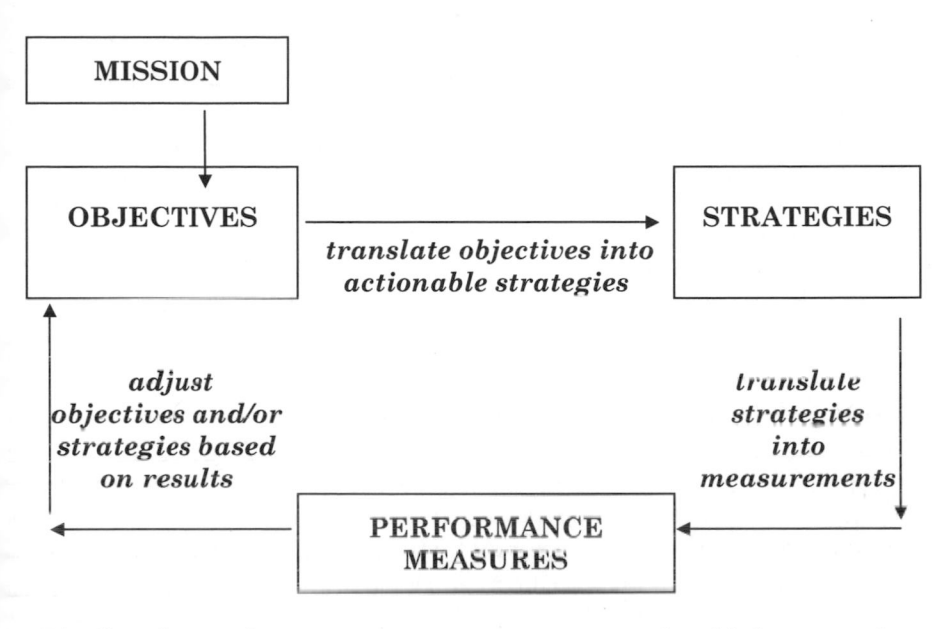

Ideally, the performance measurement system should focus on the *critical or key success factors* that represent the actions that must be performed to yield the highest probability of success or the key results that determine success. They are the areas where "things must go right" in order for the business to succeed.

Selecting Performance Metrics

Once areas have been selected for measurement, based on their strategic importance, performance metrics must be established: Deciding what precise metric will be employed to report on the chosen measurement dimension? While each company's set of measures should reflect its own strategies and processes, some principles of design hold true for all companies, for example:

1. Measures should mirror both internal and external concerns.

2. Measures should be both financial and non-financial.

3. Measures should be both leading and lagging.

Establishing and Communicating Targets

Measures must be used in context; they must be compared against a standard of expected performance. At the most basic level, targets can be set relative to past performance. However, this can breed an ethos of incrementalism — making small adjustments when more radical improvements may be demanded. There are three important factors associated with the standard setting process: Acceptance, achievablity (degree of difficulty) and equity. Acceptance relates to the principle of gaining "ownership" for the performance metric and standard. This issue is often achieved by some form of participation in the standard-setting process. Achievability is concerned with the overall level of difficulty of the targets. Generally, the higher the target, the higher motivation to achieve. However, the targets must be realistic and perceived as realistic. Equity is concerned with fairness within the organisation. In other words, targets should be comparable across similar business units.

Implementing an Evaluation-Reward System

Since all accounting information is "behavioural" by definition, mechanisms must be put in place to evaluate performance and to administer rewards. The purpose of implementing such systems is to reinforce positive performance and to modify negative behaviour. The linking of rewards in the form of recognition, monetary benefits and/or promotion is generally accepted in the literature. Practical implementation is, however, particularly dependent on organisation culture and the management philosophy of the firm. However, where companies have decided to make a significant portion of a manager's remuneration flexible – determined by performance — a balance of measurements helps to ensure that target performance in one area is not achieved at the expense of performance in another area (e.g., sales targets reached by selling at prices that are below acceptable levels, production volume targets met by compromising on quality standards, etc.). Measures on which any particular manager's remuneration depend should only be extended as far as that manager's sphere of influence extends. Rewarding managers (or penalising them) for results achieved over which they have no control runs counter to the motivational goals of rewarding performance.

Designing an Information System

Any formalised measurement system requires a well-developed information and reporting system in order to collect and report the important information that managers need.

13.4 THE BALANCED SCORECARD

The Balanced Scorecard was developed as a result of a research project in 1990 carried out by Professor Robert Kaplan from the Harvard Business School and David Norton (a management consultant) into advanced performance measurement techniques. The study was grounded in the belief that existing financial measures were hindering companies' abilities to create future economic value. The research project was conducted in conjunction with 12 American businesses that were regarded as being at the leading edge of performance measurement. Their pioneering article (Kaplan and Norton, *Harvard Business Review*, Jan/Feb.1992) has generated a great deal of interest and practical adaptation. Subsequently, their book (Kaplan and Norton, 1996) provides an integrative framework for developing a Balanced Scorecard within organisations in order to facilitate the translation of corporate strategy into results. In many ways, the development and use of a balanced scorecard is an attempt to restore relevance into the practice of management accounting.

The essential thrust of the balanced scorecard is based on two fundamental propositions. First, as most people realise, "what you measure is what you get" and, secondly, managers need a broad range of performance measures in order to manage their business. Traditional accounting measures of performance are and will always be important to managers but they have limitations. For example, traditional management accounting numbers are accused of being irrelevant since they are not directly related to the company's strategy and therefore are not powerful enough on their own to push corporate change. Since financial measures ignore, for example, customer and competitor perspectives, they fail to generate early warning signals of changes in the marketplace. In other words, traditional management accounting reports can be described as reporting the "end result" rather than the "means" but do not explain how the result was achieved, or more importantly, what should be done differently in the future. In addition, it is argued that traditional accounting measures focus too much on short-term rather than longer-term measures and can give rise to short-term decisions that are harmful to competitiveness and innovation. They may encourage companies to achieve short-term profitability at the expense of, for example, research, development and advertising expenditure. This would eventually impact on market share, sales, and company profitability. Thus, in additional to traditional financial measures of performance such as cash flow, it is also important to measure non-financial dimensions such as customer satisfaction and also employee satisfaction.

By way of analogy, they refer to an airline pilot who has a variety of dials and indicators in the cockpit for airspeed, altitude, direction, position, destination, fuel and so on. All of these are needed for a successful arrival and relying on a single performance measure can be potentially fatal. No single performance measure can provide a clear target for sustained competitive advantage in any organisation. In the Introduction to their book *Translating Strategy into Action* (1996), Kaplan and Norton use the following scenario:

> "Imagine entering the cockpit of a modern jet aeroplane and seeing only a single instrument there. How would you feel about boarding the plane after the following conversation with the pilot?
>
> Q: I'm surprised to see you operating the plane with only a single instrument. What does it measure?
>
> A: Airspeed. I'm really working on airspeed this flight.
>
> Q: That's good. Airspeed certainly seems important. But what about altitude. Wouldn't an altimeter be helpful?
>
> A: I worked on altitude for the last few flights and I've become pretty good on it. Now I have to concentrate on proper airspeed.
>
> Q: But I notice you don't even have a fuel gauge. Wouldn't that be useful?
>
> A: You're right, fuel is significant but I can't concentrate on doing too many things well at the same time. So on this flight I'm focusing on airspeed. Once I get to be excellent at airspeed, as well as altitude, I intend to concentrate on fuel consumption on the next set of flights".

The Balanced Scorecard is intended to provide answers to basic questions relating to four different perspectives as depicted below and in Exhibit 13.3.

Exhibit 13.3 The Balanced Scorecard

PERSPECTIVE	FOCUS
Financial	How do we look to our shareholders?
Customer	How do new customers see us?
Internal	What activities must we excel at?
Learning and growth	How can we continue to learn and improve?

Exhibit 13.4: The Balanced Scorecard

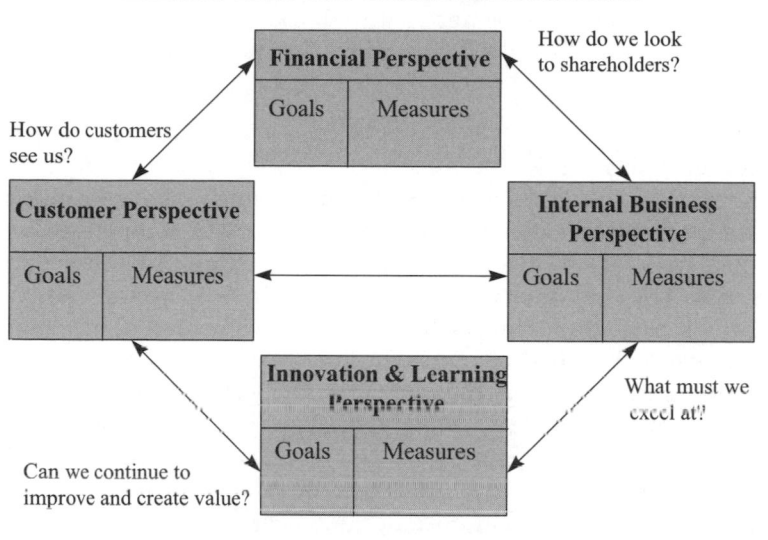

Source: Kaplan and Norton (1992)

Financial Perspective

While "profit" as a performance measure has been criticised, it is important to remember that it is an important source of finance. Retained profit improves the cash flow position of companies and offers greater flexibility in the source of finance for corporate investment. Easier access to finance facilitates greater investment, which boosts productivity, competitiveness and employment. In a macro context, company profits reflect the health of the economy. Financial measures are, typically, directed along four themes

1. Sales growth and mix

2. Cost reduction

3. Asset utilisation

4. Overall financial position.

Non-Financial Measures

The balanced scorecard complements these financial measures with three other perspectives that are essentially non-financial measures of performance. The greater emphasis on non-financial measures of performance is understandable since individuals do not generally think in terms of the financial aspects of their work. Rather, they are concentrating on the issue of production rates, on-time deliveries, quality and schedule changes. Such measures are useful indicators of long-term financial performance. In addition, non-financial measures are generally unaffected by variations in the relative price of input factors.

Customer Perspective

In the customer perspective, managers identify the customers and market segments in which the business unit will compete as well as the measures of the business unit's performance in those targeted segments. The customer perspective is intuitive, especially since most companies now proclaim to be customer-orientated. This customer perspective is designed to highlight how customers perceive the business and focus on specific measures that reflect the factors that really matter to customers. One could say that this perspective is at the heart of the scorecard. Success in any business depends on the ability to establish, maintain, and build relationships with customers. However, customer satisfaction does not necessarily mean that your satisfied customers are committed or loyal. On average, a business loses 20% of its customer base each year. Past research suggest that up to 90% of lost customers do not bother to tell a company why they left but they will, however, complain to at least 10 friends and business associates. To compound the problem, in today's competitive environment, you cannot count on new customers to take the place of lost ones. Four generic dimensions across all kinds of organisations can be cited for the customer perspective:

1. Customer satisfaction – since this is considered to be the crucial performance measure for predicting the future success of most companies.

2. Customer profitability.

3. Customer retention.

4. Customer acquisition i.e. new customers.

Internal Perspective

The internal business perspective is designed to focus on those critical internal activities that must be performed in order to satisfy the expectations of its customers and stems from a *value-chain* orientation, and includes cycle time, quality and efficiency of operations. This internal perspective is primarily an analysis of the company's internal processes. One must focus on the processes that are critical for achieving customer and financial objectives. It is recommended that the BSC for internal processes should focus on the entire value chain which starts with the innovation process (identifying current and future customer needs), through the operations process (delivering existing products and services to customers), and ends with post-sales service (offering services after the sale that add to the value that customers receive from a company's product and service offerings). In other words, we focus on measures for the internal processes that will have the greatest impact on enhancing customer relationships and will achieve the organisation's financial objectives. This perspective encompasses three principal business processes, starting with the identification of customer needs through to customer needs satisfied.

There are three main classes of activities in the value chain:

1   **The Innovation Process.** Creating entirely new products and services to meet the emerging needs of current and future customers.

2. **The Operations Process.** Delivering existing products and services to existing customers, efficiently, reliably, and responsively.

3. **The Post-Sale Service Process.** Satisfying customers after the sale with prompt attention to their concerns and as needed with field service and technical support.

Because the value chain exists to produce a product for the customer, it makes sense to evaluate the activities in the value chain from the customer perspective. If we think of the value chain ending with the final customer, we can think of each link in the value chain as the customer of the previous link. If each link in the value chain focuses on meeting the needs of its customers, the organisation will deliver the product that the final customer wants. This is a simple, but powerful way to provide focus and co-ordination in an organisation that may have, literally, thousands of activities in its value chain.

Learning and Growth

The financial, customer, and internal business process objectives of the *Balanced Scorecard* will typically reveal large gaps between existing capabilities of people and systems, that will be required to achieve targets for required performance. To close these gaps, businesses will have to invest in re-skilling employees, enhancing information technology and systems, and aligning organisational procedures and routines. These objectives are articulated in the learning and growth perspective of the *Balanced Scorecard*. Organisational learning and growth come from three principal sources: employee capability, information system capabilities and employee motivation and procedures. At the heart of this perspective are employees. The learning and growth perspective highlights the fact that, in the face of intense competition, firms must make continual improvement to existing products and processes and have the ability to introduce new products in the future. Typical measures for the learning and growth perspective include employee satisfaction and retention, skill development and information systems capability.

"Balanced" in Three Ways

The BSC is "balanced" in three ways. Firstly, there is a balance between internal and external measures. Secondly, it is balanced by the various perspectives, which include financial and non-financial measures. Finally, the scorecard is balanced in terms of time i.e. it reflects the past, the present and the future i.e. the financial perspective is a result of past decisions and represents the historic performance. The customer and internal process perspectives constitute today's dimension. The learning/growth perspective represents what we must do in the future that will have a future financial impact. Thus, it is important that the BSC be seen not only as a record of results achieved. It is equally important that it be used to indicate expected results.

Advantages and Problems of the BSC

The balanced scorecard integrates traditional financial measures with operational and softer customer and staff issues, which are vital to the growth and long-term competitiveness of the firm. The balanced scorecard requires each company to look at itself from four different perspectives and to answer four basic questions. Having understood what is important for the business, performance measures are established to monitor performance and, targets must be set for improvement. These must then be clearly communicated to all levels of management and staff within the business. This enables managers and individuals to understand how their own efforts can impact on the targets set in respect of each perspective. The balanced scorecard then becomes the primary document in the regular reporting system of the company.

In order to develop the balanced scorecard, one needs to concentrate on the key performance indicators within the organisation. By critical and innovative thinking it should be possible to identify a limited number of key variables that reflect the critical success factors of the firm. These key variables (or key success factors) are the limited number of areas in which results, if they are satisfactory, will ensure successful competitive performance for the organisation. They are the few critical areas where 'things must go right' for the business to flourish and if performance is not adequate, the organisation's financial results will be less than desired. Only by combining, measuring and thinking in terms of all four perspectives can managers prevent improvements being made in one area at the expense of another. An automatic side benefit of this critical thinking is the development of a deeper understanding of the various dimensions of the business and what activities the individuals within the firm need to perform well if the firm is to achieve and maintain success. Also, performance measures can play an essential part in developing a widespread understanding of how the various parts of the business operate together. The experience of getting acceptance by individuals of the performance measures can and should improve communication and understanding within the organisation and establishes a common vocabulary of improvement.

A generic Balanced Scorecard is listed in Exhibit 13.5.

Exhibit 13.5: A Balanced Scorecard

Critical Success Factor	Performance measures and indicators
Financial Perspective	
Sales growth and mix	Sales volume trend
	Percentage of sales from new products
Cost reduction	Total cost as percentage of total revenue
Financial position	Liquidity ratios
	Gearing (leverage) ratios
Asset utilisation	Fixed asset turnover,
	Management of working capital
Customer Perspective	
Customer satisfaction	Customer survey index
Customer profitability	Average profit per customer
Customer retention	Number of repeat orders
Customer acquisition	Number of new customers acquired and sales value
Internal Business Perspective	
Innovation	Percentage of sales from new products
	Expenditure on research and development
Operations	Cycle time (days from raw materials to finished product)
	Labour and/or machine efficiency
	Defect rates including wastage
	On-time deliveries
Post sales service	Customer complaint response time
	Number of visits to customer
Learning and Growth Perspective	
Employee capability	Days training
	Number of graduate employees in workforce
Information systems capability	Spending on IT capability
Motivation and procedures	Employee turnover
	Employee satisfaction
	Number of meetings attended

It is now generally accepted that performance measures should be an integral part of modern internal reporting systems. These performance metrics should:

1. Be linked with corporate strategy.

2. Mirror both internal and external concerns.

3. Include financial and non-financial dimensions.

4. Be both leading and lagging indicators.

5. Be both quantitative and qualitative.

6. Make explicit the trade-offs between the various measures of performance.

In developing a range of performance measures, one should be aware of the possible dysfunctional consequences associated with any performance metric. For example, if the measure is the percentage of orders delivered on time, then there is an incentive for managers to sacrifice one late shipment for the sake of orders that can be delivered on time. Thus, on-time delivery performance looks better when nine deliveries are made on time and one is ten days late compared with ten deliveries being made one day late. In conclusion, it is interesting to note Einstein's words:

> "Not everything that counts can be counted,
> and not everything that can be counted, counts."

Conclusion

Top management should be concerned not only with the internal performance of a company but also with external information about the firm's environment. This external information is required in particular to formulate and review strategies. This travels a long way from the conventional perspective of concentrating on internal and financial measures of one's own company only. Yet the change in philosophy is not difficult to comprehend. The key notion is the focus on the company's position relative to competitors' position.

The focus of modern management accounting is to provide information concerning the company's market and its competitors, and to focus on internal data from a long-term and strategic point of view rather than the short term. The focus is on market-oriented information rather than internal data for decision-making. This external information is required in order to allow the company to respond to competition and to changes in customer demand, both of which are pressures that originate externally. But this begs the question: To what extent are accountants, either in their education and/or orientation, conscious and knowledgeable about their environment?

This proposal to expand management accounting is not a subtle device to provide a role for unwanted accountants who see their traditional recording role being replaced by computer information systems. Nor is it a suggestion that allows the accountant to graduate from administrator to manager. Instead, this information *is* required by managers and, if this leads to better decisions, the company and all its stakeholders will benefit from it. In many respects, management accounting is about looking at the future. After all, if you don't look to the future, you won't have one!

13.4 END OF CHAPTER QUESTIONS

Question 13.1

"Apart from poor management, lack of adequate financial control is the most common characteristic of declining companies".

Discuss how inadequate financial controls can contribute to the decline of a company.

Question 13.2

"I sell my product/service for what I can get. I use cost to decide whether I want to do business or not."

REQUIREMENT

Explain and discuss the cost and other information that may be relevant to the pricing decision.

(*The Association of Chartered Certified Accountants*)

Question 13.3

Explain your understanding of the term "cost driver".

Question 13.4

Outline in general terms the role of the management accountant in a typical profit-seeking organisation.

Question 13.5

Your company is considering withdrawing a major product line from the market. If the withdrawal is confirmed, closure of the relevant sales offices and production facilities will lead to the loss of 1,000 jobs in about twelve months time.

REQUIREMENT

Discuss the major factors that should be considered in making such a decision, and outline the information that the accountant might be asked to provide to assist management in assessing such a proposal.

Question 13.6

At a recent meeting of local business people from a range of industries, two executives who have had to invest heavily in high technology to support their manufacturing or commercial activity were discussing its implications.

"The effect on my business has been to significantly change its cost structure", said Ms Finn, who works in the financial sector.

"We have just invested in advanced manufacturing technology and incorporated a just-in-time stocking policy," replied Mr Mann, who is in manufacturing.

REQUIREMENT

1. In relation to the remark by Ms Finn, explain the likely change to the cost structure of her business and its implications.

2. Consider briefly any other financial effects of the move towards greater technological support of manufacturing or commercial activity.

(*The Association of Chartered Certified Accountants*)

Question 13.7

The last decade has seen increasing automation and the wide use of information technology in both manufacturing and service industries and this has implications for management and the management accountant. A number of observations have been made about this, for example it:

1. Changes the cost structure of organisations and how costs are managed.

2. Can be incorporated with a just-in-time philosophy.

REQUIREMENT

Discuss each of the above statements in a way that demonstrates your appreciation of the point being made.

(The Association of Chartered Certified Accountants)

QUESTION 13.8

You are approached by an acquaintance who has been reading contemporary management accounting journals. He is aware that you have been studying management accounting and its relationship to business. He is keen to discuss with you a few current issues concerning the scope and usefulness of:

1. Strategic management accounting;

2. Non-financial performance measures.

REQUIREMENT

Briefly explain these issues making clear to your acquaintance their role within management accounting information.

(The Association of Chartered Certified Accountants)

QUESTION 13.9: Profit and Non-Financial Measures of Performance

Recent articles in management accounting journals have suggested using a broad range of performance measures is more important to managers than profits.

REQUIREMENT

You are required to explain:

1. The arguments for using the profit measure as the all encompassing measure of the performance of a business;

2. The limitations of this profit-measurement approach and of undue dependence on the profit measure;

3. The problems of using a broad range of non-financial measures for the short-term and long-term control of a business.

(The Chartered Institute of Management Accountants)

QUESTION 13.10: Current Themes in Management Accounting

"Today's management accounting information, driven by the procedures and cycle of the organisation's financial reporting system, is too late, too aggregated, and too distorted to be relevant for managers' planning and control decisions". (Johnson and Kaplan in *Relevance Lost: The Rise and Fall of Management Accounting* 1987).

REQUIREMENT
Explain the claims that management accounting has lost relevance.

(Chartered Institute of Management Accountants)

QUESTION 13.11: New Manufacturing Environment

The new manufacturing environment is characterised by more flexibility, a readiness to meet customers' requirements, smaller batches, continuous improvements and an emphasis on quality. In such circumstances, traditional management accounting performance measures are, at best, irrelevant and, at worst, misleading.

REQUIREMENT

1. Discuss the above statement, citing specific examples to support or refute the views expressed.

2. Explain in what ways management accountants can adapt the services they provide to the new environment.

QUESTION 13.12: Criticisms of Management Accounting

It has been claimed that cost and management accounting suffers from a *financial accounting mentality* and that there is excessive focus on *short-term financial performance*. However, evidence is emerging, given the improvements in information technology, of the increased generation and use of non-financial measures of performance.

REQUIREMENT

1. In the context of the role of the management accountant explain and discuss the implications of *financial accounting mentality* and *short-term financial performance*.

2. Discuss how increasing information technology has affected the development, production and use of non-financial performance

measures, draw examples from any commercial setting. Describe how this may impact on the role of the management accountant.

(The Association of Chartered Certified Accountants)

QUESTION 13.13: Strategic Management Accounting

What is the relationship between traditional management accounting and strategic management accounting?

QUESTION 13.14: The Balanced Scorecard

Recent articles have focused on summary information for running a business and on a 'balanced scorecard' approach, using a number of performance measures.

REQUIREMENT

Explain the following:

1. The arguments for using the profit measure as the all-encompassing measure of the performance of a business.

2. The limitations of this profit-measurement approach and of undue dependence on the profit measure.

3. The problems of using a broad range of non-financial measures for the short- and long-term control of a business.

(Chartered Institute of Management Accountants)

Appendix 1

Present Value of €1 Received *N* Years hence, at a Discount Rate of *X* Per Cent per Year

n	4%	7%	8%	10%	12%	14%	15%	16%	18%	20%	21%	22%	24%	25%	30%
1	.902	.935	.926	.909	.893	.877	.870	.862	.847	.833	.826	.820	.806	.800	.769
2	.925	.873	.857	.826	.797	.769	.756	.743	.718	.694	.683	.672	.650	.640	.592
3	.889	.816	.794	.751	.712	.675	.658	.641	.609	.579	.564	.551	.524	.512	.455
4	.855	.763	.735	.683	.636	.592	.572	.552	.516	.482	.466	.451	.423	.410	.350
5	.822	.713	.681	.621	.567	.519	.497	.476	.437	.402	.385	.370	.341	.328	.269
6	.790	.666	.630	.564	.507	.456	.432	.410	.370	.335	.318	.303	.275	.262	.207
7	.760	.623	.583	.513	.452	.400	.376	.354	.314	.279	.263	.249	.221	.210	.159
8	.731	.582	.540	.467	.404	.351	.327	.305	.266	.233	.217	.204	.178	.168	.123
9	.703	.544	.500	.424	.361	.308	.284	.263	.225	.194	.179	.167	.144	.134	.094
10	.676	.508	.463	.386	.322	.270	.247	.227	.191	.162	.148	.137	.116	.107	.073

Appendix 2

Present Value of €1 Received Each Year for *N* Years

n	4%	7%	8%	10%	12%	14%	15%	16%	18%	20%	21%	22%	24%	25%	30%
1	0.962	0.935	0.926	0.909	0.893	0.877	0.870	0.862	0.847	0.833	0.826	0.820	0.806	0.800	0.769
2	1.866	1.808	1.783	1.736	1.690	1.647	1.626	1.605	1.566	1.528	1.509	1.492	1.457	1.440	1.361
3	2.775	2.624	2.577	2.487	2.402	2.322	2.283	2.246	2.174	2.106	2.074	2.042	1.981	1.952	1.816
4	3.630	3.387	3.312	3.170	3.037	2.914	2.855	2.798	2.690	2.589	2.540	2.494	2.404	2.362	2.166
5	4.452	4.100	3.993	3.791	3.605	3.433	3.352	3.274	3.127	2.991	2.926	2.864	2.745	2.689	2.436
6	5.242	4.767	4.623	4.335	4.111	3.889	3.784	3.685	3.498	3.326	3.245	3.167	3.020	2.951	2.643
7	6.002	5.389	5.206	4.868	4.564	4.288	4.160	4.039	3.812	3.605	3.508	3.416	3.242	3.161	2.802
8	6.733	5.971	5.747	5.335	4.968	4.639	4.487	4.344	4.078	3.837	3.726	3.619	3.421	3.329	2.925
9	7.435	6.515	6.247	5.759	5.328	4.946	4.772	4.607	4.303	4.031	3.905	3.789	3.566	3.463	3.019
10	8.111	7.023	6.710	6.145	5.650	5.216	5.019	4.833	4.494	4.192	4.054	3.923	3.682	3.571	3.092

Lecturers' Resource Pack

A Lecturers' Resource Pack for
Accounting Information for Managers
is available free of charge to
lecturers who adopt the text for their courses.

The Pack consists of suggested solutions to
questions in the text, printed on A4 sheets in a form
suitable for making overhead projector
transparencies.

For further information, contact
OAK TREE PRESS
19 Rutland Street, Cork
T: 021 431 3855 F: 021 431 3496

Index